Islamophobia and

MW01240580

This book provides an engaging and insightful look into the definitions, discourse, and experiences of Islamophobia and its steady rise since 9/11.

It analyses concepts and binaries that are drawn around discussions on civilization, religious dogma, violence, and race. Is there a link between Islam and violence? Why does the West feel threatened by it? The author critically examines these questions and the birth of hate politics which packages hate in a marketable format and often demonizes victims. It also looks at the role of the media in the West in perpetuating stereotypes and its consequences and the nature of war reportage in Islamic countries while deconstructing the narrative of the clash of civilizations.

Topical and lucid, this book is a must-read for students and scholars of sociology, international relations, peace and conflict studies, political science, Islamic studies, and for other readers interested in these topics.

Imbesat Daudi is a urologist, surgeon, and scientist by profession. He was born in India. educated and trained in India, Germany, and the United States. He received his MBBS degree from Darbhanga Medical College, India, a Masters and Ph.D. in physiology from Albany Medical College, Albany, NY. He completed his training in general surgery in Germany and urology at the SUNY, Syracuse, NY. He is a fellow of the American College of Surgeons (FACS), a diplomate of the American Board of Urology, and the German Board for general surgery (*Arzt fuer Chirurgie*).

Islamophobia and the West
The Making of a Violent Civilization

Imbesat Daudi

Routledge
Taylor & Francis Group

LONDON AND NEW YORK

Cover image: Getty Images

First published 2023
by Routledge
4 Park Square, Milton Park, Abingdon, Oxon OX14 4RN

and by Routledge
605 Third Avenue, New York, NY 10158

Routledge is an imprint of the Taylor & Francis Group, an informa business

© 2023 Imbesat Daudi

The right of Imbesat Daudi to be identified as author of this work has been asserted in accordance with sections 77 and 78 of the Copyright, Designs and Patents Act 1988.

British Library Cataloguing-in-Publication Data
A catalogue record for this book is available from the British Library

Library of Congress Cataloging-in-Publication Data
A catalog record has been requested for this book

ISBN: 978-1-032-31973-5 (hbk)
ISBN: 978-1-032-34630-4 (pbk)
ISBN: 978-1-003-32310-5 (ebk)

DOI: 10.4324/9781003323105

Typeset in Sabon
by Taylor & Francis Books

Dedicated to my wife, Asfa

Do not believe in anything simply because you have heard it. Do not believe in anything simply because it is spoken and rumored by many. Do not believe in anything simply because it is found written in your religious books. Do not believe in traditions because they have been handed down for many generations. But after observation and analysis, when you find that anything agrees with reason and in conducive to the good and benefit of one and all, then accept it and live up to it.

—Anonymous

Contents

Illustrations

Map

Tables

Acknowledgements

I would like to thank Dr. Jawaid Alam, Professor of History, at Jamia Millia University, Delhi, and Ajai Kumar Rai, who edited the manuscript. Dr. Alam, who has authored many books and scholarly articles, has guided me through the arduous process of writing and publishing the manuscript. Mr. Rai, a visiting professor in many universities in India and abroad, has many articles and books to his credit. He is a talented editor and his attention to detail is exceptional. He helped me to keep my focus on the subject.

Finally, thanks to my family; this had been a challenging time for them as well. I did not realize how long the entire project – from the construction of ideas to publication – would last. It has taken me almost ten years to finish the book. I began the project when I was busy with my practice and other business ventures. My wife, Asfa had to take over the role of both parents and had to contend with my absence not only when I was away but also when I was at home, but away in my world.

Prologue

The following verses from religious scripture were presented to a diverse group of people in the United States, Canada, Germany, Australia, and India during formal and informal discussions.

> Even concerning your own duty, you should not waver, for there is nothing nobler for a warrior than participation in a righteous battle.[1]
>
> O Prince, fortunate are indeed those warriors who are called upon to fight a battle like this which comes unsought, for it is an open gateway to heaven.[2]
>
> I say to you that to everyone who has, more shall be given, but from the one who does not have, shall be taken away. As for my enemies who do not want to reign over them, bring them here and kill them in my presence.[3]
>
> Do not think that I have come to send peace on earth. I did not come to send peace but a sword. I am sent to set a man against his father, a daughter against her mother, and a daughter-in-law against her mother-in-law.[4]
>
> Kill every male among the little one and kill every woman who has known man intimately. However, spare for yourselves all virgin maidens.[5]
>
> When the Lord your God gives it into your hand, kill all the men in it. Take as booty only the women, children, animals, and all that is in the city, all its spoils. Use the spoils of your enemies, which the Lord your God has given to you … Do not leave alive anything that breathes.[6]

If readers assume that these verses belong to Islamic scriptures, they are not alone; they have plenty of company. However, they would be wrong. The first two verses have been taken from the Bhagavad Geeta, the next two from the New Testament, and the last two from the Old Testament. The audiences present during this formal and informal discussion on the alleged association of Islam with violence were asked the same question. More than three-quarters of the audience declined to respond, which is understandable; commenting on controversial issues in an open forum is unpleasant. Out of a thousand people, only three individuals could correctly name the source, but never more than one of the six verses.

Those who responded could be divided into two broad categories; their answers depended on their religious affiliation. An overwhelming majority of

DOI: 10.4324/9781003323105-1

Muslims opined that these verses could not belong to the Koran or Hadith. An equal proportion of non-Muslims who responded indicated either openly or otherwise that these verses could be attributed to Islamic texts. Irrespective of what people thought about the origin of the verses, it does not mean that Islam is violent or not violent; neither does it mean that a specific religion from which these texts have been taken is violent. However, the responses these verses generated among non-Muslim audiences go a long way to show that many in the West and India believe that Muslims are violent. Are they?

Their views merely reflect their perception of Islam; their opinion was not based on valid evidence, correct information, or objective reasoning. Neither did the responders show proper knowledge of Islam or its scriptures. In essence, their understanding of Islam was based on presumptions. The basis of their views varied from deducing a logical conclusion to a firm conviction, which was based on presuppositions. Some of them acknowledged that they had assumed that these verses could only belong to the Koran. Even though they had not studied the Holy Book of Islam, most of them had no contact with Muslims. Still, they had formed their opinion perhaps from social media, television programs, talk shows, or newspaper articles.

This is not a new observation; in 1997, the Runnymede Trust published its finding on the prevalent Islamophobia in Britain; their conclusions were similar.[7] John Esposito, Edward Said, Chris Hedges, and many others authors and political commentators arrived at the same conclusion.[8]

Muslims viewed this question differently. Most of them rejected the notion that such verses could ever be a part of the Islamic ethos. The majority of Muslims, even those who have no background in Islamic theology or history, were confident that these verses could not be attributed to their Holy Book. Their reaction to these verses indicates that in contrast to the perception of the association of violence with Islamic societies that is prevalent in the West, Muslims reject the notion that violence is integral to Islamic doctrine.[9] Despite being exposed to negative coverage of Islam in Western media, most Muslims, even those living in the West, still believe that their religion stands for peace. They thought these verses could not constitute Islamic doctrine, philosophy, or traditions on which the Islamic laws are based.[10]

What conclusions could be drawn from this informal survey? First, the world is sharply divided on this issue. Second, misinformation about Muslims is widely prevalent and has not been corrected so far. Could this be a problem? The answer is a yes, as this perception has caused severe problems for Muslims worldwide. The demonization of Muslims has resulted in the invasions, occupations, and bombings of half a dozen Muslim countries besides causing inconvenience, travel restrictions, surveillance at home and abroad, limiting their human rights and economic and educational opportunities. Since none of the verses is derived from the Koran or any other Islamic doctrine, traditions, or laws, it is believed in the West that these verses are somehow related to Islam. This confirms the notion that their perception of Islam is based on assumptions. Their heuristics are wrong, at best; at worse, they are confabulations.

Can these reactions be defined as Islamophobia? The answer is maybe, as the term is vague; it is also controversial. The Runnymede Trust, which came up with the term in 1997, described Islamophobia as having three components: a) unfounded hostility towards Islam, b) practical consequences of such hostility in unfair discrimination, and c) exclusion of Muslims from mainstream social and political spheres.

Islamophobia has been redefined in their newer report, which was published in 2017. It has two definitions. The shorter one defines Islamophobia as *anti-Muslim racism*. It has raised criticism as well. The more extended definition is more comprehensive; it characterizes Islamophobia as

> any distinction, exclusion, or restriction towards or preference against Muslims (or those perceived to be Muslims) that has the purpose or effect of nullifying or impairing the recognition, enjoyment, or exercise on an equal footing, of human rights and fundamental freedoms in the political, economic, social, cultural or any other field of public life.[11]

The term anti-Islamism might impart a more comprehensive definition of bias and prejudice against Muslims, but that cannot be used. Whether deliberately or not, Islamism is being used to define extremism, terrorism, and other acts of violence of non-governmental organizations of Muslim societies. Therefore, anti-Islamism would have a different connotation. This leaves limited choices of terms to define hostility towards Islam and Muslims. Since anti-Muslim bias and prejudice are more than fear of Muslims, *anti-Muslimism* may be a better term than Islamophobia to define negative predisposition towards Muslim, Islam, and Islamic civilization; both terms have been used in this book.

Why does Islam generate a negative response? The most relevant question on this issue is whether violent images of Muslims that have found a space in the Western psyche evolved spontaneously or were created; if so, how, and why? This book examines these questions by examining factors that have defined Islam at the turn of the twenty-first century. The following algorithm has been applied to assess the truth behind the perception of Islam being violent. There may be five possible explanations:

1 *Muslims and Islamic societies are indeed violent*. Are they? This is the primary question in this debate. It needs to be addressed first, but how to prove Islamic civilization is violent or more violent than Western or Hindu civilization? If historical facts show that Muslim nations have invaded more countries than their cohorts, they should be described as more violent than the rest. In that case, the next question would be why. Is it due to Islamic doctrine or economic factors common to all groups of nations? However, if the data suggest that Muslim countries have not initiated as many violent conflicts in the world as the West has, they should not be described as violent. In that case, the relevant question is not whether Islam is violent but why Muslims are considered violent.

2   *Muslims may not be violent, but they appear to be violent.* If so, what could be the reasons? A systemic bias against Muslims may be one reason to be perceived as violent.
3   *Are Muslims being judged by a more stringent yardstick than their cohorts?* If so, why? Is it related to prejudice against Islam?
4   *The negative impression of Muslims in the Western perception may be attributed to 9/11.* Indeed, it was one of the most traumatic events for Americans. Around the same period, non-governmental Islamist groups had also participated in other acts of violence. This could have caused fear of Islam and resulted in implicit Islamophobia, which became ingrained in the psyche.
5   However, there could be another reason: *the perception of Muslims as violent people has been purposely created* for financial and political reasons. This view has been seldom discussed and widely ignored by the mainstream media.

This is a controversial topic, partly due to emotions involved in discussing religious dogmas, which can create a tunnel vision; however, it is also due to the confusion created by a lack of uniform terminology in defining civilizations. Therefore, let us first define the terms that have been used in this book.

Until recently, civilizations and groups of nations were accepted as two different entities, as the former is considered a socio-religious categorization of humanity and the latter political organizations. Bernard Lewis and Sam Huntington, the two iconic thinkers of our time, merged Islamic civilization and Muslim majority countries as if they were the same; they also used the two terms interchangeably. Furthermore, Lewis used the term Judeo-Christian civilization for Western nations; and he includes the Jewish state into Western civilization. Huntington describes Europe, North America, Australia, and New Zealand as Western-Christian civilization and the West, but he excludes Eastern Europe and defines them as Orthodox Christian civilization. The fallacy and confusion associated with their concepts have been discussed in Chapter 4.

Although civilizations should not be used to define nations, this book still uses Huntington's terminology because the book examines whether Huntington's classification of humanity is valid or not. Wherever needed, the distinctions between the two terms have been made. If there is still any confusion about an individual country, readers should refer to Map 4.1 in Chapter 4.

To evaluate the options within the above algorithm, this book has been organized in the following manner. The first chapter examines the central question of the algorithm: is the present Western perception of an association of Islamic civilization with violence a reality or paranoia of the Muslim world? Alternatively, it could be xenophobia, as the fear of aliens is present in all cultures. Whatever the answer may be, the Gallup survey taken a decade ago has also shown a deep-seated and widespread prejudice towards Islam in the West.[12] The finding of the Runnymede Trust that was first published in 1997 complements the Gallup survey. Furthermore, the Western perception of Muslims being violent is not the only bias against Muslims. It is just one of the many negative impressions prevalent in the West. It is also persistent. Even if credible data are presented to repudiate such opinions, a change of perception about Islam and Muslims does not occur.[13] It should not come as a surprise as experts agree that biases and prejudices, once formed and established, are hard to eradicate.[14]

The first question in the algorithm should be if Muslims, Islam, and Islamic civilization are indeed violent or merely perceived to be violent. This issue has been explored in Chapter 2. A valid comparison of violent conflicts of all groups of countries, which have been erroneously called civilizations, is the only way to prove or disprove if one group of nations is more violent than the others. If it is correct that Muslims are more violent than others, a higher incidence and prevalence of violence will be present within and along its borders than for nations belonging to other civilizations. The data on violent conflicts have been taken from the book, *Civilization and Violence: Islam, the West, and the Rest* (QED Books, 2013), which deals exclusively with violent conflicts of the last two centuries.

However, that is not the case with the past Muslim empires in the last three centuries, which coincided with colonialism. During this phase, Muslim countries were not able to initiate violent conflicts;[15] they had started the least number of acts of aggression, as they were too weak to invade other countries, with one or two exceptions.[16] If Muslim nations had invaded or occupied other countries, they had the full support of the Western powers. On the contrary, they were the primary victims of Western expansion during colonialism; European nations had been more violent than all other countries combined. In the twenty-first century, neocolonialism has replaced overt colonialism,[17] but the dynamic of aggression has not changed, as the military and economic power has not shifted in favor of Muslim countries.

If so, why are Muslims perceived to be violent? Those who are not negatively predisposed to Islam have offered a possible explanation. They opine that the negative perception of Muslims is the natural outcome of the outrage generated by the destruction of the World Trade Center, the Pentagon, and other acts of violence directed against the United States and its allies. Is it true? Probably not, for had it been the case, the demonization of Muslims would be confined to the post-9/11 era.

Chapter 3 traces various events that may have played a role in stereotyping Muslims as violent. Emphasis has been given to the timeline of these events. When did such articles and books start appearing? Was it before or after 9/11? The appearance of such literature before the invasion of Iraq would indicate that the demonization of Muslims was a planned strategy, probably ahead of the attack on the World Trade Center. In other words, if the current perception of Muslims as violent people is related to 9/11, the articles and other literature demonizing Muslims would appear only after the attack. That is not the case either. If so, how did fear of Muslims take root in the West, Israel, India, and their allies?

Therefore, the next question of the algorithm is: how was their demonization accomplished? Was it created? The answer has been presented in Chapters 3, 4, and 5. According to the Runnymede Trust, the demonization of Muslims has generated fear of Muslims and Muslim countries. Fear and violence may go hand in hand. As Pankaj Mishra suggests, fear of Westernization is pervasive across all cultures.[18] Sven Lindqvist and other political scientists have argued that demonization and xenophobia are interconnected. The fear of Islam, which generates prejudice, is not a novel concept. The Runnymede Trust had taken the initiative to publish an extensive report on Islamophobia three years before 9/11; this also suggests that the demonization of Muslims has been present for a long time.

In recent years, social scientists have come up with new insights about how ideas spread. Concepts, if they become viral, follow a pattern. Islamophobia, being an idea, has pursued the same dynamics. The pathway is broadly divided into three stages. In the first phase, ideas are conceived; they take roots; hypotheses become functioning theories (Chapter 3); concepts may be conceived in isolation but do not develop in a vacuum; they require a nourishing environment to develop into a theory. Who created the atmosphere of fear of Islam is the critical question.

There may be multiple sources for any idea at any given time in the initial stages, irrespective of whether they are economic concepts, inventions, or political ideology. For example, Thomas Edison, credited with inventing light bulbs, was not the first but probably the twenty-first individual to file a patent for his invention. There were at least a dozen others who were working on the same issue. However, Edison was the most successful entrepreneur in this field. He went on to lay the foundation of General Electric, which, at one time, became world's largest corporation.

Similarly, Bill Gates, who produced *Microsoft Word*, was not alone in creating word processing software; others were also working on similar products, but Bill Gates became most successful. Similarly, Steve Jobs is synonymous with the most efficient laptop, although he was not the inventor; but his products became top sellers while others failed to market their products efficiently. These examples indicate that there was a need for these products, which these innovators understood, but only a few knew how to market their concepts.

Similarly, Hitler is identified with fascism, but he was neither the primary ideologue nor the first fascist leader to grab power; the credit of defining fascism goes to Mussolini, who came to power in Italy after the First World War. There were other fascist leaders in Europe, such as General Franco in Spain and Ernesto Salazar in Portugal. Others could not come to power, but they were knocking at the door. This suggests that European air was conducive to fascist movements before the Second World War. The common factor in the rise of fascist leaders may have been economic disruption from the First World War.

Similarly, many right-wing populist leaders, such as Donald Trump, Narendra Modi, Jair Bolsonaro, Boris Johnson, Victor Orban, and others, came to power in the twenty-first century. Was that a coincidence? Alternatively, there could be a cause-and-effect relationship. What could be those factors? These examples suggest that ideas, whether political or economic, appear simultaneously in many places. Anti-Muslimism is no different. This is discussed in Chapter 3.

In the second phase, concepts evolve into marketable hypotheses. Only then are they packaged to be marketed (Chapter 4). Out of several versions of the same concept, only one or two may survive; the rest wither away. Theories that become famous have greater marketability. Their ideas are easy to understand, and they stick in the memory, irrespective of whether they are factual or not. Adhering to facts does not guarantee longevity. In the final phase, concepts are propagated (Chapter 5). Each stage has its own dynamics, which have been discussed in each chapter.

Changing perceptions of millions, if not billions of people, is a massive undertaking. Changes do not "just" happen, they are created; a lot of effort goes into making views and products become popular. Successful dissemination of ideas requires a collective effort of important segments of society. The core elements in propagating ideas are thinkers and intellectuals, who provide ideas and arguments for demonizing the targets; think-tanks, which employ lobbyists; opinion-makers, who manage and control perceptions of citizens; the media, which employ journalists to propagate the ideas; specific transnational corporations, which benefit from the demonization of the victims; financial institutions, which are major shareholders in the military-industrial complex; and finally, the establishment, which has overall control over nation's policies.

Several social scientists have studied how ideas spread. As noted, Chapter 3 examines how Islamophobic ideas were conceived. Chapter 4 examines how narratives that Muslims are violent were developed and evaluates the arguments of writers who developed the hypothesis in a presentable format. Chapter 5 examines the works of those who successfully disseminated the notion that Muslims are violent. The propagation of ideas follows the complexity and network theories; centrally placed activists play a vital role in spreading ideas, whether rational or not.[19] Based on these concepts, reviews of the arguments of ideologues, who portrayed Islamic civilization as violent, have been examined in these chapters. Since nodal networks operate as centralized units, emphasis has been given to the position of individual writers within the broader network. Who are they? What role did they play? Were they innovative thinkers or merely followers? Were they connected to each other, the media, and think-tanks?

These authors and thinkers had helped in stereotyping Muslims as a potential enemy. Their narratives claimed that a) whereas Western civilization is progressive and enlightened, Islamic civilization lacks innovative ideas; therefore, values of these two civilizations are opposite to each other, and b) consequently, a clash between Western Christian and Islamic civilizations is imminent. Do they have a point? Are the logic and data they have used valid? Whatever the answer may be, their anti-Muslim views have found a space in the popular media. At the same time, equally influential thinkers with diametrically opposite views could not leave a mark on the contemporary *Zeitgeist*. On the contrary, they were relegated to the wilderness. Why couldn't they succeed in creating a similar network (Chapter 5)? Can science explain the failure of counterarguments? How much support did their opponents receive from the media, think-tanks, and establishment?

The final question of this algorithm is, why put so much effort and resources into demonizing Muslims and Islam? Were there any financial rewards? If so, for whom? Chapter 6 attempts to answer these questions by exploring the relationship between profit-making from violent conflicts, the demonization of victims, and violence against them. Is there a cause-and-effect relationship among these three factors? Also, there are other issues related to demonization, which are equally important. For example, is the treatment given to the Muslims unique in history, or were other civilizations also demonized in the past? If so, did they also had to endure acts of violence? Is demonization confined to religion-based groups, or does it affect other types of classifications of humanity? Since demonization of people has always preceded violence, are they interconnected?

The last chapter outlines the inferences deduced from the data presented in this book. Since economic factors are the fulcrum on which human activities are based, the book explores the link between capturing wealth and demonization of victims, which is an essential element in starting violent conflicts. Has Islamophobia also resulted in transferring wealth from Muslim countries to the West or trans-national mega-corporations (TNMCs)?

Conflicts among people and societies are an integral part of human nature; they are universal and ubiquitous, but what brings violence into conflicts? Humanity can never get rid of disputes and conflicts of interest, but how about violence? Can we ever eradicate violence from conflicts? Of course, that would be an ideal situation, but is it feasible? What are the consequences of a state of perpetual war on human existence? Does a permanent state of preparation for violent conflict pose an existential threat to humanity? What effect does it have on climate? Can climate change affect our planet? If so, how? Therefore, we need to understand factors that promote people's demonization, which is the first step of all violent conflicts.

However, there is another side to this story as well. Whether one believes in the concept of a clash between Islamic and Western Christian civilizations, the West still feels threatened by Islam. That has repercussions. Subsequently, the United States and its allies have bombed half a dozen Muslim countries in the first two decades of this century; that has not stopped even today.[20] President Bush had ordered the invasion of Iraq by citing newspaper articles and classified intelligence reports that Iraq had or was acquiring weapons of mass destruction (WMDs). They were later found to be false and even concocted.[21] Can another administration also use incorrect or concocted data and invade another country? Can that be done again against another Muslim country? Indeed, it was.

President Obama and President Trump used similar strategies to attack and bomb Libya and Syria; the same group of political activists and writers have been lobbying to invade Iran. They are using the same arguments, which neo-conservative activists used to invade Iraq. The U.S. administration had argued that terrorism still poses an existential threat to the United States. Can that be true? The world remains divided on this topic. This issue can be debated till the kingdom comes, but that does not change the fact that Afghanistan, Iraq, Syria,

Libya, Somalia, and other countries have been decimated. However, this policy is not confined to Muslim countries. North Korea, Cuba, Venezuela, Bolivia, and others have endured the same problem. There are also worldwide repercussions of the ongoing violent conflicts of the twenty-first century. Its impact is not confined to Muslim countries.

Are the issues raised by these questions still relevant today? That is a $6.2 trillion question. Two decades have passed since the United States and its allies invaded Afghanistan. America claims that it is a different country today than it was after 9/11. It is in a reconciliatory mode. Their tone may be different, but is it different in substance? Only time will tell, but the current U.S. President Joseph Biden has already reversed many overt Islamophobic policies that President Trump had put in place. President Biden has already withdrawn American forces from Afghanistan. The travel ban on Muslim countries imposed by President Trump has also been lifted. Though the demonization of Islam is still prevalent in the United States, the situation for Muslims is better; anti-Muslim violence has decreased, though it is still higher than what it was before 9/11. Anti-Muslim rallies are still taking place, but their supporters are smaller in numbers. They attract opponents in greater numbers; many of them are non-Muslim.

The problem for the United States could be that the country finds itself in a permanent state of war from which it cannot extricate itself. If so, is the current U.S. policy of aggression sustainable? Probably not, if we consider that violent clashes of the last two decades had severe consequences not only for Muslim countries but also for the United States. Invasions and occupations of two countries (Iraq and Afghanistan) have lasted for almost two decades. The War on Terror has the potential of being an ongoing violent conflict. These conflicts also have a human cost – 5 million deaths and 40 million refugees.[22] It has an economic cost to the United States as well, as $6.2 trillion was spent on violent conflicts[23] while poverty is rising. This money could have been spent on alleviating poverty within its borders. The United States has spent close to $2 trillion in Afghanistan during two decades of wars.[24] That means that the United States has spent tens of thousands of dollars per Afghan on its battle to subdue them. Had a quarter of that money gone to Afghanistan's economy, the country would have eradicated poverty. How long can the United States continue with violence without becoming bankrupt?

Second, Muslims feel they have been marginalized not only in the United States and other Western nations but also in Israel, India, and their allies. Do they have a point? Muslims are being killed in substantial numbers. Massacres, carpet bombings, and assassinations by unmanned drones are still taking place two decades after the United States crossed its *Rubicon*. Those who were assassinated were never indicted in any court of law. That makes the killings illegal. Israel has incarcerated millions of people in the occupied territory of Palestine, and India is doing the same in Kashmir. They are also prohibited and immoral activities, but there is a deafening silence about mass incarcerations in the mainstream media.

Can two billion Muslims be permanently incarcerated or placed behind high-tech walls? Probably not, even though the United States possesses a military unrivaled in firepower, it could bomb any country to the Stone Age without fear of retaliation except from Russia and China. Muslim countries pose no threat; neither do non-governmental organizations except reacting with random acts of terrorism, which has minimal consequences to the West, if any. The United States spends an enormous amount of money on weapons, armed forces, and covert operations worldwide; nevertheless, the most powerful nation in human history could not occupy Afghanistan and Iraq. Both countries appear to have gone through Armageddon, as their infrastructures have been decimated, bureaucracy destroyed, and economy ruined, notwithstanding, armed with primitive weapons, highly motivated insurgents have forced the United States to leave combat zones. By the end of 2020, the American presence was confined to the city of Kabul; 80% of the rural areas are already under the Taliban's control. The United States is looking to cut its losses and leave. Therefore, one could also ask if a quarter of the world population can ever be neutralized. We do not know, but it is a question worth asking.

Third, there are also conceptual inconsistencies within the notion that Islamic civilization is inherently violent. If it is true, the world would be doomed. If one-quarter of humanity is intrinsically violent, violence would not be a temporary phenomenon; the world would be permanently engulfed in wars. Therefore, if Islam is the root cause of violence, solving the problem of violence would require, at least in principle, drastic measures, such as mass extermination or incarceration of the entire Muslim population – almost two billion of them. Both options are unpleasant, impractical, ethically repugnant, and impossible tasks. Both have been tried before and failed; they brought disaster not only to the victims but also to the perpetrators.

Muslims have noted with alarm that violence has been directed against half a dozen Muslim countries in the last three decades; violence was justified on the argument that Muslims are violent; they can only be contained with an overwhelming force. The rhetoric reminds Muslims of the situation of Jews in Europe before the Second World War when Anti-Semitism was rampant in Europe. If it is not true that Muslims are inherently violent, why are they being perceived as violent? Is the demonization of Muslims laying the groundwork for an impending attack on another Muslim country? That is a cause of concern for Muslims.

Finally, the above questions also pose a challenge to the Muslim community. The assertion that Islamic civilization is violent may not be justified and appears to be demeaning to many Muslims worldwide; it still needs to be addressed by them. If they do not take the initiative, others will. So far, Muslims have failed to do so; consequently, others have replaced them on the podium during debates on policy. People known to have anti-Muslim views are labeled as experts on Islam and were invited to discuss an alleged association of Islam with violence to represent Muslim communities. Muslim voices have been muzzled. In the twenty-first century, Islamophobia has become a fact of life for Muslims worldwide; it needs to be confronted by Muslim leaders, thinkers, intellectuals, and Muslim societies. However, amidst a series of bad news for

Muslims, there is a silver lining, as they are finding more and more support among non-Muslims for their struggle against their demonization and stereotyping.

Simply put, there are credible arguments to claim that the main factor behind the demonization of Muslims in the twenty-first century is the policy of permanent wars, which requires a perpetual state of propaganda and a constant supply of potential enemies. War-mongers, who have an incentive to find enemies, have taken over the debate on an association of violence, either perceived or otherwise, with Islam.[25] Whether true or exaggerated, there is a fear of and about Muslims among many non-Muslims. Their anxiety and concerns, either real or perceived, need to be addressed; Muslim communities must provide objective evidence supporting their stand and appropriately offer arguments to refute any claims of inherent violence. These issues are not going to be resolved until a satisfactory solution to the problem is accomplished. At the same time, the question of frequent invasions of Muslim countries on false grounds is equally crucial not only for Muslims but also for the entire world. These issues, too, are not going to fade away either – not even in those countries that have conducted invasions of Muslim countries on false grounds.

Does this book have any relevance today? The world may or may not need another book on civilization and violence. Still, it needs other views on fallacies of the concept of a clash of civilizations between the Christian and Islamic societies. Foremost intellectuals of our time have presented their opinions, both for and against, on the neoconservative notion that Muslims are violent and pose existential threats to the West. Their books are widely available and have also been referred to in this book.

However, the central point of this book is different, and is this: how could a handful of political activists spread their vision across continents within a decade? How was that possible? What strategies did they use to demonize Islam and dehumanize Muslims? What lesson can we learn from their success? Even though their argument about a clash of civilizations was dismantled within a very short time, at least in the academic circle, their ideas still found a permanent space in the human psyche. Can science explain this dichotomy? Whatever the answer may be, subsequently, more than half a dozen countries were invaded and bombed. How could anti-Muslim activists become so successful in spreading Islamophobia? This book examines this enigma using evidence that is based on emerging innovations in how ideas spread. This has become possible due to an exponential increase in the computational power of software, which can analyze a vast number of data; it has helped to understand how the human brain analyzes complex data in seconds.

The controversies associated with this issue need to be addressed, as the world faces existential problems due to the impact of wars. It can only be resolved if we understand how ideas are conceived, developed, marketed, and spread. This book focuses on these issues. To find the answer, understanding the entire problem is critical. Becoming informed is the first step of this debate; it can be done by a systematic collection of relevant facts, analysis of valid data, a transparent path of arriving at inferences, and finally, disbursement of unbiased information – an enterprise which this book has undertaken.

Notes

1 Bhagwat Geeta; 2:32.
2 Bhagwat Geeta; 2:37.
3 New Testament; Luke 19:26–27.
4 New Testament; Mathew; 10:34–35.
5 Deuteronomy; 31:17–18.
6 Deuteronomy; 20:13–14.
7 Runnymede Trust, *Islamophobia: A Challenge for Us All* (1997), https://www.runnymedetrust.org/publications/islamophobia-a-challenge-for-us-all.
8 Edward Said, *Covering Islam*, Introduction, xi–xxx; John Esposito, *The Islamic Threat*.
9 John Esposito and Dalia Mogahed, *Who Speaks for Islam?* 76–94.
10 Ibid.
11 Runnymede Trust, *Islamophobia: Still a Challenge for Us All* (2017), https://www.runnymedetrust.org/publications/islamophobia-still-a-challenge-for-us-all.
12 Karen Armstrong, *Muhammad: A Biography of the Prophet*, Chapter 1.
13 Ibid.
14 Clifford Morgan et al., *Introduction to Psychology*, 467.
15 Imbesat Daudi, *Civilization and Violence: Islam, the West and the Rest*.
16 Daudi, *Civilization and Violence*, 137–138.
17 Daudi, *Civilization and Violence*.
18 Pankaj Mishra, *Age of Anger: A History of the Present*.
19 Hong-Jian Yin et al., https://www.hindawi.com/journals/sp/2017/5046905/.
20 Daudi.
21 Barry Lando, *Web of Deceit*, Chapter 9. Also see "Covering the Kay Report," *Accuracy in Media*, October 8, 2003, https://www.aim.org/aim-column/covering-the-kay-report/.
22 https://www.globalresearch.ca/us-has-killed-more-than-20-million-people-in-37-victim-nations-since-world-war-ii/5492051. Also see https://consortiumnews.com/2018/04/25/how-many-millions-have-been-killed-in-americas-post-9-11-wars-part-3-libya-syria-somalia-and-yemen/;https://www.globalresearch.ca/numbers-of-casualties-resulting-from-americas-post-911-wars-of-aggression/5638317.
23 https://www.cnbc.com/2019/11/20/us-spent-6point4-trillion-on-middle-east-wars-since-2001-study.html.
24 https://www.nytimes.com/interactive/2019/12/09/world/middleeast/afghanistan-war-cost.html.
25 Deepa Kumar, *Islamophobia and the Politics of Empire*, Chapter 10. Also see Nathan Lean, *The Islamophobia Industry*; Stephen Sheehi, *The Ideological Campaign Against Muslims*.

1 Stereotyping of Muslims as violent

The problem and its consequences

On the evening of September 30, 2012, Randolph Linn was sitting alone at his home in St. Joe, Indiana, a small town near Toledo, Ohio, drinking beer and watching Fox News. Later in the evening, he left his home, drove to Toledo, parked his SUV near the Toledo Mosque, found an open door, and entered the mosque with a few gasoline cans. A gun in one hand and a can of petrol in the other, he looked into each room and found no one. Linn then poured gasoline on the prayer rugs and set them ablaze. The mosque was destroyed. He left the scene before firefighters arrived. His red SUV, however, was identified; he was arrested two days later. Linn admitted to the arson, pleaded guilty, and was sentenced to twenty years in prison. The court ordered him to pay $1.4 million for restitution.[1]

Was it of any significance that he was watching Fox News? Possibly, yes. The network is known for anti-Muslim views, but Linn may also have consumed about forty-five cans of beer before he embarked on his misadventure. Did alcohol play any role? That is also possible. However, many people do both – drink beer and watch Fox News, but do not burn mosques. Did Islamophobia, which is widely prevalent in the United States, play a role in his decision to burn the mosque? Probably! Since angst can also trigger anger, was anger the motivating factor? How about ignorance? Perhaps! During his trial, Linn's dabbling in issues pertaining to Islam and Muslims made it clear that he had no idea about Islam. However, most Americans also do not have any clear idea about Islam, but they do not go on a rampage. Linn had never met a Muslim in his life, but he declared that all Muslims are terrorists and are killing Americans around the world. He claimed that his act was in retaliation for what Muslims have been doing to Americans.[2]

It was sheer luck that no one was hurt on that day. Others were not as lucky if they happened to resemble Muslims. On August 5, 2012, Wade Michael Page entered a Sikh temple at Oak Creek, Wisconsin, and opened fire on men and women who had assembled to prepare a communal meal, which is open to all, Sikhs and non-Sikhs alike. Police arrived promptly at the scene. Page was shot by the police, though he died of a self-inflicted wound to his head. Before his death, however, he had gunned down five men and one woman.[3] We do not know his reason for going on a shooting spree in a Sikh temple; it is buried with him.

DOI: 10.4324/9781003323105-2

But why? Is it because all male members of the community were wearing turbans? It is an integral part of their faith. Is it a coincidence that Wade chose a Sikh temple as his target? Probably not! Did the portrayal of Muslims as violent people, which generates intense Islamophobia in the U.S., play a role in his decision to go after Sikhs? Probably! Of all the immigrants, Sikhs resemble the most to the stereotypical image of Muslims and Middle Eastern men, and they have been the worst victims of hate crimes in the United States after 9/11. A Sikh, Balbir Singh Sodhi, was the first victim of violence by a vigilante after 9/11.[4] Those who had killed Sikhs and Hindus later told the police that they believed they were killing Muslims.[5] Ignorance perhaps! For them, they are all "others."

Turbans and beards have been the symbols of Islamic culture in the Western perception ever since Arabs and Turks came knocking at the periphery of Europe, although people of other faiths also keep a beard and wear a turban, and most Muslims do not use turbans. For example, Sikhs are not Muslims; they have been killed not because of their faith but because they have been perceived as Muslims. Was the shooting at the Sikh temple solely due to mistaken identity? Possibly! However, one does not have to wear a turban and grow a beard or look like a Muslim to be assaulted in the United States. Besides, what does a typical Muslim look like? Brown or turbaned? Not necessarily! Many of them are whites or Orientals. Muslims are the least monolithic groups of all their cohorts; they belong to all races – black, white, brown, and in between.

Random acts of violence against Muslims, Middle Eastern-looking men, and hijab-wearing women have become very common in the United States and on the other side of the Atlantic.[6] Numerous acts of violence have taken place against Muslims after 9/11 in the United States and other Western countries. Is there an inherent bias against Muslims in the United States? What makes Linns and Pages of the world commit hate crimes of such magnitude against people they have never met before? Are they genetically programmed to kill "other" people? Of course not; at least not according to the facts.

Is the violence, which is directed against Muslims in the United States and Europe, xenophobia? Probably, as merely being brown is enough to be assaulted or even killed by self-proclaimed American zealots. Many Indians have been attacked and even killed in the United States in the last few decades. Hindus, one of the few ethnic groups supporting President Trump, have also been victims of hate crimes.[7] Occasionally, they may have been mistaken to be Middle Eastern and Muslims, but many times, Hindu Indians have been assaulted because they are immigrants or looked like one. For example, vigilante groups, who also claimed to be white nationalists, targeted Hindus in New Jersey.[8] They called themselves the *Dotbuster*, referring to the red vermillion dots (bindis), which Hindu women wear on their foreheads.

Immigrants are not the only victims of hatred. On October 27, 2018, Robert Bowers walked into the Tree of Life Synagogue in Pittsburgh and opened fire, killing eleven Jewish worshippers.[9] It was the deadliest attack on the Jewish community, but not the last. Six months later, a nineteen-year-old white male walked into another synagogue and opened fire, killing one person.[10] Anti-Semitic violence has also increased in the United States in the last decade.[11] Jewish citizens are not the only Americans who have been targeted for violence. Dylan Roof walked into Emanuel African Methodist Church in Charleston, South Carolina, and killed nine black worshippers.[12] Even several white Americans have been killed in rampages over the last few decades.[13]

In other words, random acts of violence in the United States and the West are not solely due to fear of Muslims or vengeful anger towards them. Other ethnic groups, immigrants, and people of color have also been targeted.[14] At stake, therefore, is something else as well, not merely hatred of Islam and Muslims. Further, these events do not fully explain the state of violence in the United States either, as two-thirds of all acts of terrorism against civilians are committed in the United States by the so-called Christian groups; almost all perpetrators are "white" Americans.[15] Their actions are seldom perceived as terrorism. Why? Is it because their acts are not violent enough?

Therefore, the widespread perception of Islam as a violent religion may not be appropriate; neither is blaming Muslims as inherently violent correct. If so, why are Muslims being labeled as violent? There are two possible explanations: a) contrary to all evidence, these killers may still believe or may have been led to believe that Muslims are at war with them, the "white" Americans. After all, the concept of a clash of civilizations between the West and Islam was vigorously promoted by the opinion-makers before the invasion of Iraq and Afghanistan; b) the other possibility is that forces, which are universal, such as globalization, or the inequality of wealth, affect all groups of people. These factors were present in other parts of the world, but not in the West; now, they are also affecting American society. As Pankaj Mishra argues, these forces are subtle, invisible, and beyond the comprehension of ordinary folks.[16]

Indeed, the problem and consequences of the demonization of Muslims are more complicated than it appears. As noted by many political thinkers, this view was actively promoted by the Bush administration and senior government officials, politicians from both the Republican and Democratic Party, pro-Israeli think-tanks, right-wing members of Christian leadership, members of the Council of Foreign Relations (CFR), as well as neo-conservative supporters of the U.S. foreign policy establishment and the media. During the preparatory phase of the invasion of Iraq, the mainstream media in the United States was filled with biased opinions and fake news, which was designed to demonize Islam, Islamic civilization, and Muslims.[17]

For example, during an interview on national television, Jerry Falwell, a famous name within the Christian religious establishment, declared that Mohammad, the Prophet of Islam, was a terrorist and loved violence.[18] He neither revealed his sources of the information nor did he indicate that he had ever studied Qur'an. He is not alone in expressing such sentiments about Islam and Muslims without providing any facts. Franklin Graham, Jimmy Swaggart, Pat Robertson, and other notable names of the United States' Christian movement have also expressed similar views.[19] They have shown that they do not possess even a rudimentary knowledge of Islam.

These are influential people; they are the opinion-makers who move their flocks to vote for candidates of their choice. These men have a podium to themselves, and many of their followers respect their views. Ordinary folks come to listen to them. Their words are the parameters on which perceptions of citizens are gauged. These religious leaders have helped to change the political landscape of the United States, as 90% of their followers vote for the Republican Party. They were instrumental in not only getting President Bush but also President Trump elected to the White House, even though the latter may not have led a life of a "good" Christian. In essence, contrary to facts, some Americans perceive Islam and Muslims as the enemy of America, which was promoted by religious leaders.

Such populist rhetoric brings accolade and money to their campaigns. Political leaders from both parties may or may not believe or even care whether Muslims are violent, but expediency demands that they should base their political platform on the notion that Muslims pose a threat to the security of the country and that Islam is incompatible with the West or they are inherently violent.[20] Many junior members of the Bush administration, as well as followers of these holy men, had based their career on the Islamophobic platform; they may also have harbored similar views about Muslims earlier but could not express. Indeed, the pulpit was not the only institution that has taken up the task of denouncing Islam as a violent religion and Muslims as violent people. After the destruction of the World Trade Center, American politicians on both sides of the aisle come up with innovative rhetoric in demonizing Muslims to show that they are more stringent on the so-called Islamic terrorism than their competitors.

For example, Michelle Bachman, the Republican candidate for the highest office in the United States, was warning about an alleged Muslim plan to impose Sharia laws in the United States and the intention of the Muslim Brotherhood to infiltrate the American government.[21] How Muslims would achieve the supposed goal was never explained; neither was she asked to substantiate her claim. Her assertion is difficult to believe, as Muslims as a group are one of the most disenfranchised segments of American society. They have no influence in the corridors of power. Her speeches were a classic case of demagoguery; they helped her surge ahead in polls, but she soon faded. Other candidates with more outlandish innuendos took the lead in polls.

She was not alone among the politicians vying for the highest office of the United States to use populist rhetoric. Demonizing Muslims had become a favorite tool of politicians; demagoguery played a pivotal role in the 2016 presidential election in the United States. Ted Cruz, the Senator from Texas, who was also running for the White House, announced that he would carpet bomb Iraq and Syria.[22] So did Mark Rubio, Chris Christie, Bobby Jindal, and almost all other candidates in the fray. They overlooked the fact that President Obama had already pulverized these countries. Dr. Ben Carson, another candidate for the presidency, went one step further, as he declared that a Muslim should not be allowed to hold the highest office of the land, which is against the Constitution.[23] If elected, he was supposed to defend it. He stole the limelight for a short period, surged in the polls, and then faded.

Candidate Trump, with the most outlandish statements, took the lead over everyone and won the 2016 election. During his campaign, he promised that he would not let Muslims enter the country. In essence, he was implying that all Muslims are terrorists, or at the least, they should be assumed to be terrorists until proven otherwise. Trump provided no evidence to substantiate his stand on Muslims, but those who attended his rallies lapped up his promise. He drew huge crowds; more than one-third of all Americans still support him. Other candidates were equally bullish about expressing anti-Muslim sentiments, which means politicians do not apprehend any backlash if they present even outrageous Islamophobic statements.

On the contrary, such statements bring them applause and donations. These populist politicians express opinions that resonate with the views of Islamophobic warriors; their career and financing of their campaign are based on propagating negative images of Muslims. They had been effective in remaining in the limelight partly because of the coverage they get from the press.

For reasons that are hardly discussed in the mainstream media, those who express negative views about Islam find generous space in the mainstream media. Those who oppose such views are relegated to the alternative media. These are independent newspapers and magazines; they are not controlled by the corporate media giants. They have minimal market share and operate at the fringes of society; this is not by choice, but the corporate media do not back their views. Anti-populist positions in the United States can become a financial disaster for media barons; anti-Muslim rhetoric was the only game in town as the preparation of the invasion of Iraq was going on. Those who opposed the invasion were silenced.

How involved is the media in demonizing Muslims? Did the mainstream media play any role in swaying vulnerable people into believing that Muslims are to be feared as they are violent? One way to look at this question is to compare how the media covers violence by Muslims and non-Muslims.

In the fall of 2013, the United States army charged two of its officers for the first-degree murders and conducted their court-marshals: Major Nidal Hasan and Sergeant Robert Bales. Both were indicted for killing more than a dozen people. Both accepted their crimes. That is where the similarities end. Major Nidal was sentenced to death. The victims of his rampage were his co-workers; all were Americans. On March 11, 2012, Sergeant Bales, who was stationed in Afghanistan, had snuck out from his camp to a nearby village, Panjwari, and started shooting at the sleeping villagers. By the time the carnage was over, sixteen people, all Afghans, lay dead. Bales was also charged with the killings; he also admitted his guilt and was sentenced to life in prison without parole.[24] Why did Bales get the life sentence, but Hasan the death sentence? One does not know, but is this surprising?

The far more critical issue is how their respective crimes and trials were covered in the mainstream media; they were indeed very different, even though there are many similarities between these two people. Both were Americans by birth and grew up in the United States. Both joined the army by free will.

However, there is one significant difference: Major Nidal Hasan was a Muslim, while Sargent Robert Bales is a Christian. Did their religious beliefs make a difference in how both crimes were presented in the media? We do not know, but their acts were not covered objectively by the mainstream media. Whereas the shooting spree at Fort Hood was attributed to Major Hasan's radicalization without providing any proof, the killings by Sargent Bales were blamed on the stress of war.[25]

Indeed, Bales had reason to be psychologically affected by his job. He had served four rounds of deployment in the war zones; he may have been suffering from brain injury or post-traumatic stress disorder.[26] Four years after his trial, Sergeant Bales appealed against his sentence on the ground that he was taking medication for malaria, which, according to his lawyer, "made him do" the killings.[27] On the other hand, Major Hasan's crime was not portrayed in the media as the fallout of the stress of serving in the military during war-time. His shooting spree was attributed to him being a Muslim. Tunku Varadarajan, a professor at New York University, describes the state of mind of Nidal Hasan in an article in *Forbes Magazine* titled "Going Muslim." It is remarkable that he had never met Hasan or had a conversation with him, but he explains in detail the state of mind of the accused.

The title of the article itself defines Varadarajan's interpretation of the action of Major Hasan. For him, this shooting was not a single event by a single individual who happened to be a Muslim, but a typical act of inherent violence hidden within all Muslims. It implies that any Muslim, even those living in the United States for a long time, can become violent at any given moment. According to his theory, even those Muslims, who were born and had lived in the West, are not immune from this "disease." Why? He does not explain. Genetic predisposition, perhaps? If not, is it cultural programming? He never explained the science behind his theory of "going Muslim." He based his arguments on unexplained assumptions, as he implied that Nidal Hasan and his acts of violence on that fateful day represent Islam and over 1.8 billion Muslims. Neither did he give any other example of Muslims being involved in such actions to substantiate his argument that the shooting was the manifestation of *inherent violence* hidden within the Muslim psyche. Deepa Kumar spells out Varadarajan's state of mind:[28]

> The most virulent form of this green scare was articulated by NYU professor Tunku Varadarajan. In a November 2009 Forbes article titled "Going Muslim," Varadarajan argued that what precipitated the tragedy at Fort Hood was not the racist harassment that Hassan faced in the army or the emotionally debilitating pressure of his job as an overworked army psychiatrist, but rather a condition that he suggests is inherent to all Muslims: the tendency towards violence. He argued that Hasan did not "go postal" – that is the breakdown and become violent (the term became famous after a 1986 shooting by a postal worker). Instead, Varadarajan argued, Hasan was enacting, in a cold and calculated manner, the teachings

of Islam. He was "going Muslim." As Varadarajan puts it, "This phrase [going Muslim] would describe the turn of events where seemingly inte-grated Muslim-American – a friendly donuts vendor in New York, say or an officer in the U.S. Army at Fort Hood – discards his apparent integra-tion into American society and elects to vindicate his religion in the act of messianic violence against his fellow Americans."

Could the difference in the media coverage of the two events be attributed to the nationalities of the victims? The killings of Americans are different from the murder of Afghans who are not "us" but "them." That may not be the case all the time. For example, Aaron Alexis, a Navy veteran and a contractor serving for the Navy, also went on a rampage, killing twelve people at the Naval ship-yard in Washington, DC, on September 16, 2013. Most of his victims were also military personnel or contractors. The coverage of his acts of violence in the American media was objective; he was appropriately portrayed as a delusional individual hearing voices.[29] His portrayal in the media was even sympathetic; he was described as a "Buddhist who loved to meditate."[30]

Indeed, the coverage of violent events perpetrated by Muslims in the mainstream media is palpably different from that of non-Muslim groups. Shooting at the workplace by employees is common in the United States and is usually referred to as "going postal." This term relates to an earlier event in which an employee of the postal service ran amok, killing his co-workers. People who use violence at work-places and in schools, which is becoming more frequent, are usually portrayed as having mental health issues or having pathological resentment against their super-iors or co-workers.

But it was different for Syed Farook and his wife Tashfeen Malik, who opened fire in 2015, killing fourteen people at a banquet hall where the office conference was going on. According to the police reports, Farook came at 8.30 A.M., attended the meeting for a short time, left, and then returned with his wife. Both were armed and opened fire. The shooting was described as an inspired terrorist event, but the authorities did not provide any evidence. Was it? The American authorities reported that he might have visited the website belonging to Anwar al-Awlaki, the Muslim cleric who claimed to be affiliated with Al Qaeda. We do not know if Farook watched the Awlaki talks, but if he did visit the site, does it automatically mean that he supported or was influ-enced by Al Qaeda? Or was he ready to die for the Jihadi ideology? Many non-Muslim killers, on the other hand, have confessed the killing by citing Biblical verses, but Christianity has never been blamed for inciting violence. No one ever referred that they were going *Christian*.

Therefore, the relevant question is: were Farook and Malik going *Muslim*, as Varadarajan portrayed, or were they going *postal*? In theory, it could have been either, but the U.S. media assumed that it was a terrorist event and the couples were going *Muslim*. However, many questions have remained unanswered and unexplored. Why did Farook suddenly leave the function and go home to pick up the guns? Was there a simmering dispute between him and his co-workers?

Was there an exchange of words at the meeting that flared up and spiraled out of control? One does not know and will never know. The police did not investigate this angle, and if they did, they have not communicated it to the public. The media did not address this issue either. On the contrary, the couple was portrayed as radicalized Muslims, although their connection to Al Qaeda has never been established. Nonetheless, this shooting is also believed to be an Islamic event.

Muslims involved in terrorist acts had personal reasons to retaliate, which is the most critical reason behind their acts of violence. Najibullah Zazi and Faisal Shahzad, who were convicted as terrorists, were affected by the bombings in Afghanistan and Pakistan.[31] The bombings had killed their friends and family. However, the portrayal of killers in the Western media as radical Islamists, if they happen to be Muslims, is not unusual; it is a routine. Their killings are described as Islamic events. When Omar Mateen, an American born to Afghan Muslim parents, who opened fire at a gay bar in Florida, his acts of violence were described as an event influenced by the teachings of Islam, which was dubbed as a homophobic ideology. Never mind that Mateen was a disturbed individual; he may also have been gay himself and often frequented the same bar.[32]

On the other hand, the killing of nine black worshippers in South Carolina by Dylan Roof and bombing events in Austin, TX[33] by Anthony Conditt[34] are never described as Christian events; neither were these men portrayed as people who were radicalized by fundamentalist Christianity. The latter blew himself up during a standoff with the police, but the media did not describe the event as suicide bombing. A virulent brand of Christianity radicalized both killers; they frequented websites, which are also popular among radical groups; they are also widely accessible on the internet.

Indeed, shootings, if and when done by non-Muslims, are not described as Christian events, even if they are done in the name of perverted teachings of Christianity. There have been dozens of mass killings in the last few years; most of them were done by practicing Christians. Some of the shootings, such as the bombing of abortion clinics, were inspired by their warped interpretations of Christian texts. Were they going *Christian?* Indeed, many white Americans, all Christians, have shot their way into the record books. Still, they are not believed to be inspired by radical Christian preachers. Timothy McVeigh bombed the Alfred Murrah Federal Building in Oklahoma City, killing 168 people,[35] or Stephen Paddock killed fifty-nine people at a concert in Las Vegas;[36] Dylan Roof opened fire at a church, killing nine African American worshippers;[37] Nikolas Cruz killed nineteen students at Parkland, Florida.[38] Any of the hundreds of shooters who happened to be Christian by birth are not described as Christian or Jewish warriors. The list goes on and on.

Are the Muslims being judged by different parameters? Nathan Lean asks another question: why is it that ten years after 9/11, fear, mistrust, and hatred of Muslims were at their highest ever? He has the following answer:[39]

As it turns out, the decade-long of Islamophobia that rattled through the American public is the product of tight-knit and inter-connected right-wing fear merchants. They have labored through since the planes hit the towers to convince their compatriots that Muslims are gaining a dangerous influence in the West. Bigoted bloggers, racist politicians, fundamentalist religious leaders, Fox News pundits, and religious Zionists, theirs is an industry of hate: the Islamophobia industry. James Zogby, President of the Arab American Institute, said that "The intensity [of Islamophobia] has not abated and remains a vein that's very near the surface, ready to be tapped at any moment." Juan Cole, an author of Engaging the Muslim World and a professor of modern Middle Eastern and South Asian history at the University of Michigan, agreed. American, he said, "has been given the message to respond this way by the American political elite, mass media and by select special interests."

In the current political climate, Islam has become a punching bag for anyone and everyone who aspires to stay in the limelight. It appears as if we are living not only in the age of fake news but also in the age of demagoguery. In the twenty-first century, the verbal firepower of demagogues is directed against Muslims. A few decades ago, communists and socialists were targeted with equal intensity, and now the villains are the Russians, Chinese, and Venezuelans. Neoconservative crusaders have succeeded in their endeavor to isolate anti-Muslim violence from the anti-war movement, as there was hardly any protest from politicians and social activists in the media against the invasions of Iraq and Afghanistan and the bombing of half a dozen Muslim countries. Even the anti-war movement, which was very vocal during the Vietnam War and the civil wars of Central America, maintained a deafening silence over the deliberate killings of civilians in the war zones.[40]

Simply stated, there is a difference between how violent events are covered in the mainstream media if they are perpetrated by Muslims or by non-Muslims. Does the difference in the media coverage make a difference in how ordinary folks perceive Islam and Muslims? Can one also argue that this perception has caused the mayhem that the world is experiencing today? These are not the only questions. Whether Islamic civilization is violent or not is at the root of many contentious debates in the United States. But is it? That needs to be addressed first.

Therefore, the question is: are Muslims indeed violent, or are they only perceived as being violent? There is a distinction between the two, but since perception matters more than reality, the end effect of creating an image is no different from the schism between reality and its perception. Men who went on a killing spree and politicians and political activists who indulge in the business of fear-mongering are not alone in believing that Muslims are violent or prone to become violent. A large segment of the American public has been led to believe the same.

Here are some numbers: almost five years after the invasion of Iraq, no less than 41% of Americans believe that Saddam Hussein had strong links to Al

Qaeda, 26% of adults in the United States believe that Iraq had weapons of mass destruction (WMDs), and 24% of them thought that several of the hijackers who attacked the United States on 9/11 were Iraqis. None of them was an Iraqi national. Their many other claims are also false.[41] For example, the percentage of people who believe that Iraq was involved in the destruction of the World Trade Center (WTC) is exceptionally high among U.S. soldiers. Almost 90% of U.S. service personnel still believe that Saddam Hussein had some role in the 9/11 attack. Three-quarters of American soldiers serving in Iraq in 2005 felt that they were in Iraq to stop Saddam Hussein from protecting Al Qaeda.[42]

These and other data also confirm that the American perceptions about Muslims are not based on facts; they have been formed on illusions promoted in the media by the powers-that-be. More than half of Americans were convinced that Saddam Hussein supported the nineteen hijackers who crashed four jetliners into the WTC and the Pentagon, killing almost three thousand people.[43] True, the number of people who believed the myth of Islamic violence decreased by nearly half by December 2005; still, a quarter of all Americans believed that Saddam Hussein either masterminded or helped to execute the attacks on the WTC.

The results of these surveys are more troublesome if one considers that the Kay Commission, which was set up by President Bush to investigate the so-called intelligence failure concerning the presence of WMDs in Iraq, reported that the allegations of the presence of such weapons were incorrect.[44] They may even be deceptive. In other words, even though the President accepted that the United States invaded Iraq, a country that had nothing to do with any acts of aggression against the United States, a decade after 9/11, the majority of Americans still believed that the government was justified in invading Iraq.

These are not the only examples of deeply embedded beliefs that are widely prevalent in Western perception but have no factual basis. For instance, Americans believed that the United States was about to be attacked by Iraq, which was not only false but also ridiculous. After its defeat in the First Gulf War (1990), Iraq had no means to attack any country, much less to invade or even bomb the most powerful nation on the planet. How would Saddam Hussein send his military across the Atlantic without being annihilated? By a flying carpet, perhaps. Neo-conservative thinkers and activists have played a crucial role in creating the violent image of Muslims.[45] They have also been guiding America's foreign policy over the last two decades. Is there a cause-and-effect relationship between the two events?

Before answering the question, let us explore who these neo-conservative activists are, what they want, and whom they represent. Members of the neo-conservative movement can be divided into two broad groups: a) Pro-Israeli Zionists, whose central, if not the only goal, is to preserve Israel's dominance in the region; b) super-nationalists whose primary goal is to maintain America's unchallenged military power. Their interests are coordinated by the American-Israeli Political Action Committee (AIPAC) and the military-industrial complex, and oil lobbies. Their interests overlap. Both groups have called for higher funding for the military, development, and deployment of the most advanced weapons and expansion of military bases around the world. They have also promoted the privatization of America's wars. Their policy has been a bonanza for those corporations which form the military-industrial complex. They are the same groups of companies that control the mainstream media and weapon manufacturers, intelligence gathering, homeland security. Disaster-management companies have become an integral part of the military-industrial complex. They also provide soldiers on contract and manage the aftermath of wars and natural disasters.

Political activists who are portrayed as patriots, and act like super-nationalists, are also highly qualified individuals. Still, they have hardly provided evidence to prove the concomitance of violence with Islam. Neither have they produced any objective studies to substantiate their arguments (see Chapter 4). No comparative analysis of violence within and among different nations and communities has ever been done by them to prove or disprove whether the presence of violence in Islamic countries is more than what is prevalent in other countries. True, a handful of authors, such as Sam Huntington, have presented a few studies with data. However, the credibility of those data has been questioned by neutral observers.[46] Their works have generated criticism in academic circles, but their assertions were accepted with great fanfare by the popular culture and in the mainstream media. Fallacies associated with their work have been discussed later.

On the other end of the spectrum of this debate are critics of the current foreign policy of the United States. They claim that America's policy is the primary reason for violent conflicts around the world and argue that the policy of shoot first and talk later is fundamentally flawed. It has caused numerous wars around the world and has been detrimental to the interests of the West as well. In the last two decades, almost five million people have been killed, and fifty million have become refugees altering the demographic landscape of Europe.[47] Muslims may be the object of the demonization today, but until recently, the perceived fear and scorn of the United States was directed primarily against the communists. Since three of the four prominent nations were located in the East (China and Korea) and Southeast (Vietnam) Asia, racial bias played an essential role in diabolizing enemies. The rhetoric against Asians was hardly any different from what was used against Japanese Americans. During the Second World War, Germans were also transformed into monsters. In between the First and the Second World Wars, Jews were similarly vilified. Anti-Semitism was rampant not only in Germany but in many Western countries, including the United States.

These critics may have a point that violence is not the answer. Using force had been tried in the past by former colonial powers; that strategy not only failed over time but also backfired, as violence eventually engulfed Europe as well. More Europeans died in the two World Wars than all wars of the last two centuries. These critics argue that the current American foreign policy, which is similar to the gunboat diplomacy of the British Empire, is equally flawed. If the approach of using violence failed in the twentieth century, as in the case of former colonial powers, why would it not also fail in the twenty-first century? If the past is any indication, the policy of using force as the first choice will also be detrimental to the West in the future.

However, there are other sides to using force. Violence had been extremely profitable for colonial powers. It maintained the Western hegemony over the rest of the world for over three centuries. Apologists of imperialism have argued that violence was the *Zeitgeist* of the eighteenth century. Colonial powers were not the only ones to have used violence, which was essential for slavery and colonialism. Slavery and the slave trade, which were associated with extreme violence, gave a jumpstart to their economy, and the latter was the reason why the West remained the dominant force in the world after slavery was abolished.[48] Therefore, violence may have been worth the effort. Violence brought prosperity to Europe. According to Mark LeVine, the total amount of wealth extracted from Asia and Africa by the West is so vast that it cannot even be assessed. Utsa Patnaik documents in her book, *A Theory of Imperialism,* that the British Empire extracted and transferred approximately $45 trillion after 1765,[49] when it defeated the Mughal forces at the deciding battle of Buxar and forced the Mughal Emperor to sign the right to collect taxes (Diwani) from the province of Bengal.

However, in the end, this policy brought disaster to the colonial masters as well. As Hannah Arendt argues, the practice of using force in the colonial territories set the precedence of the policy of *might is right* in international conflicts.[50] Eventually, this policy affected Europeans – the two World Wars, which transformed the balance of power in the world. This helped China and India to emerge as political and economic powerhouses of the twenty-first century. Former colonies became independent. Still, the United States and NATO allies are in the permanent state of war.[51] The goal of the financial elites is to maintain economic gains.[52] This is what they have been doing for the last three centuries; wars have brought immense wealth to them.

A permanent state of war is a sound economic policy to the top 1% of the population, but it is detrimental to democracy, no matter how powerful and prosperous the nation may be. Weaker nations may be the first victims of violence, as wars are based on the principle of *might is right*. The initial gains of wars go to the powerful combatants. However, violence eventually engulfs them as well by altering their ability to make decisions as violence becomes a way of life. Take the example of Europe. As long as European nations avoided fighting on their soil by dividing the world into zones of influence, Europe remained peaceful, which brought prosperity. Peace in Europe lasted for over a hundred years, but power is addictive, and so is violence, especially if it is associated with power. The policy of might is right resulted in colonial wars and consequently domination of colonial subjects for centuries. However, it also paved the way to use force in Europe against those Europeans who could not resist. It resulted in the worst slaughter in human history during the First World War, only to be superseded by far more extensive massacres during the Second World War.

Can a parallel be drawn between the current state of perpetual war by the United States and European Powers during the inter-World War period? The question is that if it has any relevance in the current context. The United States has invaded, sent its military, or bombed more than a dozen countries in the last two decades. There has not been a single year in which the United States has not been at war or used force against other countries. Worse, it has become customary to remain in a permanent state of war. Its military continues to be deployed in far-away places. Not a week goes by when the President or some other senior officials do not threaten a country or the other of dire consequences. However, Americans go on with their lives as if nothing is happening. The American economy now is based mainly on wars and preparing for wars, not unlike the Roman Empire before it finally disintegrated. The parallel, once again, is academic.

Simply put, whatever the reason, these false perceptions about Muslims in the West are the result of a deeply entrenched fear of Muslims, which in turn is related to a sustained campaign of disparaging of Muslims as violent people. The other possibility is that some Muslim countries might have committed more acts of violence than their Western cohorts. Unfortunately, no valid studies have been presented to substantiate those assertions, which portray the inherent violence of Muslims.

Views of opinion-makers about Muslims are at variances from historical facts. Is it because one could, in theory, argue that Muslims behave violently, even if it cannot be proven? The fundamental question remains: are Muslims inherently violent? There are two distinctly opposite views on this topic. On one end of the spectrum are the neoconservatives in the United States, their supporters in Israel's right-wing political parties, and Christian Zionists. They argue that Muslims are perceived to be violent because they are violent. Some of the transnational corporations (TNCs) have also embraced their views, which are not only in the defense industry, including companies involved in weapon manufacturing, intelligence, homeland security, defense contracting, and disaster management but also in the energy sector and the media.[53] As a group, they are described as the military-industrial complex; they have significantly benefited from the ongoing violent conflicts between the West and Muslim-majority countries.[54] Is there a cause-and-effect relationship between profit-making by mega-corporations and the war industry? Prominent thinkers of our time, such as Chalmers Johnson, Naomi Klein, Chris Hedges, and others, believe that there is evidence to claim that it does.

Deprecating a group of people is a costly affair; it requires control of the media, skilled workforce, financial resources, and methodical execution of a long-term plan. Neoconservative authors have promoted violent conflicts as a *clash of civilizations* between Islam and the West.[55] They have the backing of people who have deep pockets. Those who are on the front line in fabricating the innuendos get generous financial support not only from TNCs but also from real-estate tycoons. They make their fortune from acquiring land from the Israeli government in the Occupied Territory at throw-away prices, building settlements, and selling them at a considerable profit.[56] In general, these TNCs are controlled by the financial sector of the corporate world.[57]

The same entities also control the mainstream media, whose support was crucial in making these theologians, politicians, intellectuals, and journalists influential in their respective countries.[58] Men and women who control the media are capable of creating perceptions about events and people. They not only influence the *Zeitgeist*; they create it. They decide what should be perceived to be right or wrong. They dominate popular culture. Their words carry weight, as they are called upon by the mainstream media to comment as experts on Islam and terrorism even though they have no requisite credentials. Without providing any evidence, these men and women claim and propagate that the attitude of the so-called *Islamic civilization* towards violence is enshrined within the framework of their religion. Therefore, Muslims will not change their belief and cannot change their behavior because they are fanatics in their faith.

Their assertion implies that any peaceful dialogue with their Muslim opponents is impossible, which means that Muslims can only be dealt with a superior force.[59] The *War on Terror,* which President Bush started, was justified on the same principles. Israel's acts of continued violence against Palestinians are also based on the same notion.[60] President Obama, who received the Nobel Peace Prize, pursued the same policy with equal vehemence as he bombed half a dozen Muslim countries.[61] He, too, had based his policy on the argument that dialogue for a peaceful solution with Muslims is not possible, as they are irrational and prone to violence. The only difference was that President Obama used a softer tone than President Bush, but his policy affected more Muslim countries and far more people than his last four predecessors. A softer tone may have brought President Obama Nobel Prize. The trend is expected to continue, as the present President Donald Trump has also promised to use violence in dealing with Muslims.[62] His justification for using violence against Muslims is no different from that of President Obama.

Still, one could argue that Muslims are inherently violent, and the reason they did not commit as many genocides because they could not; others restrained them. Therefore, an equally important question in the debate over the association of violence with Islam is whether Muslim masses condone violence?

In theory, a lower number of violent activities in Muslim countries does not automatically mean that Muslim communities worldwide have denounced violence to achieve their economic goals. A relative decrease in violence in the Muslim world could also reflect a lack of capabilities or opportunities for committing acts of violence or an increase in vigilance by their opponents or both. What do people in Muslim-majority countries think about violence against innocent bystanders?

Gallup Research also wanted to know if Muslim masses around the world approve of violence. They designed a study based on valid statistical principles and surveyed over fifty thousand people from thirty-five different Muslim countries about their attitudes towards violence.[63] The selection of people for the survey was random. Their data were scientifically gathered; the numbers are authentic, and their study transparent. Other sources also confirmed the authenticity of their data; therefore, they fulfill all the criteria of valid research. For comparison, the authors also asked the same question to Americans.

Analyzing the data collected by Gallup Research, John Esposito and his colleague Dalia Mogahed showed that violence against civilians is justified by only 7% (one in fifteen adults) of the population across the entire Muslim world. In contrast, the percentage of U.S. citizens who justified violence against civilians is three and a half times higher (24% or one in four adults).[64] The authors concluded that the Muslim public opinion remains overwhelmingly against violence in general and non-participating civilians in particular. Muslims have held on to a non-violent response to acts of violence despite the occupation of Iraq and Afghanistan and recent attacks by unmanned drones, which have killed thousands of people, including civilians in Muslim-majority countries, namely Afghanistan, Pakistan, Somalia, Yemen, Palestine, et al. by the United States and NATO forces.

An equally important question is: on what ground do those Muslims who condone terrorism justify acts of violence? To find the answer, the authors went back and asked those individuals who defended violence against innocent civilians as to why do they approve acts of terrorism against civilians. They reported that within the specific group of 7% of the Muslim population of the world, who believe that violence against civilians is justified, almost all of them explained the rationale behind their justification on political grounds.[65] More importantly, they did not base their arguments on any Koranic verses or the Islamic doctrine and theology.

Esposito points out that this distinction is essential for practical reasons; for those who argue that violence is justified on political or economic grounds, a compromise with their enemies is possible. However, if the issue at the root of discords among combatants is purely religious or even if violence against innocent bystanders is being justified by religion, reconciliation, at least in theory, is not possible.[66] These data tell a different story. Despite a deeply ingrained perception in the West that Muslims are violent, the reality is that even at the height of violence against civilians in Muslim countries, which was conducted by the West, 93% of Muslims believe that violence against civilians of the West is not the solution to political and economic problems of their societies. This number is 76% for the people in the United States.

The American perception of Muslims being violent has also proven to be false. Far more people have been killed by the bombing campaigns undertaken by the United States and its allies in the last two decades than all terrorist groups could ever do over centuries. Therefore, the current Western perception does not reflect the reality of what happened before, during, and after the invasion of Iraq. Neither do they explain the causes of violent conflicts. These data only underline that the current perception of Western Powers, The West believes that violence is prevalent in Muslim-majority countries. However, it may not be the reality, and the *attitude* of the Western citizens about the two billion-strong Muslim community, may not be accurate, as they are based on that rhetoric.

Notes

1 https://www.washingtonpost.com/national/on-faith/mosque-arsonist-randolph-linn-sentence.
2 https://religionnews.com/2013/04/17/mosque-arsonist-randolph-linn-sentenced-to-20-years/.
3 https://www.splcenter.org/fighting-hate/intelligence-report/2012/sikh-temple-killer-wade-michael-page-radicalized-army.
4 https://www.nytimes.com/2001/09/17/us/sikh-owner-of-gas-station-is-fatally-shot-in-rampage.html.
5 .www.washingtonpost.com/…/suspect-in-kansas-bar-shooting-of-indians-apparently; *Iranian*, Feb. 28, 2017.
6 https://www.nbcnews.com/news/us-news/hate-attacks-muslims-u-s-spike-after-recent-acts-terrorism-n482456.
7 //www.washingtonpost.com/…/suspect-in-kansas-bar-shooting-of-indians-apparently; *Iranian*, Feb. 28, 2017.
8 https://www.hinduismtoday.com/modules/smartsection/item.php?itemid=638.
9 https://www.nytimes.com/2018/10/27/us/active-shooter-pittsburgh-synagogue-shooting.html.
10 https://www.foxnews.com/us/worshippers-recall-fatal-attack-on-california-synagogue.
11 "Antisemitic incidents Hit All Time High in 2021," ADL Report, https://www.adl.org.
12 https://www.nbcnews.com/storyline/charleston-church-shooting/charleston-shooter-dylann-roof-moved-death-row-terre-haute-federal-n749671.
13 https://www.nbcnews.com/storyline/texas-church-shooting.
14 https://immigrationoffice.org/2019/01/violence-against-immigrants-in-us.
15 https://www.washingtonpost.com/national/in-the-united-states-right-wing-violence-is-on-the-rise/2018/11/25/61f7f24a-deb4-11e8-85df-7a6b4d25cfbb_story.html.
16 https://www.theguardian.com/politics/2016/dec/08/welcome-age-anger-brexit-trump. Also see Pankaj Mishra, *From the Ruins of Empire*, 299–310; Mishra, *Age of Anger: A History of the Present*, 13–31.
17 Juan Cole, "Islamophobia and American Foreign Policy Rhetoric: The Bush Years and After," in John Esposito and Ibrahim Kalin (eds.), *Islamophobia*, 127–140. Also see Paul Street, "Yes, There is an Imperialist Ruling Class," https://www.counterpunch.org/2015/10/06/yes-there-is-an-imperialist-ruling-class/.
18 John Esposito and Dalia Mogahed, *Who Speaks for Islam?*; also see *Newsweek*, October 21, 2002, 40.
19 *Newsweek*, ibid.
20 John Esposito, *The Islamic Threat*, 218–220.
21 https://www.citjotv.com/2019/03/26/michelle-bachman-blows-the-whistle-on-hillarys-em-assistant-and-sharia-law/. Also see https://www.huffingtonpost.com/2011/11/03/michele-bachmann-sharia-law-constitution_n_1074009.html.
22 https://theweek.com/articles/592964/ted-cruz-wants-nuke-middle-east.
23 https://www.theguardian.com/us-news/2015/sep/20/ben-carson-no-muslim-us-president-trump-obama.
24 "Soldier Gets Life Without Parole in Deaths of Afghan Civilians," *The New York Times*, August 23, 2013.
25 "Accused G.I. 'Snapped' Under Strain, Official Says," *The New York Times*, March 15, 2012.
26 "Soldier Held in Afghan Massacre Had Brain Injury, Marital Problems," *ABC News*, March 12, 2012.
27 Greg Miller, "A Gruesome War Crime Renews Concerns About a Malaria Drug's Psychiatric Side Effects," *Wired*, August 15, 2013.
28 Deepa Kumar, *Islamophobia and the Politics of Empire*, 162.

29 Eric Tucker, "Aaron Alexis, Navy Yard Shooting Suspect, Thought People Followed Him With Microwave Machine," *The Huffington Post*, September 18, 2013 (retrieved September 22, 2013).

30 Molly Hennessy-Fiske and David Zucchino, "Aaron Alexis: An adept Buddhist chanter and an angry man with a gun," *Los Angeles Times*, September 16, 2013.

31 https://archives.fbi.gov/archives/news/stories/2009/september/zazi_092409. Also see https://www.nytimes.com/topic/person/faisal-shahzad.

32 Gary Detman, "Omar Mateen had behavioral issues in school, records show," *CBS12*, June 17, 2016.

33 https://www.nytimes.com/2017/01/10/us/dylann-roof-trial-charleston.html.

34 https://heavy.com/news/2018/03/mark-anthony-conditt-austin-bomber-bombing-suspect-name/.

35 https://www.theguardian.com/world/2001/jun/12/mcveigh.usa.

36 https://www.huffpost.com/entry/stephen-paddocks-point-may-have-been-how-easy-it-is_b_59d366cbe4b092b22a8e394f.

37 https://www.nytimes.com/2017/01/10/us/dylann-roof-trial-charleston.html.

38 https://heavy.com/news/2018/02/nikolas-cruz/.

39 Nathan Lean, *The Islamophobia Industry*, 9–10.

40 https://www.quora.com/Why-was-there-no-anti-war-movement-in-the-US-during-its-war-in-Iraq.

41 Barry Lando, *Web of Deceit*, 216–221.

42 Esposito and Mogahed, *Who Speaks for Islam?* 155.

43 Lando, ibid.; Chalmers Johnson, *Nemesis*.

44 https://www.armscontrol.org/print/1488.

45 See Chapters 2, 3, 4, and 5.

46 Edward Said, *Covering Islam*, xii–xxii.

47 Imbesat Daudi, *Civilization and Violence*, Table 6.2, 239; there are at least six sources given in table format; they give different figures, which is based on the number of years the authors have included. Sources taken from https://www.Informationclearinghouse.info; also see https://www.globalresearch.ca/us-has-killed-more-than-20-million-people-in-37-victim-nations-since-world-war-ii/5492051.

48 Mike Davis, *Late Victorian Holocausts*, 296–298.

49 https://www.aljazeera.com/indepth/opinion/britain-stole-45-trillion-india-181206124830851.html. For a detailed discussion see Utsa Patnaik and Prabhat Patnaik, *A Theory of Imperialism*.

50 Hannah Arendt, *The Origins of Totalitarianism*.

51 Gore Vidal, *Perpetual War for Perpetual Peace*, 22–41.

52 J.P. Sottile, "America's Military-Industrial Addiction" (Information Clearing House, December 4, 2017; originally published at Consortium News); also see Naomi Klein, *The Shock Doctrine*, 300–304.

53 Peter Phillips, *Giants: The Global Power Elites*, Chapter 2.

54 Tom Burghart, "As Defense Budget Soars, Security Companies Reap Huge Profits, Go Offshore" (Information Clearing House, February 15, 2010).

55 Samuel Huntington, *The Clash of Civilizations and The Remaking of World Order*, Chapters 3 and 4.

56 "The Brothers who Funded Blair, Israeli Settlements and Islamophobia" (Information Clearing House, August 13, 2015); Robin Eastman Abaya, "Israel's Willing Executioner: AIPAC invades Washington" (Information Clearing House, March 16, 2012).

57 James Petras and Kimberly Soeiro, "The Global 1% Ruling Class, Exposed," *Censored 2013*, 235–248; Peter Phillips, *Giants*, Chapter 2.

58 Eric Zeus, "America's News is Heavily Censored" (RINF, September 18, 2015); Adam Ramsay, "Cambridge Analytica is what happens when you privatize Military propaganda" (Information Clearing House, March 31, 2018; originally published at MintPress).

59 Raphael Patai, *The Arab Mind*, Chapters VI, VII, and VIII.
60 Chris Hedges, "The campaign to exterminate Muslims" (Information Clearing House, April 19, 2019).
61 Nicolas J.S. Davis, "Obama's Bombing Legacy" (Consortium News, January 18, 2017).
62 Lee Camp, "Trump's Military Drops Bomb Every Twelve Minutes" (Truthdig, June 19, 2018).
63 Esposito and Mogahed, *Who Speaks for Islam?* IX–XIII.
64 Esposito and Mogahed, Chapters 1 and 5.
65 Esposito and Mogahed, ibid.
66 Esposito and Ibrahim, *The Challenge of Pluralism*, 120, 130, 131.

2 Violence

Islam, the West, and the rest

On July 22, 2011, nearly a decade after 9/11, Andre Behrend Breivik loaded homemade bombs in a van and headed for the government buildings in Oslo. He parked his van and detonated the bombs, killing eight people. He then traveled to the island of Uteya, where the Workers Youth League was holding a summer camp. After three hours, Breivik arrived at the island and began to shoot the participants, killing another sixty-nine people and injuring 319. The attack was meticulously planned and executed; it had taken him a decade to finish the project. According to the Norwegian government, the total cost of the operation was 130,000 euros, which was partly financed through his access to nine credit cards. Before the shootings began, he had posted a manifesto detailing his political philosophy. His primary motivation was to save Europe from Muslims.

Can Breivik alone be blamed for the massacre? Probably not! Did external forces inspire him? Are they also to be blamed? If so, who are they? His manifesto suggests that he got his inspiration from several writers and a handful of Islamophobia movements of the United States, Europe, Israel, and India.[1] They had created an atmosphere in which the demonization of Muslims took a foothold in the Western psyche. The Center for American Progress published a report in 2011 on the newer variant of Islamophobia, titled *Fear Inc.: The Roots of the Islamophobic Network in America*. The report names of activists, their organizations, writers, and sources of funding. The movement received $57 million from seven donors. The report also suggests that these organizations are tiny in number but wield significant influence.

Breivik's manifesto, which he released minutes before he embarked upon his murderous journey, gives a glimpse of his source of inspiration. He cites several writers (Robert Spencer alone was mentioned 162 times), at least three think-tanks, and various Islamophobic organizations, such as Frank Gaffney's *Center for Security Policy*, Daniel Pipes' *the Middle East Forum*, Robert Spencer's *Jihad Watch*, Pamela Geller and Spencer's *Stop Islamization of America*, Steven Emerson's *Investigative Project on Terrorism*, and David Yerushalmi's *Society of Americans for National Existence*.[2] Several of them had also targeted the left parties and activists along with Islam. Why did Breivik target Norwegians? Kumar explains:[3]

DOI: 10.4324/9781003323105-3

The attack on the left, particularly the academic left, has been led by groups, such as the David Project and Campus Watch. Kramer's book *Ivory Tower on Sand* was followed by *Unholy Alliance: Radical Islam and the American Left* (2004) by ex–leftist David Horowitz and Andrew McCarthy's *The Grand Jihad: How Islam and the Left Sabotage America* (2010). ....

Breivik carried this argument to the logical conclusion when he assassinated teenagers at a camp run by the social-democratic Norwegian Labor Party.

Are these activists scared of Islam, or is it rhetoric to achieve political goals? If their writings are to be taken literally, they believe that Muslims have shown violent behavior in the past;[4] they are also fanatics and are determined to bring Islamic laws into the country. That may be one reason, but there could be some tangible factors. They are afraid that their way of life is in danger; mass migration of Muslims in Europe and North America would change the demography, and Christians could become a minority. Islamophobia ideologues' arguments were straightforward, unambiguous, and easy to understand: Muslims are violent because Islam promotes violence (Chapter 4). As for proof, their argument was: what else is needed other than 9/11 to prove that Muslims are violent?

An overwhelming majority of Muslims reject these notions as nonsensical. They argued that two billion people should not be defined by a single event such as 9/11. No matter how traumatic or heinous this crime was, it was committed by a tiny fraction of 1% of the Muslim population; they belong to the fringe elements of the society. Fifteen of the nineteen men came from a single country, which has maintained strong economic and military ties with the United States for seven decades. Muslims also argue that using a cherry-picked event to blame sixty-odd nations to be violent has no logic: notwithstanding, it was being used to define Muslims as a threat to the United States and its allies. Why? We will see, but a decade after such articles and books were first published, American GIs were patrolling the streets of Kabul and Baghdad. Iraqi President Saddam Hussein was hanged, and a new Iraqi government was installed. Subsequently, its transnational corporations signed lucrative contracts to develop Iraqi oil fields.

Several non-Muslim authors have also refuted Islamophobic arguments. They have also addressed the issue of violence by the West, for instance Chris Hedges,[5] Gore Vidal,[6] Edward Said,[7] Robert Fisk,[8] Jürgen Todenhöfer,[9] William Blum,[10] Andrew Bacevich,[11] Ward Churchill,[12] Chalmers Johnson,[13] Noam Chomsky, Michael Mann,[14] Adam Hochschild,[15] Joel Andreas,[16] and others. Furthermore, several others have been documenting acts of violence by the United States and its allies on the rest of the world. They have also concluded that the West has been the biggest offender in the last three hundred years. The British Empire waged one major war every year across the globe during its golden age, which coincided with Queen Victoria's reign.[17] After the United States took over the mantle of the leader of the West, it has been the most aggressive nation on the planet. Muslim countries, especially those which happen to be in Israel's neighborhood, have been the primary victims of aggression.

Selective omissions of facts, which result in an incorrect inference, have been routinely used to demonize various groups of people in the past. Examples of the last century are the demonization of Jews before the Holocaust, Germans and Japanese during the Second World War, communists during the Cold War, and Asians – Chinese, Koreans, and Vietnamese – during the war in Korea and Vietnam. Muslims and Arabs have replaced the face of the demonized objects after the demise of communism. After the fall of the Berlin Wall, neoconservative ideologues have created myths about Muslims, which portrays them not only as violent but also a threat to the United States and its allies.

Similarly, referring to acts of terrorism, which only a minuscule number of Muslims have committed,[18] has played a prominent role in demonizing Islam by promoting an association of violence with mainstream Muslim societies when none exists. For example, a study by the Triangle Center on Terrorism and Homeland Security found that by February 2011, only eleven Muslims attempted to commit acts of violence on American soil since 9/11. In his book *The Missing Martyrs*, Charles Kurzmann, a professor of Sociology at the University of North Carolina, noted that Global Islamist terrorists managed to recruit one in 100,000 Muslims since 9/11.[19] Compare these numbers with the mass shootings in the United States. Two gunmen killed twenty-nine people in El Paso, TX, and Dayton, OH. These were the 247th and 248th mass shootings in the country. Most of the perpetrators were white Americans.

Wherein lies the truth then? Somewhere in the middle, of course, but where? Close to 100% or 0%? Therefore, a better question would be *how to distinguish facts from fiction* for the following reasons. Humanity may have reached our galaxy's outer limits and has achieved many miracles in the scientific fields, but it has not found any remedy for violence; it is still an integral part of human behavior. Thus, labeling any civilization or a group of people violent would be unfair unless its acts of violence are compared with equivalent actions of other cohorts to show that a particular group of countries has conducted more violent conflicts than others.

Second, violence may be universal and ubiquitous, but it is not a permanent fixture of any society. For example, Huntington, in his book, *The Clash of Civilizations*, has cited the data from Ted Robert Gur, who had collected violent clashes in various countries between 1993 and 1994 only. He categorized them according to the religious affiliation of its citizens and analyzed them (Chapter 4). Huntington opines that it is a clash among civilizations. Since a state of violence is cyclical, so is the state of peace; it is inappropriate to claim that a specific civilization is violent or not violent unless their violent acts have been observed over centuries. Therefore, the data cited by Huntington does not make sense.

By the same arguments, the linking of violence with Islam cannot be established by merely enumerating violent conflicts of Muslim nations, as violence is a fact of life for every religious and cultural group in the world. Furthermore, the presence of violence in any society does not automatically implicate its sacred text or theology; neither does the absence of violence refute violent behavior. As such, a cause-and-effect relationship between violence and teachings of Islam needs to be proven before it can be stated that Muslims are violent or Islam promotes violence.

How about religion itself? Does it foster violence? A large segment of humanity claims to be living in a post-religious phase of human development, which they argue is a more enlightened society than religious societies. It is common within this group to believe that religion is the cause of many violent conflicts or wars are fought for religion. Is it true? Not according to facts. Data suggest that secular societies and governments have shown as much, if not more, inclination towards using violence if their interests have been challenged.[20] Two World Wars, and the Soviet and Chinese political regimes, are few examples of violence in secular societies. More people were exterminated during these four conflicts (the two World Wars, Korean and Vietnam Wars) than were killed during all other wars of the last two centuries. Therefore, it would be wrong to implicate Islam or any particular religious doctrine for being inherently violent.

In summary, the following principles must apply for a valid conclusion about an association of violence with any particular civilization:

1   The simultaneous appearance of two factors such as violence in a society is not proof of a cause-and-effect relationship; coincidence does not automatically mean causality.
2   Valid comparisons require a precise definition of combatants and appropriate parameters of violent conflicts. The above factors should be ascertained first; only then will the data on acts of violence be compared appropriately.
3   The correct inference is based on verifiable facts and objective evidence; appropriate parameters and valid comparison of acts of violence are essential.
4   Biases in collecting data must be eliminated.
5   Acts of violence of civilizations must be compared among each other over a more extended period.
6   To avoid inappropriate comparison, data should be analyzed on established statistical principles.

Finally, subjective statements must be eliminated from debates. Therefore, arguments based on sacred scriptures have no place in any objective discussion; bringing faith in debates changes the conversations into subjective rhetoric. Objectivity is lost for several reasons. There would always be many interpretations of religious texts – from the most enlightened to the most obscurantist ones. There is no confusion about the ideals of any religious doctrine; that is for everyone to read. However, its interpretations by scholars, applications by leaders, and practice by ordinary folks alike, have another dimension. Indeed, there is a difference between the teachings of a religion, its ethos, and its practices by billions of followers. The latter combines both pathos and logos. One can argue whether religious scriptures are words of God or not, but all interpretations of religious texts are human endeavors. Thus, they will always be fallible. Therefore, to use religious texts to claim another religion to be violent may be neither correct, nor fair.

Second, since ethos and logos are two different components of any religion, it is inappropriate to compare ethos (the teaching of faith) with pathos (practices of followers of other religions). That is comparing apples with oranges. Nevertheless, several authors have compared the teachings of one religion with the practices or traditions of another religion in demonizing and stereotyping opponents. That may be either due to ignorance or a deliberate attempt to demonize their enemies (Chapter 4); it is often encountered while comparing Islam and Christianity.

For example, it is common to compare the events of 9/11, which were carried out by a tiny fraction of 1% of the Muslim population, with the enlightened principles of democracy, which is erroneously claimed by neoconservative activists as a uniquely Western phenomenon. Once again, such a comparison can neither be fair nor valid. Terrorist attacks should be compared with the killings by drones, which is a Western approach. Al Qaeda's rhetoric and justification of acts of terrorism should be compared with the rationale for indiscriminate bombings by the West, which has resulted in many civilian casualties. Justifications do not legitimize violent behavior. Slavery, colonialism, genocides during the colonial period, holocausts, and the looting of the colonial territories by Europeans were all justified by similar arguments. Now, they have all been declared to be illegal and immoral acts.

Third, those who are negatively predisposed to Muslim interests for financial and political reasons and towards Islam for theological reasons would always find excuses to reject counter-arguments, even if they are clear, appropriate, and unambiguous. Similarly, few verses can still be taken out of the context from any scripture, which could then be presented as if a religion condones violence. Such impressions become more pronounced if the correct context is not provided either deliberately or inadvertently. Different groups of people on either side of the divide can use it to their advantage. Also, the temptation is too high for unscrupulous leaders to use them to justify violence for personal benefits or secondary gains.

Therefore, the only way to prove an assertion that Muslim countries, which have been erroneously called Islamic civilization, is to provide verifiable data to compare the number of people killed by each group (in the context of the debate on so-called *civilizations*) over an extended period. Whether violence in the Muslim world is more or less prevalent than in the rest of the world is the first step in the quest of finding the answer to this problem. This issue has been analyzed in my book, *Civilization and Violence: Islam, the West, and the Rest*. Violent conflicts around the world of the last two centuries were compiled, categorized according to so-called civilizations, and compared with each other.

The results are presented in Tables 2.2 and 2.2, which document conflicts of the nineteenth and twentieth centuries. They have been arranged according to the number of casualties during war and war-related events. The validity of the data is based on Pareto's Principle, which states that 80% of all human activities are committed by 20% of the people. If we document major acts of violence in a given period, we can have a reference point for all massacres and genocides.[21] Indeed, the number of casualties in wars decreases precipitously below the 20% limit.

Table 2.1 Major conflicts of the nineteenth century arranged according to number of victims and countries/empires

	Year	Number of victims	Countries or alliances	Remarks	Reference
1	1876–1900 1700–1800	30–50 million (famine in India) 50 million	British Empire	Related to wars of conquests and famine Mostly from famine	Davis, *Late Victorian Holocausts*, 91–140
2	1850–64	30–50 million	The British and the Chinese Empire	Taiping Rebellion, the British were directly involved in putting down the rebellion	Davis, 113
3	1864–1908 1864–1960	4.5 million in the nineteenth century (out of a total number of victims, 20–30 million)	King Leopold of Belgium	Congo Free State	Hochschild, *King Leopold's Ghost*
4	1803–15	3–5 million	France	Napoleonic Wars in Europe and the Middle East	Gates, *The Napoleonic Wars*
5	1816–26 1818–40	1–2 million	Shaka Kingdom Mfecane Wars	Victims were almost all Africans in Southern Africa	White, *The Great Big Book of Horrible Things*
6	1811–23	1 million	Spain	In Venezuela, during wars of independence	White
7	1830 onwards	300,000 to 1 million	France	In Algeria: invasion, wars for colonization, pacification campaigns, and famines	Le Cour Grandmaison, *Coloniser, Exterminer*
8	1844–1852	750,000 to 1 million	British Empire	Ireland during Potato Famine	Woodham–Smith, *The Great Hunger*
9	1811–70	500,000 to 1 million	Spain, the War of the Triple Alliance	In Paraguay, Argentina, Brazil, and Uruguay	White
10	1810–21	500,000	Spain and civil war	In Mexico; the War of Independence and Civil War	White

	Year	Number of victims	Countries or alliances	Remarks	Reference
11	1850–1900	500,000	China with the British Empire in a secondary role	Multiple rebellions in China	Davis
12	1853–56	500,000	Russian Empire and allies versus combined British, French, Turkish, Sardinian, and German forces	Invasion of Crimea in the Caucasus	McCarthy, *Death and Exile*
13	1862–66	350,000	The United States	American Civil War	Zinn, *A People's History of the United States*
14	1870–71	100,000	Franco-Prussian	Prussian Empire against the French	Clodfelter, *Warfare and Armed Conflicts*
15	1800–1900	250,000	The British Empire in Australia	Extermination of Aborigines	Lyndall, *The Aboriginal Tasmanians*
16	1800–1900	240,000	The British Empire in New Zealand	Massacres of the Maori population	Lindqvist, *Exterminate All the Brutes*
17	1868–78	200,000	Spain	In Cuba: war of independence	White
18	1859–66 1873–90	200,000 in both wars	Holland	In Java In Aceh	White
19	1806–12 1828–29	170,000 130,000	Russian Empire	Russo-Turkish Wars	McCarthy
20	1840–1900	120,000	Turkish Empire	Suppression of Independence movements in the Balkans and Greece	McCarthy

Table 2.2 Violent conflicts of the twentieth century presented according to number of casualties*

	Death tolls (million)	Wars or events	Dates	Remarks
1	55–70	Second World War	1937–39 to 1945	White, *The Great Big Book of Horrible Things*, 400–426[22]
2	22–40	Soviet Regime under Joseph Stalin	1924–53	Includes WW II, repression of opponents, and deportation of various nationalities[23]
3	20–40	Communist China: Mao Tse Dung era	1949–76	Repression, Great Leap Forward, and Famine[24]
4	13–18	First World War	1914–18	Includes massacres of Armenians and Greeks (by Turks) and of Turks (by Greeks and Armenians) that took place later 1919–1921[25]
5	10–15	Belgians in Congo Free State	1900–08	The massacres started in the 1880s and continued well into the 20th century[26]
6	7–10	Russian Civil War	1918–21	Between Bolsheviks and their opponents[27]
7	5–8	China: War Lord	1917–37	Among warlords before the civil war[28]
8	3–4	2nd Indochina War	1960–75	The United States and France versus Vietnam[29]
9	2.5–3.5	Korean War	1950–53	The Western Alliance versus Communist China and North Korea[30]
10	2.5–3.0	Chinese Civil War	1945–49	[31]Communist (Mao) versus Nationalist (Chiang Kai-Shek)
11	2.1–2.5	Expulsion of Germans from Europe	1945–47	From Russia (POWs and Germans living in Russia and Eastern Europe)[32]
12	1.7–2.0	Congolese Civil War	1998–99	Ongoing violent conflicts since independence[33]
13	1.5–1.8	Cambodia: Khmer Rouge	1975–79	One of the worst civil wars[34] (highest rate of death of population – 25%)
14	1.5	Afghanistan: Soviet War	1979–89	Afghans were supported by the US and laid the foundation of future civil wars[35].
15	1.2–1.4	Ethiopian Civil War	1962–92	After Emperor Haile Selassie was deposed, there have been at least two coups and civil wars as well as a war of independence[36]

	Death tolls (million)	Wars or events	Dates	Remarks
16	0.8–1.0	Mexican Revolution	1910–20	—[37]
17	0.5–1.0	Sudan Civil War	1983–99	Arab North versus Christian-Animist South[38]
18	0.5–0.8	Pakistan–Bangladesh War	1971–72	Urdu/Punjabi-speaking West Pakistan versus Bengali from East Pakistan[39]
19	0.5–0.8	Iran–Iraq War	1980–88	President Saddam Hussein started the war, supported by the West[40]
20	0.5–0.6	Rwanda Massacre	1994	Hutu versus Tutsi[41]

Presented in Table 2.3 are major conflicts of the West and Muslim countries during the twenty-first century. The ratio of people killed by the West is no different from that by the other two centuries. This will make more sense if these numbers are examined with the number of conflicts in which Western nations have participated.[42]

Presented in Table 2.6 is the head-to-head comparison of the number of people killed in violent conflicts of the West and Muslim countries, or Western Christian and Islamic civilizations, as neoconservatives prefer to call them. The numbers are the sum total of the casualties, which have been presented in Tables 2.1 and 2.2. No such comparison has been provided by those who claim that Muslims are violent. True, there have been one or two articles, which have presented data, but as Edward Said in his book *Covering Islam* had argued, these studies were designed to prove a point, that

Table 2.3 Number of people killed by Western and Muslim countries (Islamic civilizations) (2000–2015)[43]

Nations and alliance	Number of opponents killed	Place of conflict	Remarks
The West, NATO, and alliances	1,800,000 (by 12.24.11). The overwhelming majority of casualties (95%) were civilians	Iraq: 1,445,590 Afghanistan: 280,000 Syria: 250,000 Pakistan: 30,000[44] Yemen: 10,000 Somalia: 10,000	These numbers have been taken from Information Clearing House, which updates the data regularly[45]
Muslim-majority countries or non-governmental groups	Soldiers: 7,000–8,000 Mercenaries: 2,000–3,000 Civilians: 5,000	See Table 2.2	Source: Information Clearing House

Table 2.4 Use of force by Western countries against nations belonging to other civilizations after 1950

Country	Conflicts	Remarks
USA	Korea, Vietnam, South China Sea, Cambodia, Laos, Iran (twice), Iraq (twice), Libya, Lebanon (twice), Sudan, Panama, Colombia, Haiti, Grenada, and the Philippines	1950–2003: more than 26 times[46] 1989–2003: 9 times[47] 1976–1989: 6 times[48] Includes small-and large-scale conflicts in which US forces were involved (bombing campaigns are not included here)
Great Britain	Egypt/Suez Canal, Falkland/ Argentina, Iraq, Gulf/ Kuwait	Long after it announced its withdrawal from colonies, its colonial war went on. It does not include colonial wars before World War II[49]
France	Algeria, Egypt, French West Africa, Madagascar	Its forces have attacked civilians. France left its colonies after the Algerian debacle[50]
Belgium	Congo	Among the worst atrocities committed by any colonial power[51]
South Africa	Angola and Mozambique	During its Apartheid-era[52]
NATO	Bosnia, Kosovo, Macedonia, and now Libya (2011)	Even though the United States played an important role, the operations were conducted under NATO[53]
Israel	Palestine, Syria, Egypt, and Lebanon	It is the only country in the twenty-first century which occupies another country (despite UN sanction)[54]
Portugal	Angola and Mozambique	Portugal was reluctant to leave its colonies. In almost all cases, it left after it was forced to leave[55]

Table 2.5 Muslim-majority countries occupying non-Muslim countries after 1950

Indonesia (supported by the West)	East Timor	The only Muslim country to occupy a non-Muslim country. The UN forced Indonesians to leave East Timor after 25 years[56]

Islam is violent, which was already concluded and established before the debates began.[57] Finding an answer was not their goal.

A few points are pertinent with respect to these tables: first, the casualty figures presented in these tables are the raw data; they are not an interpretation of facts, which are subjective, and can be manipulated. There are wide variations in the number of people killed during each war; both ends of the spectrum of casualties have been presented in the book, *Civilization and Violence, Islam, the West, and the Rest*, to provide a complete picture. Authenticity is not the issue with the data, which have been presented in these tables. Even if the

Table 2.6 Direct comparison of violent conflicts of Muslim and Western countries*

	By Western nations	By Muslim countries or by organizations from Muslim societies
Total number of people killed since 1800	Over 250 million; possibly 350 million	Between 5 million and 6 million
Total number of people killed since 1900	100 million, out of which 20 million were Muslims	Between 1 and 5 million out of which fewer than 20,000 were Westerners
Total number of people killed since 1950	Between 10 and 12 million in Vietnam, Laos, Cambodia, Central America, the Middle East, and Africa	10,000 Westerners (civilians) and 10,000 soldiers and mercenaries, includes Israeli civilians and soldiers
Number of people killed in the twenty-first century	Between 1.5 and 1.8 million Muslims were killed by the U.S., Britain, and others in Iraq, Afghanistan, Pakistan, Sudan, Syria, Somalia, and other places; 98% civilians	5,000 Westerners in various "terrorist attacks" around the world and 7,000 soldiers and mercenaries from NATO countries by Al Qaeda
Number of countries attacked since 1800	Over 50 countries and over 200 times	Fewer than a dozen
Number of countries attacked since 1900	40 countries over 100 times (20 of them Muslim countries)	One, none against the West
Number of countries attacked since 1980	15 (8 of them Muslim countries)	One, none against the West
Number of countries attacked since 1990	9 (5 of them Muslim countries)	None
Number of countries bombed by the West (does not include countries attacked by the West)	Since 1990: 6, Since 1980: 12 Since 1900: 20	None
Number of times countries intervened or attempted to overthrow governments	Since 1990: 5 Since 1980: 10 Since 1900: 50	None

lowest numbers of casualties of the West and the highest number of Muslim countries are taken, the conclusion that the West has committed more massacres and genocide will not be affected. The difference in the killings between the two cohorts in the last two centuries is vast.

Since Muslim countries are not more violent than the rest of their cohorts, the next question is: why are they being perceived to be violent? Whether the perception of Islam as a violent religion came about on its own or is the byproduct of a planned campaign to demonize Muslims is the issue discussed in the next chapter.

Notes

1 https://www.thehindu.com/news/national/norwegian-mass-killers-manifesto-hails-hindutva/article2293829.ece.
2 Deepa Kumar, *Islamophobia and Politics of Empire*, 179.
3 Kumar; 178.
4 Lewis, "The Roots of Muslim Rage," https://www.theatlantic.com/magazine/archive/1990/09/the-roots-of-muslim-rage/304643/. Also see Kumar, Chapter 7.
5 Chris Hedges, *War is a Force That Gives US Meaning*.
6 Gore Vidal, *Perpetual War for Perpetual Peace*.
7 Edward Said, *Orientalism*.
8 Robert Fisk, *The Great War for Civilization*.
9 Jürgen Todenhöfer, *Why Do You Kill?*
10 William Blum, *Killing Hope*.
11 Andrew Becevich, *The New American Militarism*.
12 Ward Churchill, *A Little Matter of Genocide*.
13 Chalmers Johnson, *The Sorrows of Empire*.
14 Michael Mann, *Incoherent Empire*.
15 Adam Hochschild, *King Leopold's Ghost*.
16 Joel Andreas, *Addicted to War*.
17 Niall Ferguson, *Empire*, 211.
18 Nathan Lean, *The Islamophobia Industry*.
19 Nathan Lean, ibid., 9.
20 Imbesat Daudi, *Civilization and Violence*, Chapter 5.
21 Daudi, Chapters 5 and 6.
22 John Keegan, in *The Second World War*, estimated 50 million; Rudy J. Rummel estimated 84 million in *The Blue Book of Freedom*, 99.
23 Matthew White, *The Great Big Book of Horrible Things*, 382. Also see E. Margolis, "Ukraine's Unknown Holocaust," https://newslog.cyberjournal.org/eric-margolis-ukraines-unknown-holocaust/
24 White, 429–438. Also see Ilya Somin, "Remembering the Greatest Mass Murders in the Human History," https://www.washingtonpost.com/news/volokh-conspiracy/wp/2016/08/03/giving-historys-greatest-mass-murderer-his-due/.
25 White, 344–358. Also see Alan Axelrod, *The Complete Idiot's Guide to World War I*; Michael Mann, *The Dark Side of Democracy*, Chapters 5 and 6.
26 White, 325–333. For details see Adam Hochschild, *King Leopold's Ghost*.
27 White 359–369. For details of genocide, see Richard Pipes, *Russia under the Bolshevik Regime*; also see "Lenin: Numbers, Data, and Images of the Crimes of the First Communist Dictator," https://www.outono.net/elentir/2020/04/22/.
28 White, 372–381.
29 Rummel, "Freedom, Democracy, Peace, Democide and War," http://www.hawaii.edu/powerkills/SOD.TAB6.1A.GIF.
30 Ministry of National Defense of Republic of Korea, http://www.imhc.mil.kr/imhcroot/data/korea_view.jsp?seq=4&page=1 (retrieved February 14, 2007).
31 http://www.scaruffi.com/politics/massacre.html.
32 White, 422– 424; Margolis, ibid.

33 Benjamin Coghlan et al., "Mortality in the Democratic Republic of Congo: a Nation-wide Survey" (*Lancet*, 367 (9504): 44–51, 2006), http://conflict.lshtm.ac.uk/media/DRC_mort_2003_2004_Coghlan_Lancet_2006.pdf (retrieved December 27, 2011).

34 Bruce Sharp, "Counting Hell: The Death Toll of the Khmer Rouge Regime in Cambodia" (April 1, 2005), http://www.mekong.net/cambodia/deaths.htm. (retrieved July 5, 2006).

35 Fisk, Chapter 2, 35–71.

36 Benjamin A. Valentino, *Final Solutions*, 196.

37 https://www.necrometrics.com/20c1m.htm.

38 White; https://www.necrometrics.com. Also see M. Mamdani, *Good Muslim, Bad Muslim*.

39 White, 481–483. Also see Jagjit Singh Aurora, "The Fall of Dacca," *The Illustrated Weekly of India,* December 23, 1973, quoted in K.C. Pravel, *Indian Army after Independence*.

40 White, 512–513. For details see Fisk, Chapters 4 and 8; T. Ali, *The Clash of Fundamentalisms*, 152.

41 "Rwanda: How the genocide happened," BBC, April 1, 2004, gives an estimate of 800,000, and "OAU sets inquiry into Rwanda genocide," *Africa Recovery* (12(1), August 1998), 4 estimates the number at between 500,000 and 1,000,000. Seven out of every ten Tutsis were killed.

42 Daudi, Chapter 4.

43 Daudi, 237; these data have been taken from the Information Clearing House (ICH) website.

44 White, 481–483.

45 http://www.justforeignpolicy.org/images/iraqdeaths.gif, available at Information Clearing House blog.

46 Gore, *Perpetual War for Perpetual Peace*, 22–41.

47 Andrew Becevich, *The New American Militarism*, 19.

48 Curtis, *Unpeople*, 313.

49 Curtis, 312–317.

50 White, 282–284; Fisk, Chapter 14; Olivier Le Cour Grandmaison, *Coloniser, Exterminer: Sur la Guerre et l'etat Colonial*, 90, 98, 146-152; Sven Lindqvist, *Exterminate All the Brutes*.

51 Hochschild, 283; Pakenham, 585–601.

52 Mamdani, *Good Muslim, Bad Muslim;* Richard Leonard, *South Africa at War*.

53 Johnson, *The Sorrows of Empire* (Metropolitan Books, New York, 2004). Also see https://balkaninsight.com/2013/03/25/number-of-victims-of-nato-bombing-still-unknown/.

54 Gwynne Dyer, *Future: Tense*, 208–210; Fisk.

55 White, 476-477; Mann, 490–498.

56 Mann, 490–498.

57 Edward Said, *Covering Islam*, li–lviii; for detailed discussions on this topic, see Introduction.

3   The birth of Islamophobia
Sequence of events

The conclusion from the data presented in the previous chapter is unambiguous: the United States, its European allies, former colonial powers, and their current allies have been responsible for most of the violent conflicts of the last two hundred years. Their acts of aggression both on and off the battlefield were unparalleled. These nations were instrumental in making the previous two centuries the most violent period in human history. Whatever the reasons for their acts of violence, the result was the largest territorial expansion by any group of nations in human history.[1] By the end of the First World War, the West and Russia had gained control of over 80% of the world's area.[2]

However, in spite of clear evidence of the extensive acts of violence by the West, the prevailing perception is that Western nations are non-violent; they abide by international treaties, follow laws of the land and respect human rights. Most of its citizens even assume, reflexively perhaps, that if the West has been involved in any violent conflict, its use of force must have been necessary and ensuing massacres unavoidable. That may be changing as the reasons trotted out to invade Iraq and Afghanistan have been proven to be false. It is indeed an enigma for many Muslims that even the most extreme forms of violence of the Western nations have been wiped from their collective memory.

In contrast, Muslims who were the primary victims of Western aggression are portrayed in the mainstream media to be inherently violent. This perception is especially prevalent in the United States, which is responsible for the most violent conflicts of the last half a century.[3] Since the Western perception of Muslims and Islam is not even remotely connected to the facts and reality, the questions are: 1) why are Islam, Muslims, and so-called Islamic civilization considered to be violent, while the West is perceived to be peace-loving and non-violent? 2) How could such blatantly false notions gain acceptance in Western perception?

There could only be two possibilities: either the current image of Muslims as violent people was deliberately created, or it has evolved spontaneously on its own for whatever reasons – a lack of knowledge of other societies, ignorance of different cultures, fake news, or outright lies. Many political activists in the United States have promoted the concept that the negative image of Muslims may be directly related to terrorism or random acts of violence, such as the

DOI: 10.4324/9781003323105-4

beheading of prisoners by ISIS and other groups; therefore, the most relevant point in this debate is to ascertain when exactly did the campaign of dehumanization of Muslims begin. Was it before 9/11 or after? This chapter examines the answer to this issue by exploring the timeline of the appearance of negative images of Muslims as violent people.

Indeed, there are two distinctly contradictory views on this topic. Critics of the American foreign policy and Muslims, in general, believe that the current violent image of Muslims was deliberately created by pro-Israeli political activists of the United States and Britain. They controlled the mainstream media of the English-speaking world, which are owned and managed by only six transnational corporations.[4] Many decision-makers of these corporations have shown pro-Israel bias.[5] They may have a point. If we consider that even though only a tiny fraction of 1% of the Muslim population are engaged in random acts of violence, still 57% of all news stories in the mainstream media in the West about Islam, Arabs, Muslims, and Muslim-majority countries are related to violence or acts of terrorism.[6] The process and arguments of the branding of Muslims as violent people are the same as they were before 9/11.[7] It indicates that the demonization of Muslims in the Western media began well before 9/11.

Was this a planned strategy to brand them violent? Here are some related facts: the participation of Muslims, as individuals or as a group, in acts of terrorism in the United States is the lowest among their cohorts.[8] That percentage is no different than it was before the destruction of the World Trade Center. Most acts of terrorism are committed in the United States by the White-Supremacist groups such as Ku Klux Klan, neo-Nazi or similar organizations; all of them claim their allegiance to Christianity, albeit to its distorted version. This fact has not changed in the last fifty years. Anti-abortion and anti-gay movements are a close second.

On the other end of the spectrum of this debate are the members of American policy establishments. They can be broadly divided into two influential groups: a) neoconservative ideologues representing primarily pro-Israel interests and b) neoliberal intellectuals representing corporate interests. The former is represented by the American Israeli Political Action (AIPAC), which is the umbrella group of various pro-Israel lobbies. The Council of Foreign Relations (CFR) represents the other entity. Since its inception, it has provided senior officials and diplomats, U.S. administrations of both Republican and Democratic presidents.[9] Likeminded lobbies and other organizations support both groups. Both organizations have promoted the concept that Islam is a violent religion.[10]

Their main argument is that Muslims are fanatic about their faith, much more than any other group, but they do not provide a valid comparison. Islam, they claim, is inherently a violent religion. Therefore, it breeds violent people. Bernard Lewis, one of the leading members of the neoconservative movement, claimed that Muslims tend to become violent during periods of stress. On the other hand, Tunku Varadarajan argues that Muslims can become violent at any moment, irrespective of time and space. He characterizes random acts of violence by individual Muslims as *going Muslim*.[11]

In other words, the core argument of both groups is that Muslim countries can only be dealt with a superior force; any dialogue with them is useless because they are fanatics and their leaders are irrational.[12] This particular argument was used in justifying the invasions of Iraq and Afghanistan and in the bombings of another half a dozen Muslim countries.[13] In the case of Iraq, the Bush administration had claimed that Iraq possessed weapons of mass destruction (WMDs), which was proven to be false.[14] Those so-called facts presented by officials may even have been concocted.[15] The promoters of the invasions had also argued that Saddam Hussein, the Iraqi leader, could not be trusted as he had used chemical weapons on civilians in the past. They further claimed that since the Iraqi leader is irrational besides being violent, he could use those weapons against the United States, even if it meant the annihilation of the country.

The justification of the invasion of Afghanistan was based on the claims that Afghan society is fundamentally violent by nature, and its leaders were in cahoots with terrorists; therefore, any dialogue with the Taliban would be futile. The U.S. officials who opted to go for the invasion and not for dialogue have argued that since Afghan leaders had given protection to Osama bin Laden, leader of Al Qaeda, the leading terrorist organization, they too were guilty by association. That assertion was also shown to be false, as Afghan leadership was willing and ready to hand over Osama bin Laden if the United States could provide proof of his alleged crimes.[16] However, President Bush chose to invade Afghanistan. In essence, both wars were the wars of choice and not of necessity. The leadership of both these two countries knew that they did not possess any means to be a threat to the United States or its allies.

Although in the same camp, others reject the notion that any group of people, even Muslims, could be inherently violent. However, they argue that the West did not create the image of Muslims as violent people; it evolved spontaneously. Reasons behind the negative impression of Muslims, they claimed, may or may not be correct, but to most Americans, they appear to be valid, especially after 9/11. Many of them even agree that Muslim countries may have genuine grievances against the United States or their former colonial masters; in the past, they had controlled the political process as well as resources of their land, either directly or by proxy by installing autocratic rulers. Many rulers of the Muslim world enjoy very close liaisons with the West; they were placed by the United States or former colonial powers. They are generally portrayed as progressive and modern. These intellectuals even agree that the majority of protests in the Muslim world against the Western policies have been non-violent, but they argue that the negative perception of Muslims of the West is understandable and Muslims have to live with this reality.

There are other reasons for Muslims to be viewed as violent people, even though such an assertion can only be a gross generalization. For example, there is an increase in the prevalence of civil wars in half a dozen Muslim-majority countries in which the interests of transnational mega-corporations (TNMCs) play a vital role. There are reasons to believe that TNMCs had been involved in many civil wars. Violence in places that have never been heard of by Americans makes breaking news in the mainstream media. At the same time, it is hardly ever mentioned that random acts of violence against civilians are an integral part of all civil wars; Muslim countries are no different. However, acts of violence by Muslim groups are widely covered by the media in the United States as if violence is unique to Muslim societies.[17] For whatever reasons, so-called fake news about Muslims is also widely reported in Western media.

Western perceptions of Muslims: is it associated with 9/11?

An oft-cited argument is that the image of Muslims as violent people may solely be due to the events of 9/11 and other acts of terror that Al Qaeda has conducted. It is even agreed that the acts of terror are being done by the fringe elements of the Muslim community, but for most non-Muslims, these terrorist groups represent Muslims and Islam. It is especially true for Americans who may not even have rudimentary knowledge about other people, including Muslims, who are defined as "others."

Indeed, the event of 9/11 has cast a lasting shadow not only on Western perceptions but on others as well. The terrorist groups may be just a tiny fraction of 1% of the Muslim population; still, the spectacular acts of violence overshadowed non-violent ways of life and non-confrontational protests of the silent Muslim majority. Indeed, images of the two burning towers of the World Trade Center have been imprinted on the Western perception; they have been played so many times on the screen that it is hard to avoid, much less forget, what happened to those innocent civilians who happened to be in the World Trade Center on that fateful day. The image of a man jumping to his death has given sleepless nights to people around the world.

The destruction of the World Trade Center in a spectacular fashion, in which almost 3,000 American civilians lost their lives, was destined, and probably also designed, to generate an intense knee-jerk reaction from the United States and leave a lasting memory. Al Qaeda, the group responsible for 9/11, may have planned the entire event with the possibility of an intense exposure in the media in mind. Al Qaeda was indeed quick to claim responsibility for the attack in the name of the Muslim community. The Bush administration obliged even though Al Qaeda or even a far-right party has never been elected in any country.

Since the entire episode was repeatedly relayed on television as breaking news, one could argue that the destruction of the World Trade Center may have created the perception of an association of violence with Muslims. However, facts speak otherwise, as bias against Muslims was already present in the United States before 9/11. Edward Said, John Esposito, Chalmers Johnson, and many other prominent thinkers of the last century have written about the concerted effort by neoliberal and neoconservative authors to portray Muslims as violent, fanatic, and anti-modern.

Indeed, a decade before 9/11, neoconservative writers, intellectuals, and political activists were already warning of an impending clash of civilizations between the West and Islam.[18] There is a reason for their accurate prediction. Many of these authors went on to join the Bush administration in policy-making positions.[19] The assumption that 9/11 was a clash of civilizations had already taken a firm foothold in the minds of many Americans, although Osama bin Laden had claimed that he had planned the destruction of the World Trade Center and the Pentagon in response to: a) the presence of U.S. forces in Saudi Arabia, the home of Islam's two holiest shrines; b) the carpet bombing of Iraq after the First Gulf War had ended and before the Second Gulf War began (the bombings killed at least half a million people); and c) the five-decade-long occupation of Palestinian land by Israel which was possible only due to unquestioned support from the United States.

Manufacturing a violent civilization: the process

Is there a cause-and-effect relationship between the demonization of Muslims and violence against them? Consider the events of the last three decades: the invasion of Iraq and Afghanistan by the United States and of Somalia and Mali by its allies, the toppling of Muammar Gaddafi in Libya, the attempted regime changes in Syria and Iran, and the War on Terror, which has degenerated into indiscriminate bombings of Muslim countries. Two facts stand out of these violent conflicts: 1) the demonization of Muslims has coincided with acts of aggression against Muslim countries; 2) the portrayal of Muslims as violent people was used in justifying various forms of violence against Muslim countries.

Branding potential enemies in a negative light is not specific to our time, but associating violence to a nation, nationality, religious affiliation, or so-called civilization is unique to the *Zeitgeist* of the post-Second World War era. During the colonial period, violence was celebrated as an essential element for the progress of humanity, provided such acts were directed against non-Western societies.[20] Foremost liberal thinkers of the colonial era, such as Herbert Spencer (*Social Statics*), Eduard von Hartman (*Philosophy of Unconscious*), and many others, supported or justified violence against people of color.[21] However, the carnage associated with the last two Great Wars has made violence abhorrent to ordinary citizens. After the introduction of nuclear and other modern weapons, the loss of lives was too high to endure. Since then, violence is associated with a strong adverse reaction.

Negative branding of an enemy, whether real or imaginary, is not only common but also essential before violence can be unleashed. That may not have been as crucial centuries before, but the process of demonization has become more critical over time. It appears that any violent conflict, which is essential to control other people's land and their resources, cannot be initiated, at least openly, unless the use of violence has been adequately justified. Indeed, after the conclusion of the Second World War, which witnessed the worst form of violence in human history, people had no appetite for violence. The demonization of Muslims should be viewed from these historical and economic perspectives.

Presented below are the events, in chronological order, which may explain how the image of Muslims as violent people was introduced and then sustained.

Event 1

The credit of initiating the very concept of associating violence with Palestinians as a people goes to Benjamin Netanyahu, the current Prime Minister of Israel.[22] He was the first to claim that terrorism and Palestinians go hand in hand. Until then, the opponents of the West and the United States may have been branded as violent, but they were defined in terms of political ideologies: communists and anarchists. They were generally branded as anti-democratic and people against modernity. In contrast, opponents of communist regimes, in general, were lauded as believers in modernity and even progressive, even if they were autocratic rulers. Allegiance to a free-market economy defined friendship between the West and the rest, even if the rulers were brutal killers. Even their heinous crimes were forgotten and forgiven.

In the 1970s, branding people as inherently violent was an alien concept. Netanyahu tossed up the idea of the association of violence with Palestinians, which received a lukewarm reception around the world. There was an anti-colonial mood. In most places, anti-Western protests were led by leftist intellectuals and activists. Pan-Arabism was a socialist-inspired movement that had its root in the Pan-Islamic and Pan-Arab anticolonial movements of the late nineteenth century. Pan-Arabism, which threatened Western interests in the Middle East, had evolved from an anti-colonial ideology into an anti-capitalist movement. These men and women were also fiercely nationalists. In contrast, traditional and religion-based movements usually did not participate in the freedom struggle against colonial rule, partly because Islamists generally viewed nationalism as un-Islamic. In many places, they had remained neutral.

The change in the political landscape of the Arab world began in 1956. Defying the fading British Empire, President Nasser nationalized the Suez Canal. In response, Britain, France, and Israel invaded Egypt and occupied the Suez Canal. Their victory against Egypt was a foregone conclusion; Western forces overran the Egyptian army. However, they could not enjoy the fruits of their success. The United States forced them to leave the Egyptian territory, which ended the British hegemony.

That was the most important consequence of this war; since then, the United States has replaced the British Empire as the leader of the West. Britain has played the role of a loyal follower of the United States. The British have benefited from what they portray as a "special relationship," but they should know better. Their material gain has come at the cost of their independence. For all practical purposes, Britain has become a vassal state, if not a colony of the United States.

After the Second World War, the Middle East, like the rest of the non-Western world, was divided into American and Soviet camps. In the 1960s, Iran, Saudi Arabia, and smaller monarchies of the Arab world were firmly allied with the United States. By then, the other monarchies such as Hashemite dynasties of Iraq and Syria, King Farook of Egypt, and King Idris of Libya were dumped into the dustbins of history and replaced by leftist movements. Left-leaning political ideologies, if not communism, had found fertile ground in the rest of the Muslim world. Egypt, Syria, Iraq, Libya, Sudan, and Yemen, many former monarchies, were experimenting with some form of socialism, raising concerns in the West. Even in Iran and Afghanistan, communist parties were very influential. The other Muslim countries, Indonesia and Malaysia, also had influential socialist movements. They were supported by the Soviet Union.

Then came the Six-Day War (1967), a war that changed the Arab world and altered the political landscape of the Middle East. Israel acquired Sinai from Egypt, Golan Heights from Syria, and the rest of the Palestinian land – Gaza and the West Bank, which until then was administered by Jordan. The inability of the Soviet Union to protect Egypt, its primary client state in the Middle East, was noticed with disbelief by the Muslim world. Suddenly, communism, whose influence in the Middle East was on an upward trajectory, lost its footings. The debacle in Egypt may have been the single most critical reason for the decline of the Soviet influence in the Muslim world.

After the Six-Day War, Palestinians had fewer options than any of their neighbors. Israel occupied their entire land. Palestinians responded to the annexation of their territory with protests – both violent and non-violent. The legitimacy of the Palestinian cause of becoming an independent nation made sense to many people, especially in the post-colonial period; their cause was slowly finding support in the West, more so in Scandinavia, Germany, France, and Italy, where Communist parties had always been influential. Israel responded to the Palestinian non-violent resistance with violence. The branding of Palestinians' struggle for their independence as terrorism was the first step in demonizing them as violent people.

Israel's ability to annex Palestine against the world opinion became possible only because of the unquestioned support of the United States, which in turn is due to a combination of the influence of pro-Israel lobbies on the American political landscape, foreign policy establishments, and the mainstream media and perception managing industries. The Israeli lobby operates in the United States as a single cohesive unit.[23] Not only do they have teams of skilled political operatives but also unlimited financial resources. They also wield extraordinary influence on the mainstream American media. Their success in their battle to influence Americans and garner their support may be traced to the creation of the perception that Palestinians are violent and can only be dealt with violence.[24] It was not until later that the dehumanization of Palestinians and their institutions was converted into Islamophobia, which is a form of demonization. Since Palestinians had no political and economic muscle, the Israeli lobby could operate without any resistance.

In the 1970s, Netanyahu was a rising star of the extreme right-wing of the Israeli political spectrum. He was also the president of the Jonathan Institute, a think-tank based in Israel. It was established well before think-tanks became an industry and a powerhouse in the United States. In 1979, Netanyahu organized a seminar under the banner of the institute. It became a significant event for Israel, as the conference was attended by George Bush Sr. (the Vice President-to-be),

Senator Scoop Jackson, a neocon idol, and like-minded politicians from the United States. Many "experts" on terrorism emerged at this conference, such as Richard Pipes, Norman Podhoretz, and Ben Wattenberg. Since then, they have positioned themselves as "experts" on the Middle East and terrorism. They do not have any academic background or on-the-job training. A large number of Israeli politicians attended the seminar.

The focus in this conference was on Yasir Arafat and *Al Fatah*, the Palestinian movement that was established to gain Palestine's independence from Israel. The group was getting acceptance from non-aligned groups of nations such as Yugoslavia, India, Indonesia, Ghana, and other countries worldwide, but its popularity had also seen a surge in Europe; that became the main concern for Israeli politicians. An increase in the legitimacy of the Palestinian cause, the demands of the Palestinian Liberation Army (PLO), and the acceptance of Palestine as an independent nation resonated in various parts of the world.

The emergence of the PLO as a political powerhouse was a severe threat to the financial interests of many groups and people in Israel and the United States – real-estate tycoons, who had already invested in Arab Jerusalem and wanted to expand in the West Bank, where they could buy land cheaply. Others who are negatively predisposed to Palestinian rights are right-wing Israeli politicians, Christian Zionists of the United States, who were financially supported by pro-Israel mega-donors, pro-Israel lobbies, and foreign policy experts of the United States. Their policy resonated among the military-industrial complex. These groups were also firm believers in keeping a powerful military.

Speakers at the aforesaid seminar also focused their criticism on George Habash and Nayef Hawatmeh, the two most influential personalities of the Palestinian movement. Both were dedicated leftist intellectuals and organizers and commanded respect from their friends and foes alike. They still do. Many speakers compared the PLO to Nazi Germany, a ridiculous idea; while the Germans possessed the second most potent war machinery and were an industrial powerhouse, the PLO was purely a non-governmental entity. They had no tax base and relied upon donations. Still, their notion that Palestinians are the incarnation of Nazis found a willing audience in the United States. These speakers also promoted the idea that terrorism was being initiated by the PLO, which they argued had already become a problem for the democratic world. Netanyahu called for democracies to begin rallying against terrorism.[25]

During the conference, only one speaker cited Islam as the problem. It was not even mentioned that Islam could promote violence. Instead, communism remained the devil incarnate and a dangerous concept. No association of violence with Islam was mentioned; that concept was not born yet, probably because there was no need for Islamophobia. In the 1960s, many Muslim countries were firmly aligned with the West against the Soviets. Turkey was an integral part of NATO. The Shah of Iran and the house of Saud made up the vanguard of the American power in the Middle East. Pakistan was an ally of the West and a member of the Baghdad Pact. Demonizing Muslims was neither prudent nor possible.

Event 2

It took more than a decade for Netanyahu to organize another conference on the same subject. Why it took so long is no secret. Palestinians had strong support in the non-Western world. Israeli leaders may have felt that the political climate may not have been conducive for the meeting. Important non-aligned leaders such as Nehru, Marshal Tito, Sukarno, Nkrumah, and others were supporting a separate independent state of Palestinians.

The next meeting was held in Washington DC in 1984.[26] The idea behind holding the conference in Washington was to make it easier for American politicians and intellectuals to participate. For the first time, Islam became an important issue at this conference. Unlike at the earlier meeting, an entire session was dedicated to the topic of an association of Islam with violence. It was titled *Terrorism and the Islamic World*.[27]

Benyamin Netanyahu opened the conference and set the tone by arguing that modern terrorism was exemplified by Palestinian groups and claimed that the PLO has roots in two violent ideologies: communist totalitarianism and Islamic radicalism.[28] That was strange since the Islamic fundamentalist organizations were non-entities in the 1980s. By then, Islamist organizations had not justified acts of violence by citing Islamic scripture. Al Qaida was yet to be born; neither were there any signs of a future Daesh (ISIS) nor germination of Taliban ideology among Afghans. Acts of terrorism in the Middle East were localized in the occupied territory and Israel, conducted by Palestinian groups in which both Muslims and Christians participated.[29]

Terrorism was a major factor in other parts of the world, but not in the Islamic world except in Palestine. Acts of terrorism were in response to military junta and dictatorship, which ruled their countries with extreme brutality. For practical reasons, most dictators declared themselves dedicated anti-communists. Their intention could be traced to finding support from the West, which they received without preconditions if they allied against communists. Mere verbal allegiance was enough to see support from Western establishments. The result was a polarization within the so-called Third-World countries between supporters of Western-style democracy on the one hand and communists on the other. Western support for brutal dictators was the main reason why so many movements in newly independent nations drifted towards the Soviet camps.

During the 1960s, most members of the Palestinian resistance were leftists; none were radical Islamists; Islamism as a concept was not even born then. Their association with the socialist movement helped the PLO in garnering support from non-aligned nations and socialist countries. Islam played no role in the resistance to the Israeli occupation. Many important leaders were Christians. George Habash and Nayef Hawatmeh, the leaders of the two most important Palestinian factions, the *Popular Front for the Liberation of Palestine* (PFLP) and the *Democratic Front for the Liberation of Palestine* (DFLP), were also Christians;[30] so were many other members. Wadi Haddad, who was in charge of its armed wing, was also a Christian. A sizable faction of Lebanese armed groups was led by Christians as well. Similarly, the Ba'ath Parties of Syria and Iraq, which were later demonized by the United States as the axis of evil and were portrayed as an example of everything wrong with the Muslim world, were founded by Michael Aflac, a Syrian Christian. Its ideology was influenced by European thinkers, such as Ernest Rennin, who had no sympathy for Islam.[31]

After the Iranian revolution, the United States and Iran broke up their diplomatic ties, but the damage, if any, was confined to the U.S.–Iranian relations; the rest of the Muslim world remained neutral or aligned with the West. After the Soviet invasion of Afghanistan, the alignment changed again. The United States poured its resources into Afghanistan, and the Afghans and Muslims supplied volunteers. Hardcore radical Islamists found an ally in the CIA. The Soviets had to retreat; eventually, the Soviet Union ceased to exist.

A decade before 9/11, the relationship between the West and the Islamic world suddenly took on a hostile trajectory. Common sense dictated that the defeat of the Red Army should have been a profoundly positive impact on the relationship between Muslim-majority countries and the United States. That did not happen. On the contrary, an avalanche of articles and books started appearing in the United States, demonizing Muslims and Islam (see Event 3 below).

Until the 1970s, Israel had worked hard to maintain a good relationship with the Soviet Union. Israel had a reason to do so; it wanted the Soviets to allow as many of its Jewish citizens as possible to migrate to Israel. By the early 1980s, all Soviet Jews who wanted to relocate from Russian territories had already left the Soviet Union. There were also other reasons for Israel to ignore its ties with the Soviet Union. The mighty Red Army had ceased to be of any danger to Israel. The 1967 War had exposed the weaknesses of Soviet military hardware, but above all, the failure of its intelligence. Nasser was never warned of the impending attack by the Soviet leadership; on the contrary, he was assured by them that the danger of Israeli attack is non-existent.[32] The impotence of its diplomacy also became evident when Israel ran over the Egyptian army and refused to leave the occupied territories. With a firm commitment from the United States, Israel did not need Soviet cooperation.

Bernard Lewis was also present at this conference. He came from the traditional British colonial service. After coming to the United States, he had established himself as the foremost intellectual guru of the Zionist movement. In the conference, he provided the philosophical basis of Islamophobia as well. In 1984, he was still an obscure academician in the United States, although he was well-known in the Zionist circles. His earlier works, which received universal accolades, were confined to the Ottoman Empire and Turkey. However, in later years, especially after moving to the United States, he made his name by promoting the notions that Muslims hold irrational resentment toward the West and Islam is a violent religion. The thrust of his later works had been associating Islam with acts of violence of the past Muslim empires and the modern Muslim-majority countries.

Lewis has a style of his own. In his long and illustrious career, he has seldom made a distinction between the teachings of Islam and the practice of the religion by empires headed by Muslim emperors. He ignored the fact that all politicians – Muslims or non-Muslims – interpret their religious scripture to suit their political ends. By citing cherry-picked historical events from the 1,500 years of history of the past Muslim empires, Lewis presents his explanation of current events of Islamic history as if nothing has changed in Muslim societies in the last millennium.[33]

In promoting the idea that Islam promotes violence, Lewis picks up obscure past events as examples and follows them with comparisons of actions of contemporary Muslim groups.[34] Such comparisons, which do not follow established statistical analysis, are not valid, as they are designed to impart specific impressions to readers.[35] These are the established methods of misleading even knowledgeable people. These steps are well known in scientific communities.

Valid comparisons of actions of all cohorts are essential to finding facts; it requires analyzing data within the parameters which are similar for all groups. In other words, one cannot compare apples with oranges. Lewis has not followed this essential requirement. For example, he does not compare the teachings of Islam with the teachings of Judaism or Christianity; neither does he examine or compare the actions of past Muslim empires with the activities of past Christian empires. Genocidal practices in Algeria, India, Iraq, or Sudan were never compared.

Instead, Lewis compares selected and idealized versions of the teachings of Christianity (with emphasis on love and compassion for humankind) with horrendous acts of past conquerors, who happened to be born into Muslim families. This form of comparison is neither fair nor valid. Whether by design or otherwise, he did not address the rationale behind the comparisons he opted to mention in his talks. Without providing any evidence, Lewis argued that Muslims tend to be violent during periods of stress. The validity of his arguments is discussed in the next chapter.

Of course, no one was invited to the meeting who would challenge his claims or point out the fallacies behind the assumption on which he had based his theories. He also claimed that Muslims are inherently violent since their actions, violent or otherwise, are based only on Islamic theology. However, he did not provide any evidence to support his claims; and if there were any references, their origin was questionable. For example, he argued that Islam is associated with violence by claiming that Islam is a political religion. Since the Prophet founded a state, he should be viewed primarily as a politician and not a spiritual leader.[36] Lewis also argued that since the leaders of terrorist groups claim to represent Islam, it is appropriate to call acts of terrorism by all political groups from Muslim countries "Islamic terrorism" if Muslims are the perpetrators.[37] Even random acts of violence of individuals, he argued, should be branded in the same way. The basic stand taken by Lewis is that violence is an integral part of Islamic theology.

Lewis further argued that terrorist acts, if perpetrated by Christians and Jews, should not be described as "Christian terrorism" or "Jewish terrorism."

Why? He never explained the rationale behind his arguments, at least not satisfactorily. Is it because Moses and Jesus did not found a state? But the Prophet did not form any empire either. Election chose his successor, and therefore, the first four rulers belonged to the Caliphate. The first three caliphs were not his progeny. After the death of the fourth caliph, the next administrator, Amir Muawiyah, seized power, abolished the election-based caliphate, and established a dynasty.

Besides, what does the founding of an empire 1,500 years ago have to do with actions in the twenty-first century? He never addressed this issue either. Even in his later years, he continued to explain the events of the Muslim world of the previous centuries by citing statements allegedly made by the Prophets and his companions in the seventh century.[38] With time, his arguments have become more focused on associating violence with Islam.

In this conference, Lewis's arguments were supported by many like-minded historians who were prominent political activists from the United States and Israel. They were specifically invited by the organizers to show that there is universal support to the idea of an association of violence with Islam. Two names stand out: Elie Kedourie and Panyotidis Vatikiotis. Both of them were known sympathizers of neoconservative ideology and supporters of neocon ideologues.[39] Both men claimed that many, if not all, acts of terrorism are located in the Arab world, which was not true; still, they argued that terrorism and violence are unique to the World of Islam.[40] They further claimed that since Islamic theology is associated with fanaticism, any rational discussion with Muslims is not possible. Therefore, these men claimed that fighting terrorism will require an overwhelming force and acts of violence by democracies, and it will be a long-drawn process. These were welcoming words for the defense industry; it meant profits for them.

This conference was critical in laying the foundation of Islamophobia, which exists in the United States today. Since then, neoconservative activists have focused on promoting the concept that Islam encourages terrorism; since terrorism is violence and violence equals fascism, Islam equals fascism. *Islamofascism* was a new term coined by the Bush administration. Over time, they were able to promote Islamophobia in the various forms that we see today in many countries worldwide. Once their central concept – that Islam is a violent religion – was accepted by the mainstream, they were able to convince others that all Muslims should be dealt with by force. Since then, neoconservatives and their sponsors have argued that since Islam is an inherently violent religion, Islamic people pose an existential threat not only to Israel but also to the West. These neoconservatives have been able to convince people that the West and Israel are justified in invading and bombing Muslim-majority countries.

Event 3

Benjamin Netanyahu may have started associating terrorism with nationality or a group of people (in his case, Palestinians), but the credit for associating violence with a particular religious belief, in this case, Islam, which prevails in the

Western perception today, may go to Bernard Lewis.[41] He started the current round of discussion on the so-called association of Islam with violence with a speech he delivered in 1990, his Jefferson Lecture. Lewis was awarded the prestigious annual prize that year by the National Endowment for Humanities (NEH). Since he was the keynote speaker, his lecture attracted special attention around the world since it is the highest honor given by the United States government every year to a distinguished person in the field of human sciences. The award was given to him when the Berlin Wall fell. Most governments of Muslim countries were still Western allies.

The impact of his 1990 lecture was different from that of the talk he delivered at the 1984 conference. The latter was not a publicized event; its impact though significant was primarily restricted to foreign policy establishments and pro-Israel lobbies. In his lecture, he had predicted an impending clash of civilizations between Islam and the West. The conflict, he claimed, is imminent due to an inherent incompatibility of Islam with democratic values and modernity and, therefore, by default with the West. He argued that the Western values are built on European enlightenment of the nineteenth century and rational modernity of the Western civilization and culture, and not on irrational beliefs, which he argued, exemplifies Islamic civilization. Some of his ideas were taken from nineteenth-century thinkers who were justifying colonialism. They had justified Western acts of violence in the name of bringing civilization to the colonial subjects.

The title of Lewis's lecture was "Western Civilization: A View from the East." This title seemed innocuous, but the content of his speech was anything but benign. The content of Lewis's talk was malignant. It was designed to generate Islamophobia. Even though his words were respectful toward Islam, his contempt for Islamic people was palpable. In his talk, Lewis continued to argue that Muslims are violent people, which, he claimed, is due to the fanaticism of their religious belief, which he claimed is unique to Islam.

Unlike the current Islamophobic warriors who are not averse to using derogatory language for Islam and Islamic civilization, Lewis's arguments were presented without inflammatory rhetoric. His speech jumpstarted the current round of discussions associating Islam with violence in the American media, which was dominated by neoconservatives. They have branded themselves in the United States as foreign-policy experts. A belligerent tone was introduced to debates by his followers.

His lecture was focused on the so-called Islamic fundamentalism. At the time, the topic appeared to be strange not only to Muslims but also to his many Western audiences. Until then, fundamentalism was not associated with Islam. Even the Islamic radical movement was not an issue for the United States at that time. U.S. foreign policy establishments, in the early 1990s, were firmly aligned with monarchies who would later bankroll Al Qaida and the Taliban, which are defined as fundamentalist organizations. They were fighting side by side with the United States against their common enemy, the Soviet Union. Notwithstanding, Lewis argued that the West is destined to clash with Islam. As expected, his lecture received extensive coverage in the press.

Soon, Lewis was joined by like-minded writers and activists who also predicted an impending clash of civilizations between the West and Islam; but it was Lewis's lecture that started Islamophobia in its virulent form, created anxiety about Muslims, and helped to establish the stereotyping, which has depicted Muslims as inherently violent people. Lewis understood the power of fear and the reaction it generates among ordinary folks.

Once again, Lewis presented selective events of the history of Muslim empires taken out of context to prove his point of view.[42] Because of his international stature as a scholar and an orientalist, Lewis commanded attention; he had been promoted by many political groups, especially by pro-Israeli groups in the United States, as an authority on the Middle East and other Muslim communities. Lewis was in a unique position to influence a wider audience. His reputation was due to his academic experience, penmanship, and his service to the British Empire.

During the later stages of the colonial period, Lewis had served in the British Foreign Service and became a British intelligence agent during World War II. After the war, Lewis joined academia, which gave him the credentials to speak with authority on Islam and the Middle East.[43] His area of expertise was Turkey and the Ottoman Empire. He devoted his writing mainly to the Arabs and Israel's Arab neighbors in later years, even though he neither lived in any Arab country nor spoke Arabic.[44] That was not unusual for intellectuals who served former colonial powers, as the prevailing belief in the nineteenth century was that any non-Western society could be evaluated by studying its language and scriptures alone.[45] Most pieces of literature that came out during the colonial era were gross generalizations of colonial subjects. Not all of them had focused on Muslims; other groups were equally demonized.[46]

These advisors to the former colonial powers were referred to as orientalists.[47] They formed an essential component of the colonial system. According to Edward Said, who coined the term Orientalism, orientalists were the policymakers of the colonial powers and included historians and political and social scientists. They exerted significant influence not only in Europe but also in colonies, where they dictated how colonial territories should be administered, how subjects should be treated, whether violence could be used, and if so, how or how violence should be justified.[48] Since the British Empire was the largest piece of real estate in the world, British orientalists had most influence until the Empire ceased to exist. They contributed significantly to the colonial system, as their job was to formulate policies for their employers and to provide them with arguments to justify their presence in colonies.

Orientalists had a culture of their own. They might have a condescending view of their colonial subjects, but their *gestalt* was presented with a softer or benign tone. Lewis's language reflects that training. On the theoretical level, orientalists had a far more in-depth knowledge of alien lands; indeed, they have produced extensive work on the culture and religion of the people they once ruled. Despite their so-called *deeper* knowledge, there were profound deficiencies in their understanding of the people they were writing about.[49] Many of these prolific writers may not have ever traveled to the countries in which they were presenting their dissertations. Their work reflects a gross generalization of their subjects – Muslims and non-Muslims alike. The fundamental fallacy in their knowledge is only now being recognized after the colonial system ceased to exist.[50]

Orientalists led the campaign of demonization of colonial subjects. Since Muslims were the biggest losers during the colonial era, the demonization of Muslims was also a fact of the colonial experience, which had consequences. Many forms of stereotyping of Muslims, which are widely prevalent in the West today, may have their roots in colonialism. Prejudices against colonial subjects, including Muslims, were rampant. Even though the work of orientalists lacked substance, their opinions formed the basis on which policies were established. Their words became a reality for colonial masters. Since colonial subjects, who were the objects of their writings, had no political or economic power, orientalists' influence on the colonial system went unchallenged. These men and women became indispensable to their employers. Their words became the law of the land – laws which, in some cases, persist even after their independence.

Orientalists were also trained to justify acts of violence, which were routine in colonies, as violence that had to be committed by colonial powers to rule over their restive subjects. At the same time, they had to justify their recommendations of using violence to the public back home so that those colonial policies could make sense to them. Even then, public opinion was as crucial for wars of colonialism as it is today; since not all citizens benefited from colonial wars, they were not as enthusiastic as colonialists to keep their country involved in colonies. Besides, in the twentieth century, the European presence in territories was becoming increasingly expensive and violent.[51] Without the justification of violence, colonialism may have ended long before.

After the dismantling of the British Empire, there was no empire to run. They lost their jobs; there was no use for orientalists in the British Foreign Service. They had to move to the United States or Israel, the only two countries where their skills were still in demand. Lewis joined academia after the Second World War and became a professor of Middle Eastern Studies in London. In 1974, Lewis packed his bags, moved to the United States, joined Princeton University, and became Cleveland E. Dodge Professor. His position gave the opportunity to mentor many neoconservative activists who went on to become members of the American foreign policy establishment.

Lewis also authored many books on Islam, Arabs, and the Middle East, but his area of expertise remained Turkey and the Ottoman Empire. His subsequent writings laid the intellectual foundation of Islamophobia and paved the way for politicians to justify unconditional support for Israel. Only later did other neoconservative intellectuals and authors came on board. They built upon Lewis's work. In the early 1990s, Lewis generated intense interest, but it was confined to scholars, academicians, and certain groups of political elites in the United States. His speech as the keynote speaker at the NEH conference and the subsequent article went almost unnoticed in the Muslim world.

The revised version of his lecture was published as an article in *The Atlantic Monthly*. It was titled "The Roots of Muslim Rage." He argued that 1.5 billion Muslims worldwide are a monolithic community no matter where they live or come from and are culturally (and perhaps genetically) predisposed to violence (see next chapter).[52] Edward Said, John Esposito, and many other thinkers pointed out the danger of such characterization, but their protest found little space in the mainstream media. An evaluation of this particular article is discussed in the next chapter.

Bernard Lewis branded contemporary Islam and Muslim society as virulently violent, but he used kind words, which is the hallmark of British orientalists. Despite the respect he professes for Islam, the impression Lewis leaves on his readers is that Islam is an outdated belief that promotes violence. Lewis provides neither any data nor historical facts to substantiate his assertion. For example, his main argument is that Muslims become violent during the stress of upheaval and disruption. How many of them remain docile, and how many of them take up arms? How about people from other "civilizations"? Do they or don't they become violent during stress? If so, how many? He does not provide an answer to any of these questions.

Lewis's entire essay is based on a gross generalization of 1.5 billion people. They make close to one-quarter of humanity, call three continents their ancestral home, are spread over almost sixty Muslim-majority countries, and form significant minorities in another fifty countries. During the period of expansion over a thousand years, Muslims had spread across Asia, Africa, and Europe, absorbing different cultures and languages. Muslims speak hundreds of languages and thousands of dialects. They live in the richest as well as in the poorest countries of the world. Of all religious groups, Muslims may not be as diversified in terms of interpretations of their religious texts, but they are the most diversified groups of people in terms of race, nationality, ethnicity, and language. Whereas Western and Orthodox Christians are whites, Confucian and Shinto civilizations belong to the Asian race, and Hindus are so-called brown, Muslims belong to all races, and call three continents (Asia, Africa, and Europe) their home. Nevertheless, Lewis claimed that all Muslims think and act in a similar fashion, if not an identical one. Above all, he claims that each Muslim becomes violent and justifies assassinations and kidnappings simply because he or she, the perpetrator, is Muslim.

One of Lewis's intellectual fallacies is that he made no distinction between the events of the seventh century when religion played a vital role and the early twentieth century when religion played a minor role. Most Muslim-majority countries have secular constitutions. Indeed, a sizable number of people born in Muslim families are agnostic, if not atheist. Also, Lewis explains events of the twenty-first century such as globalization and terrorism with thousand-year-old examples of Muslim history as if Muslim societies have not changed in the last 1,500 years. Is it because Muslims – all 1.8 billion of them – are incapable of change? Lewis does not address this issue either.

Irrespective of whether one believes these arguments to be irrelevant or not, his words had a powerful impact. The impression-making industry of the West, which has unusually high numbers of people from pro-Israel lobbies, supporters of the military-industrial complex, and so-called foreign policy expert groups, took his lead and started branding Muslims as violent. Thus began the Islamophobic industry, which became highly lucrative. Islamophobia in its most virulent form laid the foundation of the current campaign of the demonization of Islam. However, there was a clear distinction between Lewis and those who followed his lead. While Lewis was knowledgeable and his language remained sophisticated, his followers were not. Their words were crude but equally effective. Both appealed to different groups of people.

Much has been written about the clash of civilizations and the inherent violence of Islamic civilization in the last two decades. It is also true that both the West and Islamic empires have been serious contenders for the domination of their backyards, which happen to be close to each other. Since they have been next-door neighbors, they have often clashed. During periods of conflict, both have negatively defined their enemies. The current demonization of Muslims in the Western perception is no different. It is based on images and stereotyping that Bernard Lewis presented; it began when he delivered the Jefferson Lecture. How influential was Lewis in demonizing Muslims? Deepa Kumar believes that he changed the paradigm.

Kumar argues that contemporary Islamophobia is based on five myths about Islam:[53] Islam is a uniquely monolithic religion, promotes misogyny, is incapable of democracy, Muslims are inherently violent, and incapable of reasoning because they believe in Islam. All these myths have no validity, but they are firmly rooted in Western perception. They may have been present in the Western perception before, but Lewis's articles solidified them. He also inspired a generation of writers to follow his lead, which led to the current Islamophobic atmosphere in the West on both sides of the Atlantic.

Event 4

As the Soviet Union was collapsing in the 1980s, the United States needed a new direction. In the last year of the Bush Sr. administration, Dick Cheney, who was the Secretary of Defense, assigned his two assistants, Paul Wolfowitz and Lewis "Scooter" Libby, to formulate a new defense policy for the coming decades. These two men and their boss were the founding members of the neoconservative movement, which was just being established. Many of them had worked for defense-related industries. Some of them were also members of the Likud Party of Israel.[54] The common denominator of this group was their close association with the military-industrial complex and with the extreme right-wing of the Israeli political scene.

Though well-known in foreign policy and defense establishments of the United States, these two men were still relatively obscure bureaucrats of the Department of Defense. They were assigned to formulate the United States policy, which was needed, as the Soviet Union was expected to implode. They proposed a strategy to create or foster a World Order that was to be built around the unchallenged military power of the United States. The proposal, *Defense Strategy for the 1990s: Regional Defense Strategy*, was published in January 1993.[55] Then, peace-dividend, which was expected to come from cutting defense spending, was an issue in the United States. The country was still spending a sizable portion of the budget on counterbalancing threats, which many believed did not exist. Cheney, Wolfowitz, and Libby went on to become senior officials in the Bush Jr. administration.

Common sense dictated that the United States could have scaled down its military spending, as the Soviet Union, its arch-rival and the only nation that could have posed an existential threat, ceased to exist. Instead, this obscure group recommended that the United States should not only continue spending on the military but also significantly increase it. They argued that the country should aggressively seize the opportunity created by the implosion of the Soviet Union to become a military power that could not be challenged by any nation. They argued that an increase in defense spending would be good for all of humanity.

They also claimed the security of the so-called free world could only be secure by continuing the massive permanent military presence all over Europe (Germany) and Asia (Japan, Korea, and the Philippines), where the United States already had a physical presence. They recommended acquiring more bases. These strategists also argued that the country should be prepared, and more importantly, willing to use force against any country which could pose a threat or even a potential threat to the nation. Future competitors, if any, they argued, should also be dealt with accordingly.

For a long time, the policy paper, which remained hidden from the public for a long time, made no distinction between the current allies such as Germany and Japan and potential allies such as India or other nations that could be described as foes or future foes. True, they had focused on governments that were aspiring or had aspired to possess weapons of mass destruction. The countries in the latter category included Iraq, Iran, Libya, Syria, and North Korea. They were also apprehensive about China, which was only a potential competitor in the 1980s. The report also proposed that the United States should be prepared to establish a New World Order and recommended that it overpower any potential enemy or even competitors if and when the countries are unwilling to comply with the New World Order.[56] Do the invasions of Iraq and Afghanistan reflect their recommendations?

Their recommendation was built upon the readiness, but more importantly, the willingness of the United States to use preemptive strikes not only against its enemies but also against any potential enemy, even if those countries had not attacked the nation. Irrespective of its legality, they argued that it is politically prudent for the United States to eradicate any threat by preemptive strikes even against any country that has the potential to become an enemy. Undefined was the most critical point of their concept: who defines a potential enemy? Is it the President, Congress, and foreign policy establishment or the so-called *deep* state which holds the most significant influence (some would say "real power") in the United States?

Their recommendation meant severe consequences for the world: if the United States can arbitrarily define its potential enemies and preemptively strike a particular country, do other nations have the same right? If not, why? Which country would stop using its forces to launch a preemptive strike against an intended target? What would happen if another country comes to aid the nation being attacked by the United States? Would the United States attack the other country as well? These strategists did not address any consequences of using force on nations not willing to accept American hegemony. Indeed, preemptive use of force by a country against another was a radical idea in the 1980s. Governments had abandoned this practice after the Second World War, with a few exceptions.

What role should the United Nations have when countries are defining other countries as their potential enemies? After World War Two, the United Nations came into existence. International borders became sacrosanct; their integrity could not be violated unless another nation has directly attacked the country. The practice of crossing borders by using force was the reason behind perpetual wars in the nineteenth and the early twentieth centuries. That has been forbidden by a United Nations bylaw. This particular bylaw, which is an integral part of the UN charter, is the most critical reason why the world is far more peaceful and safer today than it ever was before the UN was established. Despite the success of its policy of banning preemptive strikes, the old concept of crossing the border (because the United States has the means to do it) had already taken root in the minds of neoconservative activists. This mindset evolved only after the demise of the Soviet Union, its only competitor.

The U.S. has the means to annihilate the world many times over; no other country could even come close to what its military is capable of. No country has attacked the United States since the end of the Second World War. Why invest then so many resources in the military when the United States was the sole superpower? Neoconservative and neoliberal activists were candid about their intention: they wanted to keep the United States as the unchallenged military power in the world. The only enigma is why they recommended acquiring so much more firepower, even though the United States was already an unchallenged superpower.

The stated goal of the neoconservative movement has been to bring the so-called "democratic revolution" to the world.[57] Indeed, its members have become engaged as the holy warriors for democracy. Ever since they occupied top positions in the Bush administration, the United States has pursued their recommendations of invading and bombing sovereign nations under the pretext of fighting terrorism or the War on Terror. Most of the victims of their policy have been those of Muslim-majority countries which happened to oppose Israel's occupation of Palestinian land. These countries are Iraq, Libya, Syria, and Iran. Is it a coincidence? Of course not; neoconservatives have been very open with the ideas of using force, especially against Muslim-majority countries. They had focused their attention on the Arab world.

The real question is whether we can believe their stated explanation: do they mean that the United States should use its military power only for the sake of bringing "democracy" to the world? Are there some other unstated motives? We will not know the answer, but these authors have proclaimed that an unchallenged power of the United States in the late twentieth century should be used judiciously. The country should take full advantage of its good fortune.

However, opponents of their policies argue that their plan would bring disaster to the United States. Pat Buchanan also questions their motives as he notes that these activists have proposed regime changes in some Muslim countries that happen to be in Israel's neighborhood.[58] According to General Wesley Clark, who was the supreme commander of the NATO forces in Europe during the Iraq War, the Bush administration was planning to invade seven Muslim countries in five years after the occupation was complete.[59] What does that mean for the United States? The proponents have remained silent on this topic. Their policy is of significant advantage to Israel and not to the United States.

The stated policy of the neocon activists seems preposterous in itself, but some of the other proposals presented were far more radical than it is generally realized in the United States. Some of them are outright insane. For example, some of them even recommended using nuclear, biological, or chemical weapons to thwart any potential competition from the rest of the world. It was a classic case of *Machtpolitik*. They justified their argument for the world hegemony on the ground that the United States can; is it because the United States is a champion of democratic virtues?

In essence, the excuses presented by proponents of the invasions of Iraq and Afghanistan and for pre-emptive strikes were no different from the arguments presented for slavery, colonialism, or anti-Semitism. Phrases such as the "White man's burden" and "spreading civilization among savages" were used by the past colonial powers to enslave millions of people and colonize other countries, which may have cost hundreds of millions of lives.

By following their recommendation of preemptive strikes, the United States was reverting to the *Machtpolitik* of the eighteenth century, which brought disaster not only to colonies but also to all of Europe. Until the United States invaded Iraq and Afghanistan, it was generally believed that the world had already evolved from using force to solving problems; that assumption was proven wrong after the American troops marched into Iraq. Reverting to the century-old policy has meant not only a continuous state of violent conflicts but also a constant state of apprehension and preparation for wars, which requires precious resources to be diverted from development to the military-industrial complex. It has the potential to destroy even the most powerful empires of any time.

As wars are a drain on the economy even for victors, the question is: why would these foreign policy experts, if they are indeed experts, recommend such measures which would destroy or have the potential to destroy the economy of their own country? Critics of neoconservatives – on both the right and left – have argued that their chief concern lies not with the United States but with Israel, which is the only country to have benefited from the current American policy of invasions and bombings of countries in the Middle East. The Bush administration's policy had been a boon to Israel, at least in the short run. Whether the consequences of such policies will remain buoyant even for Israel in the future is an open question.

The other question is: if the United States does the killing and the spending of money on invading other countries, who is benefiting from wars? Pat Buchanan argues, it is Israel.[60] Of course, the authors elected to avoid this small but most important detail of this document. These foreign policy experts should know better; preemptive strikes had failed to keep peace in the world before World War II; instead, they brought immense misery to the world. Why would it be any different now? The constant state of war had destroyed powerful empires and nations of the world in the past.[61] The use of violence to settle minor disputes led to the First and the Second World Wars. They wiped out every mighty empire that had ruled over the world in the last centuries – Nazi Germany, the German Empire, the Czarist Russia, Imperial Japan, the Ottoman Empire, the Austrian Empire, and even the British Empire. Great empires remain great because they avoid fights, not because they get involved in wars.

This policy document was supposed to remain a secret, but it was eventually leaked to the media, probably by concerned bureaucrats. There was significant resistance to their concept even in the Congress and from liberal thinkers and political activists as well as from traditional conservatives. The latter made it a point to distinguish themselves from neoconservatives.[62] Senator Robert Kennedy called it a mistake. Senator Robert Byrd of West Virginia called it myopic, shallow, and disappointing. He was very critical of their goal, as he argued: "The basic thrust of the document seems to be to remain the sole superpower in the world, and we are willing to put at risk the basic health of our economy and well-being of our people."

The criticism of this policy was so sharp that Wolfowitz thought that his political career was over.[63] With President Clinton in the White House (1992–2000), such ideas remained confined within the narrow circle of neocon political activists. Their policy may not have singled out Muslims and Islamic civilization, at least openly, but it had laid the foundation of future wars for the so-called democracy, which could be directed against any Muslim-majority country. Any nation could be declared an opponent of democracy, invaded, and bombed to the Stone Age.

Many Muslim countries, mainly Israel's neighbors, belong to this group; they became the primary target of regime change and intervention – all in the name of democracy – Muslim countries were not the only ones. Ukraine, Georgia, Cuba, Venezuela, and other left-leaning governments of South America also became their targets.[64] However, the primary targets remained a handful of Muslim-majority countries that had opposed Israel's expansion policy. The demonization of Muslims as violent people had begun even though no cause-and-effect relationship between Islam and violence had ever been established.

Event 5 (1993–1995)

At first, the recommendations of the working committee entrusted by Dick Cheney to formulate policy during the Bush Sr. administration (Event 4) were not taken seriously. It was partly because the men who wrote the above policy paper were believed to belong to the fringe elements of the far-right of the American political scene. In the early 1990s, they were not taken in earnest. They may have been part of the foreign policy team of President Bush Sr., but they were at the periphery; they did not make the inner core of confidants. The so-called pragmatic men such as James Baker Jr., Lawrence Eagleburger, Brent Scowcroft, Thomas Pickering, and others made up President's inner circle. True, Dick Cheney was the Secretary of Defense, but he had not turned into a neoconservative activist during President Bush's term.

As President Clinton came to power, neocon foreign policy advisors who were at the periphery of Bush Sr. administration were replaced by yet another group of the so-called *pragmatic experts* from the Council of Foreign Relations (CRF), the other foreign policy establishment. Despite resistance to their plan from the pragmatist group, their rivals, the neocon activists, did not abandon their long-term goal of unseating many Arab regimes, which happened to oppose Israel's occupation of Palestinian land. Saddam Hussein was their first target, but not the only one.[65]

These men and a few women went on the offensive in the mainstream media, generating anti-Arab rhetoric resulting in Islamophobia. Between 1993 and 1995, many articles began appearing in newspapers across the United States which were sympathetic to their causes. By then, neoconservatives had formed right-wing think-tanks, which mushroomed in the nineties. These think-tanks were flushed with money from large-scale donations from like-minded billionaires and other mega-rich people. Many people who funded these groups were supporters of Israel; they openly argued for the annexation of Palestinian land.

Others were openly advocating maintaining defense spending at the level seen during the Cold War. By the late 1990s, these entities had become very influential in American politics. They also controlled, either directly or indirectly, prominent journals, newspapers, magazines, and other news outlets such as *The Wall Street Journal, The Weekly Standard, Commentary, The US News and World Report, New York Daily News,* and others.[66] Mainstream newspapers such as *The New York Times, The Washington Post,* and others were also dominated by writers who had shown sympathy for Israel.[67]

Although many important articles came out supporting neocon ideology and agenda during this period, two stand out. Zalmay Khalilzad wrote the first one. An Afghan by birth, he is a prominent neoconservative and a founding member of the think-tank, *Project for the New American Century* (PNAC). Khalilzad is also a former executive of Unocal, a corporation with interests in the energy sector. He wrote a paper "From Containment to Global Leadership: America & the World After the Cold War." He argued that the United States should move aggressively to control the resources of the entire planet.[68] He also recommended preemptive strikes to control the resources of the countries if the United States needs them or to occupy the land by force obviously, even if "others" were living on the land for thousands of years. Khalilzad singled out the Arab world for this treatment since the United States needed oil, which is in abundance in the Middle East.

The second article was written by the two most important members of the group: Bill Kristol and Robert Kagan. Both are neoconservative ideologues and possess a solid ideological pedigree. Their parents were the founders of the Trotskyite movement in the United States. Both argued that the United States should strive for global domination, a benevolent one, of course, which they claimed is useful not only for the United States and its ally Israel but also for the rest of the world. Their article, "Towards a Neo-Reaganite Foreign Policy," was published in *Foreign Affairs*, an influential journal, which is published by the Council on Foreign Relations (CRF).[69] Once again, these authors did not bother to explain how "other" nations will react to their suggestions. Maybe they took it for granted that others will accept the over-lordship of the United States as these countries had swallowed in the past the colonial rule of Britain and France.

Why would newly independent nations, which sacrificed so many lives for their independence from the British and French colonial rule, accept over-lordship of the United States without resisting? They did not address the question. Was it because overwhelming fire-power, which the United States possessed, would take care of minor problems? Did they realize that for establishing hegemony, violence would be required? It was not addressed by them or by other neoconservative writers who were echoing their suggestions and dominating the mainstream media.

Neither did they address the other obvious fact that their policy would invariably put other nations, especially Israel's neighbors, on the other side of the battle line. How would they react? Should they be placated or restrained? How would they be dealt with? Should the United States invade these countries, which it did? Alternatively, should the West send its special forces to get them in line, which it also did? Should the opponents of the policy be kidnapped? Indeed, the United States had the *Rendition Program*; the number of people abducted may be as high as 1,800.[70] Should the United States send drones to eliminate unpleasant people? The United States has been using drones to eliminate its opponents in at least seven countries. Many of the victims were known opponents of the Middle-East policy of the United States.

Since these authors did not elaborate on these minor details, it appears that in their scheme of things, the American military might be able to take care of not only invasions and occupation, with the violence, of course, but also the consequences of those invasions. Indeed, the United States invaded two countries (Afghanistan and Iraq) and its allies another five – Lebanon and Palestine (by Israel), Somalia (by Ethiopia and Kenya), and Niger and Mali (by France). The United States had already planned to invade seven countries in five years. All of them opposed Israel's policy in the Middle East.

The underlying argument to invade these countries was based on the fear of Islam and Muslims. These men and women began their campaign of Islamophobia. They argued that Muslims are violent and that Arabs can only be dealt with by force.[71] Since then, Islamophobia took a virulent form.

Event 6

In the mid-1990s, Benjamin Netanyahu assigned Richard Perle and Douglas Feithe, the two prominent neoconservative political activists, to prepare yet another policy document for the extreme right-wing faction of the Likud Party of Israel; their goal was to annex the entire West Bank. In July 1996, they completed their assignment. The policy document was titled *A Clean Break: A New Strategy for Securing the Realm*. For achieving their goal of annexing the entire West Bank, these authors recommended a regime change in Iraq, which they argued should be the first step, as Saddam Hussein, the Iraqi president, was the weakest link among all Arab leaders. The Iraqi military was decimated during the First Gulf War. It was never mentioned in the document, which was meant for internal use, that Iraq or any other Arab country could threaten Israel or the United States. These two men went on to become advisors to President Bush Jr. This document outlined the strategy to unseat and eliminate Saddam Hussein.

Indeed, it was this argument on which the Bush administration justified the invasion of Iraq. Besides advocating the annexation of the West Bank and Gaza by going back from the Oslo Accord, the paper also recommended regime changes in Syria, Iran, Lebanon, and the occupied territory of Gaza and the West Bank (not necessarily in this order). However, they also argued that the United States should start with the invasion of Iraq, as Iraq had become the weakest country in Israel's neighbors after the First Gulf War. After the relentless bombing campaign by the Clinton administration, Iraq, they argued, was a sitting duck. Saddam Hussein was isolated, and therefore Iraq was easy to conquer. Keeping up with recommendations outlined in the policy paper, Ariel Sharon had repeatedly requested President Bush Jr. to divert his attention to Iran since Saddam Hussein had been taken care of, which the Bush and the successive U.S. administration attempted to do.

Event 7

In 1997, President Bill Clinton was in his second term, and the bombing of Iraq was in full swing. As many as one million people may have been killed, out of which half a million were children. The excuse given by the United States was that the use of forces was needed to maintain a no-fly zone over Kurdish and Shiite areas of Iraq so that the Kurdish and Shiite remained safe in their enclaves. A few people, all former democrats, now claimed to belong to the neoconservative wing of the Republican Party, formed a think-tank to promote their political views. The new entity was called *the Project for the New American Century* (PNAC). Prominent members of this exclusive club were Dick

Cheney, Paul Wolfowitz, Lewis "Scooter" Libby, Elliot Abrams, Donald Rumsfeld, Peter Rodman, Paula Dobriansky, Zalmay Khalilzad, Jeb Bush, William Kristol, Robert Kagan, and others. Many of them would hold high positions in the first term of the Bush Jr. administration,

The members of this exclusive club could be divided into two broad categories: pro-Israel activists and the right-wing super-nationalists who have promoted the high level of defense spending by the United States, which brings exceptionally lucrative profit to the military-industrial complex. Neoconservative writers belong to the first subgroup; they are the children and grandchildren of Trots-kyites who once believed in socialism or claimed to be socialist. Their primary goal in the 1990s was to support Israel in annexing the Palestinian land. In the 1970s, however, they had spearheaded anti-war movements and had spoken against the U.S. involvement in Southeast Asian conflicts. The popularity of their cause peaked during the Vietnam War. Their critics claim that their opposition to the Vietnam War was to support the Soviet Union in return for allowing the Russian Jews to leave their homeland for Israel. Most of them settled in the United States.

In contrast to the former leftists, people from the latter group are traditional conservatives. They had always opposed the Soviet system of planned economic order; they can also be described as super-nationalists. They also believed in maintaining a powerful military and opposing the communist movement in the so-called Third World, which they argued could only be achieved by supporting a powerful army. After the collapse of the Soviet Union, the interests of both groups had merged, as they found a common enemy in Islam, even though no Muslim-majority country had attempted to challenge the United States.

In the early 1990s, both groups had a common interest: they wanted to project America's military strength around the world, although their actual goal may have been different., They found common ground to combine their political forces. For neocons, America's overwhelming power was essential to decimate Israel's Arab neighbors so that the annexation of Palestinian land could not be challenged. For super-nationalists, their primary interest has always been to maintain America's mighty military-industrial complex for which at least the current level of defense-spending was essential.

Whether these men and women may also have a personal stake in funding for a powerful military-industrial complex has not been discussed in the main-stream media. However, it has been pointed out in the alternative press that many of the warriors of democracy had their roots in the defense industry, intelligence, homeland security companies, and defense contract corporations. All of them profited every time U.S. forces were sent on foreign soil. Of course, the bill for its international venture was paid by American taxpayers.[72]

Both groups were quick to recommend using the American military around the world to shape the future, which they called *the new American century*. American interests and its so-called "principles" could only be achieved by maintaining a powerful military. In other words, the stated goal of both groups was to create a unipolar world in which the United States was to act as the sole policeman of the planet, irrespective of what other nations might think or whether they would object. Any dissent of this policy was expected to be taken care of by the United States, by force, of course. Whether other countries would consider such policy as an attack on their national interests or even on their sovereignty was not addressed by the authors. What consequences such policies would have in the rest of the world was blatantly ignored.

Despite universal criticism of their policy, these authors and activists successfully got the United States involved in some Muslim-majority countries – Libya, Somalia, Yemen, and Syria. It may have taken another decade or so, but the United States and NATO have destroyed many of these countries. Using the U.S. military was based on their stated goal: promoting democracy in the Muslim world, by force, of course, which in turn was built upon the fear of Muslims. Islamophobia was carefully created and managed. The groundwork for the invasion was established well before 9/11.

Event 8

In January of 1998, many prominent neoconservative political activists wrote an open letter to President Clinton, urging him to undertake steps for changing the Iraqi regime of Saddam Hussein.[73] Many of them were the founders of the PNAC.[74] In their letters, they argued that if Saddam Hussein remains in power, the safety of American troops in the region and of America's friends and allies like Israel and "moderate" Arab states would be in jeopardy. They also pointed out the possible economic stakes for the United States if a conflict erupts in the future, as a significant portion of the world's oil supply either comes from the Middle East or passes through these areas. Therefore, they argued that, during future conflicts, oil supply could be at risk.[75]

Their recommendation was based on the assumption that Iraq possessed WMDs, but no proof was ever produced. Their claim was later found to be false and probably fabricated. The letter urged President Clinton to use force even if the United States could not get approval from the Security Council. The letter did not mention that any regime change in Iraq through invasion would be against the UN Charter and, therefore, an illegal act, as the United States is a signatory to the UN Charter.

Is it any wonder that Iraq was invaded on the pretense of having WMDs? Probably not, if we consider that the letter was signed by people who went on to become important members of the Bush Jr. administration: Donald Rumsfeld (Secretary of Defense), Paul Wolfowitz (Deputy Secretary of Defense), Lewis "Scooter" Libby (Chief of Staff of Vice President), Elliot Abrams (Special Advisor to the President on the Middle East), John Bolton (U.S. Ambassador to the UN), Peter Rodman (Assistant Secretary of Defense), Paula Dobresnski (Undersecretary of State), Zalmay Khalilzad (U.S. Ambassador to the UN, Iraq, and Afghanistan), Jeb Bush (Governor of Florida and President's brother), and Richard Perle (Chairman of the Defense Policy Board).

Table 3.1 Officials in the Bush administration (2000) who also signed the open letter to President Clinton urging him to remove President Saddam Hussein of Iraq from power

Name	Position in the Bush administration	Remarks	Profession/career
Elliot Abrams	Special assistant to the President, Senior Director and then-Deputy National Security Advisor on the Middle East (in the Bush administration)	One of the defendants in the Iran-Contra Affair pledged guilty to two counts of misdemeanors. He recommends military action against Syria	Lawyer, political activist, and member of the pro-Israel think-tank. Special envoy to Guatemala in the Trump administration
Richard Armitage	Deputy Secretary of State (2001–2005) in the Bush administration	According to President Musharraf, threatened to bomb Pakistan if he did not cooperate with the invasion of Afghanistan	Career military officer and intelligence. He works or worked for L3 Communication, a defense contractor, and Conoco Phillips (oil)
William Bennet	Secretary of Education in the Reagan administration	Author, and a firm supporter of family values and privatization of public-school education. Claimed that it is a moral duty of the U.S. to support Israel and "Palestinians' are "Jordanians"	A career in government, author and social activists, Radio show and political analyst with CNN
Jeffery Bergner			Professor, finance (Bergner and Brockney), and a registered foreign agent for Taiwan
John Bolton	Under Secretary of State for arms control and international security Promoted as U.S. Ambassador to the United Nations under President Bush and Trump	Had to leave after controversy, played a role in the inclusion of a statement that Iraq procured yellowcake uranium from Niger	Lawyer, political activist, and think-tank industry, PNAC, American Enterprise Institute, Jewish Institute for National Security
Paula Dobriansky	Under Secretary of State for Democracy and Global Affairs in the Bush		Government and academia, think-tank industry

Name	Office/Position		Background
Francis Fukuyama		Declared his opposition to the War on Terror following the massacre during the occupation of Iraq	Comes from academia and conservative think-tank industry
Robert Kagan		Continues to be a firm supporter of the War on Terror and on Arab countries. Supports Likudniks and Israel's settlement policy in occupied territory	Comes from the media; author and journalist. Founder of the PNAC
Zalmay Khalilzad	Special Assistant to President, ambassador to Afghanistan, Iraq and then to the United Nations in the Bush and Trump administration	One of the few Muslims associated with the neoconservative movement. He is an Afghan by birth	Comes from the oil industry (Unocal now Chevron), which invested in building pipelines through Afghanistan
William Krystol		Most influential neocon intellectual. Author of many books; supports Israel's settlement policy	Comes from the media; Editor of the *New Republic* financed by Rupert Murdoch. Co-founder of PNAC
Richard Perle	Chairman of the Defense Policy Board in the Bush administration	Argued to attack Mecca and Medina just to show that the United States has the power to do so	Comes from government, defense industry, and the American Enterprise Institute. Formed a venture capital firm, Trireme Partners
Peter Rodman	Assistant Secretary of Defense	Known for Anti-Muslim and Anti-Arab documentaries	Comes from the media. He is a journalist and political activist.
Donald Rumsfeld	Secretary of Defense in the Bush administration	Resigned after public protests and after the loss of the Republican Party in the 2006 elections	Comes from the defense and pharmaceutical industry – Gilead Sciences
William Schneider Jr.	Chairman, Defense Science Board during Bush administration	Concluded that Iraq could develop intercontinental ballistic missiles, which could be a threat to the U.S.	Government service; advocates the use of nuclear weapons in limited space even today

(Continued)

Table 3.1 *(Cont.)*

Name	Position in the Bush administration	Remarks	Profession/career
Vin Weber	Member of Advisory Board to Secretary of Energy Past member of Congress from Minnesota		Lobbyist by profession
Paul Wolfowitz	Deputy Secretary of Defense in the Bush administration. He was also an official in the Bush Sr. administration.	Quit in the Second term. He was nominated by President Bush as Head of the World Bank; he had to resign after controversy related to appointing his girlfriend	Comes from academia; after resigning from World Bank, joined the American Enterprise Institute
James Woolsey	CIA chief in President Clinton's cabinet	Claimed that Saddam Hussein was connected to the bombing of Oklahoma and the 1991 bombing of the World Trade Center	Intelligence and defense, formed consultancy group, chairs an advisory board of an Israeli security firm
Robert Zoellick	Deputy Secretary of State	Promoted as the Chairman of the World Bank, when Wolfowitz had to resign	Came from the finance world: Goldman Sachs and Fannie Mae

Soon, an avalanche of articles and books started appearing by these activists and their supporters in important newspapers (see next chapter). All of them were recommending the removal of Saddam Hussein. The underlying argument for the invasion of Iraq was that Iraq might have acquired WMDs, but their assertion, either by design or otherwise, invoked Islamophobia and other myths about Islam which had been promoted for a decade. They argued that Iraq, which was decimated during the 1991 Gulf War, was powerful enough to attack the United States, especially since the Iraqi President was irrational and violent. The fear of Muslims and Islam was carefully created in the Western perception well before 9/11 and the invasion of Iraq (2003). Islamophobia was also aggressively promoted by supporters of these men and women; the fear of Islam and the irrationality of Muslims played an important role in convincing American citizens to support the invasion of Iraq.

Event 9

In September of 2000, almost one year before the United States was attacked, the PNAC produced another document – *Rebuilding America's Defenses: Strategy, Forces, and Resources for a New Century*. This paper also argued for preemptive strikes against the so-called "rogue states" and a reorientation of U.S. armed forces and other resources toward those specific nations, all of which except North Korea are neighbors of Israel and happened to be Muslim-majority countries. Why would Muslim countries, which individually spend on their forces only 1% of what the United States and its allies spend on their armed forces, opt for war against the West? Attacking the United States would be suicidal. However, their explanation was the same: because they are Muslims, who are inherently violent and irrational, and since they may have acquired or are about to acquire WMDs, the West was in mortal danger. By then, fear of Muslims had already become a reality for many in the West. Islamophobia was carefully propagated by neoconservative foreign policy experts.

Until then, U.S. military resources in Europe and Asia were still directed toward Russia even though the Soviet System had collapsed a decade earlier and the Russians were dying to join the Western orbit – which was the nucleus of the world's economic power. It also suggests that spending on defense by the United States may not have anything to do with security. The authors provided an alternate target for the potential use of American firepower. They argued that American effort is needed to be directed towards new and potentially more dangerous competition from China and Muslim countries, which incidentally have adversarial relations with Israel. The governments of these countries had shown no interest in opposing the United States; the only problem may have been that they had vigorously protested Israel's annexation of Palestinian land.

They recommended that the United States should maintain unchallenged nuclear superiority, which the country already has; more importantly, it should exercise its power if needed. They called for developing newer generations of nuclear weapons that could be used in more confined areas such as cities and a more mobile air force that can deliver such weapons. They also argued for a global missile defense system not only to defend the American homeland but also to project the U.S. power around the world by creating U.S. Space Forces to control space. They also argued for establishing a network of military bases worldwide and for marginalizing the United Nations.[76]

Neoconservative activists, who by then were dominating the media and foreign policy establishments in the United States, promoted their world view that has encouraged Islamophobia and other myths, which have become an integral part of the Western perception of Islam. The intention behind generating fear is to control its citizens and prepare for doomsday. Influential people were discussing these recommendations before the events of 9/11, which suggests that the destruction of the World Trade Center, though tragic, cannot be blamed for the demonization of Muslims in the United States.

Event 10

In 2001, President Bush had just started his tenure at the White House. After taking over the office, he asked his Vice President Dick Cheney to draft an energy policy for the country. The Council on Foreign Relations (CRF), which is supposed to be staffed by pragmatic policy experts and not by neoconservative ideologues, presented a report on the energy needs of the country. The paper was titled *Strategic Energy Policy Challenges for the Twenty-first Century;* it called for an aggressive approach toward obtaining resources for the country even if those resources are located in other parts of the world. It also called for the reassessment of energy in American foreign policy[77] Dick Cheney organized a series of secret meetings to draft the energy policy.

This report has not been released by the Bush administration, which had fueled speculation that the United States was planning to control, if not occupy, oilfields of Iraq long before Al Qaida attacked the United States. The Obama administration also refused to make this report public.

Event 11

On September 11, 2001, the United States was attacked by Al Qaida with four jetliners; three of them smashed into the World Trade Center and the Pentagon; the fourth one crashed in rural Pennsylvania. It is assumed that it may have been headed for Washington DC. Osama bin Laden immediately claimed responsibility for the attack on behalf of Al Qaeda. President Bush pledged to smash the terror network. A meeting was organized by Donald Rumsfeld, Paul Wolfowitz, and Richard Perle to prepare for the response. In attendance were senior members of the Department of Defense, military establishments, and the State Department. There were also policymakers, members of academia, and foreign policy establishment. The meeting was supposed to be a secret.

According to Bob Woodward, the meeting was called by Rumsfeld and his deputy, Wolfowitz.[78] Both men were convinced that the Department of Defense was intellectually incapable of providing ideas and strategies to take advantage of the situation and deal with this crises of this magnitude.[79] Three individuals provided political strategy and intellectual justifications of acts of impending violence which the United States was about to unleash on Iraq: Bernard Lewis, Fareed Zakaria, and Fouad Ajami. The first two individuals, according to Sheehi, provided the roadmap of the invasion of Iraq and the War on Terror. Sheehi writes:[80]

> Wolfowitz, Perle, and Rumsfeld's meeting were a milestone. They codified the invasion of Iraq and the overthrow of Saddam Hussein as among the highest priorities for the U.S. foreign policy in the new war on terror. … Within a week of 9/11, Zakaria, Lewis, and Ajami were already considered the brain trust for Wolfowitz's "Delta of Terrorism" paper and policy that, by November of 2001, were all but a fait accompli.

In his book, Sheehi claims that the invasion of Iraq was decided in this meeting.[81] Others believe that the decision to invade Iraq was taken before this meeting was even conceived. These three intellectuals were brought in to lay the groundwork for justifying the impending invasion of Iraq. According to this theory, these men were asked to devise a strategy to justify the invasion for public consumption. Whatever the truth, the strategy for justifying the invasion may have been developed at this meeting. The three intellectuals, who were called by the Bush administration, may have presented a roadmap for the invasion of Iraq.[82]

Sheehi also suggests that these men recommended justifying the invasion of Iraq by associating the Iraqi leader with violence. The idea that Iraq had acquired WMDs, and therefore, posed an existential threat to the United States, was already in circulation; they merely solidified the perception. They further claimed that if it was left to the sanctions, which the United Nations were imposing, WMDs could turn into a *mushroom cloud*, a term designed to generate the perception of an existential threat for the United States. An association of violence with Muslims played an essential role in building the consensus on the invasion of Iraq.

Event 12

In September 2002, a year after the World Trade Center was attacked, the Bush administration published its official policy paper titled *The National Security Strategy of the United States of America*. President Bush announced that the United States reserves the right to attack or strike any country to maintain its national interests even if the United States might not be under a direct attack. This policy of preemptive strike, which can be described as an illegal act, has been downplayed by portraying the threats of violence as benevolent hegemony. The recommendations of the above policy paper are similar to the proposal presented by members of the PNAC, which was made available to Israeli Prime Minister Benjamin Netanyahu almost a decade before (see Event 6).

This paper called for American presidents to go after any country which the president may consider a danger, even if that nation may not be an imminent and immediate danger to the country. Mere suspicion was enough to declare any country to be an enemy. The paper also announced that the United States reserves the right to ignore international treaties, even if the United States had signed and ratified them in the past if the agreement is deemed to be against the country's interests. The paper also recommended acquiring and constructing military bases beyond Western Europe and North-East Asia, where the United States had traditionally operated. This meant acquiring bases in the Middle East, Africa, and South America. The United States followed up on their suggestion. Many new bases have come into existence after 9/11, not only in Iraq and Afghanistan, which the United States occupied, but also in independent nations, such as Uzbekistan, Qatar, Djibouti, and other parts of Africa.

As recommended by President Bush and his team, the policy was designed to maintain American domination worldwide. However, these ideas were conceived and directed by the members of the PNAC. They were made and packaged in Israel (see Event 6). Three of its members, Richard Perle, Douglas Faith, and David Wurmser, had conceived the concept well before 9/11. As noted earlier, they had produced a policy document titled *A Clean Break: A New Strategy for Securing the Realm*, which later became the policy document for the PNAC. President Bush's team accepted it lock, stock, and barrel. When these authors produced this paper, they were working for Netanyahu. By then, he had become the leader of the extreme right-wing political segment of Israeli politics. They declared in no uncertain terms that Saddam Hussein should be removed from power.

Since the same group of people drafted both documents, there were many similarities in the suggestions, but there was one significant difference. In the report presented to President Clinton by the PNAC, the justification of the removal of Iraq's leader was based on the fear of Islam, which in turn was based on the portrayal of Muslims as violent people. The recommendation to the American administration was meant for the consumption of the American public. In contrast, the document which was prepared for the Israeli Prime Minister, the argument for justifying the invasion of Iraq was primarily for annexing Palestinian land, which they argued is only possible by maintaining American global hegemony. The same authors claimed that the control of the Persian Gulf and its oilfields by the United States would enhance American power.

It has been argued that the primary target of the PNAC was Syria and not Iraq, but the policy paper chose Iraq to be the first target in shaping the Middle East to their liking because they believed that Saddam Hussein was the weakest link and the most natural target. In other words, Iraq was targeted for the regime change not because the country posed any threat to the United States or Israel or it possessed WMDs or was about to acquire them; Iraq was targeted just because it posed no danger, as it had no WMDs. They assumed that Iraq would capitulate quickly, which it did. They concluded that U.S. casualties would remain very low. Iraq's army was defeated in Saddam's venture into

Kuwait. They were right: the United States lost less than 250 people during combat. It was also claimed that the policy would have an impact on the emergence of China as a world power since Chinese energy resources could come from this region.[83]

Do these neoconservative political activists believe in their rhetoric that Muslims are to be feared? Not according to facts; the superiority of American weapons and intelligence was firmly established during the 1967 War, in which Israel decisively defeated the combined Arab armies. Arab nations never had the means to pose threats to anyone, much less to the United States, NATO, and Israel, which formed the most potent military and political alliance the world has ever seen. In a rare moment of candor, during an interview with *Vanity Fair*, Wolfowitz agreed that their argument for using WMDs in justifying violence in the media, which the Bush administration was going to unleash, was based on the political reality.[84] Any hint of the presence of WMDs in Iraq meant an existential threat to the United States in perception only.

The Bush administration and their neocon supporters never believed that any Muslim country could pose a threat, much less an existential threat to Israel, especially at a time when the United States had evolved into an unquestioned supporter of Israel. In 1998, when many neoconservative political activists sent an open letter to President Clinton demanding him to unseat President Saddam Hussein of Iraq, they argued that Saddam Hussein posed an existential threat to the United States allies. The same people presented their recommendation to the Prime Minister of Israel to overthrow Saddam Hussein, but the reason they cited was diametrically opposite.

Indeed, the recommendations presented to President Clinton and Prime Minister Netanyahu to unseat Saddam Hussein may have been the same. However, the arguments to justify the future invasion given to President Clinton, which received extensive coverage in the American media, and the proposal presented to Prime Minister Netanyahu for a regime change in Iraq were different. The latter received little coverage in the American press. For the United States, Islamophobia (an association of Islam with WMDs, violence, and terrorism) was the nucleus on which arguments for invading Iraq were based. Iraq was described as a threat to the United States since Iraq, a Muslim-majority country, was about to acquire WMDs. It was also implied that Saddam Hussein was irrational and violent, partly due to his belief in Islam, even though he was a militantly secular person.

However, the argument that Iraq could be a threat to the United States or anyone else, even to tiny Kuwait, was missing in the policy paper presented to Netanyahu. Richard Perle, the author of a chapter "Iraq: Saddam Unbound," in the book *Present Dangers*, published by the PNAC, also wanted Saddam Hussein to be deposed first. It was because the Iraqi leader was the most natural target. Another member of the neocon team, David Wurmser, is the author of another book, *Tyranny's Ally: America's Failure to Defeat Saddam Hussein*. He also presented similar arguments. This book was published by the American Enterprise Institute, one of the many well-endowed think-tanks which support the neoconservative point of view. Wurmser heads its Middle Eastern Projects.

To sum up, the events, which have been presented in chronological order, were crucial in forming the Western perception of Muslims as violent people. They also show that the violent images of Muslims did not evolve spontaneously. They were carefully created and managed by public relations experts. These events of the last three decades also prove that policymakers never feared either Islam, Muslims as a people, or any Muslim-majority country. Indeed, Muslims had never posed any threat to the West in the last three centuries.

Nevertheless, neoconservative activists and intellectuals presented the claim that Muslims are an existential threat to the West. Their allegation was designed for the consumption of the American public. These men and women have been arguing that the United States and its allies, which happen to be the most potent alliance the world has ever seen, need to fear Muslims. They are inherently violent, and their propensity for violence could not be altered as it is based on Islamic theology.

The association of violence with Islam became a standard script for using force not only in Iraq but also in some other Muslim-majority countries. They argued that since these countries are either ruled by dictators or are failed states, they should also be dealt with by force. The current state of Islamophobia prevalent in Western perception is an example of the power of *dogwhistle* politics. The association of Islam with violence has been repeated so often, in so many forms and different forums, that whenever the word Muslim or Islam is spoken, an image of violence follows.

The transformation of Muslims in Western perception as violent was a gradual process that began long before the jetliners crashed into the World Trade Center and the Pentagon. The success of Bernard Lewis and Sam Huntington and their influential supporters, who belong to the neoconservative movement, in changing the direction of American Foreign policy is beyond imagination. Their success was partly due to the methodical preparation of the groundwork, which had been carefully and meticulously conducted. It was prepared over the last four decades.

Articles and books dehumanizing Iraqis, Arabs, and Muslims, were primarily based on invoking Islamophobia. They are discussed in the following chapters. They followed a well-defined script: Iraqis are Muslims and, therefore, anti-democratic, Islam promotes violence and irrationality. The main point of their arguments was that Iraq has or was about to acquire WMDs. Since Saddam Hussein is irrational and has used chemical weapons earlier, he can use them again. Therefore, he can become an existential threat to the United States; a change of regime in Iraq is essential.

Notes

1 Samuel P. Huntington, *The Clash of Civilizations and the Remaking of World Order*, Tables 4.1 and 4.3, 83–84.
2 Huntington, ibid.
3 John Esposito and Dalia Mogahed, *Who Speaks for Islam?* x.
4 https://fortune.com/longform/media-company-ownership-consolidation/.

5 https://www.europeandefenceleague.com/2018/03/17/jewish-control-of-the-media-in-the-united-states-and-therefore-around-the-world/.

6 Amy Julia Harris, https://www.revealnews.org/article/islam-judged-more-harshly-than-other-religions-in-terrorist-attacks/; also see Esposito and Mogahed.

7 Huntington, 254

8 Andrew Fitzgerald, https://listverse.com/2013/03/24/10-terrorist-organizations-operating-in-the-us/; also see https://start.umd.edu/news/proportion-terrorist-attacks-religious-and-right-wing-extremists-rise-united-states.

9 http://www.bilderberg.org/roundtable/wwcfrsos.html; for detailed discussion see James Perloff, *The Shadows of Power*.

10 Tunku Varadarajan, "Going Muslim," *Forbes*, November 9, 2009.

11 Varadarajan, ibid.

12 Raphael Patai, *The Arab Mind*, Chapters VI and VII.

13 Sheldon Rampton and John Stauber, *Weapons of Mass Deception*, Chapters 2 and 3.

14 Ibid.

15 Craig Paul Roberts, "A Majority of Americans Do Not Believe the Official 9_11 Story" (International Clearing House, January 8, 2019); also see https://truepublica.org.uk/global/some-interesting-new-information-about-9-11/.

16 https://www.aljazeera.com/news/asia/2011/09/20119115334167663.html.

17 Doug Saunders, *The Myth of the Muslim Tide*, 100–103. Deepa Kumar, *Islamophobia and the Politics of Empire*, 52–54, 162–165.

18 Edward Said, *Covering Islam*; John Esposito, *The Islamic Threat*, 213–222.

19 Rampton and Stauber, 41–48, 53–58.

20 Sven Lindqvist, *Exterminate All the Brutes*, 122–127.

21 Ibid.

22 Kumar, 120–122.

23 J.J. Goldberg, *Jewish Power*, 197–226. For a detailed impact see John Mearsheimer and Stephen Walt, *The Israel Lobby and U.S. Foreign Policy*.

24 Patai, ibid.

25 Kumar, 120.

26 Kumar, 121.

27 Kumar, 120–122.

28 Kumar, ibid.

29 Robert Pape, *Dying to Win*, 264–265.

30 https://www.palestineremembered.com/al-Ramla/al-Lydd/Story173.html.

31 https://www.nytimes.com/1978/04/02/archives/wadi-haddad-palestinian-hijacking-strategist-dies-directed-first.html.

32 Tariq Ali, *The Clash of Fundamentalisms*, 315–332.

33 Said, *Covering Islam*, xxxiii.

34 Said, xxxii.

35 Said, xxxi.

36 Bernard Lewis, "The Roots of Muslim Rage," *The Atlantic Monthly*, September 1990, 49–67; Benjamin Netanyahu, ed., *International Terrorism*, 66. Also see Bernard Lewis, *The Jews of Islam*, 5, 11–13.

37 Lewis, "The Roots of Muslim Rage."

38 Lewis, ibid.

39 Ellie Kedouri, "Political Terrorism in the Muslim World," in Netanyahu, ed. *International Terrorism*, 70.

40 Ibid.

41 John Esposito, *The Islamic Threat*, 219.

42 Esposito, 219; Said, *Covering Islam*, xiv, xxxi.

43 Said, xxxi.

44 Said, xxix, xxx.

45 Said, xxxi. Also see Lewis, "The Return of Islam," *Commentary,* January 1976; Kumar, 29–33.
46 Lindqvist.
47 Edward Said, *Orientalism*, 2–4.
48 Ibid., Chapter 1.
49 Kumar, ibid.
50 Said, *Orientalism*, 26; Kumar, 43–44.
51 On violence in Congo by Belgians see Adam Hochschild, *King Leopold's Ghost*; in Kenya, see Carolyn Elkin, *Imperial Reckoning*; in Algeria see Marnia Larzig, *Torture and the Twilight of Empire.* For a broader perspective of European violence in Africa see Lindqvist, *Exterminate All the Brutes*; for massacres by English settlers in Australia, see Lindqvist, *Terra Nullius.* Also see Lindqvist, *A History of Bombing.*
52 Lewis, "The Roots of Muslim Rage," 49–67.
53 Kumar, 120; Said, *Covering Islam*, xxx–xxxii.
54 Rampton and Stauber, 47–63.
55 Bernard Weiner, "How We Got into this Imperial Pickle" (Information Clearing House, May 27, 2003), https://www.informationclearinghouse.info/article3544.htm.
56 Barton Gellman, "Keeping the U.S. First; Pentagon Would Preclude a Rival Superpower," http://www.yale.edu/strattech/92dpg.html.
57 Patrick Buchanan, *Where the Right Went Wrong*, 37–60.
58 Ibid.
59 Wesley Clark, "Seven countries in five years," https://www.youtube.com/watch?v=9RC1Mepk_Sw https://www.salon.com/2007/10/12/wesley_clark/.
60 Buchanan, ibid.
61 Joseph Tainter, *The Collapse of Complex Societies*, 193–216.
62 Buchanan, 47–59.
63 Kumar, 116.
64 John Perkins, *The New Confessions of an Economic Hitman.* This book has chapters for each country divided in chronological fashion.
65 Buchanan, 47–59.
66 Goldberg, 279–304; Peter Ford, "Weapons of Mass Deception: Media on Trial" (International Clearing House, June 8, 2018); https://israelpalestinenews.org/watch-suppressed-al-jazeera-film-details-the-israel-lobbys-covert-war-to-manipulate-americans/?eType=EmailBlastContent&eId=028aecdf-0784-402f-9213-0af528c7810a;
67 "Allison Weir on the Media Bias in Covering the Palestine Occupation" (video), https://www.youtube.com/watch?v=AdwcUDdC0Ek. Several articles on this topic can be found on the website *If Americans Knew*, https://ifamericansknew.org.
68 https://www.rand.org/pubs/monograph_reports/MR525.html.
69 https://americanaffairsjournal.org/2018/07/robert-kaplans-world/.
70 https://www.justiceinitiative.org/voices/20-extraordinary-facts-about-cia-extraordinary-rendition-and-secret-detention.   https://www.washingtonpost.com/news/worldviews/wp/2013/02/05/a-staggering-map-of-the-54-countries-that-reportedly-participated-in-the-cias-rendition-program/.
71 Patai, ibid.
72 Tom Engelhardt, "America's 'War on Terror' Has Cost Taxpayers $5.6 Trillion and it's Earned Us Absolutely Nothing," *The Nation* (May 16, 2018).
73 PNAC to President Bill Clinton; the latter can be seen at https://www.informationclearinghouse.info.
74 Rampton and Stauber, 47–63.
75 Gwynne Dyer, *Future: Tense*, 127.
76 Dyer, *Future: Tense*, 127–129.
77 Weiner, ibid.
78 Stephen Sheehi, *Islamophobia: The Ideological Campaign Against Muslims*, 44–45.
79 Sheehi, 44.

80 Sheehi, 45.
81 Sheehi 45–50.
82 Ibid.
83 Dyer, 129.
84 https://www.independent.co.uk/news/world/middle-east/wmd-just-a-convenient-excuse-for-war-admits-wolfowitz-106754.html.

4   Marketing hatred

Islamophobia and hate politics

The events that formed the nucleus of the arguments associating violence with Islamic civilization were presented in the last chapter. Their timeline shows that the image of Muslims as violent people was methodically created; it did not evolve on its own, nor was it due to 9/11 or any other random acts of terrorism perpetrated by Al Qaeda or its sister organizations. The demonization campaign had begun decades before the bullets started flying in Kabul and Baghdad or the planes found their targets in New York and Washington DC.

Several anti-Muslim activists were active in the 1970s and 80s. Some of them organized the events, while others presented their ideas wherever they could (Chapter 3). However, they were still unknown entities; their influence remained confined to the likeminded groups. Initially, they may have focused their effort in garnering support from politicians and bureaucracy. They gained valuable support from think-tanks which had mushroomed during this period in Washington DC. Their efforts were supported by pro-Israel lobby groups and transnational mega-corporations engaged in defense industry and disaster management. Only two writers succeeded in taking their concepts to the next level by presenting anti-Muslim rhetoric to the public.

This chapter identifies those two intellectuals who packaged the anti-Muslim ideas to be marketed. It also evaluates why they succeeded while others failed. This can only be done by analyzing their concepts, the ideology behind their concept and method, the validity of their arguments that established Islamophobia in its current form, and the logic behind the arguments of their opponents. Writers and political activists who propagated the hypothesis of Islamophobia are discussed in the next chapter. Several books are available on this topic. However, they have used only logic to argue their stand. This book analyzes the issue of how Islamophobia became viral.

Since confusion may arise if terms are not applied appropriately, let us first define the terms that have been used in this chapter. They are misinformation, misperception, deception, propaganda, and attitude. They are not the same; there are subtle differences among these terms. Misperceptions are false beliefs, and misinformation is incorrect information; they are either lies or manipulation of facts, such as selective omissions and cherry-picking of facts. Misinformation can cause misperception, but not always. Deception is an intentional effort to create

DOI: 10.4324/9781003323105-5

misperception, and propaganda is a presentation of information in a biased way to affect the belief of people. According to Ian McCulloch, a social scientist, attitude is an affinity towards stimuli that affects neural processing.[1]

The need for establishing Islamophobia

The fear of Islam is not new; Islamophobia in Europe has waxed and waned as it has been lurking beneath the surface in the Western psyche for centuries. Maybe, it is because the past Islamic Empires were the only *civilizations* or nations to have established hegemony in Europe. First, the Moors established their presence in the Iberian Peninsula, Sicily, and Southern France. They had even reached near Paris before they could be defeated. Next came the Ottoman Empire from the east; they conquered Eastern Europe, parts of Russia, Ukraine, and the Balkans. The Turks even reached the outskirts of Vienna. They were finally defeated in 1683 by the combined forces of European armies. Even in the twentieth century, European colonial powers had a hard time subjugating restive Muslim subjects. The trend of resisting alien powers continued in the twenty-first century. Citizens have given the West a determined resistance in Muslim countries even though Muslim rulers have aligned themselves with the United States and other Western powers.

Fear of Muslims has taken different forms and varied in intensity over time, but Muslims have seldom been described as violent until recently. An association of violence with a Muslim community was first alleged in recent years after the Iranian Revolution, which transformed the oil-rich region. It brought Ayatollah Khomeini to power in Iran, a Muslim-majority country, and resulted in the abdication of the Shah of Iran, who was one of the most important allies of the United States in the Middle East. The new rulers promptly nationalized the oil industry, expelled Americans, and branded them *the Great Satan.*

In return, Iranians were branded religious fundamentalists and fanatics. Was the loss of oil contracts the reason for stereotyping Iranian society fanatic? Since intentions can only be inferred and not measured, the answer can only be a speculation. However, until then, Iranians were portrayed as progressive; so was the Shah, even though he was installed by overthrowing a democratically elected government.[2] The newly installed Iranian monarch occupied the throne little over two decades, but during his reign, he had turned Iran into an autocracy; dissent was not tolerated. Consequently, tens of thousands were incarcerated or killed. His security agency, the SAVAK, which was trained by the United States, was one of the most efficient and brutal police forces in the region.

As friends became foes, accusations and counter-accusations followed from both sides. The stereotyping of Muslims followed the nationalization; consequently, the Iranian image in the media took a nosedive – they were branded as religious zealots, primitive, violent, and anti-democratic. Whether there was a cause-and-effect relationship between the nationalization of the Iranian oil industry and the demonization of Iranians is still being debated, but the Iranian Revolution cost American transnational corporations dearly. Iran was a significant market for American finished products, especially in the defense sector, nuclear energy, autos, and engineering equipment. The trade between the two nations came to a standstill. There was a palpable hatred in the United States against the new Iranian regime. However, during this period, the stereo-typing of Muslims was confined to Iranians; the rest of the Muslim world was not the focus of the negative branding. How could they be? Many other Muslim countries were still allied with the West.

Has the Iranian revolution anything to do with their demonization? Many Iranians believe that the loss of contracts with Iran at a throw-away price was the main, if not the only reason, behind the portrayal of Iranians as religious zealots and fundamentalists and Iran as a violent and backward-looking anti-democratic society. To Iranians, this appeared especially ironic since they had managed to overthrow the earlier monarchy by peaceful means and establish a functioning democracy in the country before Shah was brought from exile. The monarchy came to Iran through a CIA-engineered *coup d'état*,[3] which overthrew a popular democratically elected government. The demonization of Iranians was spearheaded by politicians and the oil industry. The latter had gained lucrative concessions from the Shah,[4] which they lost under the new Iranian regime.

A decade later, the negative portrayal of Muslims in the American media took a back seat. In 1979, the Middle East's political landscape changed after the Soviet Union invaded Afghanistan; Americans joined hands with Afghans against their common enemy. The United States provided funds, weapons, training, and intelligence; the Muslim world sent its men to fight the commu-nists. These volunteers were branded as freedom fighters, the *Mujahedin*. Their leaders with beards and turbans were invited to the White House. President Reagan was effusive in praising them. They were compared with the founding fathers of the American Republic.

A decade later, the Soviet Union departed from Afghanistan. The Red Army was defeated, adding yet another name to the list of mighty armies that came to occupy the gateway to India; all of them were eventually defeated and buried in the graveyards of empires in the valleys of Hindukush. The cost of war to American taxpayers was negligible, but the price of victory to Afghans was enormous. Afghanistan was bombed to the Stone Age; nearly two million Afghans died during the war and a quarter of Afghans became homeless.[5] For Americans, the Soviet–Afghan war was a success beyond imagination. America had accomplished its cherished goal of destroying communism. Soon after, the United States packed its bags and left Afghans to their fate. A deadly civil war followed, which killed more Afghans than the Soviet invasion and occupation did.

The fall of the Soviet Union, which boasted one of the most powerful armies ever assembled under one command, was swift. The dismantling of the com-munist empire began as the Red Army withdrew from Afghanistan; it was fol-lowed by the fall of the Berlin Wall (1989). The deconstruction of the Soviet system was complete within two years. In 1991, Gorbachev resigned, and Boris Yeltsin took over the truncated Russian Federation. The world watched in awe as one of the most powerful nations imploded. Surprised? One should not be; as

Alfred McCoy notes, sudden collapse of powerful empires is not unusual: that is how they vanish.[6] It took the Portuguese one year, the French colonial power eight, and the British Empire seventeen years to implode.[7] History also shows that great empires are seldom destroyed from outside; they commit *hara-kiri*. Crossing the Amu River was Soviet Union's Rubicon; it was an act of suicide.

After the fall of the Berlin Wall, an association of violence with Islam again became a rallying point for a new generation of ideologues; they called themselves neoconservative. Alleged violence of Islamic civilization became a hot topic in the American media. This time, the object of demonization was not a specific country but Islamic civilization. The turnaround in the portrayal of Arabs, Muslims, and Islam was equally quick; it caught many policymakers of Muslim-majority countries by surprise. There were no new conflicts between the West and Muslim countries. On the contrary, the United States came to the rescue of Bosnians and Kosovars against Serbia. The Palestine–Israel conflict was the only sore point, but it was old news. Also, Iran posed no threat to the United States; the Iranian Revolution had failed to attain sizable followings in the Muslim world.

Notwithstanding, Afghan freedom fighters, the *Mujahedin*, were rebranded; they became the *Taliban* and terrorists. Whether the United States and the West or Muslims should be blamed for the deteriorating relationship between the two groups of nations may be debated, but that is a moot point; the stereotyping of Muslims was going on for decades.[8] There were drastic changes in the image of Muslims in the Western perception in a short period from progressives to fanatics and violent, followed by freedom fighters, then back to violent and terrorists.

The ongoing rebranding of Muslims indicates that a) the perception of people, friends and foes alike, may not be factual; it is subjective; b) it can be short-lived; c) contradictory impressions of Muslims did not evolve spontaneously, their negative images were deliberately created; d) manufacturing of impressions depends on the political alignment, which depends on financial interests of the combatants; and e) the impressions are interwoven with the interests of the elites of the society.[9] Rapid remodeling of Muslim images in the Western perception raises the following questions: how can one explain the changes in the Western psyche about Muslims from one extreme to the other within a short period?

There are two distinctly different views on this issue. On the one side are the neoconservative ideologues; they argue that Muslims appear violent because they are violent. Their argument is that if there is a cloud of smoke, there is a fire; therefore, if Muslims are believed or appeared to be violent, there must be some truth to it. On the other side are equally talented authors who argue that there is neither fire nor smoke; there is only an illusion of smoke. The delusion of fire stemming from non-existent smoke is only a hallucination based on myths created by misinformation and backed by false news and unsubstantiated facts.[10] In the process, overzealous opinion-makers benefited from the consequences of stereotyping and demonization of Islamic civilization.

Which point of view is correct or based on facts? We will see, but the difference in the views of the two opposing camps is not only unusual but also understandable. Since the topic is also controversial, discussions often become passionate. The noise generated by emotions drowns objectivity in debates. Still, the enigma is why the notions presented by neoconservatives went viral, but the concepts of their opponents could not spread. There are two possibilities: a) either neoconservative ideas were correct and backed by facts and their opponents' ideas were false or appeared to be false, or b) irrespective of the truth behind the idea of Muslims being violent, neoconservative ideologues prevailed because they were supported by powerful forces of the establishment – the executive and legislative branches, the media, big capital, and state bureaucracy. Their opponents had no such luck; on the contrary, they were marginalized by the mainstream media.

Which of these two possibilities is correct? To answer this question, one has to be acquainted with the fundamentals of neoconservative hypothesis, as well as the arguments of their opponents. However, arguments alone may not be enough in solving the mystery of how ideas spread. Recent studies have shown that there is more to ideas becoming viral than the sheer strength of the arguments behind them. Therefore, one has to unlock the mystery of how ideas, with and without credible arguments, spread and news, fake or otherwise, can be propagated. We also have to find out why one set of ideas catches on even though it may not have any facts to substantiate the logic behind the notion. In contrast, other concepts, which may be based on verifiable data, fade into oblivion.

In other words, there may be factors beyond ideas that play a role in spreading concepts such as implicit bias against Muslims. Is it inherent in the Western psyche? Systemic biases could be too subtle to be realized by ordinary mortals, even though they are equally powerful. There are many examples of implicit biases ingrained in Western thinking. Michelle Alexander and Ian Lopez have shown the presence of implicit racism in the West that formed the basis of institutionalized prejudice against blacks.[11] Does the West also harbor implicit Anti-Muslim biases? Can that explain Islamophobia?

Opinion-makers and political activists are divided on this issue. Most of them have promoted neoconservative authors as visionary; however, others have denounced them as anti-Muslim warmongers. Both groups of writers have presented their arguments in favor of their position based only on logic. However, their reasoning lacks scientific analysis of the system in the spreading of ideas. There are still several unanswered questions. For example, these authors could not explain why the demonized images of Muslims became deeply rooted in the Western psyche and widely prevalent. It also does not explain why anti-Muslim ideas took over even those countries, where Muslims lived side-by-side with their non-Muslim neighbors with relative peace for centuries. Logic alone is not enough to settle the debate why stereotyping Muslims has been a success.

Packaging and marketing Islamophobia: primary sources

Even though the demonization of Muslims as violent was pursued by many political activists, commentators, and media pundits, giving this specter a credible format can be traced primarily to two political thinkers and academicians of the second half of the twentieth century: Bernard Lewis of Princeton University and Sam Huntington of Harvard University. Long before Islam became synonymous with violence in the West, Lewis was talking about the irrational behavior of Muslims during periods of stress, and Huntington was predicting a clash of civilizations between the West and Islam. Their genius lies in marketing Islamophobia in a successful format.

Lewis presented his ideas in a lecture he gave in 1990 in Washington DC. That speech was followed by an article, "The Roots of Muslim Rage," which was published in the magazine *The Atlantic Monthly*.[12] The article was a further clarification of his ideas. In his talk, Lewis had blamed the Islamic doctrine and theology for creating irrational rage among its followers, which he argued results in violence.[13] Lewis also coined the term "clash of civilizations."[14] Huntington took this concept a step further by predicting an imminent *clash* between Islamic and Western Christian civilizations. These two authors also argued that both civilizations are fundamentally incompatible, as their values are diametrically opposite to each other.[15] What those values are, they did not elaborate.[16]

Huntington's conclusions about Muslims and Islamic civilization are the same as that of Bernard Lewis. There is hardly any difference between the assertions of Huntington and Lewis or their followers. Their claims complement each other. Both have portrayed their version of Islamic civilization as a monolithic entity, which gives Muslims a solitary identity that is based solely on religion. The only difference between the two is how they present their arguments. Whereas Lewis presented his beliefs with what he describes as logic but provides minimal data to support his assertions, Huntington has provided data to prove his hypothesis. Could Huntington and his colleagues prove the assertions using data, which Lewis and his followers could not prove with their logic? Since there is a similarity in their arguments, this chapter evaluates their works together.

A third name could also be added to this short list: Giselle Littman. She may not be as well-known as the other two, but her impact on generating Islamophobia in Europe is equally important. She has been writing with her Hebrew pseudonym *Bat Ye'or* (daughter of Nile). During the period when Lewis and Huntington were pointing out the so-called differences between Islam and the West and predicting imminent clashes between the two, Littman produced a number of articles and books, which promoted the concept that Muslims are deliberately migrating to Europe at a furious pace to convert all of Europe into an Islamic land. This demographic shift, she argued, would be completed within a few decades,[17] and Europe could soon become an Islamic continent unless steps were taken immediately to stop Muslim migration. Her claims of Europe turning into an Islamic continent has been proven to be wrong,[18] but her assertion of Muslim exodus to Europe has generated intense Islamophobia in Europe; it became a war cry for the extreme right-wing super-nationalist groups in various European countries.

Littman's works were designed to generate anxiety among Europeans about their future and to promote a sense of impending doom for the West in general and Europe in particular. She gave the name *Eurabia* to Europe. Inadvertently perhaps, she may have played a crucial role in the resurgence of extreme right-wing parties, which have fascist and anti-Semitic tendencies. Muslims may be their primary targets in the twenty-first century, but anti-Muslimism can quickly turn into anti-Semitism, as these fascist parties carry a latent form of anti-Semitism. Therefore, Littman could be blamed, partly perhaps, for turning Europe into a bastion of ultra-right ideology. It appears that she is trying to divert anti-Semitism by inciting hatred against Muslims. However, hatred of one group can be easily substituted with promoting violence against the others; that only accentuates the intensity of hatred against every group.

The three of them were the first thinkers to provide three unique and separate forms of Islamophobia; when combined, these notions formed the intellectual foundations of prevailing pathological perceptions such as Islamophobia, hatred of Muslim, arguments for the invasions of Iraq and Afghanistan, and justifications of acts of violence committed against half a dozen Muslim countries. These people were the strategists for the Islamophobic industry. They have transformed a benign form of xenophobia into a most virulent type of Islamophobia, an emotion that should have no place in a civilized society. Their arguments were used for demonizing Muslims as violent people.

These three authors are the originators of the stereotyping of Muslims as violent; they became the intellectual gurus of the next generation of writers and political activists who are responsible for the explosion of Islamophobic literature that has inundated the West in general and the United States in particular in the twenty-first century. Together, they and their followers have also changed the *Zeitgeist* of our time. They have taken advantage of the prevailing Western anxiety about their future, which does not stem from threats of Muslim countries; they are too weak to pose any threat to any nation, much less to the United States, which has the most powerful armed forces and a strong economy to support its military.

These authors had trained their invectives against Islam, Muslims, and Islamic civilization, the terms which they have used interchangeably for Muslim-majority countries. It may be because of their pro-military-industrial complex agenda and pro-Israel stand. Islamophobia and irrational fear of Muslims were the basis of the demonization of Muslims. These three authors and their followers were successful in branding Muslims as violent, anti-democratic, proponents of autocratic rule, misogynists, fanatics, and opponents of modernity. The question is whether their assertions are based on facts or myths.

That leads to the next set of questions: how did these authors measure the acts of violence of civilizations? Have they presented historical facts to substantiate their arguments? If so, were the data that they used legitimate or based on inappropriate assumptions? Were their methods scientifically analyzed and statistically valid? These questions have been addressed in this segment. The issues raised by the above questions might become clearer if we understand what is meant by civilization. It has remained a vague term, perhaps, intentionally.

The vagueness of the term civilization has been used by people with different agendas to present their points of view. How did these authors and their followers define the term civilization? What do they mean by Islamic civilization? Do they mean Muslim countries? If so, is Islamic civilization identical to or different from Muslim-majority countries? The other sets of questions are: how did they conclude that Islamic civilization is violent? Since civilizations do not have a central bureaucratic structure, armies, or militia, how can Islamic or any civilization be violent? The enigma is how these authors were able to convince the entire Western world. The rest of the chapter deals with these questions.

Huntington's *Clash of Civilizations*

Huntington published his book in 1997. It remained obscure for a decade even though the content of the book was widely discussed in academic circles. By the middle of the 1990s, Bernard Lewis's arguments (see Chapter 3) had been discredited within academia. However, he remained popular among neoconservative activists. The events of 9/11 and the President's decision to invade Iraq changed the fate of Huntington's book. Suddenly, the book and the ideas contained in the book became viral.

Whether Huntington's assertions are valid rests on the following factors: are his data correct, or are they concocted? Irrespective of whether his arguments are appropriate, are the data he presented based on facts? Alternatively, he may have used what is dubbed as alternative facts, which is a euphemism for lies. Huntington has based his hypothesis on the assumption that humankind has one identity. The following segment evaluates the concept of solitary identity to understand the idea of a clash of civilizations.

The credit for coining the phrase "clash of civilizations" may go to Bernard Lewis (Chapter 3), but Huntington transformed the term into a household name. He gave credibility to and acceptance of this concept to a broader audience. He had predicted an impending clash between the West and the Muslim world in an article that was published in 1993, almost a decade before 9/11. Whether he had the wisdom to predict future events or the knowledge of the impending changes in the U.S. policy from his association with neoconservative ideologues, who wrote the open letter to President Clinton demanding to remove President Saddam Hussein from power and then went on to become an essential part of the Bush administration (Table 3.1), cannot be stated with certainty, but his prediction catapulted his book to the fore as one of the most critical works and him as a political writer.

Did he influence President Bush and his team? Possibly! Can the onus for starting the invasions of Iraq and Afghanistan also lie on Huntington? Probably; his book was the rage during the early years of the Bush administration. President Bush was seen carrying the book around before the invasion of Iraq. However, the far more critical impact of Huntington is his idea of a solitary identity of all humanity, which has permeated into the Western perception. His concept of solitary identity has caused the *otherization* of nations and groups of people within countries. Solitary identities have formed the basis of an *us versus them* mentality.

Huntington presented his views first in the form of a question in the 1993 article, "The Clash of Civilizations?" published in the prestigious journal *Foreign Affairs*,[19] which is the flagship publication of *The Council of Foreign Relations*, an organization which is believed to be representing the interest of the establishment. In 1997, Huntington presented the same concept in book form; it had the same theme but a slightly different title. Missing in the title was the question mark. Was it an indication that the author had two years later found the answer? Alternatively, Huntington may have been predicting an impending clash of civilizations.[20]

One could argue that Huntington was right; less than a decade after his article was published, the World Trade Center was attacked by Al Qaeda. However, there are other issues linked with this concept. There were a series of friendly interactions between the CIA and the Islamist organizations. Al Qaeda was created by the CIA;[21] the Pakistani secret service was the conduit for funding American aid to Gulbuddin Hikmatyar,[22] Abdul Rashid Dostum, and other warlords.[23] Together, the CIA and Mujahedin were able to defeat the Soviet Union in Afghanistan. Then both allies parted ways. One of the ironies of the political landscape of the twenty-first century is this: Al Qaeda was created by the United States to fight the Red Army in Afghanistan, but a decade later, they were at each other's throats. Why did Al Qaeda go against the CIA, an organization that had created and transformed the Islamist organization into a global player?

Whether Huntington was right in predicting the impending confrontation is not the point; the issue is if Huntington's view that 9/11, subsequent invasions of Afghanistan and Iraq, and the War on Terror can be classified as a clash of civilizations. He, like Lewis, has suggested that the difference between the West and Islam can never be reconciled, and violence is the only way to tackle Muslims. That alleged difference between the West and Muslim countries was the main argument on which President Bush and President Obama formed America's Middle East policy. It has resulted in the invasions, bombings of half a dozen Muslim countries, and the killing of five million people.[24] Over thirty million people have lost their homes.

Problems with hypotheses

In this book, Huntington compartmentalized humanity in precisely defined units of civilization, which he classified on the religious affiliation of the inhabitants. Religion formed the basis of the solitary identity of all people. His views were presented in an intelligible format, but it was written in a quasi-scientific language with tables, graphs, charts, maps, and diagrams. The book has left a substantial impact, albeit for a short period; nevertheless, it impacted millions of people over two decades. The book's format gave an illusion of objectivity to those readers who have little knowledge of scientific methods and statistics – a group to which most of us belong.[25]

Is his classification of humanity, which was based on a single identity, correct? To some, it was wisdom; to others, it was theory doctored. One could argue, who cares for theoretical discussions; Huntington's arguments made sense. Above all, Huntington was right. He had predicted an impending clash of civilizations between the West and Islam. Consider the following events: within a decade of the publication of his book, the United States, which he characterizes as the leader of Western Christian civilization, was attacked by Al Qaeda, a so-called Islamist organization, which has been described as the representative of the so-called Islamic civilization by the rival groups. Neo-conservative ideologues immediately blamed Al Qaeda for the event of 9/11 without proper investigations; the latter wasted no time to take the credit in the name of defending various Muslim communities around the world. The rest is history; by the time President Obama left the White House, Israel's neighbors Syria, Iraq, and Libya were decimated.

Since inferences drawn in Huntington's book appear to be based on scientific principles (even though they are not), and his views generated respect in the West. His presentation of the so-called historical facts in scientific jargon gave the book an impression of the scholastic aptitude of the author. Amartya Sen, in his book, *Identity and Violence: The Illusion of Destiny*, opines that debates on the book that were taking place in the living rooms of the West gave the participants the delusion of intelligent discussion and an aura of intellectual accomplishment. Edward Said, in his book *Covering Islam* points out that during the preparation of the invasions and bombings of civilian areas, social media was filled with fake news and unsubstantiated facts; ordinary folks in the West would cite passages and data from Huntington's book to convince others that Islamic civilization is violent; therefore, Iraqis and Afghans deserve what is happening to them. The arguments presented in his book were used to justify the violence of their government. The book became a best-seller in the wake of the destruction of the World Trade Center.

The success of his book, which came a decade after its publication, can be traced to the following two factors: a) Invasions and bombings by the United States that followed 9/11, were perceived by many, and described by important members of the Bush Administration, as a clash of civilizations. Others claimed it was a clash of Islamic values with the so-called Western values; whatever the terms or jargon meant, remained unclear. b) The presentation of Huntington's views with data gave an impression that his conclusions are based on scientific analysis, and therefore, his vision of the world order is correct.

The book also changed the Western perception of Islam. Denouncing Islam as a violent religion was no longer a taboo, not only among laypersons but also among intellectuals and political leaders. Consequently, Muslims became an easy target not only in the West but also in other parts of the world, especially in places where Muslims have been battling their governments, which Muslims allege denied them the rights that others enjoy. However, the real question remains: irrespective of the impression the book gives, is Huntington's worldview correct? He may be right about the confrontation, but how do we know that it was not a coincidence?

Indeed, there are a number of fallacies with Huntington's assumptions. He has based the division of humanity only on religion and classified human societies into civilizations that are defined exclusively on the religious affiliation of people living in particular geographical areas. His hypothesis, in theory, could be valid only if people practicing a single religion exclusively inhabit geographical regions of the world. He also argued that there is a causal relationship between religious affiliation and civilization, which, he also claimed, forms the building blocks of nations and their alliances.[26] Are these assumptions correct?

First, according to his classification, Western Europe became Western Christian, Eastern Europe became Orthodox Christian, while India and China became Hindu and Confucian civilizations, respectively.[27] The rest of the old world became Islamic civilization, which lies in the center of the world map. What was left became a Buddhist civilization, which remained confined to a few pockets in Asia. Huntington had assumed that religious groups are strictly confined to specific geographical areas (Map 4.1).

Second, he categorized Africa and Latin America separately and independent of the religious affiliation of the inhabitants. That idea appears neither appropriate nor valid. He has based his entire argument on the concept that people belonging to a particular religious affiliation live in a specific geographical area. He does not give any reason why the classification of these two civilizations should not be based on religion, while other cohorts are. South America has been defined as Latin and Africa, sans Muslims, as African civilizations. However, if two out of the six habitable continents were not categorized by the same yardstick, how could his theory have any credibility?

Map 4.1 Distribution of religious-based communities across the world
A similar map was used by Huntington in his book, *The Clash of Civilizations*.

Finally, he divides the world with precise borders drawn on the map among civilizations and calls these borders fault lines. He assumes there will be violent conflicts across these fault lines, which he also based on religion. Is this concept true? There are two relevant observations: 1) True, people across fault lines may be fighting with each other, but are they fighting for religion, or are they fighting for basic and tangible issues, such as the distribution of resources of the disputed land? 2) There are places that do not lie along the fault line; they are also in the state of confrontation based on the same religious identities. What is the difference between violent conflicts along the fault lines and those not along the fault lines? Huntington is silent on this issue.

Huntington argues that fault lines are prone to violent conflicts because people living around fault lines come from two different civilizations. He cites a number of examples to prove the validity of his assertions; however, he omits those fault lines which do not conform to his hypothesis. This is manipulation by omission. He also claims that the groups on either side of the fault lines have been fighting with each other for centuries.[28] This is wrong as well. Even if we assume that Huntington's theory is correct, are they fighting for religious or economic factors? If so, are the reasons for their conflict the same as they were centuries ago, or the cause for conflicts has changed? Huntington does not address this issue either. His theory also implies that the geographical location of civilizations plays a vital role in violent conflicts.

Huntington claims that Muslims have been at odds with every other civilization. That may be true, but he does not elaborate on the relevant factors behind violent conflicts. Since geographical factors decide the number of neighbors, civilizations that have a central location will have more neighbors. Whether the combatants belong to the same or another civilization does not matter. The incidence of violence is the same. Those with more extended borders would have more neighbors, therefore, more conflicts than other civilizations. Huntington does not address this issue either.

For example, if we look at the Old World on the map, countries of the so-called Islamic civilization appear in the center, and all other civilizations are at the periphery. The so-called Islamic civilization borders nations belonging to every other civilization except Shinto (Table 4.1). In essence, Muslim countries have more neighbors than any other cohort, which comes to nine out of a total of ten cohorts. That is not the case with other civilizations: Western Christian civilization has only two; Orthodox Christian, Confucian, Hindu, and Buddhist civilizations have between four and five. Each civilization has fought wars with its neighbors. A better question, therefore, should be which civilization has invaded countries that were not in the neighborhood. The groups of nations that stand out are the West and Japan.

Furthermore, the New World is located at a distance from other groups; they are separated by oceans, therefore, in theory, at least, the United States should have fewer international conflicts, but that is not the case. It has invaded more

Table 4.1 Neighbors and conflicts in non-Islamic civilizations

Religion-based civilization	Number of neighbors	Conflicts	Conflicts with neighbors
Western Christian	2 (Eastern orthodox, Islamic)	Orthodox Christian: Serbs (Croats)[29] Soviet Russia (1918–89). Islamic: Turkey (1914–18), Palestine (1920–48), Egypt (1956);[30] all colonial wars in Asia and Africa[31]	100%
Orthodox Christian	4 (Western Christian, Islam, Sinic, Buddhists)	The West: Croatia and Slovenia Islamic: Bosnia, Kosovo, Turkey, Chechnya, Sinic: China Buddhists: Mongolians, many indigenous groups	100%
Confucianism	4 (Islamic, Buddhist, Hindu, Shinto)	Islamic: Sinkiang (succession movement)[32] Buddhist: Tibet (1959 to date)[33] Hindu: India (1962)[34] Japan: Nanjing, World War II	100%
Hindu	5 (Western Christian, Islamic, Sinic, Buddhist, miscellaneous groups)	The West: The British Empire Islamic: Pakistan, Sinic: China (1962) Buddhist: Sri Lanka Tamil vs. Sinhalese[35] Miscellaneous: Sikh (Khalistan),[36] Secessionist movement in Nagaland, Mizoram in East India[37]	100%
Shinto	4 (Western Christian, Orthodox, Sinic, Buddhist)	The West: The U.S., Australia, Britain Orthodox: Russia (1904,[38] 1939–45) Sinic: China, Manchuria Buddhist: Korea	100%
Buddhist	4 (Hindu, Confucian, Orthodox, Islamic)	Hindu: in Sri Lanka Confucian: Tibet Eastern Orthodox: Mongolia, parts of Russia Islamic: Burma, Thailand[39]	100%

nations in the twentieth century than any other country. So did the British Empire during the colonial period; Ireland, a nation belonging to the Western Christian civilization, was one of the first nations to be colonized by Britain. In the second half of the nineteenth century, the British Empire was involved in one major war every year.[40]

There are other reasons for the importance of geographical locations of the so-called "civilizations" in initiating violent conflicts. Before the advent of mass transportation, violent clashes were localized for the most part to neighbors only. Countries located in the center, surrounded by other countries, had to protect from or expand their interests at the cost of their neighbors. It is, therefore, logical that countries located in the center could have a higher incidence of conflicts, civilizational or otherwise, with their neighbors. He does not acknowledge this fact.

Neither does he mention in his book that since Islamic civilization has more neighbors, it could have more conflicts with its numerous neighbors. However, they do not have more conflicts relative to their number and neighbors.[41] Muslim countries have been the least aggressive groups of nations in the last three centuries, partly because they do not have the means to pursue wars to achieve their economic goals. In contrast, the Western world has been the most aggressive group of nations in the last two centuries because they had the most powerful weapons among all countries. Therefore, Huntington's views on an association of violence with Islamic civilization do not make sense. He has selectively omitted facts.

His notion about so-called civilizational violence also appears to be without any merit for the following reasons. First, all conflicts between nations in the last two centuries were fought over the control of land and the distribution of its resources and not over religion. It is hard to find any example in the last century in which a war was conducted to convert a group of people to Islam or Christianity or any other religion. Even in Afghanistan and Iraq, which have been branded as a clash of civilizations between Islam and the West, religion is not the issue. However, although wars are not fought over religion still, faith is often used in branding people in a certain way and to justify the violence that cannot otherwise be justified.

Violence at an individual level may be due to greed, lust, hedonism, or other negative emotions, but violence at the national level is primarily due to economic factors; the issue in violent conflict between two nations is the control of land and its resources, which are distributed within society among various subgroups, which may be formed on the basis of common identities. These identities may be based on multiple factors. At times, the origin of identities may be religious affiliations of the subjects, but not always. There are other equally relevant identities for the distribution of resources of the society; they are based on different factors: ethnicity, language, the color of skin, political beliefs, or any other factor which divides humanity.

These identities may be used for the distribution of resources of society. In that case, the warring factions could be divided based on those characteristics; they also have the potential to turn into confrontations. The role of religion in wars is to justify violence. However, if religious texts cannot justify wars for any reason, combatants have always found a way to justify wars through many populist and noble causes such as fighting for democracy, bringing civilization to savages, defending political philosophy, a particular way of life, or for nationalism. As Samuel Johnson said, patriotism (to which religion can be added) is the last resort of scoundrels. Actual reasons behind conflicts, violent or otherwise, which are always land and its resources, are not identical with arguments for justifying aggression.

Do Huntington's arguments make sense? There are many fallacies in his arguments. Let us review Huntington's assertions from a geographical perspective.

Fallacy: civilizations are not monolithic units

One of the most crucial contributions of Huntington in deconstructing the violence taking place around the world is to convince people that Islamic civilization has bloody borders and interiors.[42] His assertion rests on the following two concepts. First, Islamic civilization is inherently violent because it has its origin in the desert.[43] Why should that be the reason for their violent behavior? He never made it clear. He compares the prophet with Jesus, but that comparison is not appropriate.[44] Whereas Moses could not reach the Promised Land and Jesus died fighting loan-sharks and did not enjoy the power of the state, the prophet of Islam laid the foundation of the first republic, in which the nascent Muslim community shared power with three different tribes and communities. In that respect, he should be compared with Lord Krishna or Ram, the Hindu gods, who had to pick up arms to defend *dharma*. Second, Huntington also claimed that all civilizations are based on culture, which he argued depends on the religious affiliation of its people.[45] That may not be correct either.

Huntington categorized humanity on a solitary identity a) by claiming that all civilizations are located in a specific geographical area and b) based the divisions in the religious beliefs of the people living in a particular area. The underlying principle has been challenged by many contemporary thinkers, such as John Esposito, Edward Said, Amartya Sen, and others. According to them, the problem of his classification begins with the hypotheses on which he has based his study. His first concept that Islamic civilization is violent has been addressed in Chapter 2.[46] The data show that Muslim-majority countries or the so-called Islamic civilization were not the most aggressive groups of nations. The credit for being the most violent, at least in the last three centuries, goes to Western nations. In contrast, Muslim nations have been the primary victims of violent conflicts of the previous two centuries.[47]

This segment examines his second assertion, which stipulates that civilizations confined themselves within specific geographical areas. His inference has been based on the assumption that people of the same faith live together, but is that correct? Do people of the same faith live exclusively in specific geographical areas? Presented in Table 4.2 is the list of non-Muslim-majority (Muslim-minority) countries and their Muslim population, and Table 4.3 the list of Muslim-majority nations and their non-Muslim population.

Table 4.2 shows that Muslim-minority countries, which by definition do not belong to Islamic civilization, have a significant Muslim population. For example, India has almost 180 million, if not more, Muslims, a number which is only exceeded by Indonesia and probably Pakistan. There may be more Muslims living in India than in Bangladesh, which is the third-largest Muslim-majority country. The number of Indian Muslims may be equal or close to equal to the number of Muslims living in Pakistan since a sizable Muslim population has

Table 4.2 Muslim-minority countries and their Muslim population[48]

	Country/ (world ranking)	Total population (millions)	Muslim population (millions)	Remarks
1	China (1)	1300	30–60; may be even higher[49]	Between 1.6 and 6%. Their exact number is challenging to assess. According to Uighur sources, there are 26 million Uighurs in Sinkiang alone. They constitute only a minority of all Muslims. There are at least ten major groups of Muslims in China
2	India (2)	1100	150–180	The influx from Bangladesh: the exact number is speculative at this stage,[50] and the higher birth rate has seen their number increase
3	United States (3)	300	5.8–8	2%; could be higher, as many Muslims have been reluctant to provide their religious affiliation after 9/11
4	Russia (8)	143	16–20	Between 12 and 15%; they were severely prosecuted during and after the communist era and after the Chechnya War
5	Germany (12)	82	4.02	Mostly immigrants; almost 6%. Many immigrants tend to hide their religious belief
6	Philippines (14)	80	4.6	The official version is an underestimation. The total number could be as high as 12%[51]
7	Ethiopia (17)	71	28–30	Almost 40%
8	Thailand (19)	62	3.9–5	Officially 5.1%, but could be as high as 12%.[52] Thailand (along with Myanmar) has one of the worst anti-Muslim records in the world today[53]
9	France (20)	60	3.5	Almost 6%; Anti-Muslim parties have made significant gains
10	United Kingdom (21)	60	2.7–3.0	1.6–2%
11	South Africa (27)	45	0.8 to 1	Almost 2%[54]
12	Tanzania (32)	37	13.5	30–35%
13	Kenya (34)	32	27.3	7–10%
14	Uganda (40)	25	3.9	10.00%
15	Mozambique	20	5.2	22.80%

Table 4.3 Muslim-majority countries: minority population[55]

	Country	Population (world ranking in millions)	Muslim (%)	Minority (%)	The religious affiliation of minorities	Constitution
1	Indonesia	212.1 (4)	82–86	13–18	Christian, Hindu, Buddhist	Secular
2	Pakistan	141.3 (7)	95	4–5	Hindu, Christian	Islamic
3	Bangladesh	137.4 (8)	88	13–15	Hindu, Christian, Animist	Secular
4	Nigeria	113.9 (10)	50–52	48	Christian, Animist	Secular
5	Iran	70.3 (15)	97	1–3	Jews, Baha'i	Islamic
6	Egypt	67.9 (16)	90	10–15%	Coptic Christian	Secular
7	Turkey	66.7 (17)	99	1	Christian, Jews	Secular
8	Sudan	31.1 (31)	70	30	Christian, Animist	Islamic
9	Algeria	30.3 (36)	98	2	Christian	Secular
10	Morocco	29.9 (37)	97	3	Christian, Jews	Secular
11	Uzbekistan	24.9 (39)	97	3	Christian	Secular
12	Iraq	22.9 (43)	98	1	Christianity	Secular
13	Malaysia	22.2 (47)	60	40	Hindu, Chinese	Secular
14	Afghanistan	21.8 (48)	99	1	Hindu, Sikh	In transition
15	Saudi Arabia	20.3 (49)	97	3	Hindu, Christian	Islamic
16	Yemen	18.3 (53)	97	3	Christian	Secular
17	Kazakhstan	16.2 (55)	70	30	Christian, Buddhist	Secular
18	Syria	16.2 (55)	85–88	12	Christian	Secular
19	Cameroon	14.9 (61)	90	10	Christian, Animist	Secular
20	Niger	13.2	90	10	Christian, Animist	Secular

not been included in any of the Indian census figures. Besides, many Muslims from Bangladesh are permanent residents in many parts of India, especially in its northeastern provinces. Similarly, many Indian Hindus are now heading to Bangladesh as its economy is improving.

Besides India, a large number of Muslims inhabit other politically important countries as minorities. Examples are the United States, China, Russia, France, Germany, Kenya, South Africa, Uganda, and Ethiopia. Of the top ten most populous countries in the world, Muslims are either in the majority or form a large minority population of that country. The entire Sub-Saharan African region has a significant number of Muslim citizens. Other smaller countries like Holland, Belgium, Macedonia, Bulgaria, and Thailand have substantial Muslim-minority populations as well.

Four countries – Indonesia, Pakistan, Bangladesh, and India – have more than 100 million Muslim citizens each. China has not been included in this list, but the total number of its Muslim population is higher than the official figure, which is thirty million. It is widely accepted that there may be more than sixty million Muslims living in China; others claim that the actual number may be closer to a hundred million. Uighurs, one of the major groups, alone claim to be over twenty-five million. This number is, of course, disputed by China. Half of all Chinese Muslims belong to the Han ethnicity; it is the predominant group of the country, which Huntington defines as Confucian or Sinic civilization.

In other words, the two most populous countries of the world, China and India, are predominantly non-Muslim or Muslim-minority countries but have sizable Muslim populations. According to Huntington's classification, these two countries are Hindu and Confucian civilizations, respectively. Since he has not included Indian and Chinese Muslims within Islamic civilization, almost one-sixth of the total Muslim population of the world belong to these two countries, which are outside of the core Islamic civilization. How should these 250 million Muslims be described? Are the Muslims from India not Muslims but Hindus? Of course not! Does it make any sense to follow Huntington's classification then? Their brothers and sisters across an artificial border are described as Pakistanis, which forms the nucleus of Islamic civilization. Genetically also, there are no differences between the Muslim population of India and Pakistan.

Should the Muslims in China be classified as Sinic or Chinese? That has not been addressed by Huntington either. Muslims in China believe they are Chinese Muslims. Besides, one-third of the total Muslim population of the world lives in countries where they are minorities. Since Muslims living as minorities in conflict zones or Western countries are hesitant to divulge their religious affiliation, their number may even be higher in these countries. It is especially true if their government has a dispute with its Muslim community. That includes the United States, China, and the former Soviet Union (Russia). The problem in India is different. Indian Muslims were given equal protection by the constitution, but some political parties have distorted the laws, which had protected their rights. In some countries, there is an official policy of under-reporting of its Muslim populations. The examples are Russia, Thailand, Burma, Bulgaria, Macedonia, and other countries of the conflict zones.[56] In these countries, their number is significantly higher than officially reported.

My assumption is that Muslims would not mind being described as Chinese, but they would reject the notion of being classified as Confucian. The former term defines their nationality, which, in their case, is correct; the latter term refers to religious identity, which, in the case of Chinese Muslims, is incorrect. The same is true about Indian Muslims. Hardcore Hindu fundamentalist groups have argued that Muslims in India should be described as Hindus since they live in India. That concept is rejected by Muslims who consider themselves Indian Muslims but not Hindu. The difference between Hindu and Indian or between Confucians and Chinese identities is important for Muslims who inhabit these two countries.

Huntington's concept could be valid, at least in theory, if those Muslims who belong to the so-called Hindu and Confucian civilizations are demographically insignificant, which they are not, or are politically, culturally, and economically non-entities. That may not be correct either, as Muslims in these countries are an integral part of society. Some former presidents of India, many cabinet ministers, important officials including police chiefs and generals, film stars, sports person-alities, and CEOs of many large Indian companies had been and are Muslims. These corporations employ thousands of non-Muslims, who may challenge the notion of religion-based civilization. That is also true for Chinese Muslims.

These data point out the fundamental problem with Huntington's theory. How could his classification of civilization be correct and statistically valid if one-third of Muslims do not inhabit the defined geographical areas of Islamic civilization? Therefore, the division Huntington used to classify humanity, which was based on the religious affiliation of the citizens, is not only invalid but also nonsensical.

How about Muslim-majority countries? Huntington's concept can also be negated by the presence of equally varied and diverse populations within Muslim-majority countries. The Organization of Islamic Countries (OIC) has almost sixty members. In many Muslim-majority countries (Table 4.1), there are sizable non-Muslim citizens who form a significant segment of their coun-try. Indonesia has the distinction of having the highest number of Muslims in the world. Its total population is about 210 million; still, Muslims constitute approximately 80% of that total number. However, more Christians live in Indonesia than the total population of many Christian countries. Are Indone-sian Christians not Christians? If so, how should they be called: Islamic Chris-tians or Christian Muslims?

Demographically, only a handful of Muslim countries are entirely Islamic. Turkey, Algeria, Afghanistan, and Saudi Arabia belong to a select group of countries that have more than thirty million people (by 2018 census), and their Muslim population is close to 100%. The irony is that two out of the four countries are avidly secular states. Turkey had forbidden the wearing of the Hijab in government offices until recently. In the ninety years of Turkish history, the Turkish army has intervened a dozen times to ensure that Turkey remains a secular nation. Algeria has a similar history. It has an ongoing battle with Isla-mist groups since the 1990s. Only Saudi Arabia claims to be an Islamic state, but it is firmly allied with the West. So is Egypt, the most populous and powerful Arab state. Egyptian generals Sadat, Mubarak, and Al Sisi were supported by the United States.

There are a few other countries, such as Maldives and Mauritania, which boast close to 100% Muslim population. Almost all of them have secular constitutions. The population of each of these countries would be less than that of the city of Karachi, Dhaka, or Lagos. That may not be as interesting since these cities are in Muslim-majority countries, but more Muslims live in Moscow (1.5 million) and New York City or Toronto (half a million people each) than in Maldives or Comoros.

The other more populous countries have many non-Muslim citizens. Examples are Bangladesh (15% or even more non-Muslims), Nigeria (40–50%), Egypt (10–15%), Sudan (30%), Uzbekistan (20%), Iraq (at one time 10%), Malaysia (45%), Kazakhstan (30%), and Syria (10%). The demographics in other smaller countries are no different. The examples are: Lebanon (40%), Palestine/Israel (10%, only an estimate), UEA (50%), Chad (30%), Ivory Coast (40%) and others. The majority of Muslim countries have a secular constitution as well. Therefore, in the context of this debate, the question is also the same: who are these people? How can we classify them? Do they belong to Islamic civilization or non-Islamic civilization?

The above paragraphs, which summarize the distribution of the Muslim population around the world, contradict the concept of dividing humanity strictly on the basis of religion or calling them religious civilizations. These data also confirm that any rationale to divide people into groups based on any solitary identity – religious affiliation or other identities – is an obnoxious notion. Such division of the world's population into religious civilizations is inaccurate. It follows Huntington's classification at best only 50% of the time. It is because one-third of the total Muslim population live in Muslim-minority countries, and a large number (up to 50%) of non-Muslims inhabit Muslim-majority countries,

These facts raise several other related questions. What are the identities of non-Muslims residing in Muslim countries and within the borders of the so-called Islamic civilization? Are they Islamic or non-Islamic? Who is more Islamic – non-Muslims living in Islamic civilization or Muslims living in other parts of the world? Are Muslims living outside of the designated Islamic civilization areas less Islamic? Can these 250 million Muslims, who live in India and China, making one-sixth of the total Muslim population of the world, be defined as Hindus or Hinduized Muslims and Confucians or Confucian Muslims? Simply put, if one follows Huntington's criteria of classification of humankind, there is going to be confusion due to the vagueness of his selection criteria.

Therefore, calling Muslim-majority countries Islamic civilization is false as these terms are not identical. Dividing humanity through civilization, which forms the nucleus of Huntington's hypothesis, is inaccurate. Since the concept is fundamentally false, the inferences that Huntington has drawn from his hypotheses that Muslims are violent because they belong to Islamic civilization are false as well. Not only is Huntington's assertion not supported by the data, but it may also be deceptive, especially if he has knowingly extrapolated his inferences from those data if he knew these were incorrect. There is no evidence to claim one way or the other. It may have been a mistake, but how a person of his stature could fall for such an elemental error is intriguing but possible.

The premise of his argument of religion-based civilization is inaccurate for another reason. Historically, minorities in Muslim-majority countries have shaped the culture and events of Muslim nations. At the time of the initial expansion of the Arab empire, societies they conquered were culturally far advanced from the Bedouins, who were confined to the desert during the pre-Islamic period, lived in isolation. Locals contributed significantly in forming the culture of their new amalgamated societies or empires, which is described by Huntington as "civilization." Being one of the youngest religions (civilization by Huntington's account) among the major groups, Muslims have taken their cultural traditions from every indigenous society, which eventually became a part of Islamic empires.

Therefore, Muslim countries have cultural diversity, equal to, if not better than the other groups. The core belief of Islam is the oneness of God, and since Islam professes that it is not a new religion, but merely a continuation of all other religions of the world, Muslims found it easy to assimilate cultural ideas and traditions of other societies, as long as its core monotheistic belief was not challenged. That is why even after 1,500 years, Islam is still the fastest-growing religion. It is because Islam is flexible in accepting new entrants; its rituals are few but rigorous. It is also the least dogmatic religion. Anyone who agrees with the oneness of God and Mohammad as the Prophet is a Muslim. Rigid dogmas come from cultural traditions and not from the ethos of the religion. Huntington has portrayed cultural dogmas as theological facts.

More so, the practice of Islamic rituals is different around the world. Muslims in Turkey have been influenced by Byzantine Orthodox Christianity, in Persia by Zoroastrians, in India by Hinduism, in Malaysia by Buddhism, and in Indonesia by Hinduism and Buddhism. All these nations practice a different form of Islam, although the essence of Islam, which is the oneness of God and Mohammad is His Prophet, is never compromised, but their cultural rituals differ significantly.

However, diversity in Muslim countries is not unique. Whether it is *so-called* Hindu, Confucian, African, or Latino, each one of them has similar variations in its populations and rituals. Therefore, to brand any country with a solitary religious or civilizational identity is a mistake. Each so-called civilization is unique in its way; it is due to the contribution of many groups of people. Let us again take the example of India. Huntington defined it as the quintessential Hindu civilization, but the demarcation is not as precise as the author would like us to believe.

Huntington should have known better. He is a political scientist; still, he defined civilizations as monolithic units based only on religion, which is especially not right for a country like India with many religious traditions. The same is also true for the entire Subcontinent. Pakistan and Bangladesh may be Muslim countries, but their cultural heritage is shaped by Hinduism and Buddhism. They have influenced each other. Amartya Sen points out:[57]

> It would be, in fact, quite futile to try to have an understanding of the nature of and range of Indian art, literature, music, films, or food without seeing the range of contribution coming from both Hindus and Muslims in

a thoroughly intermingled way. Also, the interaction in everyday living or cultural activities is not separated by communal lines. While we can contrast the style of Ravi Shankar, the magnificent sitarist, with Ali Akbar Khan, the great Sarod player, on the basis of their mastery over different forms of Indian classical music, they would never be seen as a 'Hindu musician' or a 'Muslim musician' respectively. (even though Shankar does happen to be a Hindu and Khan a Muslim). The same applies to other fields of cultural creativity, including Bollywood – that great field of Indian mass culture – where many of the leading actors and actresses, as well as directors, come from a Muslim background (along with other non-Muslim ancestries), and they are much adored by a population of which more than 80 percent happens to be Hindu.

An overlap of cultural traditions in the Indian Subcontinent, not only with the Islamic societies but also with other religions and people, cannot be denied. An example is the music functions at the tombs of Sufi saints, which are not seen in the Arab world. It is the influence of Hinduism; to some it is blasphemy, to others it is an integral part of the tradition. Sikhism, Jainism, and Buddhism originated in India; India is also home to the largest Sikh, Jain, and Zoroastrian populations in the world. Although minuscule in numbers relative to India's Hindu population, their contributions in finance, business, armed forces, sports, and cultural creativity are vital to the country.

India is also home to thirty million Christians; more Christians live in India than in all of the Scandinavian countries combined. There are as many Christians living in India as there are in Canada. Their contributions to every aspect of Indian life are as vital and inclusive as those of any other religious group. Christianity was established in India centuries before it was accepted as the state religion in Europe by Constantine, the Roman Emperor (in 312 AD), or Vladimir I of Kiev, the Russian Emperor (in 988 AD).[58] Christianity came to India in the first century.[59]

China is also similar in this respect. To define China solely as a Confucian civilization makes a mockery of its cultural and religious diversity. China has five major ethnic groups; it is home to more than sixty million Muslims or even higher (the official figure may be as low as thirty million). As noted earlier, according to Uighur sources, in 1982, ten to twenty-six million Uighur Muslims were living in Sinkiang alone.[60] They are Turkic-speaking people and have their own culture. Besides Uighur, there are at least ten different broad groups of Muslims in China and many smaller groups. Muslims are found in every part of the country; half of the Muslim population belongs to the Han ethnicity, which is the predominant group. China also has other Muslim-dominated regions with their unique culture.[61] China has three other major social and religious groups – Buddhists, Christians, and Animists.

If classifying China exclusively as a Confucian civilization is false, lumping other Southeast Asian countries as Confucian civilizations also defies logic. Korea and Vietnam, which were lumped together as Sinic civilization, are also not monolithic societies. There may not be many followers of Confucianism in these countries. There is only a sprinkle of Chinese people who have made their homes across the region. Even Japan, which is one of the most monolithic societies in the world, is not as monolithic in terms of the religion of its inhabitants. Huntington described Japan only as a Shinto civilization, but there are as many Buddhists living in Japan as followers of Shintoism. Japan has a sizable Christian population as well; they are no less Japanese than other groups.

The strongest criticism of Huntington's theory has been directed at classifying Sub-Saharan Africa as an African civilization while calling others by their religious heritage. He placed all non-Muslim Africans into a single but separate category and defined African civilization as if all of them profess the African religion. The problem with his idea is that it is not true; monolithic African civilization turned out to be the figment of Huntington's imagination. Why he did not define non-Muslim Africa as a religious civilization as he does the others also defies logic. The rationale to place all African nations into a separate category has been taken by many of his critics as quintessentially an implicit racist attitude.

Alternatively, it may have been due to ignorance even though Huntington is a reputable scholar, but like many scholars who learned their trade during the colonial era, or immediately thereafter, he may have a Eurocentric view of world history. This belief was used to justify slavery and colonialism. Edward Said calls their world view *Orientalism,* which evolved during the colonial period. The idea behind portraying Africans as different from Europeans was to justify slavery and the slave trade, which was a lucrative business for a handful of colonial powers, no matter where they came from.[62] As noted by W.E.B. Du Boise, there was a rush to label themselves as white in the nineteenth century.[63]

Africa has a very vibrant culture of its own, which Huntington has either ignored, or else he may not be aware of prosperous African kingdoms.[64] Musa Mansa, the emperor of Benin, may have been the wealthiest human being to have ever walked on this planet. As people of all other regions, Africans are not monolithic. The population follows Islam, Christianity, and Animist religions. There are pockets of Jewish inhabitants, such as South Africa, Ethiopia, and Morocco. With recent Indian immigrants, Hinduism has also flourished in many pockets of the continent. The rationale to give Africa an African identity may have been proper if Western Christian civilization had been designated as European, Hindu as Indian civilization, and China not as Confucian civilization, but Chinese civilization. Similarly, he has classified South America as *Latin* and not Christian civilization, although Christianity is the predominant religion of the entire continent.

How relevant is Huntington's idea of dividing humanity through the prism of religious identity when a large percentage of minorities are an integral part of the landscape of many countries? Amartya Sen views such ideas as redundant. In his book *Identity and Violence: The Illusion of Destiny,* he points out the problem in dividing the world by religion only. He argues that such divisions may *appear* to be scientific, but they are not; in actuality, the idea of a monolithic world is wrong, irrelevant, and inconsistent with reality; therefore, it gives quite a *distorted perception* of the world. Sen also argues that the entire project is bound to be divisive; the division of humanity by solitary identity could breed violence:[65]

> Conflicts involving, say, Hutus and Tutsis, Serbs and Albanians, Tamils and Sinhalese, are then reinterpreted in lofty historical terms, seeing in them something much grander than the shabbiness of contemporary politics.
>
> Modern conflicts, which cannot be adequately analyzed without going into contemporary events and machinations, are then interpreted as ancient feuds which allegedly place today's players in preordained roles in an allegedly ancestral play. As a result, the "civilizational" approach to contemporary conflicts (in the grander or lesser variant) serves as a major intellectual barrier to focusing more fully on prevailing politics and to investigating the processes and dynamics of contemporary incitement to violence.

Sen is right on this issue as well. Today, if Israelis and Palestinians are going at each other's throats, it is not because they are disputing whether Abraham intended to sacrifice Ishmael or Isaac or they are asking for the legal documents to verify Abraham's marriage to his second wife *Hazra* (*Hagar*). Arabs are believed to belong to her lineage and the Israelites or Jews to the first. Instead, they are fighting over the control of the land of Palestine and the right to use its resources. Their fight is not about the validity of religious texts either. The conflict is over the right to live in colonial territory.

Ashkenazi Jews were driven out of their homes from Eastern Europe during the Second World War when Hitler started his campaign to establish a living space for Germans (*Lebensraum*). Anglo-American political elites agreed with Hitler; they decided to find a new home for Eastern European Jews. They chose Palestine, which was an ideal place for establishing a colony; it was under the mandate of the British Empire, and the Palestinians had no political strength or military power to challenge the mandate. The current violence is because the resources of this land are being distributed based strictly on the religious identity of its inhabitants, and the transplanted Jewish population from Europe has acquired the land on which Palestinians were living for thousands of years. The new arrivals have pushed the indigenous population from their land.

If viewed from a broader historical perspective, the presence of European Jews in Palestine is colonialism. The new arrivals from Europe continue to enjoy the lion's share of the country's resources. Palestinians, both Muslims, and Christians, have been marginalized. They have attempted to justify their claims through the religious texts; however, the Old Testament is not a real-estate document. To seek a claim on a piece of real estate in the twentieth century based solely on religious texts, which came into existent thousands of years ago, also defies logic.

Similarly, the idea that the current Israel-Palestinian conflict can be explained by events that took place thousands of years ago may be the basis for conventional wisdom and may even be convenient to justify the annexation of Palestinian land by Israelis to American citizens, but it is fundamentally false and baseless. Their arguments may fool American citizens, but they cannot distract Palestinians. However, these arguments are not for them; they have been designed for the West, which does not know the region's history. Huntington's views are designed to placate the Western conscience.

Sen points out the reason behind the popularity of Huntington's approach in mainstream media:[66]

> It is not hard to understand why the imposing civilizational approach appeals so much. It involves the richness of history, and the apparent depth and gravity of cultural analysis of it seek profundity in a way that an immediate political analysis of "here and now" – seen as ordinary and mundane – would seem to lack. If I am disputing the civilizational approach, it is not because I do not see its intellectual temptations.

Agreed! An approach of categorizing and dividing humanity into civilizational compartments gives a sense of intellectual accomplishment, even though it has no rational basis. These arguments also come in handy for blaming the victims of violence by justifying illegal acts, including violent conflicts against other people (or so-called civilization), which cannot be justified on moral grounds. Huntington's book has generated great interest in his ideas, but it has also created confusion across the globe. His world view was enthusiastically embraced by the United States even though it was proven to be fundamentally inaccurate. His ideas were challenged by leading theorists and intellectuals on the ground that he has ignored the basic principles of science and statistics, as the groups that are being compared should be well defined to minimize, if not avoid, any natural variation within groups.[67] If people are compartmentalized vaguely, the variation within groups could be so significant that it would overlap with variations between two distinct groups that are being compared.

Huntington's divisions of humanity are vague because they are based on ill-defined parameters. Since vagueness has created systemic and structural problems in his arguments, it is impossible to come to any valid conclusion. His study cannot distinguish between coincidence and a cause-and-effect relationship between two factors. Consequently, it cannot be proven that the difference (if any) is not related to natural variations within a group or among groups. Conclusions based on such data would be inconclusive, if not false. The difference between Islam and Western Christian civilizations or Islamic and Hindu civilizations may be significant at least in some parameters but relatively insignificant in others.

Lewis: The Roots of Muslim Rage

As noted earlier, the credit for starting the current round of discourses on the association of violence with Islam and imparting a bellicose tone to the debate that prevails in the West today may partly go to Bernard Lewis, a retired

Princeton University professor.[68] In this chapter, the focus is on the content of his arguments, which was presented in his article "The Roots of Muslim Rage." This article is the revised version of the speech he gave when he received the award from the National Endowment of Humanities (Chapter 3). The reaction of people who opposed his ideas is also discussed here.

As expected, his acceptance speech generated much interest, which was confined to intellectuals, academicians, and certain groups of political elites in the United States. In the Muslim world, it went unnoticed. In the article "The Roots of Muslim Rage," which was published in *The Atlantic Monthly,* he argued that 1.5 billion Muslims around the world are a monolithic community and that they are culturally (and perhaps genetically) predisposed to violence.[69] That article drew praise from his supporters and the neoconservative ideologues and sharp criticism from his critics, who believed that the content of this article posed a danger to peace in the world.

John Esposito, Professor of Theology at George Washington University, was one of the critics; he argued that the message that Muslims and Islam are violent began with the illustrations on the front cover of the magazine. He points out:[70]

> The message and impact of the title "The Roots of Muslim Rage" were reinforced by the front cover of The Atlantic Monthly, which portrayed a scowling, bearded, turbaned Muslim with American flags in his glaring eyes. The threat motif and confrontational tone were supplemented by the two illustrations that accompanied the article, ostensibly presenting "the" Muslim perception of America as an enemy. The first was a serpent marked with stars and stripes seen crossing a desert (America's dominance of or threat to the Arab world); the second illustration showed a serpent poised behind an unsuspecting pious Muslim at prayer as if to attack. These illustrations perpetuated sensationalist stereotypes and were meant to provoke the reader and reinforce a myopic vision of reality. Muslims are attired in "traditional" dress, bearded and turbaned, even though most Muslims (and most "fundamentalists") do not dress in this way. This image portrays Islamic activists as "medieval" in lifestyle and mentality.

The cover of the magazine also indicates not only the support Lewis got from the media in projecting his idea that Muslims are violent but also a commitment from the magazine and the corporate media that they are willing to provide space to these ideas even if they remain unsubstantiated and unproven. Lewis was using the adjective violent for the so-called Islam, Islamic civilization, and Muslim societies. Still, the mainstream media, public relation firms, and publishing industries, which are controlled by mega-corporations, were willing to support Lewis's assertion without insisting on critical evaluation. By the 1990s, the Soviet army had already withdrawn from Afghanistan; the corporate media started taking a stand in favor of Lewis and his supporters, and were producing Islamophobic literature. Was it a coincidence? After the fall of the Berlin Wall, the West had no immediate use for Muslim countries. The

United States did not need any ally, as it ruled the roost; it had no competition. As William Engdahl documents in his book, *Manifest Destiny*, even the mighty Russian Federation could not put up any resistance to the CIA-sponsored plot to debunk state institutions. Under President Boris Yeltsin, the Russian Republic had become a vassal state and was being methodically dismembered by the Western banks in the name of the free-market economy.[71]

During this period of shifting sands of international equations and priorities, Lewis claimed that Islam is the problem, as Islamic theology preaches violence.[72] He was also suggesting that since the so-called clash of civilizations is about religion and theology, reconciliation between the two is not feasible. Lewis was implying that had there been clashes due to land or its resources, a compromise could be reached. Lewis further argued that since religious fanatics do not compromise on their beliefs, the confrontation with Islamic civilization would invariably lead to the use of violence to subdue Muslim countries. He gave no data to substantiate his logic. Here is how he describes Islam:[73]

> [Islam is a religion] ... which inspired, in even the humblest peasant or peddler, a dignity and a courtesy towards others never exceeded and rarely equaled in other civilizations. And yet, in moments of upheaval and disruption, when the deeper passions are stirred, this dignity and courtesy towards others can give way to an explosive mixture of rage and hatred which impels even the government of an ancient and civilized country – even the spokesman of a great and ethical religion – to espouse kidnapping and assassination, and try to find, in the life of their prophet, approval and indeed precedence for such action.

In this passage, at least, Lewis comes across as respectful of Islam, but is he? His critics argue that his hidden message is not complementary. On the contrary, his words are responsible for creating negative myths and the current violent image of Islam. Besides, his assertions may not be correct, at least not according to the facts. For example, Lewis provides neither data nor historical facts to show that Muslims *suddenly* become violent during periods of stress, upheaval, and disruption. However, true to his style of making a point more palatable and effective to his Western readers, he begins the discussion by praising his intended target – in this case, Muslims, and Islam – in an objective style but then he goes on to assert, without any data or facts to substantiate his statement, that Islam is violent. Also, Lewis does not provide any historical facts in a forty-page-long article to prove his points. For example, he avers that "an explosive mixture of rage and hatred" is more characteristic of Muslims than of others. Is it? He does not provide data to justify his assertion that these emotions are directly related to their religion or culture or so-called Islamic civilization. How about economic reasons such as colonialism, which depleted the resources of the colonies?

In this essay, he has not properly defined the term *Islamic civilization*. Is it a geographical entity, religious identity, or political institution? What constitutes

Islamic civilization remains vague. Since Lewis has used the term civilization interchangeably with these three entities, the vagueness imparted by the term further confuses the issue. For example, who are those non-Muslims who reside in that space? Are they a part of Islamic civilization, even though they are not Muslims? If so, do they also get enraged during the period of stress? If only religion defines civilization, how could non-Muslims belong to the Islamic civilization behave? Did they also get enraged? What about Muslims in countries outside of the designated areas? Do they get enraged like Muslims from Islamic civilization, or do these Muslims behave like non-Muslims and do not get violent? He provides no answer.

Lewis did not address the difference between Islamic civilization and Muslim-majority countries, nor does he explain how Muslims and non-Muslims should be defined if they fall outside the orbit of precisely defined civilizations. Neither did he describe or explain *Islamic behavior*. Nevertheless, he associates the adjective "explosive" and "rage and hatred" with Muslims. Are they? If so, do these adjectives define individuals or the entire Muslim community? If Lewis is right, such behavior should be rampant among Muslims but not among non-Muslims. However, he neither explained his logic nor substantiated his rationale to associate Muslims with these behaviors, which were never defined, much less standardized. If there is indeed one particular behavior specific to Islam, it was neither pointed out nor characterized. In this article, Lewis gently guides his readers to assume that violence is an Islamic behavior or is exclusively prevalent among Muslims without providing facts or references. The author never made comparisons with data of the so-called *Islamic behavior* with the behavior of other religions or civilizations.

Finally, Lewis asserts that governments of an ancient country and spokesmen for Islam espouse kidnapping, but he never provided the name of persons or country. In a case where a Muslim ruler had ordered the kidnapping and justified on a distorted version of Islamic text, which is entirely possible, the issue should have been this: was this phenomenon unique to Islamic history or common to all cohorts? Is he or she a spokesperson for Islam? If so, was that individual elected by the majority of the Muslim community? Or was he or she selected? If so, by whom? Who has designated that individual to be the representative of Islam? Lewis is silent on this issue as well.

As an expert on religion, he should know the difference between the teachings of a faith and its practices by its followers. Acts of individuals cannot be used to demonize an entire population. Moreover, the teachings of one religion cannot be compared with the practice of groups of people affiliated with other religions even if they claim that action is being done in the name of their religion. It can be argued that the teachings of religions might be inspired by divine sources, but the practice of every religion is a human institution; therefore, they are fallible.

Furthermore, he does not even provide the data to prove his assertion that kidnapping and assassination are more common in Muslim countries than in any other countries of the world, much less to show that kidnappings and assassinations are linked to any Islamic beliefs or traditions. True, in the 1980s, kidnapping was common in Lebanon, which boasts an almost equal percentage of Christian and Muslim citizens. Was the kidnapping in Lebanon related to religious traditions or due to political problems associated with economic issues?

Besides, had kidnapping been related to religious beliefs, it would have persisted today, but in the twenty-first century, Lebanon is relatively free from crimes, including kidnapping, even though it borders war-torn Syria. Moreover, kidnapping was rampant in many Latin American, African, and Asian countries during that period. These are non-Muslim countries. Even Italy experienced a sudden surge in political kidnapping in the 1970s. Parts of Russia were also affected by this malaise after the dismantling of the Soviet Union. Lewis has not provided any comparison in this regard between Muslim and non-Muslim countries. Kidnapping appears to be related to restiveness in society and not to any religion.

However, it is the overall message of the article (that Muslims are not only irrational but violent as well), which has no bearing to facts, that is deceptive. Lewis is a very talented individual. It is indeed to the credit of his expressive ability that his views about Muslims come across as authentic and logical to the readers even though his arguments are unsubstantiated by facts. In spite of his sophisticated style, his words have no merit. As his reference to Islamic violence is indirect and subtle, and his language is not crude, his message becomes more powerful. Even though he never gives specifics about why he concludes that Muslims and Islam are violent, his style and his reputation as a respected Orientalist leave such an impression on his readers that they are led to trust him – a trust which may have been exploited in favor of his political beliefs.

Consider the following facts: he writes that men who participate in *kidnapping and assassinations* are trying to find *approval and indeed a precedent*, but he provides no specific historical facts in his forty-page article that such actions are indeed related to the Prophet. Though Lewis never openly expressed that the Prophet approved or participated in the kidnapping, the underlying message is clear. By using the words that Muslims *are trying to find approval and even precedents in the life of the Prophet*, Lewis creates an impression in the minds of his readers that the Prophet condoned violence. His assertion helped to create an impression that there may have been a precedence for kidnapping and assassination during the Prophet's time and that the Prophet might have approved them, but he provided no evidence to substantiate his assertion. His job was made easy, as most Americans have little or no idea about the life and times of the Prophet of Islam anyway.

Did Lewis exploit his position as a respected academician from Princeton University to promote his views as facts? Probably! He was a professor at the prestigious Ivy League institution and wielded influence on his readers, students, and followers. One would expect that a person of his stature would follow the basic rules of putting forward a claim with data or facts, but he never substantiates his assertions with historical events. The example given above is typical of his writings on the subject of Islam; there are other subtle suggestions in his article that are as powerful in creating an impression that Muslims are violent, and are equally deceptive. Consider the following paragraph in the same article that was published in *The Atlantic Monthly*:[74]

The struggle between Islam and the West has now lasted fourteen centuries. It has consisted of a long series of attacks and counterattacks, jihad and crusades, conquest, and reconquests. Today much of the Muslim world is again seized by an intense and violent resentment of the West. Suddenly America has become an archenemy, the incarnation of evil, the diabolically opponent of all that is good, and specifically for Muslims and Islam.

Are these historical facts? Of course not. These are Lewis's opinions. He was implying that the past wars between the Western and Islamic nations and empires were fought for religious beliefs. Were they? Not according to facts. There is an agreement among historians that all wars of the past between Christian European and Muslim Asian and Middle Eastern empires were fought to control the land and resources.[75] Even the underlying reasons behind all Crusades were economic issues. However, he chose to ignore those facts. Since Lewis has not substantiated his assertions with facts, these are his opinions, which he presented as facts. For example, he writes that *the Muslim world is again seized by an intense and violent resentment,* but the term resentment is subjective; he did not provide his parameters in defining resentment or in making any comparison of "violent and intense resentment" of "Islamic civilization" with other "civilizations."

Lewis did not answer other questions about resentments. Is there a difference between Muslim and Christian resentments? Would they be the same? Resentments of different civilizations have not been standardized. How could we know that Muslim resentments are not being judged with a yardstick different from the ones used for Christian, Jewish, Buddhist, or Hindu resentments? If the events of 9/11 are indeed a Muslim resentment, how about the Holocaust, which killed twenty million Slavs and six million Jews? Was that a Christian resentment? How about massacres of between ten and twenty million Congolese by Belgium? Were they also European resentment? Did anyone benefit from that particular resentment?

Whatever the resentment, if there was one, it was associated with the transfer of hundreds of millions of dollars to King Leopold and Belgium. In the last two decades, thousands of Palestinians have been killed by Israel. Is that the Jewish resentment? That resentment has also been lucrative, as these actions have resulted in the control of the Palestinian land by Israel's real-estate tycoons. How about 65,000 Hindus killed in Sri Lanka after the Tamil Tigers surrendered?[76] Was that a Buddhist resentment? Cambodia, under the Pol Pot regime, may have wiped out one-quarter of its population. Those specific statistics do not bode well for the prevalent peaceful Buddhist society.

Another problem is the use of the word *suddenly.* Esposito has argued that it implies that although there have been violent confrontations between the two civilizations for centuries before, today, it is Islam and not the West that is violent and the instigator of violent clashes.[77] He provides no evidence to support his claims. If Lewis chooses to impart an opinion, which he has every right to do, it would have been valid if he had declared the statements as his opinion.

It would have been even fair if he was open about his intentions of defending Western civilization. In that case, it would have been without manipulation of historical facts to promote his agenda.

Lewis uses specific words to generalize the entire 1.8 billion-strong Muslim community as a single group. He starts his discussion with impeccable statements but ends up with gross generalizations of Muslims when he claims that *today much of the Muslim world is again seized by an intense and violent resentment*. Using such sweeping statements, which help his generalization, is the hallmark of his essays about Islam in general and Arabs in particular.

Finally, Lewis brings up psycho-social analysis of contemporary issues, but he bases the explanation of current events on a time capsule that is a thousand years old,[78] as if the *Zeitgeist* of the seventh century had not changed during the twentieth century when he wrote his piece. The result is that his articles and books have helped to promote the stereotyping of Muslims and Islam, on descriptions which are based on blanket statements and crude generalization. The following passage from his article is another example of generalization and a complete lack of facts in stressing his point of view:

> The Muslim has suffered successive stages of defeat. The first was his loss of domination in the world to the advancing power of Russia and the West. The second was the undermining of his authority in his own culture through an invasion of foreign ideas, laws, ways of life, and sometimes even foreign rulers or settlers, not to mention the enfranchisement of native non-Muslim elements. The last straw was the challenge to his (a Muslim man) mastery in his own house from emancipated women and rebellious children. It was too much to endure, and an outbreak of rage against these alien, infidel, and incomprehensible forces that have subverted his dominance, disrupted his society and finally violated the sanctuary of his home was inevitable. It was natural that this rage should be directed primarily against the millennial enemy and should its strength from ancient beliefs and loyalties.[79]

Is it an irrational stereotyping of Muslims? If so, it laid the basis of prejudice. Readers should judge whether such passages are based on rational arguments, or they are crude polemics and whether the explanation contains historical truth or creates myths about Islam. Whatever arguments and examples Lewis presents in this paragraph, these are vague generalizations about 1.8 billion Muslims. His claim that Islam being violent stems from challenges in the sanctuary of home from emancipated women and rebellious children, or incomprehensible forces or anything else, is not based on facts.

Lewis was successful in building his image as a rational thinker and credible intellectual even though his affiliation to Zionist causes and ideology was well-known. His success in creating his image was partly due to the general apathy about current affairs. The American public's lack of knowledge about other "civilizations" in general and Islam, in particular, has not helped either. The result is that the campaign of promoting Islam as a violent religion has been highly effective in the United States even though Lewis provides neither valid data nor arguments in his article to prove that the emancipation of women and the rebellion of children are more prevalent or any different in the 1.8 billion-strong Muslim world than in other civilizations.

Also, he never explains why every Muslim man would automatically be enraged against the West. Do they? If so, how many of them are enraged? Is it 100% or a fraction of 1%? How about other cohorts? Are they *not enraged* when foreign powers have occupied their land? Have they welcomed their occupiers? Lewis has not given any data or facts. Besides, it does not make sense: if almost one-quarter of the world's population is truly *enraged*, the world will be in chaos. Fortunately, that is not the case. On the contrary, once colonialism came to an end, the most violent era of human history also ended. Since then, the world is passing through the most peaceful period of human history, a fact that may not be perceived as such, but this has been documented with historical events.[80] Articles like "The Roots of Muslim Rage" may be the reason why it is not perceived by American citizens that the world is far more peaceful today than it has ever been.

Many intellectuals have raised questions about Lewis's logic and his intentions. Presented below is one of the comments on this article to provide the perspective of his critics. Commenting on Lewis's technique of generalizations and polemics, another academician, C.H. Naim, gives the following analogy in his essay, "The Outrage of Bernard Lewis." His article was published in the *Journal of Columbia University*. The following paragraph, which mimics Lewis's words to describe Muslims, may explain the generalization of Islam and the folly in using polemics to portray Islam:[81]

> The American has suffered successive stages of defeat. The first was his loss of domination in the world to the advancing economic power of Japan and Germany. The second was undermining of his authority in his own country through the invasion of foreign ideas and ways of life brought in by waves of non-European immigrants and the enfranchisement of the vast African-American and Mexican-American population within the country. The third – the last straw – was the mastery in his own house, from emancipated women and rebellious children. It was too much to endure. It was natural that his rage should be directed against the millennial enemy and should draw its strength from ancient beliefs and loyalties.

Dare I submit the above as a serious analysis of President Bush's recent actions in the Middle East?

Indeed, Lewis has written extensively about those Muslims who are supposed to be "enraged" with the West, but he never answered or wrote about the factors behind the current confrontation between the West and Muslim groups: why are Muslims *enraged*? Are they enraged because they are Muslims, which Lewis suggests? Alternatively, Muslims could be enraged and resent the United

States because of its policy of unconditional support to Israel and the autocratic rulers of the Middle East. Maybe, they had lost their loved ones during the invasions of Afghanistan, Iraq, and Somalia and now because of drone attacks in Pakistan. Over five million people have been killed in Muslim countries in the last two decades. Lewis has never addressed these issues, much less answered, except through polemics. Naim also describes the generalization Bernard Lewis brought to the discussion:[82]

> After a recondite and irrelevant digression on why America is a "daughter of Europe," Lewis describes the contact between the United States and the "Islamic lands" since 1939. As a model of selective history, it too deserves to be quoted. The Second World War, the oil industry, and postwar developments brought many Americans to the Islamic lands; an increasing number of Muslims also came to America, at first as students, then as teachers, as businessmen and other visitors, eventually as immigrants. Cinema and later television brought the American way of life, or at any rate a certain version of it, before countless millions to whom the very name of America had previously been meaningless or unknown. A wide range of American products, particularly in the immediate postwar years when European competition was virtually eliminated and Japanese competition had not yet arisen, reached into the remotest markets of the Muslim world, winning new customers and, perhaps more important, creating new tastes and ambitions. For some, America represented freedom and justice, and opportunity. For many more, it represented wealth and power and success, at a time when these qualities were not regarded as sins or crimes.

These comments are poignant. As Naim points out, not only are there no rational arguments in Lewis's article to substantiate his assertions that Islamic civilization is violent and unmodern, but Lewis cites only select events of 1,500 years of Islamic history to prove his points. His examples can only be described as cherry-picking of historical facts. For example, there was no mention of the Crusades, colonialism, slavery, and the slave trade or violence associated with colonial practices and later, during decolonization, the neo-liberal wars and occupation of the Middle East by proxy.

For example, take Lewis's omission of what happened to Muslims and Jews during the Crusades. He should know what happened to Jewish people when Crusaders broke through Muslim defense around Jerusalem in the First Crusade. After European forces entered Jerusalem, defeating the Muslim army, there was a massacre of the entire Muslim and Jewish residents. During the third Crusade, Richard the Lionheart massacred civilians after his victories. In contrast, Saladin, the Muslim general, who conquered back Jerusalem in the year 1187, invited its Jewish residents back and left Christians in peace.[83] Even their property was not taken as compensation for war or war-booty, which was a common practice. During the Spanish Inquest (in the 1490s), the Ottomans invited Jewish residents of Spain after the last the Spanish forces defeated the Muslim Moors.

The Iberian Peninsula and Anatolia changed hands between Muslim and Christian empires within a few decades of each other. Muslim Spain came under Christian rule, and Christian Anatolia and Constantinople (now Istanbul) came under the Muslim Ottomans. Lewis did not mention that not a single mosque remained standing after the Spanish conquest; they were either converted to churches or razed to the ground or burnt. The story of churches is different in Anatolia; they were left untouched with a few exceptions, such as Hagia Sophia, a Byzantine church in Ottoman rule for three centuries. It was first turned into a mosque; later, it was converted into a museum. Moreover, the headquarters of all Orthodox Christianity, except the Russian Orthodox, has remained under Islamic rule for centuries, such as Eastern Orthodox, Armenian, Coptic, Serbian, and others. In the last century, the British Empire and the United States have intervened in Muslim countries to consolidate their hegemony, causing immense misery. Iran is the more recent example.

Some of the events cited by Lewis in his essay are irrelevant. The major events and their consequences that defined and formed the relationship between the United States and Muslim-majority countries in the post-World War II period are never mentioned. This, in turn, gives a very distorted picture of reality. One could only ask: what was Lewis's intention? Commenting in the same essay, Naim documents the events of the twentieth century that have shaped the relationship between the West and Muslim societies around the world. The West may have forgotten many of those events, but the victims have not; those events are etched in their collective memory. The subjugation, which took place through extreme brutality, had a profound impact on Muslim communities. Naim reminds us:

> Note the admirable neutrality of his words: "the oil industry and postwar developments *brought* many Americans to the Islamic lands" (emphasis added). The oil industry did not entail, apparently, any state policy or action on the part of the United States. The Americans did not themselves come in pursuit of oil, some third party called "the oil industry" brought them. ARAMCO was as innocuous as Coca-Cola. As for "the postwar developments," Lewis conveniently does not list any. Let us, therefore, refresh our memory. (1) CENTO, a brainchild of John Foster Dulles that linked the United States with Turkey, Iraq, Iran, and Pakistan in a Cold War posture against the Soviet Union. It involved American bases, advisers, arms sales, and U-2 spy missions. (2) Kermit Roosevelt and the CIA's destruction of the nascent democracy in Iran, and the consequent American love affair with the "King of the Kings." (3) President Eisenhower's use of US Marines in Lebanon to prop up a political structure favoring the minority Christian population. (4) No American support for any democratic, nationalist movement in that part of the world. (5) Lastly – lest I be guilty of the same lapse of memory as Lewis – the adoption of the state of Israel as America's surrogate in the Middle East.

The reaction to Naim's article was tepid; not many critics made their views known. Comments, if any, were on the ideological lines. Lewis elected not to challenge this article in public. Steve Coll is one of the very few who made his views known on this topic. He presented them in *The New Yorker* magazine, in which he pointed out that Al Qaeda had been wiped out east of Myanmar, not by the United States, but by the locals. He further argues that it is hard to find rage in airconditioned malls of Asia; most Muslims live in Asia, which has remained mostly peaceful (his words). However, anti-West riots had erupted in the Muslim world off and on.

One of the riots took place in Libya; it took comprehensive coverage in the American media, as Christopher Stevens, the U.S. ambassador to Libya, was killed by the mob. This event appeared to be well planned, as rioters used rocket-propelled grenades. Demonstrators also attacked the U.S. embassy in Cairo and looted an American school in Tunis. The immediate stimulus of the riot was a YouTube video, which was created by an Egyptian Coptic Christian. A U.S. resident, he was on probation for bank fraud. Citing this example, Coll writes:[84]

> Crowds have protested since then in several capitals, at times violently. Some of the protestors appear to have been organized by fringe political parties and radical activists; for them, "Death to America" is a mobilizing strategy. The rioting they encourage is about Muslim rage only in a tautological sense: raging Muslims do the burning and looting, but they typically attract not even a large minority of the local faithful. The faces on American screens are often shock troops, comparable to Europe's skinheads or anarchists.

Coll further argues that Salafists have returned after the North African dictators were deposed by the uprising. They had kept the Salafists behind bars. These strongmen, who were supported by the West, generate resentment against the United States. The dictators are gone, and Salafists have returned; however, as Coll points out, radicals are not popular with the locals either. Even in Benghazi, crowds had ransacked offices of Ansar al-Sharia, a jihadi militia. Salafists have remained outsiders even after the departure of U.S. friendly regimes, but it has prompted them to create unrest. Islamists have never won any election except in Egypt, if you consider Muslim Brotherhood to be an Islamist organization. Even in the Indian Subcontinent and Southeast Asia, Islamists were not able to get sizable popular votes. At the peak of the Salafist influence in Pakistan, only once were they able to get in double figures of the popular vote, that too barely. In the most recent election, Maulana Fazlur Rehman's hard-liner party was wiped out. Coll concludes:

> [T]he notion that generalized Muslim anger about Western ideas could explain violence or politics from Indonesia to Bangladesh, from Iran to Senegal, seemed deficient. It was like arguing that authoritarian strains in Christianity could explain apartheid, the Argentinian Juntas, and the rise of

Vladimir Putin.[85] Nevertheless, the meme sold, and it still sells. Last week, *Newsweek*'s cover splashed "Muslim Rage" in large type above a photograph of shouting men. Inside came advice on how to survive "Islamic hate."

Simply put, gross generalizations of Muslims and demonization of Islamic societies by Lewis have not only helped to create the impression that Muslims are violent but have also been instrumental in promoting the prevalent notion that Muslims "do not want democracy and hate modernity." His conclusions are in complete disagreement with many surveys, which have been conducted by reputable institutions of the West.[86] Lewis never mentions that despite the deep resentment many Muslims feel about the American foreign policy, they admire various aspects of American and Western society: their democratic institutions and the freedom of expression that has been given by their respective constitutions to their citizens, even if they speak against their govern-ments.[87] A recent study conducted by the Gallup poll confirms that Muslims around the world admire America's freedom of expression.[88]

Neither did Lewis mention that the real reasons behind the anger of the Muslim world against the United States are not scientific innovations, MTV, Hollywood, McDonald's, bikini-clad women, or the U.S. Constitution,[89] which since the Nineteenth Amendment of 1920 gives equal rights to women. Instead, their anger is directed at the American invasion of Iraq and Afghanistan and subsequent occupation, which led to more than one-and-a-half million civilian deaths in Iraq before the Second Gulf War; political, military, and economic support to Israel that has resulted in the brutal occupation of the West Bank and Gaza; and, finally, the *War on Terror* has become a *war of terror* on at least six different Muslim countries.

The single most important reason for the resentment many Muslims around the world harbor against the United States is its unconditional support of Israel. They also resent America's support of autocratic regimes in the Muslim world, which has brought not only misery to many Muslim societies but also the extraction of resources and transfer of wealth from their lands to the West. Wherever the United States and its allies have intervened, the lives of ordinary people in those countries have changed for the worse.[90] The irony is not lost to Muslims that they and their societies are being criticized by the West for lack-ing democracy on the ground that they are being ruled by autocrats, while these dictators were imposed on Muslim countries by the British Empire and then by the United States. Since then, these rulers have been supported by the West. Without Western support, they would have been thrown into the dustbin of history, as the Arab Spring of 2011 has shown.

Lewis is the recipient of many civilian awards for his scholarship on Islam and the Middle East by Israel and the United States – mostly from pro-Israeli lobbies and think-tanks. During the two decades after his article was published he emerged as one of the most prominent thinkers on Islam in the United States. He is closely associated with the pro-Israeli lobby (AIPAC) and con-servative think-tanks, which dot the landscape of Washington. His articles became a regular feature in influential newspapers such as *The Wall Street Journal, The New York Times,* and others. Lewis remained an influential advisor to the Bush (Jr.) administration during the invasion and occupation of Iraq (see Chapter 3).[91] According to one report, President Bush personally sought his advice before and during the invasion of Iraq.[92] His influence on President Bush may have been vital, although his essay lacked substance and failed to provide facts on which he based his arguments.

John Esposito argues in his book *The Islamic Threat* that in most discussions about the so-called Islamic threat, there is a surprising dearth of information concerning the nature of the Islamic resurgence.[93] He cites Lewis's article, "The Roots of Muslim Rage," as an example. Esposito also agrees that Lewis selectively omits facts and information and asserts that both civilizations have been equally guilty of attacking each other and other "civilizations" if and when they had the means to do so. However, Lewis picks and chooses facts to substantiate his view that it is Islam that is violent and not the West, or as Lewis chooses to describe it, "Judeo-Christian civilization." Esposito also argues that cherry-picking data and historical facts only help to strengthen the stereotyping of Muslims. He underscores the so-called facts presented in the article, "The Roots of Muslim Rage":

> Thus, there is little to contradict the stereotype of strange, backward-looking figures from another age. The reader never learns why Islamic activism presents an attractive option for many educated Muslims. The pre-dominant picture is that of radicalized, marginalized, and often violent revolutionaries, traditional in dress and at war with modernity.[94]

Both John Esposito and Edward Said make interesting observations in their respective books, *The Islamic Threat* and *Covering Islam*.[95] They point out that Lewis's views first appeared as a lecture in 1991; both its date and venue are important. The forum is important because the issue that Islam is violent was initially raised on the occasion of Lewis's delivery of the annual Jefferson Lecture, thus assuring a wider audience. The timing of raising the issue is equally important because there were hardly any outstanding issues between the United States and the Muslim world, except the lingering occupation of Palestinian territory by Israel, whose annexation policy Lewis vigorously defends.

Lewis had carefully cultivated his personal image as a scholar of Islam and Islamic history, as well as a rational thinker. His neoconservative followers have branded him as the "doyen of Middle Eastern Studies." He has promoted himself as a neutral observer, which helped him to become the most sought-after commentator on Arab–Israeli affairs in the mainstream media. However, his support for the neoconservative causes goes deep, which he does not admit. Also, his financial association with the AIPAC remained hidden from the public. His image of an aloof intellectual has persisted even after the failure of the policy to invade Iraq, which he recommended. With the exception of neoconservative ideologues, prominent thinkers on either side of the ideological divide, such as Chris Hedges[96] and Pat Buchanan,[97] believe that the Iraq War was one of the worst foreign policy disasters for the United States.[98] They even argue that the Iraq War may also be the beginning of the decline of America as a superpower.

Whether the United States is indeed in decline is debatable at best, but the country is deep in debt; it is partly due to the Afghan and Iraq Wars and the War on Terror. America has already spent almost $6.4 trillion on unproductive wars in the twenty-first century;[99] despite so much expense, American influence has slipped around the world in general and in the Muslim world in particular.[100] Lewis's critics believe that he was instrumental in preparing the United States for the invasion of Iraq and the War on Terror.[101] Lewis's writings provided the intellectual basis for the American response, which eventually killed almost five million people in half a dozen Muslim countries.[102] They argue that the mainstream media promoted him as the most important expert on Islam, a perception which he had exploited to promote his political agenda.[103]

Lewis has authored many books on Arabs, Muslims, and Islam. There is a clear distinction in how he had approached the topic of Islamic identity. He changed his views on this topic, which is not unusual. People change their position over time, but Lewis's stand on the identity of Arabs and Muslims has taken a dramatic turn-around; it changed from a pluralistic to a monolithic or singular identity. In recent years, his focus has shifted on the so-called clash of civilizations between Islam and the West. Was the change in his stance prompted by his political agenda? Promoting the notion that Muslims have a singular identity made it easier to demonize the entire Muslim communities.

In his earlier book, *Arabs in History,* which was first published in 1958, he writes about the pluralistic identities of Arabs. He continued the same narrative in his other book, *Multiple Identities of the Middle East.* The book came out before "The Roots of Muslim Rage" was published. The concept of the multiple identities of Muslims changed into a singular identity in his works that came after 9/11; Lewis was laying the groundwork for the notion of a clash of civilizations. Two important books, *What Went Wrong?* and *The Crisis of Islam,* were published in 2002 and 2003, respectively. The timeline of these two books is relevant. The United States invaded Afghanistan in 2001; Iraq was invaded in late 2003. During this fateful period, the above two books appeared.

Shortly after the invasion of Iraq, many journalists and authors have argued that the invasion was already planned nine months before 9/11.[104] They claim that it was a *fait accompli* after George Bush was elected as President, but the decisions taken by the Bush administration were hidden from the public. According to Paul O Neal, the Treasury Secretary at the time, the Bush administration started planning for the invasion of Iraq as soon as President Bush took over the White House – almost nine months before 9/11. However, the official narrative had remained that a) the invasion of Iraq was not a certainty even after 9/11, b) whether President Bush would indeed send troops to Iraq was doubtful, c) the decision to invade Iraq was up in the air, and finally d) the pros and cons of the invasion of Iraq were being debated – both in the media and within the war cabinet of the Bush administration.

Said points out that there is a gross generalization in Lewis's articles and books, especially related to Islam and Muslims. The arguments presented in these two books are no different. They were complementary to the article "The Roots of Muslim Rage," which was published a decade previously (see earlier segment). There were no new ideas in these books. Therefore, these books should be viewed as the continuation of the 1990 article, which served as the background on which Lewis built the arguments for the Bush administration so that officials could justify the invasion of Iraq. Both were written from a slightly different perspective to cover diverse angles so that the administration has an easier time justifying violent conflicts not only against Iraq and but also against half a dozen Muslim countries, a decision that was already taken.[105] General Wesley Clark, in an interview, confirmed that Lewis's followers in the administration had already planned invasion of seven countries in five years.[106] During this period, Lewis was preparing President Bush and his inner circle to defend the invasion of Iraq.[107]

The first book, *What Went Wrong?*, was published shortly after 9/11; in this book, Lewis presented Islam as a religion that is inherently violent; and since it has not kept up with time, Islam has become incompatible with the forward-looking Judeo-Christian civilization. In the second book, *The Crisis of Islam*, his focus was on so-called Islamic terrorism. Even though he agreed that acts of violence were being conducted only by the fringe elements of the Muslim communities, he still blamed Islam for terrorism.[108] Lewis's logic was that since Osama bin Laden justified his acts of violence with Islamic texts, all acts of terrorism by Muslims should be viewed as Islamic events.[109] He did not elaborate why the same logic should not apply to Jewish and Christian acts of terrorism.

By the mid-1990s, many prominent thinkers such as John Esposito, Edward Said, Robert Fisk, Pepe Escobar, Chris Hedges, Deepa Kumar, and others were challenging the above narrative not only as myopic but also fictitious. They had been presenting data that showed that terrorism was not an exclusively Islamic phenomenon. Pat Buchanan, in his book *Where the Right Went Wrong*, had pointed out that all religious groups, including the founding fathers of the Jewish state of Israel, had used terrorism to achieve their political goals.[110] During the same period, another academician, Robert Pape, came up with his landmark book, *Dying to Win*, in which he classified various terrorist organizations according to the religious affiliation of members.[111] He documented that every religion had its version of terrorist groups. Even suicide bombing is universal and ubiquitous.[112]

In his two books, Lewis went through cherry-picked historical events of Muslim empires of the last 1,500 years, but he elected to highlight only those examples which suited his assertion that Muslims are inherently violent.[113] In other words, what he wrote was not made up; those events had indeed taken place. However, they are anecdotal events and not a trend. For example, he invokes the history of assassins of a single Muslim empire of the thirteenth century. Assassins were used by the rulers of a single dynasty of Central Asia and Iran to spread terror among its enemies. These assassins were trained to kill, and after the killings, they would not leave the scene of the crime. They were captured and put to death,[114] but their acts of violence spread terror. It is the only known example of such acts in one-and-a-half thousand years of Muslim empires: Lewis presents this as an example as if it was a common event among Muslim rulers.

In other words, the problem in his writings has been either omission of facts or presenting half-truths as facts. Partial truths give a distorted image of their targets. Even minimal distortion of facts can give a wrong impression, which could be diametrically opposite to reality. Half-truths are perception-manipulation techniques. Once set in motion, the underlying strategy and political agenda are challenging to comprehend. Those who are not historians may be easily misled. Lewis's critics have given examples of how he has cherry-picked events from 1,500-year-old Islamic history in demonizing Muslims.

The demonization of Muslims is the hallmark of these books. For example, in the last two chapters of the book, *What Went Wrong?*, he argues that Muslims are unwilling to accept other civilizations as equals or grant legitimacy to the virtues of other civilizations; therefore, Muslims have failed to keep up with modernity, which is not correct. Greek philosophers are an integral part of the Islamic world. At the turn of the twentieth century, almost every intellectual and social, and political activist was following Western intellectuals. By the middle of the twentieth century, half of the Islamic world had a powerful Marxist movement. In his other book, Lewis also writes about terrorism in such a way that it gives an impression that terrorism is uniquely an Islamic phenomenon, which was also proven to be false. Besides, Lewis had also argued that Muslims are unaware of the concept of secularism; this is also incorrect.

Deepa Kumar explains what went wrong with Lewis's assertions. She argues that he may have missed the point, either by design or otherwise, that there is a de facto separation of politics and religion in Islamic theological traditions, which Lewis has elected to ignore. On the other hand, the demonization of "others" has a long tradition in the West, which Lewis has also ignored. Apologists of colonialism started the campaign to demonize Muslims; their assertions were copied by the neoliberal and then by the neoconservative activists. Both groups have continued with the same vigor to demonize Muslims. Their goal is no different: it is about controlling the resources lying under the sand of half a dozen Muslim countries; it is not about religion. It never was, neither would it ever be since religion does not provide capital to finance wars.

The role of religious authorities was limited in political spheres in Islamic empires. Kumar explains the role of ulema in Islamic societies:[115]

> The role of ensuring social discipline through religious law was pervasive, and in this realm, the ulema did indeed hold power. However, in the realm of politics, they had little sway. Instead, in terms of Muslim societies as a whole played a secondary and subservient role in relation to political leadership. This, even though Islamic treatises that emerged during this period

and later have a good deal to say about the nature of good rulers and governments and are loaded with suggestions and advice for rulers, they do not stake out a political role for the clergy. The Clergy insisted that the powerful should rule society in a way that conformed to Sharia law; they viewed their role to be censuring bad rulers rather than acting as rulers themselves. As Ayoob notes, there "was a consensus that as long as rulers could defend the territories of Islam (dar-al-Islam) and did not prevent his Muslim subjects from practicing their religion, rebellion is forbidden, for fitna (anarchy) was worse than tyranny. ... Political quietism was the rule in most polities, most of the time for thousand years, from the eighth to eighteenth century."

Kumar's explanation of the role of clergy in Islam should be viewed from the pre-Islamic *Zeitgeist* of the Bedouin society to which the Prophet belonged. Nomadic societies are egalitarian because they have limited resources; they can afford neither a monarchy nor a feudal structure. Hejaz was no different. As long as Bedouins remained nomads, they followed an egalitarian system. In the sixth century, they settled in Hejaz, and elites took over the tribal hierarchy soon after the Bedouin adopted urban lifestyle and commerce. Their weaker segments had no say in running religious places, which was the most vital source of income. The shrine gave power to its elites. Its economic system had become crony capitalism.

The Prophet and early converts to Islam, who were either slaves, women, or poor, were pushed to the periphery of the society; they were rebelling against the influence of powerful elements of the community. Time and again, the Prophet emphasized getting rid of the power structure within religion, which produces an authoritarian streak in the religious establishment. That is the reason why there is no Pope or Vatican-like authorities in Islam, which are seen in other religions. Islam had gotten rid of the power of clergy very early on; although they did come back, their influence remained local.

The power in Muslim empires was vested in the Caliph of Islam, who was a political and not a religious leader. A lack of power of clergy is believed to be the reason for the spectacular success of Islam in attracting millions of people to its fold. The excesses of holy men who controlled organized religion in Christianity and Judaism were probably known to the Prophet. He was also aware that Jesus blamed religious elites; they were collecting interests from the poor to perform religious rights and selling objects of offerings at an exorbitant price, against which Jesus rebelled. That rebellion eventually cost Jesus his life. That may also have been known to him.

Did Lewis miss these points? Probably not; at least, he should not have missed them. If so, did Lewis elect to ignore them? As a scholar of Islam, he should have known that in Islam, the relation between humans and God does not go through any middleman or church-like establishment. Therefore, the question is: why did Lewis write these books? They are filled with false data, which have created negative images of the victims. What was his goal? Was it sheer ignorance about Islamic laws that led him and his followers to make mistakes? At least in Lewis's case, ignorance may be ruled out if it is indeed true that Lewis is a scholar of Islam and Islamic history. However, his words contradict his reputation.

Lewis and his followers, such as Huntington and other neoconservative authors, are accomplished authors. They have also achieved academic success. They know what should be acceptable as facts. If so, why did they make such mistakes time and again? Did they think they could get away with such words? Is there something else that drove them to do what they did? Is it their *Weltanschauung?* Maybe, they are pursuing the neoconservative goal to demonize Islam and Muslims; they were preparing the country to accept impending violence, which the United States was about to unleash. Kumar points out:[116]

> In his book *What Went Wrong?* published shortly after 9/11, Lewis develops these arguments further and asserts that the notion of a non-religious society as something desirable or even permissible was totally alien to Islam.
>
> Huntington, who popularized Lewis's "clash of civilizations" thesis, took this one step further and argued that the "underlying problem is not Islamic fundamentalism. It is Islam, a different civilization whose people are convinced of the superiority of their culture and are obsessed with the inferiority of their power."[117]

Robert Canfield, Professor of Anthropology at Washington University, St. Louis, agrees with Kumar; he argues that although Lewis's contribution of his earlier works cannot be denied,[118] his contemporary works have taken a political undertone. Lewis's goal in these two books was to provide arguments to the Bush administration to justify not only the invasion of Iraq but also six other countries. Juan Cole of Michigan University points out that Lewis did good work early in his career, but he lost his way in his later years when he got pulled into present-day politics, especially the Israel–Palestine issue. Cole believes that Lewis began grafting medieval insight onto the modern Arab mindset.[119] Hamid Debashi, a professor of history at the Columbia University, also argues that Lewis's later works lack scholastic depth, which his earlier works possessed.[120]

However, despite well-documented fallacies ingrained in Lewis's assertions, his influence on the political culture of the post-modern United States has been profound. Canfield explains the aura of Lewis, which mesmerized the Bush administration:[121]

> … it was no surprise that in the critical months of 2002 and 2003, while the Bush administration shunned deep thinking and banned State Department Arabists from its council of power, Bernard Lewis was persona grata, delivering spine-stiffening lectures to Cheney over dinner in undisclosed locations. Abandoning his former scholarly caution, Lewis was among the earliest prominent voices after September 11 to press for a confrontation

with Saddam, doing so in a series of op-ed pieces The Wall Street Journal articles, with titles like "A War of Resolve" and "Time for Toppling." An official who sat in on some Lewis-Cheney discussions recalled, his view was 'Get on with it. Don't dither.' Animated by such grandiose concepts, and like Lewis quite certain they were right, the strategists of the Bush administration, in the end, thought it unnecessary to prove there were operational links between Saddam and Al Qaeda. These were good "bureaucratic" reasons for selling the war to the public, to use Wolfowitz's words, but the real links were deeper: America was taking on a sick civilization, one that it had to beat into submission. Bin Laden's supposedly broad base and Saddam's recalcitrant to the West were part of the same pathology.[122]

As Canfield argues, these two books played an important role in justifying the invasion of Iraq. They provided arguments to the Bush administration on how to debate the opponents of wars if and when President Bush would go after the targeted nations. It is no surprise that all these countries were challenging their policy of annexation of Palestinian land; they also happened to be Israel's neighbors. Lewis's recommendations were designed for an audience with limited knowledge of history. In these books, Lewis described selected events of the history of Muslim empires in minute detail, but he has ignored others. He elected to use only cherry-picked events as examples, which are irrelevant in the twenty-first century.

They may have been important to Muslims in the past, but these events are not pertinent to them anymore. Lewis wrote about Crusades, various battles, and treaties between Christian and Muslim empires of the last five centuries, but they are history to the Muslims, as they are to the Western citizens of the twenty-first century. Lewis talked a lot about the treaty of Carlowitz. Of what significance can that treaty, signed in 1699, be to Muslims today, or the battle of Lepanto that took place in 1577 between the Ottoman and the combined navies of European empires? A vast majority of Muslims are not even aware of these battles and treaties, but Lewis manages to convince the West that Muslims are still lamenting those events.

At the same time, Lewis did not mention events that still affect Muslims in their daily lives: the Belfour Declaration and the treaty of Sykes-Picquet, which established Israel on the Palestinian land; the struggle against colonialism; the killings in Algeria by the French or in Sudan, Iraq, Malaysia, and Yemen by the British; or the coup in Iran which deposed the duly elected leader and brought Reza Shah Pehlevi to power. There is hardly any mention of these events in his writings, except in passing. That prompts Sheehi to question if Lewis has been asleep while the Muslim world has moved ahead. How could Lewis miss significant progress Arab and other Muslim countries made during their struggle against the colonial powers?[123] Lewis remains oblivious to these events either by design or otherwise. Canfield explains:[124]

> At least until the Iraq war, most present-day Arabs didn't think in the stark clash-of-civilization terms Lewis prefers. Bin Laden likes to vilify Western Crusaders, but until relatively recently, he was still seen by much of the

Arab establishment as a marginal figure. To most Arabs before 9/11, the Crusades were history as ancient as they are to us in the West. Modern Arab anger and frustration are, in fact, less than a hundred years old. As bin Laden knows very well, this anger is a function not of Islam's humiliation at the Treaty of Carlowitz of 1699, the sort of long-ago defeat that Lewis highlights in his bestselling What Went Wrong? But of much more recent developments. These include the 1916 Sykes-Picot agreement by which the British and French agreed to divvy up the Arabic-speaking countries after World War I; the subsequent creation, by the Europeans, of corrupt, kleptocratic tyrannies in Saudi Arabia, Syria, Egypt, Iraq, and Jordan; the endemic poverty and underdevelopment that resulted for most of the 20th century; the U.N.-imposed creation of Israel in 1948; and finally, in recent decades, American support for the bleak status quo.

Given the timing of the appearance of these books, when Islam and the West had no particular areas of serious contention except the Palestinian and Israeli conflict, the question is: are Lewis's unique interests and concerns about Israel the reason why he portrayed Arabs and Islam in this fashion? Are he and his neoconservative colleagues representing American or Israel's interests? The topic of dual national interests of the neoconservative ideologues is a sore point with Zionists. Even raising this issue could be labeled as anti-Semitic. However, Zionism and Judaism are two different issues. Not all Jews are Zionists, and not all Zionists are Jews. To make the distinction between Zionism and Judaism is essential, which many neoconservatives avoid doing.

Also, Lewis is selective in quoting other people, especially Israelis. Of all people, Lewis quotes an Israeli commentator in "The Roots of Muslim Rage," which merely reflects his specific political interest. Consider the following quotation by an Israeli official:

> No matter how bad communism was, it was never a step into the early Middle Ages, and what is hard to see is how democracies of the twenty-first century will be able to live in peace with forces determined to prove that the last thousand years did not happen.[125]

This statement from an Israeli commentator, which also does not provide any examples or facts to prove the assertion, is an example of crude polemics. Of course, such a statement is expected from an Israeli official. Presenting unsubstantiated accusations as facts by combatants is not uncommon during periods of conflict, but what about Lewis? He has presented himself as an objective commentator. Besides, as an eminent academician, he is expected to be neutral. Is he? Not according to what Lewis has been writing. He never quotes an Arab or a Muslim commentator or an impartial scholar of Islam on this topic.

Besides, Lewis's association with various think-tanks, which are supported by the AIPAC, and his special affiliation with the State of Israel, are also facts that have been documented by multiple neutral observers, but these are never mentioned. Neither have his financial interests with AIPAC and its sister organizations been pointed out. Could one argue that his associations with Israel and pro-Israel lobbies in the United States may be the reason why Lewis opines Islam being irrational and violent? For example, he writes:

> It should now be clear that we are facing a mood and a movement far transcending the level of issues and policies and the governments that pursue them. This is no less than a clash of civilizations – perhaps irrational but a surely historic reaction of an ancient rival against our Judeo-Christian heritage, our secular present, and the worldwide expansions of both.[126]

Is there indeed a clash of civilization between the West and Muslim countries, which Lewis calls Islam? This question should be evaluated from the following perspectives. First, there is not a single Islam or, to be precise, a single interpretation of Islam. Lewis's Islam is different from the Islam of Muslims or what is perceived by Muslims as their religious belief. His assertion should be evaluated in the light of two separate facts: 1) there were no conflicts in the 1990s between the West and Muslim countries, except Arab–Israeli wars, if we include the Jewish nation in the fold of the Western nations; 2) Lewis has gone an extra distance to incorporate Western Christian civilization into the so-called Judeo-Christian heritage. For him and in his writings, Israel is a part of the West. Is this true? If so, on what grounds? Jews and Christians may be in an alliance today, but is this alliance permanent? Henry Kissinger, the former Secretary of State, pointed out that the United States neither has permanent friends nor permanent enemies; it only has permanent interests.

Alliances are never permanent; they are created for a reason, and when the reasons vanish, the cause for staying in alliance loses its significance. How long this particular policy of joining hands with Israel would last remains to be seen. There are reasons to be apprehensive about the future of the current alliance. Noam Chomsky had always argued that the United States had established Israel in order to keep an American outpost within the Arab world, which, he argues, is to exploit its resources.[127] If he is to be believed, Israel is not the cause but is being used as a tool. Some may disagree, but this only reminds us of the temporary nature of the Anglo-American-Zionist alliance. Democracy or not, not to persecute Jews, both in Europe and (even) in the United States, is only a recent phenomenon. Anti-Semitism has not vanished from the West.

The mass shooting of Jewish people does occur occasionally.[128] The lynching of a Jewish person had taken place as late as the 1920s.[129] Nazi Germany may have killed six million Jews during the Second World War, but other countries have equally sinister records of anti-Semitism. Western nations did nothing to save the Jews of Europe, even though they had the chance to save millions of doomed Jews. They elected to ignore pleas from the Jewish organizations. The United States, Britain, France, and other nations took the decision not to allow Jews to come to the United States or Western Europe during the War. Even Lewis agrees, during the same period, persecuted European Jewish Diaspora found refuge in the Muslim land.[130]

Lewis and others may routinely include Israel in the fold of the West, whose hallmark is a separation of church and state. How about Israel? Does the country have the separation of synagogues and state? If so, it can be described as a secular democracy. That is not the case; it is a Jewish state and not a democracy. Lewis failed to mention that there is no separation of synagogue and state or between other symbols of Judaism and the state of Israel. Israel's constitution is based on Jewish scripture and Talmudic traditions. The killing of Palestinians is discussed by right-wing politicians and by religious leaders and justified by citing Talmudic laws, which in any democratic system would not be allowed.

These facts are ignored by Christian Zionists, which only suggests that the state of Israel and Christian Zionists may have a common goal today, but they could have divergent views about the future of the Holy Land. Christian Zionists are waiting for the Armageddon in which only Christians – and not Jews (unless they convert to Christianity) – would survive. In the world of Christian Zionists, Jews are destined for violent deaths – the fact that they or neoconservatives neither discuss nor acknowledge. A lack of discussion on this topic only suggests that Christian and Jewish Zionists have their separate agendas, which are very different from each other. Today, their interests converge only on one issue – the control of the real estate of the Holy Land, but for various reasons.

Lewis and his neoconservative colleagues have argued that the current battle with Islam and the West and its ally, Israel (in his words, *Judeo-Christian civilization*), is about values that are best represented by democracy. Is this true? Of course not; democracy, as it is known and practiced in the West, is based on the principle of one person, one vote. If we judge Israel by the same yardstick, democracy does not exist in Israel. Rights given by the State of Israel to its non-Jewish citizens are very restrictive.[131] Even in non-Jewish-majority areas, only Jews have the right to own property, but not the Arabs. Israel's non-Jewish population constitutes almost one-fifth of pre-1967 Israel. If we include the occupied territories, over half of the population of Israel is barred from participating in many aspects of democracy. If we take the state of Israel only, its Arab population, who have Israeli citizenship, do not have equal rights; they have severe restrictions regarding what they are allowed to do, including how they live or earn a living and many other mundane aspects of their daily lives. Human rights abuses of Palestinians are rampant.

The hallmark of democracy is two-fold: majority rule and equal rights for the minority. One of the fundamental principles of democracy is to guarantee the fundamental rights to everyone, including to its minorities and other weaker segments of the society. Since Israel does not provide such rights to Palestinians, its original inhabitants, it cannot be defined as a democracy; it is an Apartheid state. Israel's rule in Palestine is modeled after the colonial system. Newly arrived European settlers pushed native inhabitants from their ancestral land, similar to what they did in places like Australia and the Americas; they ended up occupying the continent where natives were living for thousands of years. The result was the massacre and marginalization of the natives in their own country.

Likewise, all Palestinians in Israel are also being marginalized in their country. Human-rights groups are of the view that every aspect of daily Palestinian life has been affected by state-sponsored discrimination. Many of them have become refugees; the rest have been pushed from their ancestral homes into Gaza, a strip of land, which has become a ghetto. Despite the support which Israel gets from Christian Zionists, Palestinian Christians in Israel are equally discriminated against by the Israeli laws.[132] The state of Israel does not distinguish between Christians and Muslim Palestinians.[133] The interests of Palestinian Christians of Palestine are different from the interests of Christian Zionists of the United States.

These facts merely confirm that the reason behind violent conflicts is not religion but the land and its resources. In other words, the battle between native Palestinians and Israelis is about the land and its resources. Lewis ignored these facts. Why? Is it because of his support for the Zionist cause?

Notes

1 Ian McCulloch, "Mod7C Fake News," YouTube, https://www.youtube.com/wa tch?v=jFR99Fhn8fU.
2 Steven Kinzer, *Overthrow*, Chapter 5.
3 Ibid, Chapter 5; for a detailed discussion of events see Stephen Kinzer, *All the Shah's Men*.
4 Edward Said, *Covering Islam*, 5–7.
5 https://www.theatlantic.com/photo/2014/08/the-soviet-war-in-afghanista n-1979-1989/100786/.
6 Alfred McCoy, *In the Shadows of the American Century*.
7 Chris Hedges, https://www.youtube.com/watch?v=MFF5wGbX2W8; also see Hedges, https://www.commondreams.org/views/2017/10/02/end-empire.
8 Said, *Covering Islam*, xi–lxx.
9 Said, *Covering Islam*, 36–79.
10 Ari Rabin-Havt, *Lies, Incorporated*, 3–21; Cynthia Crossen, *Tainted Truth*. For detailed discussions on this topic see Edward Herman and Noam Chomsky, *Manufacturing Consent*.
11 Michelle Alexander, *The New Jim Crow*; Ian Haney Lopez, *Dog Whistle Politics*.
12 Bernard Lewis, "The Roots of Muslim Rage," *The Atlantic Monthly,* September 1990, 49–67. Also see Edward Said, *Covering Islam*, Chapter 1.
13 Said, *Covering Islam*, xxx–xxxiii, 136.
14 John Esposito, *The Islamic Threat*, 230–236.
15 Samuel Huntington, *The Clash of Civilizations*, Chapter 8.
16 Ibid.
17 Melanie Phillips, *Londonistan*.
18 https://www.newsweek.com/dispelling-myth-eurabia-81943;   https://www.thegua rdian.com/books/2014/apr/03/muslims-are-coming-islamophobia-extremism-dom estic-war-on-terror-review.
19 https://www.foreignaffairs.com/articles/united-states/1993-06-01/clash-civilizations.
20 John Esposito, *The Islamic Threat*, 223.
21 https://www.globalresearch.ca/america-created-al-qaeda-and-the-isis-terror-group/ 5402881. Also see: http://www.theinsider.org/news/article.asp?id=0228.
22 https://www.counterpunch.org/2003/02/14/meet-mr-blowback-gulbuddin-hekmatyar/.

23 Ibid. Also see Michael Chossudovsky, "The Spoils of War: Afghanistan Multi-billion Dollar Heroin Trade," https://www.thelibertybeacon.com/the-spoils-of-war-afghanistans-multibillion-dollar-heroin-trade/.
24 https://www.thenation.com/article/for-the-15-years-since-911-the-us-has-waged-an-endless-campaign-of-violence-in-the-middle-east/. Also see https://www.globalresearch.ca/us-has-killed-more-than-20-million-people-in-37-victim-nations-since-world-war-ii/5492051;https://www.answers.com/Q/Number_of_people_killed_in_Iraq_and_Afghanistan_wars_so_far.
25 Amartya Sen, *Identity and Violence*, 42–44, 57.
26 Huntington, 44.
27 Huntington, 44–46.
28 Huntington, 207–209, 252–254, 266–299.
29 Michael Mann, *The Dark Side of Democracy*, Chapters 12 and 13.
30 Mark Curtis, *Web of Deceit*, 312.
31 Imbesat Daudi, *Civilization and Violence*, Chapter 5, Tables 5.1 and 5.3.
32 Huntington, 246–265.
33 Ibid.
34 Ibid.
35 "Armed Conflicts Database," International Institute for Strategic Studies, http://iiss.org.
36 M.J. Akbar, *India: The Siege Within*, 167–195, also see Anurag Singh, *Giani Kirpal Singh's Eye-Witness Account of Operation Bluestar*.
37 Robert Pape, *Dying to Win*, 265 and Table 6.3.
38 For a detailed discussion see Piotr Olender, *Russo-Japanese Naval War 1904–1905*.
39 Caesar Farah, *Islam*, 272–274; for a detailed discussion on the subject see Duncan McCargo, *Tearing Apart the Land*.
40 Niall Ferguson, *Empire*.
41 Daudi, 207–212.
42 Huntington, 254–259.
43 Huntington, 263–265.
44 Huntington, 267.
45 Huntington, Chapter 2.
46 Daudi, 102.
47 Daudi, 239, 283, 315–316.
48 https://www.theguardian.com/news/datablog/2011/jan/28/muslim-population-country-projection-2030. Also see https://www.theguardian.com/news/datablog/2011/jan/28/muslim-population-country-projection-2030.
49 Farah, *Islam*, 283.
50 https://carnegieindia.org/2016/06/29/illegal-immigration-from-bangladesh-to-india-toward-comprehensive-solution-pub-63931.
51 Farah, 276.
52 Farah, 272.
53 Farah, 274.
54 https://www.sahistory.org.za/archive/history-muslims-south-africa-1652-1699-ebrahim-mahomed-mahida
55 https://www.theguardian.com/news/datablog/2011/jan/28/muslim-population-country-projection-2030. Also see https://www.theguardian.com/news/datablog/2011/jan/28/muslim-population-country-projection-2030. Also see Daudi, 104.
56 Farah, 272, 276, 287, 291, 343.
57 Sen, 47.
58 "Adoption of Christianity in Russia," https://russia.rin.ru/guides_e/6483.html.
59 Paul Zachariah, "Surprising early history of Christianity in India," https://www.smithsonianmag.com/travel/how-christianity-came-to-india-kerala-180958117/
60 Farah, 283.

61 https://www.muslim2china.com/MuslimInfo/Muslim-Cities-in-China.html.
62 Mike Davis, *Late Victorian Holocausts*, 296.
63 Marilyn Lake and Henry Reynolds, *Drawing the Global Color Line*, 1–2.
64 https://medium.com/@writingben/four-great-african-empires-that-astonished-the-world-fd374a79f89b. For further discussion see documentary for PBS by Henry Louis Gates Jr., *Africa's Great Civilizations*.
65 Sen, 42.
66 Sen, 43.
67 Sen, 41–50.
68 John Esposito, *The Islamic Threat*, 219.
69 Lewis, "The Roots of Muslim Rage," 49–67.
70 Esposito, 220.
71 Engdahl, Chapter 3.
72 Lewis, ibid., 49–51.
73 Lewis, 49–67.
74 Lewis, ibid.
75 Daudi.
76 "Fragile Peace: Sri Lanka is Beginning to Reckon with the Aftermath of a Brutal Civil War: Tens of Thousands Homeless, Tens of thousands Still Homeless," *National Geographic*, November, 2016, Also see: "Basic Math Explains Root Cause of Sri Lanka Conflict," https://www.sangam.org/2012/07/Structural_Cause.php?print=true.
77 Esposito, 221.
78 C.H. Naim, "The Outrage of Bernard Lewis," *Journal of Columbia University*, http://www.columbia.edu/itc/mealac/pritchett/00litlinks/naim/ambiguities/23berna rdlewis.html (originally published in *Social Text* 30, 1992, 5).
79 Lewis, 49.
80 Steven Pinker, https://www.npr.org/2016/07/16/486311030/despite-the-headlines-steven-pinker-says-the-world-is-becoming-less-violent. Others disagree; see https://www.theguardian.com/books/2015/mar/13/john-gray-steven-pinker-wrong-violence-war-declining.
81 Naim, "The Outrage of Bernard Lewis."
82 Ibid.
83 https://www.christianity.com/church/church-history/timeline/901-1200/saladin-cap tured-jerusalem-11629809.html.
84 Steven Coll, "The Days of Rage," *The New Yorker*, Sept. 24, 2012.
85 Ibid.
86 USA Today/Gallup poll, 2006, quoted in John Esposito and Dalia Mogahed, *Who Speaks for Islam?* 2–3; Pew Research quoted in James Bamford, *A Pretext for War*, 377.
87 Esposito and Mogahed, 140–142, 155–160.
88 Esposito and Mogahed, 165.
89 Esposito and Mogahed, 140–160.
90 Esposito and Mogahed, 140–155.
91 https://www.counterpunch.org/2007/05/17/bernard-lewis-latest-call-to-arms/ https://saberpoint.blogspot.com/2007/05/bernard-lewis-on-islam-iraq-and-bush.html.
92 Ibid.
93 Esposito. 221.
94 Esposito. 221.
95 Esposito, 221; Said, xxx.
96 Hedges, *The American Fascists*, Chapter 1.
97 Buchanan, *Where the Right Went Wrong*, Chapter 7.
98 https://www.alternet.org/2013/03/worst-mistake-us-history-america-will-never-recover -bushs-great-foreign-policy/.

99   https://www.cnbc.com/2019/11/20/us-spent-6point4-trillion-on-middle-east-wars-sin
      ce-2001-study.html.
100 https://foreignpolicy.com/2015/12/15/do-muslims-around-the-world-really-hate-the-un
      ited-states/.
101 https://mondoweiss.net/2012/04/bernard-lewis-revises-bernard-lewis-says-he-oppose
      d-invasion-of-iraq/. For a detailed discussion on Lewis's role see Stephen Sheehi,
      Islamophobia.
102 See https://www. informationclearinghouse. info; it gives statistics on the first page.
103 https://www.prospectmagazine.co.uk/magazine/thelewisdoctrine.
104 https://rense.com/general47/before.htm.
105 https://www.middleeasteye.net/opinion/do-not-weep-bernard-lewis-high-priest-wa
      r-middle-east.
106 https://www.salon.com/2007/10/12/wesley_clark/.
107 Sheehi, Chapter 2.
108 Lewis, *The Crisis of Islam*, 1–5.
109 Lewis, ibid.
110 Buchanan, Chapter 4.
111 Robert Pape, *Dying to Win*, Table 5, Chapter 4.
112 Ibid.
113 https://graduateway.com/the-nature-of-islam-peaceful-or-warlike/. For Lewis's idea
      about Islam and violence see his book, *What Went Wrong*. For other perspectives see
      Deepa Kumar, *Islamophobia*, Said, *Covering Islam*, and Esposito, *The Islamic Threat*.
114 Lewis, *The Assassins*.
115 Kumar, 84–85.
116 Kumar, 82.
117 Kumar, 82.
118 Richard Bulliet, *The Case for Islamo-Christian Civilization*.
119 https://historynewsnetwork.org/article/42328; https://historynewsnetwork.org/article/
      27148. For a detailed discussion see Juan Cole, *Muhammad: Prophet of Peace amid
      the Clash of Empires*.
120 Ibid.
121 Robert Canfield, https://rcanfield.blogspot.com/2004/11/richard-bulliet-and-berna
      rd-lewis.html.
122 Ibid., 2.
123 Sheehi, Chapter 2.
124 Ibid, 2.
125 Esposito, 221.
126 Lewis, "The Roots of Muslim Rage," 56–60.
127 https://www.alternet.org/story/147865/noam_chomsky%3A_the_real_reasons_the_
      u.s._enables_israeli_crimes_and_atrocities.
128 Pittsburgh, October 27.
129 https://forward.com/news/210334/untold-story-of-the-first-jewish-lynching-in-ameri/.
130 Bernard Lewis, *Jews of Islam*, Chapter 3.
131 https://www.hrw.org/news/2020/05/12/israel-discriminatory-land-policies-hem-pales
      tinians; also see https://theowp.org/ethnic-cleansing-of-palestinians-a-deep-dive-in
      to-how-israel-has-violated-humanitarian-laws-and-justified-appropriation; https://
      www.aljazeera.com/news/2022/1/31/israel-forces-palestinian-families-to-self-dem
      olish-their-homes-in-jerusalem.
132 D. Neff, "Christians Discriminated Against by Israel," https://Ifamericansknew.
      org/history/rel-christians.html.
133 Ibid.

5 How Islamophobia spreads

In the debate over the alleged association of Islam with violence as well as a clash of civilizations between Islam and the West, Lewis and Huntington are the two most quoted authors of this period. Both are credited with espousing the view that after the fall of communism, Islam would be the only enemy of the so-called Judeo-Christian civilization. Because of their international stature in the field of Orientalism (Lewis) and political science (Huntington), they were not only pioneers in defining the current debate, but they also laid the foundation of the current Islamophobic mood in the West. They changed the very narrative on which American foreign policy was based; it was a superlative achievement. However, the changing of the prevailing narrative was a concerted effort of the neoconservative movement.

Neoconservative writers and activists can be divided into three broad categories. The division is arbitrary. The first tier of writers are theorists; they established the concept. As talented as they may be, these two writers could not have achieved what they achieved without the help of other neoconservative writers and journalists who belonged to the second tier of the movement. The second and third tiers of writers are the real workhorses of the movement; they were instrumental in spreading this narrative and made it a popular idea. The third tier are activists on social media. They may not have written articles and books, but their role in spreading and sustaining Islamophobia was vital.

The neoconservative movement was also supported by the mainstream media, which is controlled by six mega-corporations. Together, they created a loosely connected system, which was well organized and effective. They supported each other and created an environment which helped to justify the U.S. invasion of Iraq and Afghanistan and the War on Terror. The internal resistance to war, which was a vibrant force during the Vietnam War, was nowhere to be seen. The success of their undertaking should go to the organization that was created for them.

The science behind spreading of ideas

Two theories have emerged in the last few decades that explain how ideas spread within and among communities and how various components in a multi-

DOI: 10.4324/9781003323105-6

cultural society with multidimensional units interact with each other. They are a) *the small world theory*, which states that people around the world are separated by just six intermediaries, and b) *the complex network theory*, which states that groups of people, when connected to each other, may act independently, but they are still dependent on each other. Their interdependence alters the outcome of their effort, sometimes exponentially; the end result could either be an increase or decrease in the outcome that is greater than if the impact of each element is combined.

These two theories complement each other. The first theory explains why it is easy to propagate ideas around the world. A fashion or song popular in one country becomes viral worldwide. The reason may be that people are connected by only six intermediaries and now by six clicks of a keyboard. The network theory explains the internal dynamic of propagation of ideas within and among communities. This is a relatively new field of social sciences; it could only emerge with the increasing computational power of software. Computer chips can now analyze extensive data, which was not humanly possible. They have unlocked the mystery of complex non-linear relationships among various components, which has also enabled us to understand how ideas spread, what factors influence their propagation, valid or otherwise, and how.

Combined, these two theories can explain how the stereotyping of Muslims exploded in the United States and among its allies and why those who raised their voices against the proponents of Islamophobia failed. Why could brilliant minds with exceptional writing skills not oppose neoconservative ideologues for space in the Western perception? Was it because of the strength of their arguments or because fake news travels faster than the truth? We will see; the other factor could be how human brains perceive gossip and facts. If so, were neoconservatives programmed to succeed and their opponents destined to fail?

Six degrees of separation

In 1929, Frigyes Karinthy, a Hungarian author and poet, conceptualized that people across the world are connected by six intermediaries only.[1] He presented his idea in a Hungarian short story *Lancszemak* (Chains). Whether his hypothesis was based on science or imagination is unknown; his concept did not get much traction for the next fifty years. That changed in the 1960s when Stanley Milgram, a psychologist, investigated Karinthy's hypothesis by a scientific experiment.[2] He is better known for an experiment on obedience in which he had asked the subjects to apply electric shocks to people. Many complied. He showed that ordinary people, with intact morality, did despicable acts when asked by authorities.[3] Can that explain holocausts? Probably; can that justify their actions? Of course not!

In this experiment, Milgram asked a few hundred people across the country to send a letter to a person whom the volunteers did not know. The recipients lived in Boston, over 2,000 miles away. Participants were asked to send the letter to an acquaintance; in turn, they would then send that letter to someone else whom the recipient thought could have known or expected to know the target. Low and behold, it took only six intermediaries to reach the desired destination. Milgram's experiment confirmed Karinthy's hypothesis that all of us are connected by just six connections (the technical term is nodes). With the advent of the world-wide web and social media, the number of intermediaries might have decreased to five or four. The world is indeed a small place; thus, the small-world theory was born.

The complexity theory

The second relevant observation in propagating ideas is the complex network theory; it deals with the process and dynamic of spreading ideas within and among societies. It hypothesizes that any system is a set of parts (people or objects) called *elements*. Collections of elements are referred to as nodes. Both elements and nodes are connected to each other; connectivity is defined as *relations*. If there is no order to the relationship, nodes or people follow the Newtonian law, which states that the end effect would follow an arithmetic progression (sum of the impact of individual nodes). However, if there is an order within a node and among sets of nodes, it is described as a complex system. Since each node specializes in different tasks, their relationship makes the job easy but also complicated due to the presence of more nodes with other functions.

Many species in nature follow complex systems to maintain an efficient environment for their survival. For example, tens of thousands of honey bees act in unison to keep the temperature to thirty-four degrees Celsius within hives; a flock of birds maintains a specific pattern to navigate long-distance with the least possible effort; neurons within the nervous system and various organs within bodies act synchronously to maintain homeostasis. This is also true for systems created by humans or by artificial intelligence such as global financial systems, airline operations, electrical grid, world-wide web, and others. Scientists describe the process as non-linear chaos, but this way, the system functions more efficiently. At the same time, the operation becomes more vulnerable because of the presence of more participants. Any problem at one station could disrupt the entire process. The malfunction of even a single node can be fatal for the whole system. For example, a change in one amino acid in one of more than a billion genes in the human body can make life incompatible.

There is a hierarchy within a system and nodes. Not all units are equal; some are "more" equal than others. It is estimated that only 10% of nodes or people in a community are active; the rest follow the lead nodes. A further 10% (or 1% of the total) make up the nucleus from where the leadership arises. They provide ideas and set rules – formally or informally. Peter Phillips, in his books *Giants: The Global Power Elites*, has analyzed the power structure of the world order, people who are in control of the world, and how the system works.[4] He estimates that only the top 1% of individuals own 80% of the world's wealth; they set the rules, which the world follows. This hierarchy is also evident in chat rooms on WhatsApp. Merely a tiny fraction of people within each group set the agenda of discussion. Those who oppose the rules set by the 1% feel ostracized, but their choices are limited: they can either leave the group or avoid resisting the prevailing consensus or belief.

The power of systems: non-linear chaos

Social scientists who study networking for a living opine that the strength of a system comes from interaction among the different elements that form the system. A summary of how the system works is presented next; it explains how organizations become more effective than individuals within the system if the system is organized correctly.

Elements, whether formed in nature or created by artificial intelligence, follow specific rules. First and foremost, they show *homophily*; they tend to have similar characters, summarized by the proverb *birds of the same feather flock together*. Homophily is more pronounced in larger groups than in smaller ones.[5] In the context of the discussion on Islamophobia, the example would be the neoconservative movement, which has grown in size. There is a cacophony of loud echoes. It acts as an echo chamber. Evangelical Christians and Hindutva ideologues are the newest entrants to the world of Zionism.

The neoconservative movement comprises a close-knit community of writers, intellectuals, thinkers, and political activists. Their dedication to Israel and their commitment to its expansion policy are financial and emotional bonds that have glued them together. Their interaction with other members of the network provides access to each other's resources. Like-minded people have also flocked together to give a greater impetus than individual activists could have done. It has created connectivity to other groups and produced non-linear expansion. It also enhanced the outcome in geometrical progression. The system has created a more effective and efficient movement. Pro-Israeli activists have expanded their influence beyond Israel and the United States. Other right-wing political groups such as the Hindutva forces, Islamist movement, and quasi-fascist political parties of Europe and South America have succeeded by following the same path.

Second, elements act independently; still, they are interdependent with other nodes or subgroups within the system. Complex mathematical formulas can calculate the importance of individual people or elements within each subset of the system. Since knowledge is power, whoever controls the flow of information has the power to control the system. Since information flows in all directions, influential nodes are centrally placed and connected to more nodes. The influence of each node within a system can be measured by the degree of centrality. Originators of ideas may not function as a central node; their job is to provide novel ideas. How that idea would spread depends on the system, its management, and the next level of activists. The position of the central node is reserved for managers of the system.

One of the organizations is Unit 8200 of the Israeli military intelligence.[6] This organization trains Israeli recruits in controlling information and creating news, fake or otherwise, conducive to Israel. They manage information passing through Twitter, Facebook, YouTube, and other social media networks. Many executives of these corporations are its alumni. Unit 8200 now has a strong presence in the United States as well. Besides Israeli conscripts, Unit 8200 has recruited Israeli, American, and Jewish volunteers from university campuses.[7] Their mission is described by one of the members as *Tweet, Share, and Like*.[8] Volunteers are paid $2,000 a month for five hours of weekly work. Alumni of Unit 8200 have received support from the parent organization; there have been several start-up companies, which its alumni have formed. They dominate the cyber-security industry. To enhance Israel's interests, the American Israeli Political Action Committee (AIPAC) has played the role of coordinator by uniting the corporate media, the legislative branch, think-tanks, and other segments of American society.[9]

India has its own cyber warriors.[10] The ruling party, BJP, is alleged to have created an IT cell for election purposes. In her book, *I am a Troll*, Swati Chaturvedi outlines how BJP's IT cell targets people who oppose Prime Minister Modi.[11] Sadhvi Khosla, once a dedicated follower of the Prime Minister willingly joined the troll team, but was disenchanted. She claims that volunteers were given the names of people to be attacked on line. Women were threatened with rape;[12] men were threatened with violent deaths.[13] A journalist and community activist, Gauri Lankesh was shot dead by a person who may have been closely related to its volunteer.[14] Her death was celebrated. Another journalist, Karan Anand, describes the deeply entrenched nexus of the troll army in the BJP:[15]

> BJP appointed 1.28 lakh [128,000] block-level presidents in UP, and each of these levels had IT cell workers. After their "missed call" drive, the IT cell had verified data of 1.3cr [13,000,000] people, who would later become consumers of BJP's online propaganda. With their net fully woven around the people, by the time UP went to polls, the IT cells had access to over 9000 WhatsApp groups across the state with each group having a minimum 150 members. Numerous messages were sent to these groups on a daily basis, with at least 13.5 lakh [135,000] people reading them every day. Even these people further forwarded these messages on various other groups.
>
> One member of the BJP IT cell told Newslaundry, "A lot of these messages sent by our members included propaganda against our opponents. Many had statements which were factually incorrect". Thereby, by forming these vast networks on WhatsApp and brainwashing the public, BJP's IT cell has helped the party achieve serious political gains.

There is no equality within nodes; elements do not follow socialism; they act on *Mathew's Principle*, a Biblical proclamation, which states *the more you have, the more you get*. This explains why Huntington and Lewis have many followers and references to their work, but men and women who belonged to the second or third tier of the network may not have as many citations of their articles. Nevertheless, they play a crucial role in propagating concepts substantiated by facts or not. They are the worker bees; they do all the chores in the hive but do not get attention on a public platform. Those who belong to the third tier focus on smaller communities, chat rooms, and other social media. These activists may have as many connections to influential people of the society as the second tier of activists, but not publicity.

The other properties of elements, which can also be precisely calculated, are 1) betweenness (it is the informal power of individual nodes), 2) closeness to each other (it estimates the time of spreading information to other elements or nodes, relatively influential people in any community are connected to the leader of the pack), and 3), eigenvector, which is defined as the connection to the central node; this gives importance to different elements within nodes. One of the main differences between the neoconservative writers and their opponents is that the former has a centralized approach to their effort. There may not be an official organization; nevertheless, there is a loose network by which they are connected.

Their opponents, such as Edward Said, Noam Chomsky, and others, have also presented brilliant ideas that have been fact-based, but since they may not have a centralized structure to advance their cause, they have not been as effective in propagating their views. Besides, the neoconservative movement has not only greater numerosity but also closer betweenness, closeness, and a stronger eigenvector, which also arises due to a centralized system. That includes the media as well. That approach has led to better performance of the second and third tiers of writers. Their writings appear to be factual even though they may not be correct. They cite and promote each other, which accentuates the effect of fake news. This phenomenon has been described as *pluralistic information,* which creates what is called *echo.* The neoconservative network has a louder echo and attracts more volunteers to its echo chambers.

Elements or activists, if they combine with others, enhance their impact on the outcome. This is due to their property of self-organization, which is due to *numerosity.* The other properties of nodes of a complex system are connectivity, interdependence, and adaptation, which give them their autonomy. People (nodes) within complex systems act independently while taking actions, but they are also interdependent with other activists of the same system. Anti-Muslim activists have conducted in this manner. Lewis and Huntington had provided an idea, which was expanded by the second tier of neoconservative writers and sustained by the third tier.

This particular nodal property also explains why Islamophobia hypotheses were being dispersed effectively by the second-tier political activists and writers such as Judith Miller, Francis Fukuyama, Thomas Friedman, and others. They would take one particular point from the writings of Lewis and Huntington and then expand on it. Other writers then repeated their arguments; this gives an aura of authenticity to their claims even if their statements and opinions may not be factual. This also provides an impression that more people tend to think as they think. In technical terms, the above phenomena are called *majority illusion.*

Their approach to Islamophobic narratives shows interdependence. It has the potential to enhance the desired impression. The connectivity of activists to each other produces a different level of organization within a community, which can also influence volunteers from other systems. For example, Israel's extreme right-wing politicians, settlers, and activists, and Hindutva forces have joined hands. The concept of a common enemy has joined them together. In this way, a new level of a loose connection was formed, which has created yet another level of connectivity. This phenomenon is called *emergence*. The connectivity of nodes can alter the outcome of the system, sometimes exponentially.

An increase or decrease in the outcome arises from feedback loops. That can change the effect in both directions. The examples are a sudden rise and fall of empires; the collapse of ecosystems, such as coral reefs in oceans; booms and bursts of financial bubbles in capitalist systems; the rise of communism after the First World War, and its fall after the Soviet-Afghan War; the rise and fall of fascism between the two World War period, and the rise of quasi-fascist leaders in the twenty-first century worldwide; a sudden rise of Islamophobia in the last thirty years, and a dramatic increase of neoconservative influence in American politics during the Bush administration. These are also examples of *emergence*; it is due to the connectivity to other sectors of American society.

Take the example of neoconservative ideologues and their supporters. The sum total of their collective influence had been phenomenal. Their combined effort led to the invasion of Iraq and Afghanistan, civil wars in Libya and Syria, and the bombing of half a dozen Muslim countries. Could they alone have altered the perception of the nation? Probably not, as they were supported by other segments of society – the executive and legislative branches, investors and executives of corporations controlling media, and significant capital, which controls transnational mega-corporations. The neoconservative movement alone might not have achieved what it achieved without the help of other factions. For example, Huntington and Lewis had presented their theories during the Clinton administration; some of them recommended toppling the Iraqi President; the media also supported these writers, but their suggestion of toppling Saddam Hussein was ignored. By then, they had not evolved as a potent force until George W. Bush came to the White House. Not that his predecessor President Clinton was averse to using force. After all, he had invaded or bombed four other countries.

President Bush brought the power of the executive branch to neoconservative narratives. This is another example of *emergence*. Thus, a new organizational level was created by combining the media, government, and big capital. This is another example of how the combined efforts of all the above sectors within a complex system had increased (sometimes exponentially) the outcome and the desired effect more than if individual groups had acted alone. With President Bush in the White House, neoconservative influence on the U.S. policy increased exponentially. The worldwide impact of the theory of clash of civilizations is another example of the phenomenon of combining forces to achieve a goal in a democracy.

The other property of complex systems is the adaptability of nodes to the new environment that the system has created. The change comes from two properties: independence and interdependence. The former gives the nodes autonomy, which helps individuals make changes to adopt emerging circumstances and adjust accordingly. The latter provides a guideline to stick to so that drastic changes, which could be fatal to the system, are kept in check. Combined, they affect long-term survival and functionality. An example of this property is the evolution of species in nature. Neoconservative narratives, which have been described below, should be evaluated from the perspective of the network theory.

How did their idea become viral? How much support did they get from the media, bureaucracy, government, and big capital?

The second tier of activists

The rest of the chapter deals with the arguments of activists who form the second tier of neoconservative writers. Their work should be evaluated with the interaction among them. The intention behind giving space to their views is to evaluate whether the complexity and network theories can explain why their ideas went viral. Their arguments should be viewed concerning the above two theories. Is there connectivity with the arguments of Lewis and Huntington, who should be considered the first tier of writers? Both are universally recognized as the gurus of the neoconservative ideology. They alone had provided the hypothesis that Judeo-Christian civilization is being threatened by Islamic civilization, which, according to their claims, is inherently violent.

The second tier of writers, journalists, and activists are identified next. Emphasis is given to the emergence of new forms of the same ideas, which these writers and journalists have promoted. They took over from where Huntington left off. Do they fall within the confines of the network theory? Did other writers and journalists complete the campaign of stereotyping Muslims? The rest of the chapter also discusses the opinions of their opponents and the merits of their arguments. Presented here are a few examples of other writers who have followed the neoconservative pioneers.

One of such authors is Francis Fukuyama, a professor of political science at Johns Hopkins University. His area of expertise was the Soviet Union. After the implosion of the communist system, he turned from a Soviet expert into an expert on Islam. In the 1990s, he became a fervent supporter of neoconservative political theories. For a brief period, he was widely believed to be one of the most influential intellectuals. His credentials as a professor of another prestigious university gave validity to neoconservative views. Fukuyama was often seen on neocon talk show circuits, but not anymore.

In his book, *The End of History and the Last Man,* he argued that after the demise of the Soviet Union and the collapse of the planned economy of the communist system, the West had won, and the battle for supremacy of the world was finally over, which he argued was good for humanity. His critics call his idea outrageous and a remnant of the Eurocentric mentality. So far, so good, but why demonize Muslims when Muslims played an essential role in the demise of the Soviet system? They were the cannon fodder during the Soviet-Afghan war; over a million Afghans lost their lives, and a quarter of them had to flee their homeland.

In the subsequent edition of the same book, Fukuyama claims that he has been misunderstood; nevertheless, he still believes that Islam is fundamentally incompatible with democracy and modernity.[16] He may not have openly argued that Islam is fundamentally violent, but he claims that culture is based primarily on religious beliefs and traditions, Muslim societies are anti-modern.[17] As the debate about the impending invasions of Iraq and Afghanistan was heating up in the media, his arguments about a lack of modernity in Islam complemented the notions of Lewis and Huntington that Islam promotes fanaticism among its followers. Fukuyama made it easier for the neoconservative ideologues to argue that Islam equals fundamentalism, which equals lack of modernity, which in turn equals inherent violence of the Islamic doctrine.

Fukuyama also implied that Muslims belonged to a monolithic social network. By generalizing Muslims as having a solitary identity, he made it convenient for neoconservatives to argue that the so-called "violent behavior" of Muslims is based on their religious doctrine or texts; therefore, any difference between the West and so-called Islamic civilization is irreconcilable. His reasoning was that the values of Islamic civilization are based solely on Islamic theology, which he argued, has not changed in 1,500 years. On the other hand, the values of the West – modernity, democracy, and a belief in the free market economy – are, according to him, based on rational thinking and, therefore, are constantly evolving; since Islamic civilization, unlike others, is impervious to changes, Muslims resist modernity and democracy. Fukuyama writes:[18]

> Modernity has a cultural basis. Liberal democracy and free markets do not work everywhere. They work best in societies with specific values whose origins may not be entirely rational. It is not an accident that modern liberal democracy emerged first in the Christian West since the universalism of democratic rights can be seen as a secular form of Christian universalism.... However, there does seem to be something about Islam, or at least the fundamentalist version of Islam that has been dominant in recent years, that make Muslim societies particularly resistant to modernity.

These words are self-explanatory, aren't they? But are they correct? Not according to the facts. They are subjective interpretations of modernity. There is a difference between westernization and modernization. The other problem with his argument is that he relied on nineteenth-century thinkers to formulate his ideas about the Islamic world of the twenty-first century. Those philosophers were the product of the colonial system; their notions were based on unquestioned European superiority over the rest of the world. They rejected any other ideas or civilizations worthy of discussion. Islam was demonized as a backward religion for, they argued, what else could explain the Western triumph over Muslim empires. The answer, of course, was more powerful weapons, and not powerful ideas, but that was not acknowledged.

Political thinkers of the colonial period were focused on justifying European presence in the colonies. Muslims were not the only victims. Native American and aboriginal Australian societies, which practiced an eco-friendly economic system, were characterized as ignorant and savages. Their culture has been vindicated; the West is embracing their eco-friendly concepts. African kingdoms, which had a vibrant economy until the arrival of Europeans, were not even mentioned as civilizations. The African continent was the least violent and had highly developed social networks; still, they were also branded savages and uncivilized.[19] Hindu and Buddhist philosophies were declared outdated concepts.[20] Indians and Chinese were also declared inferior to the Europeans.

There are other reasons why Fukuyama's arguments do not make sense. First, there are fallacies associated with his narratives of democracy; it is generally believed in the West that democracy started in Greece, which is only partially correct. Democracy does not belong to any particular civilization; neither did it start at one specific place. Athens may have been the first place in Europe where democracy was established, but other sites had embraced the concept. Democracy evolved at various locations during the same period when Athens was also experimenting with democracy. Athens was one of many centers, such as Vaishali in India and Bakhtara, an area around Iran and Afghanistan, where the Zoroastrian religion was flourishing.[21] Besides, not all Greeks were in favor of a democratic form of government, including Aristotle, who argued that governing could not be left to ordinary citizens.[22] Historical events suggest that the democratic form of government was the *Zeitgeist* of the fifth century B.C.

Fukuyama's explanation of modernity raises an important question: what is the proof that there is a cause-and-effect relationship between democracy and modernity? There is none, but he assumes there is one. If there is, Fukuyama did not establish it in his writings. There are many so-called modern nations and societies that are not democratic, but they find approval from neo-conservative ideologues who have branded themselves as the holy warriors of democracy. There are two reasons for their approval: a) these non-democratic nations have vibrant economies; b) they have an excellent relationship with the United States and Israel. These countries do not speak against the U.S. and Israeli policies, at least openly.

Similarly, there are many societies that are modern in outlook but do not have vibrant economies; they are ignored if they do not follow the prevalent world order. Others profess to be conservative by various social parameters, but they are very modern in the political arena. Besides, many times modern and democratic countries have evolved into fascist nations, which have willingly abandoned democratic principles. Germany was the most enlightened and modern nation in Europe in the latter half of the nineteenth century but slid into fascism after the First World War; so did Italy, Spain, and Portugal. The last two countries were fascist states into the 1970s. In the twenty-first century, modern European nations with century-old experiments with democracy are electing populist parties.

Indeed, the term *modernity* is subjective. Whatever modernity may mean to different people, the term remains undefined. The other problem with the notion is the assumption that modernity and westernization are identical, which, of course, is not true. Similarly, Western culture does not result automatically in social progress; neither does capitalism equate with democracy and equal rights for all. If there is any correlation, it is coincidental; there is no cause-and-effect relationship between the two.

Westernization, modernity, democracy, free-market economy, capitalism, and social equality are different virtues. They may appear simultaneously in some societies, but they are not causally related to each other. They may even appear to be identical, but they are not. All of them are fundamentally different concepts. Some are mere perceptions and not reality; others may be wishful thinking or a mirage. Above all, there is no cause-and-effect relationship among them. Whatever their importance for social changes, a lack of modernity and democracy in the twentieth century has provided ample justification for occupying weaker countries, which can only be done through violence by powerful nations. These arguments had been very effective in achieving the neocon goals of invading Iraq and Afghanistan and bombing various Muslim-majority countries during the so-called War on Terror. Without proper justification, the West would not have achieved its goal of occupying Iraq.

Fukuyama has since changed his views, which, as explained, was due to the destruction of Iraq that took place during the occupation. He may have distanced himself from the neoconservative movement after the failure of the neocon policy of occupation. In one of his recent articles, Fukuyama even denounced the current status of Islamophobia in the United States. He is unique among former or current neocons in this respect. As a result, Fukuyama has been criticized for his altered views by his former colleagues. In the second edition of his book, *The End of History*, he claims that the concept that history would end was a communist idea, not his; he was merely referring to that concept. Fukuyama claimed that he does not believe that human history ended after the implosion of the Soviet Union.[23] It is not clear if he has also changed his stance on the association of Islam with modernity and democracy.

Many other authors have also helped to propagate the myth of so-called Islamic violence. Far more media pundits routinely speak against Islam, Muslims, Arabs, and Palestinians. Nick Gatlin reports:

> According to a 2018 study from 416Labs, a research firm based in Canada, mainstream media such as *The New York Times, The Washington Post* and others published four times as many Israel-centric headlines as Palestine-centric ones between June 1967–2017. Additionally, Israeli sources were nearly 250% more likely to be quoted than Palestinian sources, and, in Israeli-centric headlines, the use of the word "occupation" has declined

nearly 85% since 1967. The use of the phrase "Palestinian refugee(s)" in headlines has also declined by 93% over the 50-year period.[24]

Thomas Friedman, a former correspondent for *The New York Times*, has written extensively on the Middle East. He was stationed in Beirut in the 1980s, around the time Israel invaded Lebanon. Friedman is also a firm supporter of globalization, which is the byproduct of corporate power. In return, Friedman gets support from the mainstream media controlled by a handful of corporations. He is a popular author of many books; many of them are on the best-seller list. Friedman shares views on Israel with Bernard Lewis and Sam Huntington. He also believes in a strong military and robust spending on the military-industrial complex, a trait common to all neoconservative ideologues. But he claims that he is not one of them.

In an article in *The New York Times*, Friedman has argued that the United States should selectively refuse immigration to Muslims to punish Al Qaeda, in case Osama bin Laden-sponsored attacks continue on Western targets.[25] Tom Friedman was responding to one of the bombings organized by Al Qaeda in Britain and Spain, two countries that had participated in the U.S.-led invasion of Iraq. His article is another example of a vague generalization of the entire Muslim community, usually seen in Lewis's articles. Friedman's primary argument is that Muslims from the United States should be punished for the actions of Al Qaeda. But why? What do Muslims have to do with Al Qaeda? What does an ordinary Muslim have in common with the leadership of Al Qaeda? Nothing, if he or she is not an Arab; not even language or culture, except a belief in the oneness of God. However, many share that belief, including many Hindus, Jews, Christians, or even agnostics.

Such rhetoric has laid the foundation of the demonization of Muslims. Like Lewis, Friedman also presents his opinions (that the entire Muslim world is a monolithic unit irrespective of sect, race, language, ethnicity, or nationality) as facts. He should know better; he has lived in the Middle East as a reporter for *The New York Times* during the Lebanese civil war and has written extensively about the sectarian fights in Lebanon in which sub-groups or sects within a particular religious community were pitted against each other. Friedman had reported on the interaction of various denominations within various Muslim societies. In his earlier reports, he distinguished various factions within Lebanese communities, but now he perceives and explains acts of violence by Muslim extremist groups not to be a local issue but an issue that represents the interests of every Muslim of the world.

In other words, Friedman argues that violence against Western and Israeli targets by any group of Muslims is a clash of civilizations with the West. Is it? Only a dedicated neoconservative would assume that. However, he does not describe himself as a neocon ideologue. Nevertheless, Friedman has assumed that every Muslim worldwide belongs to one broad community in the world with identical political, economic, and social agendas. That may be the reason why he argued that the United States should hold all Muslims living in the country as hostages if the U.S. faces another terrorist attack from any Muslim organization. Why? Only he knows the reason why he recommends such an unconstitutional step.

Friedman's recommendations may reflect his belief, genuine or otherwise, that Muslims around the world not only form a single community but Muslims in the United States also have the clout to change the minds of those who are in the business of attacking U.S. interests.[26] Like Lewis, Friedman did not answer the relevant question: why should the American Muslims be penalized for the acts of violence committed by other Muslims who may have a personal or political agenda against the United States? Is it because all Muslims are guilty? Is it because they are Muslims? However, he should know better. *Guilt by association*, which has often been used to justify violence and massacres in the past, has no place in the civilized world.

So why does Friedman recommend punishing all Muslims indiscriminately? Is it because all Muslims belong to a single monolithic unit? That may be a possible answer and even a solution. If it is indeed true, punishing American Muslims would affect the behavior of the terrorist group if they happen to be Muslim as well. However, are the interests of Muslims from the United States identical to the interests of Muslims in Afghanistan, Iraq, and Palestine? Of course not! The reasons behind all terrorist actions are local and not global.[27] So why does Friedman present such arguments? Does he genuinely believe that all the Muslims of the world are acting in unison to attack the United States? I do not think it is the solution; neither do millions of Muslims living in the United States. They have no interest in attacking U.S. interests.

More importantly, Friedman fails to mention one of the critical geopolitical facts: most leaders of the Muslim world are firmly aligned with the West because their interests are tied to Western interests. Besides, individual Muslims may be against a specific American foreign policy, but that does not mean that all Muslims are willing to take up arms against the United States. The total number of people who use violence in opposing the United States is minuscule, probably less than a fraction of 1%. Those who agree in theory that random acts of violence against civilian targets are justifiable to oppose tyranny are close to 7% across the Muslim World. That number is 24% in the United States.[28]

Muslims know that bombs do not discriminate; any bomb, if dropped on U.S. targets, is bound to kill American Muslims as well. Almost sixty out of 3,000 people who perished in the attack on the World Trade Center were Muslims,[29] a fact hardly ever acknowledged or even mentioned by neoconservatives. Besides, the bombing of any target in the United States makes the lives of American Muslims worse. As such, they have been blamed by neoconservatives for being too sympathetic to Al Qaeda. Being one of the weakest groups in the West, Muslims are an easy target. They have been attacked on streets by lunatic fringe elements of Western society.

Worse still, Muslims have to pay the price for being defined as the "other"; they have been stopped at border crossings by the law enforcement agencies merely based on their attire, beard, name, or the color of their skin, which is only by association in practically all cases. According to John Esposito, Muslims and those who appear to be Muslims, in general, were held in long lines at boarding areas at airports and were questioned by law enforcement officials – all in the name of the security of the country. The Police Commissioner of New York even initiated a surveillance program targeting Muslims in the Greater New York area after 9/11, an illegal act that infringed the civil liberties of Muslims, many of whom are American citizens. No wonder American Muslims usually make every effort to distance themselves from the events of 9/11.

Would those people behind the acts of violence against the West consider compromising their political goals in their country to safeguard the civil liberties of their co-religionists in the United States? Of course not; neither Al Qaeda nor its sister organizations have shown any concern for the lives of Muslims. Most victims of terrorism are Muslims in countries where these groups originated. Maybe Friedman has not made the connection yet between Al Qaeda and its victims. He recommends going after Muslims who live in the United States and are U.S. citizens. He prescribes denying Muslims immigration to the United States, which does not make sense unless used only for publicity or demonization.

Crimes committed by a tiny group of political activists from other parts of the world and blaming the coreligionists thousands of miles away is an example of presumption of guilt by association. This is not the first time such a policy has been proposed against a vulnerable group. On this issue, there is a similarity between his suggestions for Muslims and those of Nazi ideologues before the Second World War; they too had recommended curtailing the civil liberties of Jews who were citizens of Germany; many of them had served their country during World War I. Such practices are not confined to fascists; even in the United States, a full-fledged democracy demonized Japanese Americans before locking them up during the Second World War. Friedman should know better; he belongs to a group that was demonized and persecuted only one or two generations ago. *Never again* was the motto of the people who survived the Holocaust. Has Friedman learned a different lesson?

There are many other examples of writers who promote Islamophobia. Judith Miller, another well-known journalist who until recently was associated with *The New York Times*, is also a proponent of the same views, but she presents them from a different perspective. Her book *God Has Ninety-Nine Names* was published in 1996. She presented a picture of Islam which is very much like the Islam that Lewis has portrayed: monolithic, militant (look at the title, but she does not define the criteria on which she asserts that Islam is violent), and enraged at modernity (however, like Lewis, she has presented neither any definition of modernity nor any evidence to substantiate her opinion). Throughout her book, she (like Lewis) suggests that *they* (Islam or Muslims) are a threat to *our civilization*. With *our*, Miller means the United States and Israel, which is essentially the so-called Judeo-Christian civilization of Bernard Lewis. Does she have a point?

Could there be identical political interests of the United States and Israel? Hardly any. Their situation is fundamentally different. The former is a superpower and a democracy; America's interests, being a superpower, are scattered around the globe. Israel is only a regional power, focused on annexing the land in its neighborhood; consequently, it is shunned by its neighbors. Israel's interest is localized within its vicinity. Its guns are directed towards Palestinians. Miller does not acknowledge that Western powers created Israel for European Jews, who were expelled from Europe, which was their homeland for thousands of years. European powers wanted a continent free from Jews.

Consequently, Palestinians, the original inhabitants of the land, had to be displaced to make room for the colonizers, the new arrivals from Europe. Neither does she acknowledge that Israel denies fundamental rights to Palestinians as people – a political reality, which makes Israel's conflict with its neighbors very different from the interests of the United States. This issue has never been mentioned, much less addressed, by Miller in her book.

There are differences between these two authors: Lewis is more sophisticated and knowledgeable about Islam and the Middle East, though his knowledge is limited to Turkey. Nevertheless, he has effectively used his limited knowledge; his writing has an aura of authenticity. It is indeed challenging for a layperson to find inaccuracies in his writings. He is also subtle and sophisticated in presenting his arguments. Miller, on the other hand, is not. She is crude in her approach. Edward Said argues that it is partly because she has hardly acquired any knowledge beyond generality and prevailing conventional wisdom about Islam, but wants to prove that she is the expert on Islam and the Middle East. The fallacy within her arguments can only be compensated by the crude generalization of the victims. Since she has no knowledge of any of the Middle Eastern languages, and her knowledge of Arabic culture does not go beyond the stereotype, she makes numerous elemental errors. It is easier to point out inaccuracies in her articles. Her book is indeed filled with inconsistencies. Edward Said points out a few examples:

> Her [Judith Miller's] other tic is to inform her readers of everyone's religion – such and so is Christian, or Muslim Sunni, Muslim Shi'ite, and so forth. For someone who is so concerned with this particular aspect of life, she is not always accurate, managing even to produce some rather amusing howlers. She speaks of Hisham Sharabi as a 'friend' but misidentifies him as a Christian; he is a Sunni Muslim. Badr el Haj is described as Muslim, where he is a Maronite Christian. These lapses would not be so bad were she not bent on impressing us with her knowingness and her intimacy with so many people.[30]

These is not the only examples of providing incorrect facts to her readers. Her confusion about the religion of individual Arabs may have come from a lack of even a rudimentary understanding of the Arabic language or Arab societies across the Middle East, but she insists that she knows about the Arab world and, of course, about Islam. Is it because the words Haj and Badr represent the symbols of Islam? Haj in Arabic means the pilgrimage to Mecca, which is one of the five pillars of Islam. Badr is the name of the place where the first battle between Muslims and their tormentor, Quraish, had taken place. A far superior army had attacked the Prophet and his followers, but the nascent Muslim community was able to defeat them.

Miller's critics believe that she may have failed to comprehend that an Arab Christian could have a name, which to her, symbolizes Islam. However, these words are not related exclusively to Islam. It is also a part of the entire Arab society and its culture, including that of its Christian and even Jewish segments. The rituals of Haj predate Islam and Badr symbolizes a victory over any powerful enemy in any conflict. The Arabic language is an integral part of the Coptic Church or Eastern Orthodox Christianity and Maronite Christians. After all, Christianity, like Islam, originated in the Arab world, and Jesus was born in Nazareth, a town in Palestine. Jesus, like the Prophet of Islam, was also an Arab and not a white European.

Edward Said questions her intention: why did she write this book? Was it for the love of journalism or for demonizing the so-called enemies of Israel? Or, has she dedicated her professional life to finding the "truth," whatever that means? Edward Said comments:[31]

> The most crucial question about Miller's book is why she wrote it at all. Certainly not out of affection. Consider, for instance, that she admits she fears and dislikes Lebanon, hates Syria, laughs at Libya, dismisses Sudan, feels sorry for and a little alarmed by Egypt, and is repulsed by Saudi Arabia. She has not bothered to learn the language and is relentlessly only concerned with the dangers of organized militancy, which I would hazard a guess accounts for less than 5 percent of the billion-strong Islamic world. She is totally in favor of the violent suppression of Islamists (but not torture and other 'illegal means' used in that suppression: the contradiction in her position seems to have escaped her notice), has no qualms at all about the absence of democratic practices or legal procedures in countries backed by the United States, such as Egypt, Jordan, Syria, and Saudi Arabia so long as Islamists are the target. In one scene related in the book, she actually participates in the prison interrogation of an alleged Muslim terrorist by Israeli policemen, whose systemic use of torture and other questionable procedures (undercover assassination, middle-of-the-night arrests, house demolitions) she politely overlooks as she gets to ask the handcuffed man a few questions of her own.

Still, her book was not challenged in the mainstream media, even by observers professing neutrality; they elected not to mention the errors. Instead, she became a celebrity not only among pro-Israel opinion-makers who control the mainstream media but also among ordinary citizens who get their information from the same source. Thanks to the media, she has been promoted as an "expert" on Islam. There appears to be a credibility gap. Does it reflect the state of the American media? Probably, if we consider that Judith Miller authored the article in *The New York Times* which broke the news that Saddam Hussein was attempting to buy raw material for his nuclear weapon program. This information was later found to be incorrect and, by all accounts, was fabricated.

Nevertheless, the news got international coverage, and she became a star reporter. Her article formed the nucleus on which President Bush built his argument to justify the invasion of Iraq. Consequently, more than 1.5 million people died in Iraq alone.

The common denominator in the writings of Bernard Lewis, Tom Friedman, Judith Miller, and Francis Fukuyama is: not only did they produce Islamophobic literature, but they also got support from the corporate media. They may be the most important and well-known authors, but they are not the only ones to create, propagate, and support Islamophobia. Each of them also generalized 1.8 billion Muslims, demonized them by characterizing Islam and Islamic civilization as violent, and then claimed that democracy and Islam are incompatible. They also claimed that Muslims abhor modernity without substantiating their assertions with facts.

Many other journalists have expressed similar views in their specific style and have continued to do so, even after the collapse of President Bush's policy in Iraq and Afghanistan. The problem with their articles is the same; there were no facts to substantiate their arguments. Here are a few examples to convey the point. These articles were published before 9/11, indicating that the current Islamophobic attitude of the Western media is not the effect of the attack on the World Trade Center; Islamophobia predates 9/11.

Martin Peretz in *The New Republic* (May 7, 1984), describing a play he has seen, writes about Arabs:

> He [the Arab] is intoxicated by language, cannot discern between fantasy and reality, abhors compromise, always blames others for his predicaments, and in the end lances the painful boil of his frustration in a pointless, though a momentarily gratifying act of blood lust … but in the real world it is not he but his 'moderate' brother who is a figment of imagination.

Is it true or a gross generalization about a group of people? I will leave it to readers to make their own opinions. There are 200 million Arabs around the world. Ten percent of them are Christians. Does the Arabic language also intoxicate them? Does every Arab *always* blame others for his predicament?

Peter Rodman in *The National Review* (May 11, 1992):

> yet now the West finds itself challenged from the outside by a militant, atavistic force driven by hatred of all Western political thought, harking back to age-old grievances against Christendom.

Rodman neither reveals how and why he is using the specific adjectives "militant" and "atavistic" for Islam, nor does he present his reasons for claiming that Muslims are "driven by hatred for the West." If so, how many of the 1.5–1.8 billion of them are driven by hatred, and how many of them are driven by the fact that they have hardly any access to the resources of their land, which is being exploited by others? Peter Rodman has been presented as an expert on Islam.

Daniel Pipes in *National Interests* (Fall 1995) writes:

> [Islam] is closer in spirit to other such movements (communism, fascism) than to traditional religion … Like communism and fascism, it offers a vanguard ideology; a complete program to improve man and to create a new society; complete control over that society; and cadres ready and even eager to spill blood.

However, Pipes presents neither any supportive evidence to show that Islam (which has no hierarchy) has the infrastructure spread around the world to support and train "cadres" for violence, nor any comparisons with other civilizations.

Milton Viorst writes:

> Islam succeeded where Christianity failed in shackling man's power of reasoning, Muslims both Arabs and Turks readily acknowledge that judged by a range of intellectual criteria, their civilization does not measure up to that of the West, or there is basic antagonism to creative thinking that has come increasingly to characterize Islam.[32]

Once again, Viorst does not mention Islam's notable contributions to science, astronomy, mathematics, or philosophy. Viorst, like Lewis, never fails to claim that he is a great fan of the accomplishments of the past, although he uses vitriolic words for Arabs and Islam.

These are just a few examples of Western journalists, academicians, and authors who have been very vocal in portraying Islam as a violent religion. Notably, almost all these people started to share their version or interpretation of Islam at the same time when Lewis and Huntington came up with their articles and books. Further, their ideas may not have become the mainstream views at the time these articles were written, or people may not have believed that all Muslims are violent, but in the context of general apathy in the United States towards Islam (and for many other cultures and "civilizations"), these views were presented and accepted as facts. They have occupied more space than other views about Islam. In the wake of September 11, 2001, these views have become omnipresent in the Western media. It appears that these views are by no means exceptions in the political climate of the West in the twenty-first century. Other views have become dormant, if not non-existent, and have been pushed out of the mainstream media. They are seen only in alternative channels such as Links TV, Free Speech TV, Democracy Now, or RT.

These views that occupy the mainstream media have one significant tendency in common: they promote personal opinions as facts. The omissions of specific facts and the presentation of selective data to promote their ideas are the hallmark of many articles written by them. Muslims are usually presented in their writings as violent people who are a source of danger to the West in general and to the United States in particular. Almost all of them include Israel as part of the West and make it a point to use the term *Judeo-Christian* (and not *Christian*) civilization. Prominent authors, journalists, and academicians from one part of the political spectrum present the same arguments but with different perspectives. Presented here are titles of articles to substantiate the argument that portraying Islam as violent has not been based on objective and authentic data. No comparison has been presented:[33] Daniel Pipes, "The Muslims are coming! The Muslims are coming," *National Review*; "There are no Moderates: Dealing with Fundamentalist Islam," *The National Interest*; Elaine Sciolino, "The Red Menace is Gone. But here is Islam," *The New York Times*; Judith Miller, "Is Islam a Threat," *Foreign Affairs*; David Pryce Jones, *The Closed Circle* (Harper Collins) and *At War with Modernity: Islam's Challenge to the West* (Alliance Publishers); Charles Krauthammer, "The Crescent of Crisis: The Global Intifada," *Washington Post*; Peter Rodman, "Don't Look for Moderates in the Islamic Revolution," *International Herald Tribune*; Fergus Borderline, "A Holy War Heads Our Way," *Readers Digest*; Patrick Sookhdeo, "Prince Charles Is Wrong – Islam Does Menace the West," *The Daily Telegraph*; Amos Perlmutter, "Wishful Thinking About Fundamentalism," *Washington Post*; Michael Youssef, *Revolt against Modernity: Muslim Zealots and the West* (Brill); Sam Huntington, "Will More Countries Become Democratic," in *Global Dilemmas* (University Press of America); Martin Kramer, "Islam versus Democracy," *Commentary*.

Note the titles. All of them suggest a relationship of violence with the symbols of Islam such as Jihad, Holy War, Islamic terror, terrorism, *intifada*, suicide squad, or Islamic fundamentalism. Are they describing Islam objectively way or creating myths about Muslims? These are subjective opinions, which these authors have the right to have. However, none of their articles are backed by facts; they rely on anecdotal events, yet they found space in respected newspapers. Some articles and books on this topic started appearing in the West after the Iranian revolution and became an avalanche after the Soviet Union retreated from Afghanistan. Indeed, these are not isolated examples. John Esposito documents many more similar articles.[34] In his book *The Islamic Threat*, he points out:

> Belief in the impending clash between the Muslim world and the West was reflected in America and Europe by headlines such as 'A Holy War Heads Our Way,' 'Jihad in America,' 'Focus: Islamic Terror: Global Suicide Squad,' 'I believe in Islamophobia,' 'Algerians in London Fund Islamic Terrorism,' and 'France Back on the Rack' in which the author observed in the wake of the Air France hijacking:

Are such views benign? Of course not. Are they irrelevant? I will argue that they are not. Subsequent events suggest that these words serve a purpose. They were designed to create myths about Islam, which were used to justify violence against half a dozen Muslim countries. Oversimplification of issues forms generalization and stereotyping; both help to promote and foster derogatory views about intended victims. The first step in generalizing Muslim societies was to present them as a monolithic entity. It portrayed Muslims as uniquely *others*; all other steps help to oversimplify any complex issue and to hide the real reason for a particular violent conflict, which invariably has a contemporary and local cause.

There are attempts by neoconservative authors to hide those issues behind these articles. It is accomplished by providing a vague and generalized version of the conflicts between the West and Muslim-majority countries. This point is exemplified by the article, "The Crescent of Crisis: Global Intifada." It is an example of how distorting a local issue by anecdotal events in a distant world can be used to manipulate opinions in the West. This article was written by Charles Krauthammer, who, like other neocon writers, was also a vigorous defender of Israel's interests. He worked for the *Washington Post,* which its critics describe as serving the so-called *deep state.* It represents people who control mega-corporations.[35]

In this article, Krauthammer argues that *history is being driven by another force as well: the political reawakening of the Islamic world*, which he claims is more dangerous because it is pan-Islamic and global. His arguments follow the same pattern as those of Lewis and Huntington: promoting his personal opinion as a fact (that Muslims are violent) without substantiating these assertions with arguments or data. Like Lewis, Krauthammer also presents the entire Muslim population as a single monolithic unit and generalizes about one-quarter of the world's population. However, shared political views on every issue of almost sixty Muslim countries from three continents in different stages of economic development with every imaginable racial group cannot be possible, except in the paranoid world of the ardent supporters of Zionism. This concept hides the primary reason for the Arab–Israeli conflict: annexation of the Palestinian land by Israeli settlers.

Whatever the reason behind his arguments, Krauthammer wants everyone to believe that Israel's conflict with Palestinians is not about the annexation of Palestinian land. He has attempted to use the image and impression of the so-called resentment and anger of the entire Muslim world towards the United States. His argument that the Islamic world, from Indonesia to Morocco and from Chechnya to Mozambique, has embarked upon violent uprisings against the West just because all of them are Muslim. Like Tunku Varadarajan,[36] he argued that being Muslim automatically makes them prone to be violent and they become possessed by anti-Western and anti-modern sentiments. Many authors have expressed similar views, such as Hirsch Goodman, Martin Peretz, Patrick Sookhdeo, Daniel Pipes, and others.

Indeed, monolithic, misogynist, and anti-democratic Islam is a recurrent Western myth, which is just not true. So, why does such myth-making take place in the Western media? The answer is simple: promoting such ideas in a society where these authors live and make a living has a purpose. The creation of an imaginary monolithic Islam leads to a religious reductionism that views political conflicts in Iraq, Iran, Syria, Sudan, Lebanon, Pakistan, Afghanistan, Bosnia, and Azerbaijan in primarily religious terms as "Islamic-Christian conflicts." However, there is more to it than a simple explanation. John Esposito points out a probable reason behind Krauthammer's effort:[37]

> Talk of a 'global intifada' also distracts and detracts from the nature and real causes of discontent in the Palestinian intifada by implying that it was merely part of a transnational Islamic uprising rather than an Arab Israeli problem. The intifada was first and foremost an uprising of Arabs, both Muslim and Christian. The primary cause of the intifada was not Islam or Islamic fundamentalism but continued Israeli occupation of the West Bank and Gaza and the desperation of young Palestinians in particular.

Charles Krauthammer is a staunch defender of Israel's settlement policies in the occupied territories and entirely built enterprise on confiscated Palestinian land. By definition, these settlements are colonization, an outdated political strategy, which peaked in the late nineteenth century. Since then, overt colonialism has been in retreat; but it has been replaced by covert colonialism, described as neo-liberal neocolonialism. Today, Palestine is the only country occupied and colonized by people from other countries (European Jews, who as a group perished during the Holocaust). Krauthammer also ignores the fact that colonialism was the single biggest cause of violence in entire human history. Those whose land is being colonized have no option but to resist. Consequently, colonized subjects have to pay a heavy price in terms of lives and properties.

One way to understand Krauthammer's article is to view it from the perspective of his goal to influence Americans. Since American support is vital for the confiscation of land that belongs to Palestinians, blaming non-existent "global" forms of *intifada* is an attempt to obfuscate the issue of forceful seizure of Palestinian land. That land grab, which is the most important, if not the only reason for the Arab and Muslim resentment against Israel and the United States, is being overshadowed by side issues, which are irrelevant and distracting. Indeed, it is convenient for Krauthammer or other supporters of Israel's policy of annexation of Palestinian land to portray the confrontation between Israel and Palestine with abstract ideas. Former colonial masters used similar arguments.

Is Krauthammer attempting to confuse the primary issue, which is the ongoing confiscation of Palestinian land? The main point of contention in the occupied territories of Palestine is neither religion nor so-called historical animosity. The conflict is based on the contemporary event: a small group of people from another part of the world have forcefully taken over the land on which indigenous people were living for thousands of years. It was possible with the help of powerful countries and because the occupiers had better weapons. Palestinians, who are the most disenfranchised people of the world, are resisting by whatever means possible the gradual and ongoing takeover of their land by Israelis. Their effort has remained ineffective so far. Israel's annexation policy of the Palestinian land is supported by powerful real-estate moguls of the United States. They have put up massive amounts of money in real-estate ventures in the occupied territories.[38]

The mainstream media have ignored this aspect of the Palestinian conflict, but the plight of Palestinians is on the screen every day; that has not been forgotten by the Muslim world. On the contrary, it is a sore point with them. Krauthammer's arguments form the basis of the justification of violence against Palestinians, who are the weakest segment of the Israeli society. The same ideas apply to other nations that raise their voice against the mighty West in other conflicts. Denying the actual issue of land and its resources, which is at the root of all violent conflicts between the two so-called civilizations, can absolve the West if it is believed by the tax-payers that Muslims are violent, emotional, and irrational.[39] Such attempts are not new, as Edward Said has argued in *Orientalism*. James Piscatori also points out the trends of the last two centuries.[40]

> Whether it was the Ottoman attempt to thwart Christian nationalists or the Muslim attempt to gain independence from the West, Islam was fanatical because it ran counter to imperial interests. However, it was the converse formulation that became the standard explanation of Muslim conduct: Islam was hostile to the West because it was fanatical …. Consequently, Muslims came to be seen as a uniformly emotional and sometimes illogical race that moved as one body and spoke with one voice.

Krauthammer's global *intifada* should be viewed from the perspective of controlling the land and resources of other countries. The problem is compounded by the fact that there is a lack of a proper understanding of a cause-and-effect relationship between these two factors – violent conflicts in Muslim-majority countries and the religion of Islam. Violent clashes were directly related to colonialism and foreign occupation in the past; they are not related to religion. All religious groups were equally affected. However, these confrontations have been presented by these neocon political activists as violence with Islamic civilization; however, non-Islamic countries, if occupied, behaved similarly in the past. These authors have not mentioned conflicts between the West and the non-Muslim world.

A clash of civilizations between Islam and the West has become a self-fulfilling prophecy. John Esposito, in his book, *The Islamic Threat*, observes:[41]

> Political Islam now appears in the Western eyes, as the new villain, successor to communism and the evil empire; nowhere more than there do Islamists themselves, or their extreme factions, deem themselves so viscerally, so genetically at war with another civilization – that of unbelievers, the Crusaders, the Jews.

Was it any different in the past? Not, according to Esposito. He cites two examples – both were written after the First World War.[42] One of them was the Italian Orientalist Leone Caetani who described the so-called Muslim resentment against the West after the First World War when Turkey was defeated and its Arab provinces were incorporated into European empires. Resistance, both violent and non-violent, followed. Caetani describes the turmoil in the Middle East after the First World War (1918) as follows:

> The convulsion has shaken the Islamic and Oriental civilization to its foundation. The entire Oriental world, from China to the Mediterranean, is in ferment. Everywhere the hidden fire of anti-European hatred is burning. Riots in Morocco, risings in Algiers, discontent in Tripoli, so-called Nationalist attempts in Egypt, Arabia, and Libya are different manifestations of the same deep sentiment and have their objective the rebellion of the Oriental world against European civilization.[43]

The description of the turmoil in the Middle East of a century ago is similar to what is happening today. Caetani either ignored the facts or did not understand that annexation and colonization would invariably fuel resentment, irrespective of the religion of the victims. There is hardly any difference between Caetani's century-old explanation and the reasons given by Lewis, Friedman, Krauthammer, and other neocon activists in the twenty-first century. After the First World War, almost 95% of the Muslim World was taken over by the West for one reason or the other. Only four Muslim countries remained independent, but only nominally, after the Allied Powers had divided the world among themselves; they were Turkey, Saudi Arabia, Iran, and Afghanistan. Violence was the consequence of colonialism. Citizens of the occupied countries gave determined resistance to their respective colonial powers. Did non-Muslim groups, which were also occupied by the West, behave any differently? Of course not; they were equally determined to overthrow colonial powers such as in South Africa, Zimbabwe, Kenya, India, Vietnam, and South and Central America.

Caetani, like Lewis and Krauthammer, did not consider that colonizing the entire Middle East, displacing millions of people from their ancestral land, and exterminating a large number of people, could be the reasons for their resentment. However, Caetani could be forgiven as his arguments may be considered the *Zeitgeist* of the early twentieth century. "Might is right" was the established policy of the colonial era. Occupying other countries was deemed to be normal behavior for powerful countries. Caetani and other orientalists were breathing air that was laced with the concept of the innate superiority of the West.

Should neoconservatives be excused for being baffled at the Palestinian resistance? They may believe that they have already won the battle of Palestine. However, history shows that the victory in battles for the Holy Land is only temporary; rulers come and go, but the local population remains anchored to the land. The inhabitants may be terrorized and demonized, but they stay put, as they have nowhere to go.

Caetani was not alone in expressing such views. Not many people opposed massacres in the past in various colonies. Even Maxim Rodinson, a noted French Marxist, and Alex Tocqueville, a staunch defender of democracy, were no different. They were also silent on the atrocities committed by enlightened democratic nations in their colonies. However, it is easy to understand men like

Caetani; they were the byproduct of their time. They believed in the subjugation of other people as the progress of humankind as long as Europeans were not at the receiving end of violence. The outlook of their world was based on their conviction of the superiority of the white race.[44]

In contrast, the current supporters of Israel's settlement policies belong to the twenty-first century. It is hard to understand the logic behind justifying the subjugation of other people today. Israel is a colonial power, and its creation was the product of colonial mentality. Today, Israel is the only country that occupies lands belonging to other countries. Besides, Israel came into existence only after the First World War, when the colonial system was at its peak even though its demise had already begun. The world of Orientalists, neoliberals, and neoconservatives has been caught in a time warp; it has not changed with time even though the rest of the world has moved beyond colonialism and the justification of confiscation of alien land by powerful nations.

To sum up, this brief review of the literature demonstrates that the current discussion on an association of Islam with violence in the popular media has not followed the basic principle of evidence-based arguments. On the contrary, these discussions have defied every rule of logic. An inference has been deduced at the onset of debates (that Islam is violent or "more" violent), and then attempts were made in the discussion to prove their assumptions as facts. Many of those who are the proponents of an association of violence with Islam belong to special interest groups; they are at the forefront in promoting lopsided theories, which are based on a few anecdotal examples, cherry-picked events, and casual observations.

Demonizing Muslims was a well-coordinated plan which was set long before 9/11 or the first set of bombs were dropped; its execution was flawless. Lewis set the tone with his article in *The Atlantic Monthly*; others supported him, taking a single aspect of Lewis's argument and expanding it to create specific myths about Islam. The result was that a group of people acting in unison presented specific views in a symphony with a compounding effect. The contents of the articles of individual writers and political activists supplemented the idea that Muslims are violent. The mainstream media supported these authors in their endeavors. They found space in the mainstream media; at the same time, those who opposed their views found it difficult, if not impossible, to present their views, which also had a multiplier effect.

The miracles of fake news

The preceding pages present an analysis of the neoconservative hypothesis that promotes the notion that Muslims are violent. It documents how their arguments were based on gross generalization, selective omission of facts, cherry-picked data, unsubstantiated facts, and phony news. Simply put, their statements were based on opinions, innuendos, and rumors; fake news has a distinct dynamic separate from actual news. They are created to cause misinformation. Notwithstanding, fake news goes through the same pathway that all news follows. There is nothing unique about how neoconservative ideas spread in the last three decades. Fake news based on imagined facts has always been a part of human societies, but the disbursement and propagation of this type of news and information have taken a pandemic form in the twenty-first century. Today, there is hardly any society that is free from this disease.

Misinformation has always been used as a tool for selling commercial products, influencing voters, and garnering support for government policies, but now it has reached a pandemic stage, bordering on hysteria. Edward Bernays first described the process in his book *Propaganda*, which was published after the First World War.[45] He had spectacular successes in marketing products and propagating government policies. However, there is a difference. Today, even a smaller group of people can initiate fake news, which can have a cascade of reactions with troublesome implications in many directions. Earlier, only larger groups such as nations or mega-corporations had the means to use this tool, but now smaller groups can achieve similar results. This change has come from the availability of social media to ordinary consumers.

Fake news, like any idea, spreads from person to person, but how fast an idea or rumor would travel depends upon the connectivity of those who are spreading the information, false or otherwise.[46] The spreading of ideas or news follows the sine curve; so does the spread of malicious news. There is an initial lag phase, followed by a fast uptake, and then it slows down as the effect reaches a plateau. In the first phase, consumers of news, the targeted groups, are primed with unsubstantiated facts so that neurons in brains get familiarized with concepts. Its dispersion in this stage is a gradual process. The *credibility* of the originators of ideas (primary nodes) and their position in the community (*degree of centrality*) are the two most essential factors in percolating the concept among a larger audience.

Lewis first presented his hypothesis in 1990. It was followed by Huntington's article "The Clash of Civilizations?" in 1993, and then his book. It took more than a decade for his notions to become mainstream in the United States. This was the lag phase of the neoconservative movements. This is not unusual. Gandhi's concept of non-violence had its origin in the 1900s while he was in South Africa, struggling against the Apartheid regime. It took him close to two decades before he was able to launch his first non-cooperation movement. Communism had a more extended lag period.

The neoconservative movement's success in demonizing Islamic civilization is owed to its originators, Lewis and Huntington. They were ideally placed to spread and legitimize their hypotheses even though they were based on unsubstantiated facts; they had the credibility; both were academicians attached to the ivy-league universities, prolific writers with a large following, had a reputation as thinkers and intellectuals, and were well connected to the academia, bureaucracy, political parties, corporations, and the mainstream media. These institutions not only supported their concept but also managed the spread of their views. Their effort was supported by the think-tank industry that had evolved into an assertive foreign policy establishment in the United States. Their network had become power-brokers; they have become the establishment.

In the second phase, the spreading of the neoconservative views from one node to the other is faster than it is for accurate information; it is due to the presence of a larger number of second and third tiers of writers and activists and feedback loops among them. They had played a vital role in promoting the current atmosphere of Islamophobia. Their numbers had been increasing gradually after the publication of "The Roots of Muslim Rage" and *The Clash of Civilizations*. A decade later, the number of writers and activists affiliated with the neoconservative movement increased significantly.

Moreover, Islamophobia activists were organized and showed a centralized structure to their campaign. During this period, think-tanks, which had mushroomed in Washington DC, gave a boost to their campaign. Their focus has been Israel; many of the writers were Israeli citizens and showed open support to Israel's annexation policy. By 2000, the neoconservative movement had taken over the executive branch as well; Dick Cheney, who belonged to the military-industrial complex and the inner circle of neoconservative campaign to invade Iraq, had maneuvered himself into the position of Vice President. He played a vital role in America's energy and the Middle East policies of the Bush administration (2000–2008).[47]

In the final phase, the propagation of concepts slows down; its effect plateaus as it reaches the highest achievable level. It can go no further, and it does not need to spread exponentially; its impact can be sustained by maintaining a *status quo* with minimal effort. The *closeness* among writers and activists plays a more critical role in sustaining the spread of news, fake or otherwise. The pro-Zionism networking of writers, lobbyists, media, the corporate world, and political parties had expanded in the second decade of the twenty-first century, but anti-Islamic opinions are seldom seen in major newspapers or media outlets. That does not mean that Islamophobia is absent or receding; on the contrary, it is getting more robust with time; it is still omnipresent but remains invisible. It merely requires a minor trigger point to explode.

For example, Nathan Lean, in his book, *The Islamophobia Industry*, documents that suspicion of Islam and hatred for Muslims were at the peak after 9/11 and increased with the invasion of Iraq (2003). It was the topic of discussion; after the invasion was complete, the media showed restraints on the expression of overt anti-Muslim rhetoric. That changed around 2010. Lean credits the change to a tiny group of pro-Israel activists; they created a new wave of Islamophobia in the country. They picked up the opening of an Islamic Center in New York near the World Trade Center as a trigger point.[48] Others chimed in; suddenly, Islamophobia became an issue again. They used the opening of mosques and Islamic community centers in portraying that Muslims are taking over the country.

Prejudice sticks: so does Islamophobia and racism

How did a small group of anti-Muslim activists inflame so much hatred a decade after 9/11? Researchers who study how ideas spread have the answer to this enigma. Those who have propagated such views were still active, but they were not visible. Islamophobia warriors were lurking under the surface; they could come out in the open any time if needed, and they did – some for personal gains, others due to their conviction. Think-tanks, which had played a vital role in the first and second phases, played an equally active role in the third phase. However, their plan of action changed, as they merely needed to sustain the prevailing view. For that, activists use sublime strategies to keep the issue at the forefront. That was easy as they already had an army of writers and organizers who could be deployed at will. Once in a while, there will be a news item or fake news that stokes the impression that Muslims are violent, which is sufficient to keep the violent images of Muslims alive in the Western perception.

Implicit biases: racism and Islamophobia

Today, the stereotyping of Muslims as violent may have reached a plateau. The effort of those who promote the concept has receded into the background; their action is invisible, and is being maintained with minimal effort. Notwithstanding, Islamophobia will keep polluting virgin minds. If the prevalence of racism against African Americans in the West is any indication, it will take a long time to eradicate discrimination against Muslims. Similarities between anti-Muslimism and racism are a poignant reminder of the sticky nature of fake news, gossips, rumors, innuendos, and, consequently, misperception, prejudice, and discrimination.

In recent years, there has been soul searching about racism in the West; research is being done to find the reason behind the prevalence of racism and its impact on people of color. African Americans are not the only victims of racism; it has affected the entire nation. In her book, *The New Jim Crow Laws*, Michelle Alexander documents that the stereotyping of African Americans in its virulent form is two or three centuries old;[49] Sven Lindqvist confirmed her assessment. He traces the demonization of Africans as subhuman to a small group of mid-nineteenth-century intellectuals headed by Richard Knox.[50] Lindqvist further argues that xenophobia is natural, but its virulent form, such as racism, is acquired; he also documents how racist literature started appearing in Britain during the early nineteenth century to fight anti-slavery campaigns, which were gaining strength in Britain.[51]

The campaigns were successful in abolishing slavery in Britain. Theirs was an uphill battle; they met strong resistance within the British society; slavery was a lucrative business in the United States and Britain.[52] Transnational corporations were involved in the slave trade – the banking and insurance industries, shipbuilding, transportation, plantation owners and management, and other sectors of the British economy. They formed the nucleus of the slavery-industrial complex. These institutions were making profits from slavery and the slave trade. However, the main problem was that many ordinary citizens also owned slaves. Their pension plans included slaves in a distant land; this made the passage of anti-slavery bills cumbersome.

Transnational companies bought and sold slaves for their clients and rented them to plantation owners; they also managed various aspects of the slavery-industrial complex. Slavery had transformed into a world of its own within the larger world order of the colonial system; they had developed sophisticated justification of inhuman treatment of slaves based on morality; for that, they had to change its definition. Owning slaves became similar to owning stocks and bonds; the owners received dividends from renting slaves. Dividends paid to stockholders by asset-management corporations in the twenty-first century are identical. The business of slavery looked benign from a distance; the owners did not see the use of whips or hear the banging of chains tied to the neck, legs, and hands. However, they received timely checks and dividends. The anti-slavery initiative was challenging the pocketbooks of those who were dependent on the income from renting slaves.

Pro-slavery ideologues began their campaign in the nineteenth century to counter the influence of anti-slavery pioneers. They got the reprieve, as slavery was abolished in Britain, but the slave trade, which was equally profitable for the British companies, continued until the United States (1863) and Brazil (1888) abolished slavery. Brazil was the largest importer of slaves; close to 40% of Africans were destined for Brazil. Therefore, despite the abolition of slavery in Britain, the slave trade, which had a devastating impact on Africa, went on for decades; the burden of the slave-trading is still visible. The West had benefited from slave labor. They built the infrastructure of the United States, Britain, France, and other slave-trading nations. Billions of dollars went into the British, American, and European economies. Slavery and the slave trade transformed Europe into the First World. As noted by Mike Davis, slavery laid the foundation of the Industrial Revolution.[53] It also jumpstarted the most brutal form of capitalism.

The main argument to justify slavery was that Europeans belonged to a superior race, and Africans were not even human; they were branded subhuman, a species between *Homo sapiens* and primates. Many Europeans believed it.[54] Furthermore, they argued that God had created people of color to serve white people; therefore, it was morally acceptable to capture Africans, with violence, of course, and use them as slaves.[55] Similar arguments were used to justify colonialism and the servitude of colonial subjects. Lynching, which was used to terrorize victims into silence, was also justified on similar principles. The campaign to legitimize slavery was replaced by justifying indentured labor and sharecropping. It remained on an upward trajectory even in the twentieth century. Prejudice against Africans reached a plateau in the late twentieth century. The civil-rights movement challenged the Jim Crow law, which was finally removed, at least on paper, by the latter half of the twentieth century. However, its impact is present. It is visible to those who are aware of it; its effect is oblivious to the rest. In other words, racism sticks; once it has put its tentacles in a society, it is difficult to eradicate.

In recent years, the mainstream media have neither published racist literature nor openly supported groups that promote the racial superiority of whites. That is not the case with anti-Muslim ideologies. Similarly, in the last half century, hardly any literature appeared in the mainstream media promoting the superiority of the white race. However, that does not mean that racism has receded.

It has persisted in different forms; discrimination against blacks persists because racism is lucrative for businesses. Alexander argues that mass incarceration of African Americans is another manifestation of racism,[56] which shows its resilience because racism benefits groups belonging to the prison-industrial complex.

She argues that racism is ingrained in the system; it is now implicit. Police shootings of unarmed African Americans, which until recently were hidden from scrutiny, are another example of racism. Now, shootings cannot remain obscure, as they are being streamed on social media. The demeanor of police officers after the shooting unarmed civilians, who are disproportionately people of color and poor, is an indication of implicit racism. Since less than 5% of offending officers are indicted by the court of law, it confirms systemic racism. Ava Duverney has documented the same in her documentary titled *13th*.[57] Chris Hedges argues that there is hardly any segment in a Western society free from racism despite many reforms. They have not been able to eradicate racism.

How about prejudice against Muslims? Would it also be as sticky? Racism has lasted in its most brutal form well over a century after the abolition of slavery. How long will Islamophobia last? We do not know, but the similarity between the two cannot be ignored. The effects of anti-Muslim policies in their most severe form have already lasted for two decades. Invasions and bombings of Iraq, Syria, Libya, Somalia, and Afghanistan have decimated these countries; they may not have been ideal nations by Western definition, but these were functioning societies; they have been destroyed. Discrimination against African Americans in the past was justified on arguments that they are inherently savages; therefore, blacks cannot be given the same privileges that a white person is entitled to have from society. Similarly, neoconservative activists have advanced arguments against Muslims that they are inherently violent;[58] they are not going to change, therefore, they should be dealt with a superior force.

The similarities between racism and Islamophobia and its implications suggest that there is more to stereotyping a group of people who are weak but sitting on precious resources. The world cannot effectively oppose the demonization of the most vulnerable segments of humanity by simple measures and empty slogans. Prejudice against blacks has been enduring. Is it going to be any different with the followers of Islam? Not until we explore the cause and extent of the problem and take actions to stop it.

Misinformation, misperception, deception, and attitude

An essential concept in spreading ideas, malicious or benign, or real, or false, is that fake news is designed to cause misinformation, which in turn may cause misperception, but not always. At the same time, not all misperceptions are caused by misinformation.[59] Exposures to misinformation do not invariably result in misperception. That explains why many non-Muslims have resisted Islamophobia and opposed anti-Muslim rhetoric, whereas others have followed the neoconservative hypothesis. Many opponents of neoconservative and neo-liberal intellectuals are non-Muslims, such as Edward Said, Noam Chomsky,

Amartya Sen, Yvon Haddad, Deepa Kumar, Steven Sheehi, Robert Fisk, Arundhati Roy, and many more.

Misinformation can be corrected, but correction of misperception is complicated and cumbersome, at least during the later stages. Even if misinformation is corrected, it does not mean that people's perception about the objects of misinformation would revert to a neutral position; on the contrary, they can continue to harbor a negative attitude towards an idea or a person who has been the victim of negative stereotyping. If so, those who believe in anti-Muslimism would continue to harbor misperceptions about Muslims. Similarly, Muslims who believe that the West is demonizing Islam as violent to justify the conquest of their land would not change their mind.

Why? Emily Thorson of Syracuse University has an answer that is based on science. She has shown that exposure to misinformation, fake or otherwise, can cause changes in the attitude that persists even among those who do not believe in misinformation and even if they accept that the news was fake. For example, if a celebrity is charged with a heinous crime, which is later found to be concocted, and even if a court of law subsequently acquits him or her, the accused may still carry the stigma of that crime. Regardless of the verdict, even by due process, people tend to dislike the celebrity in question.

Furthermore, correcting misinformation is not effective in the long run, as the perception reverts to the baseline.[60] For example, some examples of the prevalent misinformation in the United States are that President Obama is a Muslim, and that he was not born in America; Saddam Hussein, the Iraqi President, had acquired weapons of mass destruction (WMDs) and had helped Osama bin Laden to attack the World Trade Center; Hillary Clinton, the Democratic Party's candidate for the presidency, was running a pedophile ring based in a Pizza Parlor in the Washington DC area; and the 2020 election was stolen from President Trump. These claims were proven to be false; they were based on fake news and deliberately created. Notwithstanding, highly educated and intelligent people still believe the above narrative even though the government has refuted the misinformation. Consequently, many continue to carry misperceptions.

One of the above examples has also been studied in depth by social scientists. There has been lingering confusion about the birthplace of President Obama. He was born in Hawaii to a Kenyan father and an American mother. Still, many Republicans were promoting the notion that Obama was born outside the country. That would have made him ineligible for the office of the presidency. Specific news channels, which cater to right-wing audiences, promoted this notion before the 2008 election that brought him to the White House. President Trump also made this an issue in 2016 during his election campaign. The assertion was false. Since the President of the United States can only be a native-born citizen, officials had examined his birth certificate at the time of filing for the candidacy. Notwithstanding, it became such an issue that in 2011 President Obama had to release his birth certificate to show that he was born in the United States. How did people react?

Opinion polls showed that before the release of his birth certificate, only 55% of Americans thought that President Obama was born in the United States; the rest (45%) either believed that he was born out of the country or were not sure of his birthplace. Another survey was taken soon after his birth certificate was released. The researchers asked the responders the same questions. The result showed a 17% increase in the number of people who believed that President Obama was born in the U.S. The responders were asked the same questions a third time a year later. This time, only 57% believed that he was born in the United States. In other words, 15% of people reverted to their initial position months later, even after looking at the facts. Less than 4% believed or ignored the birth certificate that proved that President Obama was born in the United States. There was even a slight increase (2%) within the group who thought that President Obama was born outside the country. Inference: facts alone are no guarantee of objectivity.

The impression about his place of birth went back to the baseline even though facts were provided, which suggests that fake news sticks in the memory. Scientists opine that this is due to a phenomenon called *belief echo*. Once an impression has been created, it does not melt away. Likeminded people tend to flock together to exchange ideas, but not all aspects of ideas. People narrow the topic of discussions on strengthening their polarized views and block arguments of the opponents irrespective of facts or validity of their opponents' views. In the context of President Obama's birth controversy, people believed what they earlier believed. The release of his birth certificate did not change their perception. It was true in all groups that were surveyed – independents, Republicans, and Democrats. But why?

Ian McCulloch of Johns Hopkins University argues that misperceptions do not change; it is a universal phenomenon and is not confined to a single event. How can that be explained? A similar dynamic is seen regarding the perception of Muslims being violent; that perception has proven to be equally enduring. There are many examples of persisting misperceptions about the Muslim world. For instance, before the invasion of Iraq, a majority of Americans believed that the Iraqi President had acquired WMDs, but no such weapons were found. This fact was accepted by the Kay Commission set up to look into why the decision of invasion was taken on claims made by questionable sources.

The Bush administration eventually conceded that Iraq had no WMDs and was not planning to acquire them. Be that as it may, a significant number of Americans still believe that Iraq either had or was about to acquire WMDs.[61] Furthermore, those who have been radicalized with Islamophobia were more likely to believe that Iraq had WMDs or that Muslims are killing Americans or are violent. They are specific subsets of Evangelical Christians, groups of supporters of President Trump, and a small group of military personnel. A tiny subgroup within this group had taken violent actions against Muslims, such as bombing mosques or shooting Muslims. They also justified their actions by claiming that Muslims are planning to destroy America.

Why have false notions about Islam and Muslims persisted in the American psyche? Similar perceptions of Muslims have found a space in other parts of the Western world, India, and Israel. However, not all Indians and Israelis were polarized. Why? The answer lies with how the human brain processes information.

Research on human perception has advanced significantly in recent years. Ian McCulloch, a social scientist, has divided the process of perception formation into three distinct stages: a) an initial phase in which priming of neurons with new information and ideas takes place; it is processed at a center located in the medial prefrontal lobe (front and middle). b) The phase of opinion formation: this is the stage of analysis; it takes place at an adjacent center which is also in the prefrontal lobe, but it is a different center. Finally, there is c) the phase of polarization: in this stage, the ideas become firm; the process occurs at a different center, where information is stored; it is located at the lateral prefrontal lobe.

The third center can neither analyze concepts nor process information, whether new or old; it can only hold information after it has been analyzed in the second center and sent there to be stored. The arguments used to explore the validity of the concept taking place in the second center have no impact on the third location. Another function of this center is to defend its position. It does this by devising methods and arguments to protect their stored ideas. It functions as an echo chamber; similar opinions are collected and analyzed, and repeated with the single purpose of strengthening the formed positions. It evaluates the opponents' views to develop counterarguments. The third center is ready to fight back any arguments against its existing position.

The role of malicious nodes in spreading fake news

Can the physiological process taking place in these three centers explain the success of neoconservative ideologues in propagating ideas even though they had presented false information? Why couldn't their opponents succeed in challenging the neoconservative positions with fact-based arguments? Why could other thinkers, equally brilliant and able, not be able to change the perception of ordinary citizens? Information about how the human brain analyzes, stores, and defends its position may answer some of the above questions.

First and foremost, those who spread fake news have an advantage over their adversaries. Time acts in their favor. They choose the timing of when and where to present their arguments; their opponents do not have that luxury, they can only react. By the time the opponents have found space to present their views, enough time may have passed that misinformation has gone through the first two stages and is already stored perception in a polarized form in the third center. The brain, which was open to new ideas had it been in the early stages, is closed to counterarguments.

For example, the hypothesis that Islam is violent was first presented in 1990 by Bernard Lewis. This was followed in 1993 by an article by Sam Huntington in the magazine *Foreign Affairs*. By the time Edward Said, John Esposito, and others could present counterarguments, two years had already gone by, and

Americans' perception had taken a firm position in favor of neoconservative ideologues. Even though neoconservative claims were based on concocted data and unverifiable facts, the advantage went in their favor. As noted, their claims are not based on scientific data. However, since their opponents were fighting polarized brains, they could not change the prevailing attitudes even though facts were in their favor.

Second, fake news, which is analogous to gossip, is juicy; it satisfies carnal pleasure; therefore, it is well received by people. Moreover, gossip travels faster than real news, which is dull and stale. McCulloch gives the following analogy: by the time fact or accurate information is tying its shoes to get out in the real world, fake news has crossed half the world. Gossip is also stickier. It attracts more attention than factual news; it is because the former acts on the pleasure center of the brain, which is the location where opioids act.[62] Those who spread gossip or innuendo appear to take an interest in what is going on in and around them become insiders; those who shun gossip may remain outsiders and may even be ostracized from the clique. Spreading fake news is both an art and science; it requires social skills. Those who are at the forefront of propagating Islamophobia belong to a small network of activists; they are well connected, may have better people skills, and understand how social media works.

Simply put, no matter how valid the argument is or how elegantly it was presented, science tells us that the opponents will fail to change the mind of readers and audiences by mere analysis of data in any format. On the contrary, counterarguments are counterproductive, as they start another set of echoes in the echo chamber. This phenomenon is called a *belief echo*.[63] In other words, the arguments of opponents only help to strengthen the polarized stand. Discussions against a polarized position merely give strength to the stored ideas by belief echo. Once polarized, the brain is ready to defend its position on controversial issues. Why?

McCulloch opines that arguments which would have been effective during the stage of analysis are counterproductive in the third stage. His analogy is charging a fortified bunker (surrounded by open space) by a frontal attack with muzzle-loaded guns while defenders are ready with machine guns. They are prepared with their counterarguments; they will retaliate with their own arguments irrespective of how valid or invalid the arguments and counterarguments are. The polarized mind breaks down arguments against their ideas even if the opponents' statements are factual. Another analogy would be trying to wake up a person who is already awake but pretending to sleep. A different strategy must be applied to change the minds, which is extremely difficult, but it is not impossible.

In other words, science explains why neoconservative ideologues and their supporters were successful beyond expectation; it also explains why prominent intellectuals of their time like Edward Said, Noam Chomsky, Robert Fisk, and other opponents of neoconservative ideology could hardly change their readers' views once subjects had become sympathetic to neoconservative ideas, even though toxic notions have a cost. It took years and trillions of dollars to realize that Iraq's invasion was based on concocted data, and their hypothesis was based on fake news. The perception that Iraq had acquired WMDs still lives on in the American psyche; it is ready to be exploited if needed. The targeted objects for the false information had convinced themselves that their position is correct and even pious.

Notes

1 https://www.hhhistory.com/2014/05/six-degrees-of-separation.html.
2 https://hbr.org/2003/02/the-science-behind-six-degrees.
3 https://nature.berkeley.edu/ucce50/ag-labor/7article/article35.htm.
4 Peter Phillips, *Giants*.
5 Berkley Haas, "The Power of Groupthink: Study shows why ideas spread in social network," *Research News*, February 10, 2021.
6 Allison Weir, https://www.unz.com/article/how-israel-and-its-partisans-work-to-censor-the-internet/. Also see https://www.deepstateblog.org/2020/02/12/how-the-idfs-unit-8200-feeds-israeli-cybersecurity-startups/.
7 Allison Weir, ibid. Also see https://www.richardsilverstein.com/2012/11/01/idf-unit-8200-coming-soon-to-a-theater-near-you/.
8 https://www.ancreport.com/meet-spies-injecting-israeli-propaganda-news-feed/.
9 J.J. Goldberg, *Jewish Power*; also see https://www.timesofisrael.com/covert-israel-based-facebook-network-stoked-hatred-for-profit-report-alleges/ https://electronicintifada.net/blogs/ali-abunimah/israeli-students-get-2000-spread-state-propaganda-facebook.
10 https://thewire.in/politics/narendra-modi-twitter-trolls-free-expression.
11 https://gulfnews.com/world/asia/india/bjps-troll-army-bullies-abuses-and-fights-dirty-with-narendra-modi-as-the-general-1.1541941374832.
12 https://www.washingtonpost.com/opinions/2020/07/07/threats-censorship-are-price-questioning-narratives-about-kashmir/.
13 https://qrius.com/bjp-troll-army/.
14 https://www.thenewsminute.com/article/bjp-response-anti-troll-campaign-exposes-dangerous-agenda-cong-leader-divya-spandana-68094.
15 https://qrius.com/bjp-troll-army/.
16 Francis Fukuyama, "The West has won," *The Guardian*, Oct. 11, 2001, https://www.theguardian.com/world/2001/oct/11/afghanistan.terrorism30.
17 Fukuyama, *The End of History and the Last Man*.
18 Fukuyama, "The West has won." Also see http://ontology.buffalo.edu/smith/courses01/rrtw/Fukuyama.htm.
19 Lindqvist, *Exterminate All the Brutes*, 121–130.
20 http://dissertationreviews.org/archives/11459; for a detailed discussion of Indians see Pankaj Mishra, *From the Ruins of Empire* and *Age of Anger*.
21 Amartya Sen, *Identity and Violence*, 51–55.
22 https://www.thoughtco.com/aristotle-on-democracy-111992.
23 Fukuyama, "The End of History?," https://www.wesjones.com/eoh.htm; for a detailed discussion, see his book of the same title (but without the question mark).
24 Gatlin, *PSU Vanguard*, https://psuvanguard.com/western-media-has-a-systemic-bias-against-palestinians/, citing 416Labs, https://static1.squarespace.com/static/558067a3e4b0cb2f81614c38/t/5c391cc4758d46ef9834907f/1547246789711/416_LABS_50_Years_Of_Occupation_Jan+9th.pdf.
25 Thomas Friedman, "If it's a Muslim problem, It needs a Muslim Solution," *The New York Times*, 9, August 9, 2005. Also see "Tom Friedman on Muslim & Terrorism: Getting it Wrong Again," https://www.huffpost.com/entry/tom-friedman-on-muslims-a_b_398642.

26 S. Alam, "Did Thomas Friedman flunk History? A Muslim Problem," *Counterpunch*, Aug. 7, 2005.

27 https://www.thoughtco.com/the-causes-of-terrorism-3209053; for a detailed discussion see Robert Pape, *Dying to Win*.

28 John Esposito and Dalia Mogahed, *Who Speaks for Islam?*

29 Rick Hampson, "For families of Muslims 9/11 victims, new pain," *The USA Today*, Sept. 9, 2010.

30 Edward Said, *Covering Islam*, xl.

31 Said, ibid., xli.

32 Milton Viorst, *Sandcastles*, quoted in Esposito, *The Islamic Threat*, 213-218.

33 Works are quoted in Esposito, *The Islamic Threat*, 218.

34 Esposito, 213.

35 Charles Krauthammer, "The Crescent of Crisis: Global Intifada," *The Washington Post*, Feb. 16, 1990.

36 Deepa Kumar, *Islamophobia and the Politics of Empire*, 162.

37 Esposito, 224.

38 https://www.mintpressnews.com/jared-kushner-peace-envoy-funder-illegal-israeli-squatt ers-palestine/235335/. Also see https://whoprofits.org/company/remax-israel-impact-prop erty-developers/.

39 Esposito, 227.

40 James Piscatori quoted in Esposito, 227.

41 Esposito, 222.

42 Esposito, 222.

43 Quoted in Esposito, 227.

44 Lindqvist, *Exterminate All the Brutes*, 121–150.

45 Edward Bernays, *Propaganda*.

46 John Berger, *How Ideas Spread*.

47 For a detailed discussion see Chapter 3.

48 Nathan Lean, *The Islamophobia Industry*, Introduction and Chapter 5.

49 Michelle Alexander, *The New Jim Crow*, Introduction and Chapter 1.

50 Sven Lindqvist, *Exterminate All the Brutes*, 127-131. For the fundamental mistake of this notion see Richard Knox, *The Races of Men: A Fragment*.

51 Sven Lindqvist, *The Skull Measurer's Mistake*, 5–9.

52 Alexander, *The New Jim Crow*. Also see David Olusoga, "The History of British Ownership has been Buried: Now its Scale can be Revealed," *The Guardian*, July 12, 2015.

53 https://historyofyesterday.com/how-slavery-fueled-the-industrial-revolution-a0190a 9b48a1. Also see Mike Davis, 296.

54 Lindqvist, *Exterminate All the Brutes*, 130, 140–141, 147.

55 Lindqvist, ibid., 9, 127, 132, 135.

56 Alexander, 1–19.

57 Ava Duverney; *13th*, Netflix.

58 Samuel Huntington, *The Clash of Civilizations*, 253–257, 263–265.

59 Ian McCulloch, "Mod7C Fake News," YouTube, https://www.youtube.com/watch? v=jFR99Fhn8fU.

60 Emily Thorson, "Belief Echoes: The Persistent Effects of Corrected Misinformation," *Political Communication*, November 2015.

61 https://news.gallup.com/poll/8623/americans-still-think-iraq-had-weapons-mass-des truction-before-war.aspx. Also see "Half of Republicans Still Believe WMDs found in Iraq," https://www.politico.com/story/2015/01/poll-republicans-wmds-iraq-114016. "Yes, Iraq Definitely Had WMD, Vast Majority of Polled Republican Insist," https:// www.huffpost.com/entry/iraq-wmd-poll-clueless-vast-majority-republicans_n_1616012.

62 https://www.bustle.com/articles/64444-people-love-celebrity-gossip-and-theres-a-tota lly-valid-scientific-reason-why.

63 Emily Thorson, ibid.

6 The tirade of war, propaganda, and avarice

The assessment of the literature presented in the previous chapters documents how a small group of political activists started a campaign to shape the current image of Muslims as violent people and that of Islam as a violent religion. Their assertions were a willful demonization of the entire Muslim community. It is no different from the branding of Jews as *Untermensch* or loan sharks by the Nazi propaganda establishment before the Second World War or of Africans as savages and subhumans before industrialized slavery became entrenched in the Anglo-Saxon world.

The demonization of Muslims was a gigantic undertaking; people behind the process formed a complex network (Chapters 4 and 5) and guided and coordinated authors, journalists, and political activists and the control of the mainstream media. Even though Muslims are the most diverse group among their cohorts still, these authors were able to characterize 1.8 billion people as a single monolithic unit.[1] This process began decades ago. Their effort was methodical, sustained, and very effective, as today, more than half of all Americans have an unfavorable view of Islam and Muslims. Almost one-third of them still believe that Iraq was involved in the destruction of the World Trade Center, although Iraq had no weapons of mass destruction (WMDs). All these perceptions, as noted by the Kay Commission, were false.[2] The process can be broken into the following steps:

1 *Compartmentalization* of *the world's population* by dividing the entire humankind into subgroups based only on their religious belief system: the division may appear logical but ignores significant variations within each group.
2 *A gross generalization* of up to a billion people within each compartment: according to their theory, religion provides the only identity to each. Like everyone else, Muslims were given their Islamic identity. Their other identities, no matter how important or relevant, did not matter.
3 *Overlooking facts that negate compartmentalization*: the authors disregarded a wide variation within every compartment. Islam is presented as a monolithic entity, although Muslims are spread all over the world. Islam calls three continents its home; it has every racial group as its followers (Whites, Africans, Orientals, and Asians). There are at least fifty-five

DOI: 10.4324/9781003323105-7

Muslim-majority countries in the world. One-third of Muslims live in non-Muslim countries as minorities, who have different priorities and perceptions from Muslims who live in Muslim-majority countries.

4 *Stereotyping of all groups*: without substantiating their claims, the authors claimed that Muslims are violent, Hindus are docile, Buddhists are peace-loving, and the West is progressive. Facts do not support their assertions. These images are based on false assumptions or imaginings.

5 *Oversimplification* of the projected character helped to stereotype the entire Muslim world and create the term Islamic civilization, which has not been clear and is usually misleading.

6 *Subjective characterization of Muslims and Islam*: the adjectives used by these authors to describe Muslims were subjective, such as *militant* Islam, *enraged* Muslims, Islam is *incapable of modernity, rise of fundamentalism* in Islam, or phrases like *Muslims have feelings of inferiority* or *Muslims think that their religion is superior* or *violence of Islam* is related to its *doctrine*. Consequently, they cannot be measured. Therefore, the impressions generated by innuendos could be easily manipulated.

7 *Substantiating innuendos with anecdotal observations*: for example, *Muslims are inherently radical and intolerant of other religions*. He claims his assertions by highlighting a single event from small groups of individuals. The actions of a fraction of 1% of the Muslim population are then projected onto the entire Muslim world.

8 *Presenting opinions as facts* without providing data to substantiate statements: for instance, *Islam is violent,* but why not Christianity or Judaism? Objective parameters for the claims were not given. If they meant Muslims are more violent than others, there were no comparisons.

9 *Omitting data that negate their views and opinions*: for example, when talking about Islam and violence, these authors avoided discussing the universal nature of violence and the prevalence of fundamentalist movements across all religious groups. However, these authors emphasized that violence is the character of Islamic civilization.[3]

10 *Repetition of the same opinion in the media* by many *like-minded* authors and journalists. Individuals who promoted these arguments were called upon to deliver their views as experts on Islam, terrorism, the Middle East, or related subjects, although they have no credentials. These men and women presented the same messages *again and again*. They reiterated similar arguments, which gave an impression that what these people are speaking is the truth and that a large group of people also believe that Muslims are violent.

11 *Promoting opinionated authors as neutral experts* even though these so-called experts have a personal agenda in portraying Muslims as violent and anti-democratic. These "experts" come from the same pool of political thinkers who work for special interest groups, lobbies for the military-industrial complex, and think-tanks. They are financed by billionaires who have political and financial interests in waging wars

against these Muslim countries. Therefore, the challenge in understanding the dynamics of the demonization of Muslims is not only the
discussion itself but also the subtle manipulation of the content of the
debate and the hidden intention of the participants.

12 *Denying access to the mainstream media*, which is owned and controlled by
mega-corporations, to people with opposing views and different opinions.

13 *Controlling the topic of debate* and negating their perspective does not
occur during the discussions. The talks are restricted to specific issues that
they would like audiences to know.

14 *Control of social media*, which has taken over the role of the source of
news in the twenty-first century. Contents of the information that originated from these organizations, which lack oversight, may not only be
false, but also deliberately concocted, which gives a false impression.[4] The
control of information, which influences human perception, is being carefully dissipated by social media. It is the key to manufacturing consent.[5]

If seen in isolation, each of the above steps appears to be benign and innocuous,
as they are designed to appear rational and reasonable; but combined, they
formed an image of Muslims in the Western perception that was violent, irrational, and fanatic. Those who have labeled Muslims violent also promoted the
concept that Muslims abhor democracy and oppose modernity. These activists
laid the intellectual foundation of the most malignant form of Islamophobia.[6]
At the same time, these men and women also predicted impending acts of violence against the West; this had its intended effect. Their arguments were used
as an excuse to invade Iraq and Afghanistan and the *war on terror*.

As a consequence of the policy, up to five million people were killed, and
close to fifty million became refugees.[7] The entire Middle East is in turmoil.
These observations raise the following questions:

1 A lot of effort and resources have gone into demonizing Muslims and Islamic civilization. Why take so much pain and put in so much effort in portraying Muslims as violent? What was the purpose of demonization?

2 Since economic factors are the primary motivation of all human activities,
is there any financial incentive for neoconservative activists in demonizing
Muslims? Did the West benefit from the process? If so, which segment?

3 The West has been in a permanent state of war for the last three centuries.
Not all of their victims were Muslims. Were their other victims also
demonized before their land was invaded?

4 Since the West is involved in invasions and occupation for centuries and
since violent conflicts cannot be started without propaganda, is the West
also in a perpetual state of propaganda? Has the demonization also continued for over two centuries? Is there a cause-and-effect relationship
between the demonization of people and violence against them?

The issues raised by the above questions will be discussed next.

The demonization of victims, justification of violence of the aggressors, and capture of wealth of vanquished: are they connected?

The control of the land belonging to other nations and the capture of resources of the defeated people are the ultimate goals of all empires. They cannot survive without expansion. Since this goal cannot be accomplished without violence, the question is: is there a link – direct or indirect – between violence, the demonization of people, and the capture of their wealth? An intriguing aspect of this issue is: how could a permanent state of war be sustained for centuries? Was the perpetual state of conflicts associated with a permanent state of justification of wars? If so, how can that be maintained for so long?

The data presented in the previous chapters are unambiguous: Western nations have been the most aggressive groups of countries in the last three centuries. Even during the previous three decades, the United States has been involved in as many as thirty violent conflicts;[8] many, but not all, were directed against Muslim societies. The West has also demonized several non-Muslim countries and dehumanized their leaders. There is a distinct pattern: those countries, Muslim or non-Muslim, which were invaded or bombed, were first demonized. Those that were spared the wrath of the West were not. It appears that demonization is the first step in starting a violent conflict. No country was attacked without being demonized first.

Before the Second World War, the British Empire, the French Republic, and other colonial powers had been continuously at war with Asian and African nations for over two centuries. Their goal during the colonial era was to capture as much land as possible and preserve and expand their colonies. Colonies provided them slaves, who were treated as a commodity, and in later years, a cheap labor force and a captive market. The British Empire alone went to war at least seventy times during the reign of Queen Victoria, which lasted over six decades. The idea behind wars was to preserve and expand their colonies by any means – even with brutality – at a time while European nations were making progress in providing rights to their citizens.

Colonial expansion had to be justified to their citizens, especially if they are not benefiting from the occupation. Justifying wars or other forms of violence was a full-time job for colonial powers. They employed the foremost social scientists, economists, and political thinkers of their time to serve in their colonial offices. These intellectuals formulated colonial policies, but their main job was to justify the presence of colonial powers in their colonies. As Edward Said documented in his seminal work *Orientalism*, they invented excuses to manipulate perceptions of the citizens and colonial subjects.[9] Their excuses can be divided into two distinct objectives: a) demonization of the potential victims as subhumans worthy of elimination for altruistic reasons such as the progress of humanity and b) justifying acts of violence as the only option left for the colonial powers.

These men and women did a remarkable job of justifying the violence of European nations if we consider that even though the West had perpetrated most acts of violence during the colonial period, these intellectuals were able to convince the world that the victims, and not the perpetrators, were inherently uncivilized and violent. Edward Said called this dichotomy *Orientalism*.[10] Colonial powers committed the most heinous crimes in human history after deliberation and profited from violence, but they were branded genetically and morally superior to other races. That aura of racial superiority has persisted for centuries in some quarters, even after the collapse of the overt colonial system, which followed the Second World War. This war witnessed the most uncivilized behavior of human history, conducted by Europeans, including the British Empire and the United States, which have promoted themselves as the most civilized race.

During the colonial period, the justification given for invasions of alien lands was that colonial subjects, who were the actual victims of violence, were *savages* and *uncivilized*; therefore, the officials argued that the occupation was essential in teaching *civilization* to colonial subjects. If their arguments are to be believed, the colonial powers were doing a favor to their colonial subjects by staying in the colonies. Was that the reason for the presence of the West in their colonies? Of course not; these colonial wars resulted in the transfer of immense wealth from colonies to the colonial powers. According to LeVine, the total value transferred from the colonies to Europe was so large that it could not be measured.[11] How transferring resources would help to civilize colonial subjects was never addressed.

Since the end of the Second World War, the United States has taken over the leadership of the West; it has remained involved in as many violent conflicts. There is hardly any year that the country was not actively engaged in wars.[12] Its excuse for interventions in those foreign lands, which did not pose any threat to the most powerful nation, is that these violent conflicts were essential for the country's security and democracy; they also argued that the United States is merely defending democracy.[13] Apologists have also argued that the United States is not an empire[14] and that the country has not profited from these wars. That may be true. In the past, taxes levied on the colonial subjects went into the treasuries of their colonial masters. However, unlike other empires of the past, transnational mega-corporations (TNMCs) located in the West have benefited from these wars.

Apologists of the U.S. policy also argue that the preservation of democracy is its sacred duty because 1) democracy is the solution to all problems of human societies; 2) non-democratic countries create most problems; and finally, 3) the United States has to take over the role of the custodian of democracy because it is an exceptional country. However, these assertions are not based on facts. Democracy does not ensure civilized behavior; democratic countries are equally violent.[15] By and large, autocratic rulers have shown good behavior in the international arena. Their acts of violence have been directed towards their people, as dictators are busy consolidating and preserving their power; they are too busy to focus outside the borders. Leaders of democratic countries, on the other hand, treat their citizens with kid gloves, as they have the power to vote them out. Their acts of violence are mainly directed towards their neighbors or the outer world, which cannot strip them of their power.

The enforcement of an arbitrary world order, which benefits powerful countries, is a standard policy of every mighty empire. That has not changed in the twenty-first century. After the Second World War, the United States took over the role of the enforcer of the current world order. Since then, the country has been in a permanent state of war; so was the British Empire during the colonial period when it acted as the enforcer of the *civilizing mission*. The excuses for using violence have changed. While the British Empire used the term civilizing mission as its excuse to occupy other nations, the United States uses *defending democracy* as its excuse to bomb or invade other countries. The intentions behind justifying the violence of the British Empire and the United States are economic factors, which helped them to remain as the foremost economic powers.

No matter which derogatory adjectives may be used to define their victims, the terms are not relevant; they only serve the purpose of justifying their acts of violence and demonizing the victims. Indeed, the purpose of demonization of victims is the same with the United States and the British Empire; so is the justification of their acts of violence. Both nations have been justifying their various acts of violence – invasions, occupations, and bombings – for centuries. The current campaign of dehumanization of Muslims is not new. Branding Muslims as violent people has become a war cry.

A. Demonization and violence

To appreciate connections between the demonization of victims and violence against the demonized, consider the following historical facts of the last fifty years: the campaign of demonization of the so-called Islamic civilization began in earnest only after the Soviet forces withdrew from Afghanistan. Before that, demonization was focused on the Soviet Union and the communist system. During the Russian occupation of the Central Asian nation in the 1980s, Afghan volunteers were branded as *freedom fighters*. They were called *Mujahedin* and were welcomed at the White House with open arms. Throughout the 1980s, Afghans were close allies of the West against the Soviet Union in the war in Afghanistan.

Volunteers from the entire Muslim world were encouraged to come to fight the Soviet army. The United States organized a string of base camps in Pakistan and Al Qaeda was born. The ragtag Afghan irregulars defeated the mighty Red Army in the war, which lasted a decade. More than a million Afghans lost their lives,[16] and a quarter of its population became refugees. The Soviet losses were close to 20,000.[17] In 1989, the last Russian units crossed the bridge over the Amu Darya river and left Afghanistan. Soon, the Berlin Wall fell, and the geopolitical situation changed. Unlike other imploding superpowers of the past, the Soviet Union elected to crumble and not fight its disintegration, a decision that saved thousands of lives. After the fall of the Berlin Wall, the Soviet Union imploded. The United States had no use for Afghan warriors. Having achieved its goal of destabilizing its arch-rival, the United States also packed its bags and left.

As noted in earlier chapters, soon after the departure of the Soviet forces from Afghanistan, anti-Islamic campaigns began in earnest in the West. Bernard

Lewis chose to deliver his famous lecture after the fall of the Berlin Wall, and Huntington presented his prediction in his book of an impending clash between the West and Islamic civilization. *Mujahedin,* the freedom fighters of the past, were instantaneously turned into the *Taliban,* the terrorists. A few years after the first wave of reports claiming Muslims and Muslim-majority countries are violent appeared on the front pages of newspapers across the United States, President Clinton imposed sanctions on Iraq and ordered bombings to *enforce a no-fly zone* to save Iraqi civilians. As a result, close to a million civilians were killed.[18] American bombing campaigns lasted almost a decade.[19] Madeleine Albright, the Secretary of the State, was asked in an interview by Leslie Stahl if the death of half a million children was worth the price of removing Saddam Hussein. She is on the record to say that she thought it was.

During President Clinton's term, American marines landed on the beaches of Somalia to *stabilize a failed state.* Consequently, whatever stability Somalia had achieved after the departure of its dictator disintegrated, the country became an actual failed state. President Clinton also ordered the dropping of Tomahawk cruise missiles on Sudan to destroy the so-called *chemical weapon* factory, which turned out to be the only pharmaceutical facility producing life-saving antibiotics in the country. He also ordered the bombing of other targets in Afghanistan and Somalia to *subdue terrorists.* He also bombed Serbia to *tame an autocratic ruler,* indicating that his bombing policy was not about Islam versus Christianity; it was about imposing the hegemony. Incidentally, Clinton was the first president to bomb a European nation after the Second World War.

All these events took place under one president. A decade later, President Bush Jr. ordered the invasions of Afghanistan and Iraq. Within days, U.S. Rangers and British Tommies were patrolling the streets of Kabul and Baghdad to *bring democracy* to these two nations. However, instead of bringing genuine democracy, puppet regimes were installed; the bombings killed over a million and a half civilians during the occupation of these two countries. Bombs were raining down from the skies on Afghanistan, Pakistan, and Yemen and killing civilians *to make the world a safer place* from terrorists. According to one estimate, close to 80% of the victims were innocent bystanders.

President Barack Obama, who got the Nobel Peace Prize, followed President Bush into the White House. He pursued the same policy. Obama let NATO forces bomb Libya to *bring democracy.* He also sent American troops to Syria to *defeat ISIS,* the terrorist group. How the ISIS fighters found a safe passage from Iraq to Syria remains unclear. How the so-called terrorists got hold of American and Israeli weapons as they were retreating from Iraq also remains an enigma.[20] This has led to speculation that there was an association between these two groups, which were portrayed as arch enemies. President Obama also increased the use of drones to assassinate young Muslims to eliminate terrorist threats. Most of those killed by unmanned planes were also civilians.

What was the intention behind these killings? Was it to eradicate potential and future terrorists? We do not know, but the victims had not committed any acts of violence so far either against the United States or against anyone before they were exterminated, which leads its critics to question: how could anyone determine which person can become a terrorist in the future? No algorithm has been devised that can predict the future actions of an individual. Why were these young men targeted? We do not know. Since no trials ever took place, we will never know. These people were declared suspects and executed without providing any proof of their crimes; these killings can only be characterized as assassination. Did the country benefit from drone attacks? Not according to facts. Drones are the projects of three corporations; these have prospered.[21] They have combined their resources and formed a lobby, which promotes the use of drones in wars. The War on Terror has been good to them; their profits have soared.[22]

The invasions of Iraq and Afghanistan had not faded yet from the collective memory, and the NATO forces started bombing Libya. France and Britain spearheaded the effort, but President Obama was not an innocent bystander. His Secretary of State, Mrs. Hilary Clinton, had taken the initiative to overthrow the legitimate Libyan government. Libya was declared a repressive state and Muammar Gaddafi was a dictator. The Libyan leader may have been an autocrat, but the country had excellent universal health care and free education for all. Libya was bombed; its president was brutally assassinated. His killing was broadcasted live on television.

What did Gaddafi do to get this treatment? Was it to keep the world safe from nuclear weapons? Probably not! He had already dismantled its nuclear weapons program. Was it related to his stand on selling his oil in other currencies instead of dollars? Mike Lofgren believes that the cause of his death was his insistence on using Petro-dinar for exporting Libyan crude oil. If so, was his assassination meant to be a lesson for other heads of state? Libya may have been "liberated" from Gaddafi's rule, but the country is now in chaos, which has also affected France, as the refugees are pouring into Europe. The Libyan territory has become a launching pad for migrants and refugees to go to Europe. The recipe for the destruction of Libya and the demonization of its leader were perfected in Iraq. The demonization of Muslims and Arabs had preceded acts of violence against Muslim countries in the twenty-first century.

Syrian president Bashar-al-Assad may have been the next on their hit-list. Parts of Syria were destroyed to contain a dictator. Even though the country has been severely damaged, its president has survived, at least so far. Before the current chaos began, Syria was functioning as a reasonably successful socialist country. Although it had a diverse population, there was stability. Like Iraq and Libya, Syria had also managed to install universal health care and free education. The campaign of toppling the Syrian regime started with the same formula that was used in Iraq but with a Syrian twist. First came the demonization of Assad. He was accused of using chemical weapons against his people; that allegation, which neocon ideologues presented with great fanfare, has never been proven to be correct. Neither was it ever confirmed by independent observers. On the contrary, independent observers have provided proof that the use of chemical weapons could be traced to rebels, who have been supported by Western nations.[23]

For a short period, it appeared that the fate of Assad was sealed, and he would end up being either exiled or hanged. However, he has survived so far, thanks to Iranian and Russian support. The process of regime change in Syria is remarkably similar to what happened to Iraq and Libya: the demonization of the leader and dehumanization of its population, followed by the invasion or bombings. The resulting chaos in Israel's neighborhood was predictable, except that President Assad has so far survived.

In the last ten years, over five million people were killed in Muslim countries; most of them were civilians, and more than half were women and children. Bombings created fifty million refugees. Were these events a series of coincidences? Not according to critics of the current American foreign policy. They believe that the formula of bringing chaos was established long ago, and the United States had transformed itself from a republic to an imperial power, much like the Roman or British Empires did before their demise as the world powers.[24] Chalmers Johnson, Chris Hedges, and others have argued that the U.S. economy, like that of an imperial power, cannot survive unless there is a perpetual state of violent conflict.[25]

Imperialism needs violence, and violence requires justification, which is done by demonizing the victims. It needs support from its corporate world to survive. If the British Empire had strong support from its colonial-industrial complex, which had deep roots in the country, the United States has reached a permanent state of war partly due to an unchallenged influence of its military-industrial complex, not only on the Congress but on the entire society. The weapon manufacturers also have a strong lobby. Besides, weapon-producing units are spread over the country, creating jobs, which have made it difficult for the members of Congress to vote against the decisions taken by the military-industrial complex. Wars help the bottom line of those corporations that are engaged in wars.

Are these events part of a clash of civilizations between the Western Christian and Islamic civilizations? Of course not; violent conflicts of the West are not explicitly directed against Muslim countries. Besides, such clashes have been going on for two or three centuries. American Presidents – from Clinton to Trump – were not the only ones to bomb other countries in the name of saving democracy in recent decades. Almost every president since the Philippines War[26] has done the same; only their excuses were different.[27] A similar campaign was started four decades ago by Ronald Reagan against tiny Grenada and later by George Bush Sr. against Panama, another small nation of Central America. These countries were defined as a threat to the United States. Their leaders were demonized similarly; they have been declared either communists or drug dealers. These are not Muslim countries. Before Grenada, Vietnam, Korea, and Central America were demonized.

A similar campaign was initiated against the duly elected leader of Ukraine by the Obama administration. He was also toppled; instead of fighting back, he fled the country and found asylum in Russia. Venezuela has also been targeted. There was a military putsch in 2004 against the former Venezuelan president, Hugo Chavez, who claimed that the coup was executed by mercenaries sympathetic to the oil industry and Venezuelan elites. U.S. officials have denied any involvement in the coups. There was another assassination attempt and yet another failed coup in 2018 against Nikolas Maduro, the successor to Hugo Chavez.

There are many active conflicts around the world; not all can be blamed on the West. Some of their allies have taken advantage of the current anti-Muslim stand of the United States to spread chaos for their benefit. That may not be unusual as powerful nations have their satraps, who lurk behind the scenes to take advantage of the situation. They usually receive the crumbs after the United States, its NATO, and other close allies have devoured their share. There is a tendency among satraps to provoke new conflicts if it could help them, which is understandable.

Neoconservative ideologues, who harbor an exclusive pro-Israel agenda, have had a stronghold on America's foreign policy and defense establishments. Their influence reached its zenith under President Bush. According to Richard Clark, a senior member under the Bush administration, these activists were planning to invade seven Muslim countries in five years, topple their governments and replace the legitimate rulers with the so-called *democratically elected* leaders, who would be friendly to Israel.[28] Their stated goal may have been to bring democracy, but in the way they brought democracy to Iraq and Libya; their critics argue that their actual goal was to bring chaos to Israel's neighborhood. These ideologues have succeeded in the regime changes in Iraq and Libya and came close to toppling the Syrian regime. Toppling the Iranian regime may have been their ultimate goal.

A Western-style democracy for nations could be a good idea, but why should they be first designated as rogue states? A noble intention, perhaps, if it was true, but there are two-fold problems with their idea: 1) acts leading to any regime change are illegal activities; and 2) for whatever reasons, the premise of having so-called elected leaders to represent the nations has never worked out for countries being offered democracy. The best way to achieve democracy is to leave people alone. Historically, if left to find their way, nations have managed to do very well with a few exceptions. The so-called elected leaders of the non-Western world, if they are chosen by the West to run for the highest office of the land, invariably turn out to be autocrats – Suharto, Ferdinand Marcos, Hosni Mubarak, Al Sissie, Pervez Musharraf, Pinochet, and others. They support the Western policies; in return, they are supported by the West; the United States underwrites their life insurance by keeping a small contingent nearby. Corporations and banks provide hefty sums of money to such leaders to keep their army happy, well-fed, and inside the barracks, to be unleashed on citizens if and when they go out of line and challenge the world order.[29] This policy has turned into a protection racket; their clients are authoritarian rulers of the world. They are happy to follow anyone who supports them to stay in power.

Neoconservatives are not the only ones to take advantage of the current anti-Muslim stand of the United States. Other nations were quick to jump on the preserve-and-save-democracy bandwagon. They formed alliances with the West to defeat their rivals and neighbors, Muslim and non-Muslims alike. It was no coincidence that other countries also observed increased military activities against their restive Muslim populations around the time the United States had invaded Iraq.

For example, the Israeli army was sent into the occupied territories to punish the entire captive Palestinian population.[30] Israeli jets bombed Lebanon. No sooner had President Bush looked into the eyes of Vladimir Putin and declared that he could trust the Russian President, Putin sent Russian forces into Chechnya around the time American troops were invading Iraq. The Ethiopian and Kenyan armies are still present within the Somalian territory. The Philippines sent its army to Mindanao, where Muslims form a sizable minority and control many cities. They have been fighting for independence for decades. During the same period, India was threatening to teach a lesson to Pakistan, and it sent the military to put down the insurgency in Kashmir.

It appears as if these nations were waiting for a green signal from the United States to invade or occupy their foes. The above examples indicate a close link between the demonization of victims and violence against them. The question is: why demonize a country and start violent conflicts? Wars are a burden to society anyway unless the aggressors benefit from violence. What are the benefits of violent conflicts? Is there a connection between the accumulation of wealth and violence?

B. The permanent state of war

The United States went to war in Iraq and Afghanistan and half a dozen other countries in the twenty-first century. American policymakers may disagree with their critics as to why the country went to war, but not that they went to war in so many places in the last two decades. Despite the debacles in these countries, the United States remained firmly anchored in the war-torn areas. Why? U.S. officials continue to claim that they only wanted to bring democracy. Their critics argue that their arguments are excuses; the ultimate goal was to control oil fields or help Israel subjugate its neighbors.[31] The other purpose could be to support its defense industry; the show must go on. The military-industrial complex got the lion's share of the budget to manage the War on Terror.[32]

Neoconservatives, who run America's foreign policy establishments, may not accept that the United States is in a permanent state of war. However, they are firm supporters of the War on Terror, which has become a war on many Muslim countries since 1991. It is now a permanent fixture of American foreign policy. Barbara Lee, the only member of the Congress who voted against invading Afghanistan, argued that American involvement could make it a never-ending war. Indeed, a single individual can explode a homemade pipe bomb in a God-forsaken place, which can then be used to retaliate or as an excuse to bomb or even invade another Muslim country. The War on Terror has the potential to keep the country in a perpetual state of war. So had *La Mission Civilisatrice* (civilizing mission), which kept the colonial wars going for two centuries.

The justification of violent confrontations perpetrated against half a dozen Muslim-majority countries by the United States and its allies was built upon the demonization of Muslims, Islam, and Islamic civilization. As noted in Chapter 3, that campaign started decades before the destruction of the World Trade Center; the subsequent response by the United States was expected. America's recent violent conflicts have continued with high intensity since President Clinton was in the White House. It indicates that the United States is not only in a perpetual state of war, but is also in a permanent state of propaganda, the sole purpose of which is to demonize nations and to dehumanize their people who are against Western policy. Branding Muslims as violent should be seen from this perspective. In the past, so-called villains were communists; today, they are Muslims; tomorrow, they could be Russians, Chinese, or anyone. The demonization of future victims would also be based on made-up threats.

The purpose of using fake threats of impending attacks on U.S. soil is to influence the perception of its citizens in favor of war, the purpose of which is to achieve economic or political benefits for elites of the society. Claiming that there is an existential threat to the nation is a part of the preparation for impending war. Noam Chomsky calls it *manufacturing consent*.[33] The process is not confined to the United States; it is common to every powerful empire. Demonization lays the foundation of upcoming violence, which benefits corporations, but is a disaster to the country.

Whether or not wealth can be successfully extracted from wars, violent conflicts could be divided into productive and unproductive wars. Empires in their early stages are judicious in the use of violence; in the latter stages, violence is used by the fading empires to subdue their victims. The Athenians sent an armada of 200 ships to Sicily to punish the rebellious subjects; the fleet was lost. The French wanted to tighten their control over Algerians, who were demanding equal rights. France responded by sending its dreaded paras and foreign legion, but the French rule in Algeria imploded. In 1956, Egypt nationalized the Suez Canal; the British along with France and Israel responded by invading Egypt, but they had to retreat. The political cost of withdrawal to the British Empire sapped its life. Numerous historical events confirm that the empires become less judicious during the decay phase. The American invasion of Iraq can be placed in the same category.

The road to the decay of empires is long and gradual. The end comes suddenly. The British Empire reached its zenith during the late nineteenth century. It had its first major roadblock in South Africa, while the Empire was at the peak of its power. The Boer War became Vietnam. This was noted by men who went to establish anti-colonial movements around the World. The British won, but barely. After the First World War, they added the entire Middle East. The first half of the twentieth century witnessed numerous wars in which the British Empire was involved. Most of them were unproductive wars; the purpose was to preserve the territories that the British Empire had managed to wrest from people who could not defend.

The Mughal dynasty, which ruled India between the fifteenth and eighteenth centuries, is one of many examples that confirm the assertion that unproductive wars are disasters for the country or empires. The Mughals ruled India for over 250 years. The first seven emperors of the dynasty have been described by historians as the *Great Mughals*.[34] Two of them, Akbar and Aurangzeb, remained on the throne for a little over five decades each. Akbar's reign witnessed an exponential increase in India's GDP. He also laid the foundation of a stable empire that lasted for the next two centuries, partly because he was very astute in using violence. The second half of his rule was remarkable for the lack of violent conflicts. He used the last half of his reign to consolidate his gains.

On the other hand, his great-grandson, Aurangzeb, ruled over the largest swath of land – from the southern tip of the Indian Subcontinent to the border of Iran. He had twice as much land under his control as Akbar had at the peak of his power. India's GDP was close to 27% of the world under Aurangzeb, but he had an army of over a million soldiers, which was a burden to the treasury. In the middle of his reign, Aurangzeb crossed the Narmada river, which divides India somewhere in the middle. It was supposed to be a short war, but the emperor could never return to his capital, which he left to conquer his nemesis Shivaji; the Maratha king died soon, but the Mughal army could not return. The second half of his rule also witnessed numerous unproductive wars, which helped to drain the empire. Five decades after his death, the empire ceased to exist. The economy was in ruins; unproductive wars were draining the treasury.

In his book *The Collapse of Complex Societies*, Joseph Tainter has looked into the decay of sixty-nine superpowers of their time – from the Mayan civilization to the British Empire. He describes the factors associated with the decline. Tainter points out that the collapse of every powerful empire was associated with a perpetual state of war.[35] Chalmers Johnson agreed; he opines that the collapse is due to imperial *hubris*,[36] which promotes irrational thinking among ruling elites. In his book *Nemesis*, he compared violent conflicts of the United States with the British and Roman Empires and documented that the incidence and prevalence of wars show an upward trend towards the end in both cases.

Chris Hedges has described constant wars as an overreach of empires, which he argues, no country can afford, no matter how powerful and wealthy.[37] He cites many examples of increasing incidence of unproductive before the collapse of empires. When the collapse comes, the contraction of imperial overreach is swift: one year for Portugal, two years for the Soviet Union, eight years for France, eleven for the Ottomans, and seventeen years for the British Empire.[38] If Alfred McCoy is to be believed, it will be twenty-seven for the United States – from 2003, when the U.S. army crossed its *Rubicon*, the Iraq–Kuwait border, to 2030, which is, of course, an arbitrary number based on estimation of debt, other obligations, and cost of running an empire and its tax base.

Indeed, wars are expensive for the nation's treasury;[39] unless replenished, wars become a drain to the country. Mired in constant violent conflicts, even the mightiest empires wither away. At some point, there is no easy prey to be conquered; wars of conquest become unproductive. Pat Buchanan, a conservative writer and politician, agrees; he was one of the few media pundits who had argued against the invasion of Iraq for this reason. He may not be against violence if it helps the nation; he is only lamenting the loss of hegemony of the West. Buchanan argues that the leaders of the British Empire squandered the advantages of the West over the rest by starting the two World Wars.[40] However, he does not acknowledge that the current advantages of the West over the rest of the world stemmed from violence perpetrated on colonial subjects.

Facts back Buchanan's views. In his book *A Century of War*, William Engdahl has also documented that the British Empire started both Wars to derail the rise of Germany as an industrial superpower.[41] Mike Davis argues that satisfied with the captive market of India and China, British industry failed to innovate and became unproductive. German and American economies had overtaken Britain by the end of the nineteenth century. In his seminal work, *Tragedy and Hope*, Carroll Quigley has confirmed the assertions of all these writers.[42]

These are not new ideas; they have been put forth for centuries by numerous thinkers. Ibn Khaldun, the fourteenth-century Arab philosopher, described the phenomenon of perpetual war as a sequela of any long-standing imperial power in its end-stage.[43] He describes it as the *senility* of empires; Ibn Khaldun probably meant the Alzheimer's disease of old age. He argued that multiple centers of power emerge within empires with time, making it difficult for the rulers to govern the country efficiently. Khaldun also pointed out that once the senility seeps into the system, the power brokers would like to maintain the status quo, which helps their agenda. Therefore, the problem would not go away even if the rulers are aware of the decay and even if they are addressing the issues. Khaldun argued that the rulers could not control the collapse as the problem lies with the system; the entire system needs to be overhauled, which is a complex undertaking. Rulers usually make cosmetic improvements; therefore, the disease continues unabated. The decay of powerful empires should be viewed as nature's way of circulating power and wealth around the world.

Therefore, the invasions or acts of war by the United States and the British Empire are not a series of coincidences. On the contrary, these events are expected in old empires, as they are the symptoms of the deep-rooted malaise of imperial policies. They are an indicator of the underlying disease, etiology of which is common to all violent conflicts of mighty empires and nations. Since violence is essential to capture the wealth of the defeated people, demonization should be viewed as the first step in capturing wealth. These examples, at the least, indicate, if not prove, a close relationship between acts of violence by powerful combatants and the dehumanization of the potential victims, which is the most potent indicator of impending violence.

Demonization is an integral part of war; historically, it has always preceded violence. That dynamic is similar in international as well as in intra-national conflicts. So are the consequences; they are equally disastrous for the weaker combatants. Wars have the potential to destroy powerful combatants with time, irrespective of the type of conflict. There happen to be more incidences of intra-national than international conflicts after the Second World War. The decreased incidence of international disputes can be traced to the establishment of the United

Nations. Its charter has made international borders sacrosanct, which has resulted in a lower frequency of conflicts among countries.

Only six nations have crossed internationally recognized borders and established or attempted to establish their presence over a more extended period in the conquered land. They were North Korea (in South Korea), South Africa (Namibia), Indonesia (East Timor), Iraq (Kuwait), Israel (Syria, Lebanon, Egypt, and Palestine), and the United States (Iraq).[44] The United Nations forced the first four countries on the list to withdraw; the United States was allowed to stay temporarily in Iraq until the situation improved. It had withdrawn its forces but went back into Iraq, but this time with the permission of the Iraqi government, which was installed by the United States. Israel is the only country that continues to occupy territories belonging to other people. How long would it last? We do not know, but probably as long as the United States remains the only superpower and the sole enforcer of the world order.

Violent conflicts are an outdated concept, especially for international disputes, as victors have been forced to withdraw from conquered territories. Besides, since an alien power can rule over its subjects either by consent or by violence, empires are a temporary phenomenon. They may have more than a million soldiers under their arms, but empires are surprisingly fragile like any complex network. Afghanistan, which is the poorest country in the world, defeated the Soviet army, which had destroyed the German *Bundeswehr*, in a decade-long war. There is a strong chance that Afghans may force the United States, which is the most powerful country in the world, to withdraw on their terms. The breakdown of one component can destroy the entire structure of a complex imperial system.

The primary aim of wars is to capture the wealth of the targeted country; non-violent forms of confrontation are equally effective in capturing wealth. Economic sanctions, denying access to the line of credit, or currency manipulations, are more efficient and less messy in achieving the goal of extracting the wealth or punishing the victims. Oil-producing nations are more vulnerable to sanctions by international institutions, which are backed by Western governments. Drastically lowering the oil price of other oil-producing countries can cause a sudden decrease in revenues, which can damage their economy. Combined, these processes can transfer billions of dollars from a targeted country to international banks. Since the same group of super-elites control these financial institutions, they are the primary beneficiary of violent conflicts, currency wars, sanctions, and a drastic lowering of the price of fossil fuel.

Violence is still being frequently used because it serves a purpose for powerful nations; they are in a position to be aggressive without fear of reprisal. Violence, in that case, is a valuable tool for intimidation. It has been used to soften up opponents' attitudes before negotiations start, but there are other objectives. In the last three decades, acts of violence have been used to spread chaos in Israel's neighboring countries, a policy that has helped Israel in annexing the Palestinian land. Wars are the most effective way of circulating cash sitting idly in the banks. Money that cannot be lent is expensive for the lending institutions, as they have to pay interest to depositors.[45] Finally, violent conflicts help to lower the trade deficits of the weapon-exporting countries.[46] These nations have benefited from the current world order.

Since the United States has been importing fossil fuel since the 1970s, oil-producing countries have developed a trade surplus with the United States, which is also the number-one weapon- producing and -exporting country in the world. Since international trade in petroleum products is conducted only in U.S. dollars, the trade imbalance due to oil import to the United States can be offset by buying weapons from the United States. In this way, dollars are circulated back into the system. Buyers of military hardware do not have to drop bombs to justify their purchases, but they may do once in a while to justify the expenses incurred on weapons. A few bombs here or there may justify spending money on the country's defense establishment. That also helps local leaders to be in the good books of the powerful nations which manage the world order.

Intra-national conflicts are no different, except their incidence has not decreased after the Second World War; the UN did not address the problem of violence within sovereign nations at the time of its inception. Its primary focus after the Second World War was on international conflicts. Crossing borders had caused numerous wars and the two World Wars, which caused close to eighty million war-related deaths. There is no such restraint on the leaders if they indulge in intra-national conflicts, even if the casualties are high.

Countries dealing with intra-national conflicts include, among many, India, Israel, Myanmar, Sri Lanka, former Yugoslavia, Rwanda, Congo, Ethiopia, Thailand, and Indonesia; they are or were involved in violence against their citizens for one reason or the other. It may appear as if the clashes with their governments are due to differences in religion, race, or ethnicity. In many cases, governments have directed their guns towards specific religious or ethnic groups. However, disputes are neither about the practice of religion, nor are they religious wars; the primary factor behind almost all clashes is either the land and its resources or resistance to unfair distributions and allocation of resources.

Equally common are conflicts in which governments have directed their wrath towards a class of people who may be ethnically similar to the majority but belong to a different social class. They are usually poor, illiterate, and belong to the lowest rank in their society. Examples are the United States (against inner-city blacks and rural poor whites), India (Dalits, Muslims, and indigenous or tribal groups), Brazil (people of color, former slaves, and indigenous people), Mexico (indigenous population), Britain, France, and other European Union countries (refugees and third-generation citizens from former colonies), and Central and Latin American countries (Native Americans). In all these cases, police and law-enforcement agencies, which are designed to serve its elite class, are engaged in suppression and even frequent killings of its disenfranchised segment. In each country, governments aided by the power vested in the state apparatus have dehumanized their targets before unleashing acts of violence. The end game remains the same: the capture of the resources of the targeted country or people – either directly or indirectly.

In intra-national conflicts, violence against a group could also be for political considerations, especially in nations where elections are regularly held, and power is transferred subsequently. That helps the bottom line of political elites, who serve the financial elites of the country. For example, in India, Muslims, who belong to the most disenfranchised groups in the country, have been targeted by their governments. They were first branded as anti-national, terrorists, criminals, and supporters of Pakistan – India's arch-enemy.[47] Now they are being persecuted as beef-eaters. For the policy-makers, the fight is not about religion but about votes, which is essentially an economic issue. Getting elected to the parliament is the surest ticket to become super-rich in one generation.

In many countries, the authorities of the land are enthusiastic proponents of hate-mongering. For example, in Myanmar, a firebrand Buddhist monk, Wirathu, has openly incited violence against Rohingya Muslims; he also describes them as subhuman. The underlying problem in these countries, like anywhere else, is the unequal application of laws, which helps its influential segments. They usually belong to the majority community. However, once violence is established in the society or becomes the *modus operandi*, it cannot be controlled; violence gets directed against some other group.

Muslims are not the only group who have been demonized and targeted by their government. In Sri Lanka, the state had unleashed its forces against the Tamil minorities even after the war had already ended.[48] Before going into action against insurgents, the government also branded the Tamilians as terrorists and criminals. After defeating the Tamil insurgency, the same group of politicians and activists has directed their campaign against Muslims. If they are not stopped now, another round of violence is imminent, which has already begun. The minorities have also been branded most offensively in other places. In Rwanda, Hutu activists went on the airwaves to describe Tutsi minorities as *cockroaches*. In Thailand, Malay minorities are the target. They, too, are blamed for being violent, anti-state, and terrorists.

In the United States, African Americans are demonized as criminals and superpredators. President Clinton coined the term in his presidential campaign of 1996 to justify the mass incarceration of young men of color from inner cities. His tough stand on crime helped him to garner votes from white America.[49] The issue was also raised during Hillary Clinton's presidential campaign (2016). She apologized to the black community.[50] Ironically, both Clintons have been portrayed as the most black-friendly politicians, but two decades after Bill Clinton left office, blacks have a very different perspective. He was responsible for the mass incarceration of African Americans, which has devastated the black communities.[51]

Indeed, the situation of Muslims in the current world order is neither unique nor unusual. They were targeted because, in the last quarter of a century, political and economic forces were aligned against them; the conflicts were not for or because of their religion. Acquiring Palestinian land may have been the primary aim of pro-Israel neoconservative activists; Islamic civilization happened to be the most convenient target. The demonization of Islamic civilization was crucial to start a bombing campaign in the name of the War on Terror.

There were factors that went against Muslim countries, such as oil, Israel, and the military-industrial complex of the United States and Britain. One of the underlying impetuses for the West is their insatiable desire to control the supply of fossil fuel. The other factors are the power of the pro-Israel lobby groups and their influence over the political spectrum of the United States, its military-intelligence-security-industrial complex. Also, most importantly, the financial sector controls mega-corporations, which manage the military-industrial complex. The combined interests of these groups were channeled in the twenty-first century against Muslim countries by the political activists; that may not end soon, as the underlying factors have not been addressed.

Like their Jewish counterparts, Christian Zionists are also steadfast supporters of Israel's policy of annexation of Palestinian land. They have a wide following in the United States; they are passionate about supporting the invasion of countries in Israel's neighborhood. They do it for theological reasons. They believe in *Armageddon* and the *Second Coming of Jesus*, which according to their belief, would happen only if and when Jews control the entire swath of land between the Euphrates and Nile. That explains why evangelical Christians support the Jewish state and not the Christian Palestinians. Are the Christian Zionists well-wishers of Jews? Of course not! They have their own agenda.

Many Christian Zionists are *Born Again Christians;* they are waiting for the *Armageddon* in which only those who believe in Jesus as their Lord will survive. All Jews will be massacred unless they convert to Christianity; only genuine converts will be spared, but who will decide whether a person is honest or a fake convert? Will it be Jesus or his disciples? If it is left to his disciples, will it be another inquisition? Jewish people have already experienced one *Inquisition*. If that happens, the treatment awaiting the Jews may be worse than the Holocaust. Christian Zionists are warmly embraced by the Jewish States, as they serve a purpose for the ruling elites of Israel.

In essence, all forms of violent conflicts, whether international or intra-national, follow the same dynamics. They are a gross generalization of the targeted group, which helps to characterize the victims by isolating them from the rest. This is followed by their demonization, which precedes violence, whose purpose is to control the land and distribution of its resources or tax dollars.

This has been the *modus operandum* of the colonial powers in the nineteenth and twentieth centuries. It is no different today. The demonization of the victims can only be accomplished by sustained propaganda.

C. *Inexorable propaganda*

There has hardly been a year that the United States has not actively waged war ever since Mayflower landed at the shore of Virginia. The settlers intended to find a new home; it became a colony. First came the expansion of the boundaries of the new republic; then, it became an avalanche in the eighteenth and nineteenth centuries. Leaders of the United States justified their expansion with the excuse that they are preordained to rule all of North America. The concept was called *Manifest Destiny*, which led to genocidal wars against the Native Americans who were living here for thousands of years. They were defeated and banished to *reservations*.

The war against Mexico followed. By 1848, the United States had seized nearly half of the Mexican territories. By then, the republic had stretched from the Atlantic to the Pacific; only then did the United States expand beyond America – Hawaii, and then the Philippines, Cuba, and other territories that once belonged to the Spanish Empire. Between 1898 and 1934, the United States invaded Honduras seven times, Nicaragua five times, Cuba, Colombia, and the Dominican Republic four times each, Mexico three times, Haiti and Panama twice each, and Guatemala once.[52]

How could a nation stay in a perpetual state of war? Since any conflict cannot be initiated without propaganda, is the United States in a permanent state of propaganda? Most Americans will probably laugh at this question. They might even claim that a question like this reflects not only anti-American bias but is also propaganda against the United States, a country that has done so much for democracy, free-market economy, free speech, and human rights. They could argue, how could that be possible when the United States neither is a communist country nor has an autocratic system of governance?

Whether their argument is correct or not may be debated, but here are other well-documented facts. The United States has invaded or bombed seventy countries since the end of the Second World War;[53] it has invaded fifteen countries[54] and bombed half a dozen other places in the last thirty years. Those countries, which were branded as threats to the United States, belong to the least advanced countries of the world. They posed no threat to the United States, especially in the era of high-tech wars. So many invasions are not possible without demonizing victims, especially since these countries posed no threat. Could the demonization of over fifteen nations be done without active propaganda? Of course not; citizens had to be convinced that they are under existential threat from these nations before they would allow elected officials to go to war.

Common sense dictates that without an adequate demonization of the victims, resistance to violent conflicts within the country would have been too high for political elites to pursue such policies. That was not the case for the invasion of Iraq among members of Congress, who are supposed to represent people. Iraq was already believed to be a nation with WMDs, its leader a fanatic, and its people violent. That perception had found root in the American perception, as reflected by the voting pattern of the members of Congress. In the wake of 9/11, President Bush sent the Authorization of Use of Military Force (AUMF), a bill that gave the authority to the President "to use all necessary and appropriate force against those nations, organizations or persons he determines planned, authorized, committed the terrorist attacks that occurred on September 11, 2001."[55]

This bill gave sweeping power to the executive branch. It was unprecedented in American history. From then on, presidents did not need approval from Congress to wage war; they could arbitrarily decide to attack any country if they claimed that a nation is supporting terrorism, irrespective of whether that nation did or not. That bill passed with a single member of Congress opposing it. This was a blank check to President Bush to continue a perpetual war on terror, an ongoing proposition. Every president has used its authority. Indeed, wars and other forms of violent conflicts continued even in 2019, although not exclusively against Muslim countries. The United States has shifted its focus to other parts of the world, such as China, Russia, Cuba, and now Venezuela.

Why? Critics of the U.S. policy have claimed that the United States is not a republic anymore.[56] It was transformed into an imperial power after the Second World War. Since it replaced the British Empire as the leader of the Western world, it is in a permanent state of war, from which it cannot extricate itself. Critics also argue that the perpetual state of war is not spontaneous but an active process. To sustain as many wars over the decades, the United States has to propagate the so-called "virtue" and benefit of wars. That policy requires not only a continuous supply of potential targets but also a sustained or perpetual state of propaganda so that the victims could be systematically demonized and portrayed as a threat to the nation. They have to be turned into a dangerous enemy in the perception of American citizens.

Simply put, a perpetual state of war can only be sustained by a) justifying the nation's own acts of violence and b) dehumanization of the victims. The United States is not unique in this respect; powerful nations of the past have followed the same policy, which has a negative influence over an extended period, but it serves the interests of elites. Such an approach has not only economic, social, and political consequences for the country as a whole, but it can also cause emotional and psychological trauma for individual citizens. Post-traumatic stress disorder (PTSD) is three times more common among American conscripts than it is among Allied soldiers.[57] The suicide rate is equally higher among war veterans.

Demonization influences what one should think and circumvents how to think. This diminishes the ability of independent thinking, a lack of which is a disaster for any society. Hannah Arendt believes that the inability of individuals to think for themselves was the reason why Nazi Germany, though the most enlightened nation going into the First World War, produced men like Adolf Eichmann. He planned the last details of the extermination of twenty million people without firing a single bullet.[58] He showed no remorse and justified his action by stating that he was doing what his superiors ordered him to do. Arendt calls people like him *desk murderers*. Eichmann did not kill a single person personally but was one of the architects of the Holocaust that exterminated twenty million Russians and six million Jews.

Indeed, a perpetual state of propaganda alters people's perception and their way of thinking; therefore, a constant propaganda campaign is more dangerous for any society than a continuous state of war. Endless violent conflicts have become the norm for the nation. Hardly anyone in the United States feels it unusual that soldiers as young as eighteen are trained to kill and are being killed in alien lands. That is not unusual for empires. The Romans did the same before they ceased to be a republic and degenerated into an empire. So did the British Empire and the French Republic.

In most cases, soldiers do not even know who benefits from their sacrifices, much less the actual reasons for going to war. Neither do they have an idea of what they are fighting for. Most of them may not have heard the name of the country where they are being sent. They might not have come in contact with a single person of that country except through the telescope mounted on their long-range rifles. Nevertheless, they would form an opinion, mostly negative ones, from the mainstream media, which has become a mouthpiece of the military-industrial complex in the West. No one bothers to ask why young men leave their homes to kill in countries that pose no threat to them or their country. Hardly anyone knows, much less wonders, why the United States has 800 bases in foreign lands and maintains its forces in more than 150 countries, which are manned by more than 200,000 soldiers. Are they defending the United States from a country so tiny as Djibouti or Diego Garcia, from where all indigenous inhabitants have been banished? Why are the GIs there then?

Indeed, wars have a considerable cost, both tangible and intangible, to society, more so if wars are in the continuum. However, a perpetual state of propaganda can be far more troublesome for the country, as it has the power to alter the collective thinking of the country. The entire society could be led to believe in fairy-tales as well as in nonsense. For example, today, wars are being portrayed by the authorities and accepted by the citizens as a vehicle for peace. This particular concept has created a pathological state of reality. Such ideas can only promote delusions among citizens, but ordinary people are not the problem; those who run the country are. They either believe in their own rhetoric, which is based on false ideas (that the United States is under an existential threat, is an exceptional country, or has a Manifest Destiny) and fake news (Iraq had WMDs) or uses the same rhetoric to convince their followers to accept their version of the truth. Their vision for the country's future is a perpetual state of war, which in reality is unsustainable. The interests of elites lie with violent conflicts, which invariably bring disaster to their nations in the long run.

There is confusion about the etiology of countless wars; it stems from policies that are translucent. A lack of transparency has helped to accentuate the problem for its citizens. It has also allowed political elites to pursue their goal without generating resistance from the citizens. The vision of its financial elites is invariably the opposite of that of ordinary folks. That is understandable: elites benefit from wars; ordinary citizens do not.

In contrast, those who do the actual fighting pay a heavy price for wars with taxes and occasionally with their lives if they join the military. Those who start wars usually sit within the comfort of their homes; in contrast, those who are on the front lines to defend the country have to sleep in trenches. The best an ordinary soldier can expect from wars is to come back in one piece. In most cases, citizens are compelled by financial reasons to join the military. Most young men and now increasingly young women have no options – no job prospects, poverty, and a chance to educate themselves. If they are lucky, they can get a college education from the money provided after four years of active duty.

Time and again, gullible voters have fallen for the rhetoric of politicians who promote wars as the only solution to the complex problems of the modern world. Citizens tend to support the policy of violence for varied reasons: ignorance, patriotism and hyper-nationalism, xenophobia and fear of the unknown, and a fear of being overrun by aliens or for revenge. However, in most cases, their support for wars is for simple reasons such as complete faith in their leaders and the system, a lack of interest, apathy, or being too lazy to protest. In contrast, the focus of those who are behind violent conflicts is on making profits from wars. They have to convince (or force) legislatures to vote in favor of wars and provide tax dollars to fight battles.

Such a mindset promotes acts of aggression and keeps the nation under a perpetual state of war, which can only be sustained by the demonization of victims. That, in turn, can only be accomplished by sustained propaganda. If viewed from a historical perspective, the invasions of Iraq and Afghanistan are just a minor point in the saga of violent conflicts of the last three centuries. The War on Terror may be different, as it has the potential to turn into a permanent war; still, it is not the main issue. One can always find an excuse to continue violent conflicts.

Lurking behind the perpetual state of war are widely ignored facts, which are: 1) The West has continuously and serially demonized various groups of people and nations in the last three centuries. There has hardly been a year when the West has not been at war with some political entity and at the same time actively demonizing one group of people or the other. 2) Those who were demonized have also been the primary victims of the aggression of the Western nations. 3) However, either by design or otherwise, authorities, politicians, and the corporate-controlled media, discuss only their slanted views of current conflicts, which are not the real issue. They are just a symptom of the disease. Hardly anyone talks about the demonization of intended victims, which is the primary etiology of resentment that affects both sides – the victims as well as the perpetrators.

The current state of demonization of Muslims has transformed not only the United States but also the world. It has also filled them with anger and hatred towards Muslims. Demonization has created a hierarchy among nations, which helps to categorize and demonize individual countries if needed. It is like the caste system of nations: the United States is on the top, followed by other Western nations, and then come Western-friendly nations, which support the United States as the leader of the pack. Neutral countries are the next in the hierarchy; finally, nations defying (or that have the potential to) or attempting to challenge the current world order. Those who are at the bottom of the totem pole are being demonized as and when needed. They have been branded as opponents of modernity and democracy. The faces of victims may change, but all of them are easy targets for being demonized.

The real issue is not the war in Iraq and Afghanistan, no matter how damaging; the actual reason is the economic system, which is the foundation of the current world order. The system promotes violent conflicts. Had the victim not been Iraq, it would have been any other Muslim country, such as Iran, Syria, or Libya, or any non-Muslim nation, such as Cuba, Nicaragua, or Venezuela. The permanent states of propaganda and of war, which go hand in hand, have been going on for centuries. The following examples confirm that the West is in a perpetual state of demonization.

As the colonial powers aimed their guns towards Asia and Africa, colonial subjects, especially Asian Indians, Chinese, and Africans, were also dehumanized. They were declared uncivilized and inferior. It was argued that the defeats on the battlefield of the three Asian giants – Japan, China, and India – were due to their innate inferiority. Asians were portrayed to be fit for coolies only, nothing more. After the abolition of slavery, plantations needed a workforce; Asians filled the empty slots as indentured labor. They were also expected to be subservient to the white race, as were the slaves. Millions of Asians perished during the occupation. Migration followed the extraction of wealth from their land. As the Asians started coming to North America, Australia, and New Zealand, they were welcomed with racial slurs similar to what Black Americans had experienced.[59]

Germans and Japanese were similarly targeted for demonization before the Second World War. They were branded as fanatics, fascists, and hyper-nationalists. After the War, communist countries – Russians, Chinese, Koreans, and Vietnamese – were demonized with equal intensity. Four million people were killed in Vietnam and another three million in Korea. Later, South and Central Americans were branded as drug dealers or communists. They, too, have been killed in millions. The West has serially demonized various people; it was not specific to one group. The United States and its allies are still demonizing one country after another. The demonization of colonial subjects was followed by the demonization of communists and then of Islamic civilization or Muslims. That came only after the fall of the Soviet Union. Now the Russians, Chinese, North Koreans, and Venezuelans are the targets. Another era of the Cold War is in the air. Their targets are continuously changing, but the pattern has not changed as the second decade of the twenty-first century has ended.

Since violent conflicts and demonization have been a constant feature of Western policy, the attitude of the American society towards violence has changed to accommodate the prospects of impending wars. This change can be traced to imperceptible but intense propaganda campaigns that promote the use of force to solve complex issues of the country. The culture of violence has become the new norm, which is accomplished by controlling what we view and read. Children in America have viewed millions of violent images by the time they become adults.[60] Warrior culture is idolized in the West as it was during the Roman Empire. TV shows and movies are creating a new generation of gladiators; these heroes of the screen kill brown *terrorists* without any remorse; victims are portrayed as evil who happen to be people of color with strange accents. To live in a state of demonization of so-called *others* and a state of propaganda to justify violence can only create surrealism; it is dangerous, as it alters the perception of reality. However, the flip side of this perception is that the culture of violence makes it easier to find young soldiers willing to kill and be killed.

Authorities and the corporate media in the United States are portraying wars as a vehicle for peace. The Orwellian phrase, *war is peace*, has been promoted as an excuse to wage wars by the successive administrations; it has been ingrained in the Western perception. The mainstream media have nurtured this notion. The belief in irrational ideas has formed the perception of Americans. Consequently, the sanctity of life has lost its meaning. Their perception of the worthlessness of human lives was initially directed against the demonized people, but gradually the population at large is also the target. Consequences are expected: there are over 60,000 deaths every year from opioid overdose; more than 30,000 people are killed by guns every year in the United States. Mass shooting, which is defined as killing or injuring more than three people in a single event, is taking place almost once a day.[61] The suicide rate among ex-soldiers is the highest in the world.

Chris Hedges has argued that these avoidable deaths are related to the culture of violence. He believes that the prevalent violence in the society is due to underlying depression and other forms of mental disorders, which are widely prevalent in the United States, more so among veterans of foreign wars. Citing Emile Durkheim, an early twentieth-century philosopher, Hedges argues that suicides and homicides reflect an altered perception of society. It is a sign of desperation, which becomes prevalent in society as empires decay into oblivion. Fear of loss is the root of irrational behavior. Alfred McCoy, in his book, *In the Shadows of the American Century*, substantiates Hedge's arguments.

McCoy writes that those in power have put forth policies that have led to a perpetual state of war, which, he argues, can cause the American economy to collapse by 2030.[62] He believes that the fate of the United States may already be sealed due to so many unproductive wars. Until now, the United States has been printing money, which foreigners are willing to buy, but how long can that last? McCoy assumes that once the dollar ceases to be the world's trading currency, American financial power will collapse. The United States would not be able to maintain 800 bases; 200,000 soldiers scattered around the world will have to be called back. Indeed, the American dollar is being slowly replaced by other currencies for international trade; if it is true, that will mean a contraction of its economy sooner than later. The exact time period cannot be predicted.

The current dehumanization of Muslims as violent people should be seen from these historical perspectives. Groups of people have been demonized before with worse adjectives. The characterization of victims was more despicable during the colonial period; that also left a negative impression about the victims, which has continued in the twenty-first century. Negative images of people, once they become a part of the collective perception, are hard to eradicate. Impressions, once formed, continue to exist for centuries, even after they are proved to be false and even concocted.

For example, Sven Lindqvist has documented how sustained propaganda in the nineteenth century had justified the slave trade and slavery. Africans were called *savages* and branded as *subhuman* from different species. Some of them were even described as closer to primates than *Homo sapiens*. The campaign of demonization was so effective that scientific expeditions were dispatched to find *missing links*. Some social scientists were quick to brand pygmies to be mythical creatures somewhere between humans and chimpanzees.[63] This was a classic case of dehumanization.

Those in the business of slavery needed an argument to satisfy the conscience of Christians to justify not only the extreme inhuman treatment of slaves but also of slavery. Their argument was that since Africans were not humans, there was no need to treat them at par with Europeans. Even religious leaders justified the inhuman treatment of Africans – fellow human beings – by a distorted version of their scripture. They argued that God created Africans to serve Europeans, who are the chosen people. Indians and Chinese did better, but not much. In the mindset of the clergy supporting the colonial-industrial complex, they were humans but still inferior to whites, who were created to rule.

The extermination of Tasmanians, Native American tribes, and Hottentots was justified by using similar arguments.[64] They were portrayed as animal-like creatures before they were massacred to the last person. Chinese, Indians, Arabs, and Iranians were described as inherently inferior to Europeans, even though each of them boasts seven thousand years of civilization. Judaism, Christianity, and Islam were born in the Arab world, Hinduism, Sikhism, Buddhism, and Jainism in the Indian Subcontinent, and Zoroastrianism and Baha'i in Iran. The Arab contribution to science and Greek and Western philosophy were ignored or trivialized. Flourishing African empires were never acknowledged. Why?

The justification of colonialism was based on the imagined racial superiority of Europeans, which was created from a concoction of facts and assumptions by the apologists of the colonial-industrial complex. Accepting that other races and cultures have contributed to the upliftment of humanity would have left colonial powers with no excuse to stay in colonies. Hannah Arendt, in her seminal work, *The Origins of Totalitarianism,* shows that colonialism established racism in the West, and racism was created to justify colonialism. From the perspective of colonial subjects, colonialism and racism are complementary to each other.[65] What came first – the chicken or the egg – is of no value to the victims. This question is only academic.

Prominent social scientists of the colonial period promoted the innate inferiority of the so-called "other races," which comes from the smaller size of the skull or the color of skin and the height of the victims' noses.[66] That idea has been long debunked, but the perception that blacks are inferior has lingered on; they are still called *savages* in some places. We know that the racist ideologues, who were the cheerleaders of the colonial-industrial complex, were wrong; they were propagating the ideas they knew were either unsubstantiated, erroneous, or concocted.[67] The color of skin depends upon melanin, a pigment within the skin. One out of a billion-plus genes is responsible for producing melanin. This gene neither influences intelligence nor violent behavior. Was it ignorance? Perhaps, but men like Richard Knox, Joseph Arthur de Gobineau,[68] and others who pioneered promoting the notion of the inherent inferiority of Africans falsified their data to prove that Africans are savages.[69] Even the diehard racist ideologues now agree that these assertions were wrong.

There could be, of course, an alternate explanation of the claims of violent behavior of Muslims: the problem may lie with the so-called Islamic civilization. Many highly accomplished people believe in this concept. India's former Prime Minister, Atal Bihari Bajpai, once wondered if Muslims can ever live with other people.[70] We do not know what he believed as he expressed his opinion while giving a speech to the members of his party. He later retracted his statement claiming that his words were taken out of context. That retraction is neither new nor important, as politicians tend to present an argument to test the water and then retract it if it backfires. The question is if this was a Freudian slip or his assertions are correct.

There are reasons to argue against his assertions; Muslims have been living in India for centuries, by and large peacefully. Besides, even in today's toxic atmosphere, both communities are not at each other's throats in many parts of the country. The current antipathy of the Hindutva diehards towards Muslims is mainly confined to India's Hindi heartland, which is ruled by the BJP. However, not all Hindus carry such ideas. Fierce defenders of the rights and sharpest critics of the lynching of Muslims are Hindus. South Indian states are free from anti-Muslim violence. Bajpai's words reflect a softer form of demonization; nevertheless, it is still a case of demonization, especially since he was addressing his party cadre, some of whom were in the process of developing overt anti-Muslim biases. A virulent form of Islamophobia was in its infancy; it took two decades to become deeply entrenched in Indian society.

On the other hand, Bajpai may have had reasons to express such views; he could have mentioned many conflicts in which Muslims were involved with members of other groups. Indeed, the demonization of Muslims has taken a firm foothold not only in the United States and the West but also in other parts of the world where they form a sizable minority. There are many countries where civil unrests, if not outright civil wars, are taking place between the non-Muslim majority and Muslim minorities. In some situations, governments have shown open contempt for Muslims; they have rebelled, in some cases, with violence against their governments. Both sides have used violence – some more, some less. These countries are Israel (against Palestinians), India (against Kashmiris and now even against Indian Muslims), Myanmar (against Rohingya), the Philippines (against Moros), Thailand (against Malays), Russia (against Chechens), Serbia (against Bosnians and Kosovars), Ethiopia (against Somalis); the list goes on.

However, this may only be half the story. In all these places, Muslims constitute a distinct minority; they are demanding equal rights for their communities, which others enjoy as their birth-right. Authorities of these countries claim that the demand for Muslim minorities to be treated at par with other citizens is outrageous, as they are being treated fairly. If so, statistical data about jobs should show no disparity between the two groups, but that is not the case. Take the example of India. Muslims constitute 15% of the population, but after the 2019 election, there are only twenty-seven

Muslims among 543 members of the parliament, which is less than 5%.[71] They have done worse in finding jobs. India's armed forces have less than 3% Muslims; its bureaucracy has even less, around 2.5%.[72]

The author of the article that quotes the above data, Amit Saksena, took the data from the Sachar Commission report. Former Prime Minister Manmohan Singh had commissioned it to evaluate the conditions of Indian Muslims. Despite the official report, which has drawn a dismal picture of Muslims in the country, officials continue to claim that there is no discrimination. On the contrary, they have argued that the Muslim community in India has become a law-and-order problem; they should be dealt with using force (violence). The question, therefore, should not be if Muslims have a problem with their government and neighbors, as all groups are expected to have their issues with each other.[73] The questions should be: do non-Muslim groups in identical situations have a similar problem with their governments? Do they also resort to a violent confrontation? If so, why and when?

The answer to the first question is, of course, "yes." The examples are violent conflicts in Crimea, Eastern Ukraine (Donetsk), and Georgia in which Russians are engaged with other groups, which are supported by the United States.[74] The situation in Sri Lanka (Hindus and Buddhists), South Africa (Zulu and Xhosa and immigrants from Zimbabwe), Kenya (Kikuyus, Luo, and Kalenjin), South Sudan (Kier and Machar), Rwanda (Hutu and Tutsi), Zimbabwe (Shona and Ndebele), and other countries in Africa is no different. Countries in Central America (Guatemala, El Salvador, and Honduras) and South America (Andes region and Brazil) have the same dynamics. The same holds for the West: the IRA (the Irish Republican Army) in Northern Ireland or ETA in the Basque region of Spain. Robert Pape has presented similar data in his book *Dying to Win.*[75]

What could be the reason for violent confrontations among non-Muslim groups in non-Muslim countries? Islam should be ruled out as a factor, as Muslims are not a party to the conflicts. The conflict in each country is also about the same mundane issues as they are in Muslim countries, such as the demand for equality or respect of human rights, irrespective of the religious affiliation of combatants. The root cause of the clash is the unequal distribution of resources of the country between its powerful and powerless groups and not necessarily between majority and minority communities. However, in most cases, the majority community is the most powerful group in the country. The majority–minority problem is universal.

These data suggest that global issues are at stake. Indeed, there is an atmosphere of fear as well as anger in the world today, which is universal and ubiquitous. Fear is also present in powerful nations; these countries can annihilate their enemies in minutes. In the twenty-first century, the anger of the West and its allies may be directed against Muslim minorities, but that is not the main reason, at least not according to the facts. Fear of and rage against "others," especially if they are in a sizable minority, are also universal. Indeed, we are living in the age of anger, and this anger is pervasive. Every group is angry with some "other" groups, especially if they share a space with them. Why? But more importantly, why now?

Pankaj Mishra has an explanation for this phenomenon. He argues that this situation is unique to the twenty-first century; to him, the entire world appears to be in a state of anger, and rightly so. In his book, *Age of Anger: A History of Present*, he points out that this anger is ubiquitous. It is directed not only towards Muslims but also against any group that challenges their interests. For the West, the issue is in opposition to the current world order. If there is any resistance, the offenders are defined as troublemakers.

The examples are North Korea (but not South Korea), Iran, Iraq, and Hezbollah (but not Israel, even though it is the only country to occupy land belonging to the other countries; it treats 50% of its population as second-class citizens), Vietnam (but not Cambodia, even though Pol Pot wiped out one-quarter of its population), Cuba (but not Haiti, even though its human rights record under Papa and Baby Doc was one of the worst), Nicaragua (but not Guatemala or El Salvador, which have a history of right-wing controlled murder squads; their victims' number in hundreds of thousands) or Venezuela (but not Colombia, even though the country was the focal point of narco-trafficking).

Mishra may have a point. The unrest has been raging in many parts of the world in which Muslims play no role. Since the underlying incentive for many human activities is economic factors, are there financial interests of the parties involved? The answer seems to be "yes." Groups that make a living out of tracking corruption have followed the trail of money, which also funds the campaign of dehumanization of Muslims. They found that U.S.-based Islamophobia organizations generously fund many political activists who propagate these views.[76]

According to John Esposito, $142 million was generated from donors in three years for promoting anti-Muslim hatred. True, their anger is now directed against Muslims in many places in the twenty-first century, but only a few decades ago, the same group of people and organizations funded the campaign to demonize the Soviets and other related groups. After the Second World War, the object of their scorn was the Soviet Union and other communist countries; later, it was directed against Korea and China during the Korean War and then Vietnam, as the United States got involved in the Vietnam War.

These historical facts suggest that 1) there may be a relationship between dehumanization of victims and violent conflicts; 2) in the West, there is long precedence of demonization of non-Europeans, which in most cases has ended with violence, and occupation of the country or regime changes; and finally, 3) the West has been the beneficiary of the consequence of violence. These assertions have been confirmed by many authors. Every form of violence has been justified by demonizing the victims, which has become an integral part of violent conflicts. Violence and exploitation may take different forms, but whatever its form, violence has to be justified to extract the resources of the victims.

For example, Sven Lindqvist, in his book, *Exterminate All the Brutes*, has shown that violence had been the primary tool for capturing wealth from the colonial subjects.[77] Other authors such as Adam Hochschild, Marnia Lazreg, Ward Churchill, Allison Weir, Shashi Tharoor, and others in their books confirm the assertions, but they have confined their narrative to one country. Britain's role in the slave trade and the profit from industrialized slavery is especially noteworthy.

According to the data presented by Mike Davis in his book, *Late Victorian Holocausts*,[78] profits from colonization, slavery, and the slave trade not only financed the industrial revolution in Britain and other parts of Europe but also brought unprecedented wealth.[79] Industrialized slavery is violence of the worst form; every aspect of slavery was managed by violence. Like other acts of violence, slavery also had to be justified. Plantations in the Caribbean were the main reason why slavery was started and managed on an industrial scale. Slavery has always existed, but not at the level seen during the colonial period. Plantation owners were respected individuals of the British society; so were the slave traders. They were the driving force behind slavery.

Britain's prosperity also came from its banking sector, which was the most vital factor in facilitating the trans-Atlantic slave trade at an industrial scale. Rothschild's & Sons Bank, the Bank of England, Barclays, Lloyd's of London, and other respectable institutions have been implicated in the slave trade; they were the backbone of the financial system, which made the slave trade possible. Slavery was banned in 1833 in Britain, but British corporations continued with the slave trade, which was still very lucrative. Several elites and thousands of ordinary people made their money with the slave trade. Many members of the British Parliament were ardent supporters of slavery and the slave trade; they were also slave owners.

Rothschild, the richest man in the world, his banking colleagues, and other respected elites of British society such as Gladstone, Blair, Hibbert, and others, owned slaves or invested in the slave trade.[80] However, if there is a discussion about the British role in slavery and the slave trade, apologists of Imperial Britain tend to refer to a single name, Sir William Wilberforce. He became a household name as a crusader against slavery, but he was an exceptional individual. He took up a stand against slavery when it was highly profitable and flourishing. He and his small core of dedicated abolitionists fought an uphill battle and won against the powerful pro-slavery groups.

Slavery and the slave trade were essential elements in the prosperity of Britain.[81] When slavery was abolished (1833), there were 47,000 slave owners in Britain who made a living from the labor of slaves.[82] They rented their slaves to the plantations and received compensation. The system was similar to the current financial system of owning stocks and bonds. There are companies that manage portfolios and provide interest. Similarly, corporations engaged in the slavery-industrial complex managed every aspect of slavery − buying, selling, raising money, and distributing profit to the shareholders.

Slave owners fought tooth and nail to stop abolition, which was not popular with the British people. The authorities finally relented, but the parliament had to offer a deal to the slave owners. They got the compensation package from the British government, a package which may be the second-highest in British history.[83] Slave owners were awarded twenty million pounds (in 1833), but the slaves, who were the actual victims of slavery, received nothing from the deal. On the contrary, to get their freedom, they had to pay their former masters with four years of free labor.

Rothschild put up fifteen million pounds, with a hefty interest rate, of course, which took the government more than a hundred years to pay back. For example, taxpayers of the city of Bristol, which was the focal point of the slave trade, continued to pay the dues and interests until 2015.[84] The Bristol authorities announced that the city had finally paid back the slave owners. They claimed it as a positive contribution of the city in abolishing slavery. However, they failed to mention in the communique that Bristol was the hub of the slave trade; the city was one of the worst offenders. It was the most prosperous town in Britain. Its elites were responsible for one of the most brutal activities of human history. This is not to demonize Britain, the West, or to dehumanize its leaders, but to point out that violence and profit go hand in hand. The compensation to the slave owners was paid by citizens from their taxes; the bulk of the money went to the elites.

During the colonial period, the elites profited from violence and all forms of inhuman activities, whether it was colonial wars or slavery. No wonder they were the most enthusiastic participants in the system of slavery. Their actions were bad enough, but worse, the West in general and the British Empire, in particular, used innovative ideas to dehumanize Africans as subhuman and justified their own inhuman activities. The motive behind the portrayal of Africans as subhuman was to justify slavery. They were routinely portrayed as savages. That impression of Africans and African Americans persists even today. Even almost two centuries after the slave trade was abolished, the British government is still trying to put a spin on their past activities and justify or minimize their actions, which can never be justified.

Furthermore, Davis argues that the prosperity of the United States was also built on slave labor. The imposing monuments that we see in Washington DC, the nation's capital, and other American cities, were built by slaves, and incurred a negligible labor cost to the country. The banking sector of the American economy was the backbone of the business of slavery. They financed the slave trade, insured the lives of slaves during the voyage, which had almost a 50% mortality rate, and owned and then rented them to the plantations and railroad builders. Slaves were vital to the economy. The Mexican–American War was fought to preserve the system of slavery. So was the American Civil War.

Important names of mega-corporations that were involved in financing slavery were N.M Rothschild & Sons Bank, Lehman Brothers, J.P. Morgan, Wachovia (now Wells Fargo), Fleet Boston, Barclays Bank, Brown Brothers Harriman (bank), Aetna, New York Life, AIG and Lloyd's of London (insurance companies), and of course, the East India Company.[85] These corporations are still the pillars of the Western economy. The boards of directors of these corporations control trillions of dollars' worth of equity. They run the financial world. The Catholic Church owned slaves; they were sold to finance George Washington University. Besides, Yale, Brown, and other Ivy-League universities were also built by money generated by slavery. Elites who participated in the slave trade were important individuals. They went on to lay the foundations of charities and philanthropic institutions.

Davis also points out that Britain was no more the premier economy by the end of the nineteenth century, nevertheless, it maintained its economic influence. Violence played an important role. By then, Germany and the United States had already overtaken the industrial production of Britain. The free-market economy had helped the British Empire as long as it was the foremost industrial powerhouse, but by then, it was no more the case. Still, the British Empire continued with the old system of the free market. The Empire had found another source of income. It had the luxury of keeping the *status quo* since it could maintain a monopoly on the Indian economy. British losses from international trade were passed on to the Indian taxpayers. The Indian market was also used to dump British products, which no one would buy. An example is the Indian railways; British companies built the infrastructure at a very high cost and interest, which was of a low quality. The British policy of using India as its economic dumping ground helped create prosperity in the rest of the Western world.

Apologists of the British Empire have challenged this argument; they argue that the poverty in India was and still is due to the fault of Indians, Indian leadership, and political culture. The underlying allegation is that Indian industry could not compete against the West during the colonial period because Indians were incapable of competing. But that is only half the story, as Indian companies were not allowed to participate in the free-market system. India had become the financial lifeline to the unproductive British companies. This practice prolonged the economic life of the empire.[86] Davis's argument is that the control over the Indian economy may not have been the primary reason for the industrial revolution; it was slavery, but the colonial economic loop that kept India its monopoly and a dumping ground, and a leash on Indian tax-payers during the late nineteenth century, were the reasons why the British economy continued its upward spiral even after it was not the first-rate industrial power.

Indians were also forced to pay for Britain's colonial wars – the Boer War, the three wars in Afghanistan, the Opium War, the invasion of East Africa, and the two world wars. Combined, Indian tax-payers had to foot the bills of imperial misadventures to the tune of billions of dollars. Lord Lytton arrived in 1877 as the viceroy of India. The same year, famine broke out, and between six and ten million people perished.[87] During the same period, the British Empire attacked Afghanistan; India paid the cost of war while people were starving. At the same time, the Viceroy organized a grand party to commemorate Queen Victoria's ascension to the throne, while millions of people were dying for want of food.

The British government justified the deaths from famine with utmost sincerity.[88] It indicates that the West in general and the British Empire, in particular, have found themselves compelled to justify their acts of violence in whatever form, probably because violence had to be justified to satisfy the conscience of the citizens. Justification of violence was typically done by demonizing the victims, those who were killed during the violence, or those who died during the inaction of the government during a famine. Justifying violence by demonizing the victims may be unique to the West.

In his book, Davis presents numerous examples of British authorities justifying their inactions during famines. Deaths during the Potato Famine in Ireland were also caused by the planned inactivity of the British Empire. The Famine wiped out one-quarter of the Irish population. The Irish people were branded as lazy and criminals. This label followed them into the New World and lasted well into the twentieth century. During the last decade of the nineteenth century, India lost almost ten million people to famine, but the British government forced Indians to pay for the Boer War.[89] Gujarat was one of the worst affected areas. When asked to explain why the mortality was so high in Gujarat, the officer in charge explained:[90]

> The Gujarati is a soft man, unused to privation, accustomed to earning his good food easily. In the hot weather, he seldom worked at all, and at no time did he form the habit of continuous labor. Large classes are believed by close observers to be constitutionally incapable of it. Very many among the poorest had never taken a tool in hand in their lives. They lived by watching cattle and crops, by sitting in the fields to weed by picking cotton, grains, and fruits, and, as Mr. Gibbs says, by pilfering.

Droughts are caused by Mother Nature, but famines are due to human activities, in which violence and profit play a vital role. Many apologists of the British Empire have been presenting the argument that colonialism played a crucial role in developing colonies as a financial powerhouse. Niall Ferguson argues that those countries, which have followed the British Empire, have prospered. The data show otherwise. Even Huntington accepts that the superiority of the West over the rest of the world came from its advantage from their weapons and their performance on battlefields and not from their ideologies.[91]

Violence was pursued by the West not because Western Christian civilization is inherently violent but because violence was the surest way to control land and capture its resources of powerless combatants. Wars are the most convenient way to achieve economic or political advantages for powerful nations. Western countries were, and they still are, the most powerful alliance of the last three centuries. Their victory resulted in the transfer of wealth from south to north. These facts are confirmed by historical data presented by Mark LeVine in his book, *Why They Don't Hate Us*.

Despite the data that categorically disprove the assertion of the U.S. officials and neoconservative ideologues that Muslims are inherently violent, the negative perception about Islam is widespread. That may be due to demonization, which a small group of intellectuals has actively propagated; they are also politically active. They are supported by the media, influential politicians, and organizations. Prominent thinkers of our time, such as Edward Said, John Esposito, and others, were already pointing out in the 1990s that the image of

Muslims as violent was being promoted by a particular group of people, who have their own political, personal, or theological agenda.

Contemporary authors such as Deepa Kumar, Nathan Lean, Stephen Sheehi, and others agree. They have shown that the Islamophobia industry is supported by a few activists who received financial support from a handful of super-elites with some spare change to burn on their pet projects. The mainstream media and PR industry have been promoting the interests of those who have their reasons to demonize Muslims.[92] There are strong indications that economic interests play a vital role in demonization. Many of the super-elites are real-estate tycoons; they have benefited from the annexation of the Palestinian land. Others own and operate corporations engaged in military adventures. Their goal is not to win wars, but to make a profit from war, any war – not specifically against the Muslims. Extending wars is a time-tested strategy for those who benefit from violence. In the first decade of the twenty-first century, the stars were aligned against Muslim countries.

The portrayal of Muslims as violent people is also based on made-up stories, fake news, and unsubstantiated facts. This is demonization; it is the first step in conducting acts of violence. Therefore, the rhetoric that Muslims are violent cannot be taken at its face value. Indeed, the West has a long tradition of using false data to promote a perception that justifies their acts of violence.[93] A century ago, scientists and intellectuals were producing fake data to brand Africans as the missing link – between humans and primates. There was a strong financial incentive to falsify the data. Similar dynamics are at work for the portrayal of Muslims as violent people. Social scientists of our generation are using similar arguments; their assertions cannot be substantiated by facts. There is more to the Islamophobia literature than merely the rhetoric of a clash of civilizations. The pertinent observations in this respect are as follows.

First, since a permanent state of war and a perpetual state of propaganda (for demonizing successive groups of people) have been going on for the last three centuries, contemporary conflicts are not the real issue; they are only symptoms of the disease that has affected the West for a very long time. It has consequences. Whereas the rest of the world, especially the victims, are passionately engaged in defending their religion, culture, or ethnicity from verbal attacks, the elites are making money from wars without drawing attention. Defending their religion, race, or whatever identity, which has been used to demonize the victims, merely distracts the focus from the actual problem, which is the perpetual state of war for controlling the resources that belong to other people.

Second, since another goal of demonization is to maintain a perpetual state of war, policymakers have succeeded in keeping the focus of debates on the branding of Muslims as violent and African Americans as criminals. The discussion in the West is focused exclusively on the current conflicts and not on the perpetual state of conflict, in which propaganda plays an important role. Debates on violent disputes have so far avoided deliberation and introspection on this issue. If viewed from this perspective, the rhetoric of President Trump to bomb Muslim countries is just a symptom of the underlying problem. His outrageous claims and promises may stir passionate discussions, but the real issue remains unanswered; they have been relegated to the sidelines.

Similarly, by invading Iraq and starting the War on Terror, President Bush was following what his predecessors had been doing for the last three centuries: invading one country after the other, committing genocide, and justifying acts of violence with noble causes.[94] That the invasions of Iraq and Afghanistan and bombings of poor countries in the name of the War on Terror were illegal activities was never addressed. Such rhetoric was responsible for diverting the attention from violent conflicts; incidentally, the military-industrial complex has been making a massive profit for corporations, which are the real power behind policies.

Third, had the demonization been explicitly directed against the Muslims only, one could have argued that it is either a clash of civilizations between the West and Islam or that the problem lies with Muslims or their religious beliefs. Since the West has demonized other groups of people with equal ferocity, the problem may lie either with the West itself or with every other nation or civilization that has been demonized; that may not be the case. Therefore, there are reasons to challenge their assumptions on which the demonization of "others" is based.

It raises the next set of questions: what could be the engine for the perpetual aggression by the West and continuous demonization of different sets of people? The current world order is based on two ideas: democracy and capitalism. Are they responsible for violence and demonization? Are these two principles (or a lack of) responsible for the current chaos, including dehumanization and violence?

Notes

1   Amartya Sen, *Identity and Violence*, Chapter 3.
2   https://news.gallup.com/opinion/gallup/187664/perceptions-muslims-united-states-review. aspx. For further discussion see John Esposito and Dalia Mogahed, *Who Speaks for Islam?*
3   Samuel Huntington, *The Clash of Civilizations*, 174–184. For problems associated with Huntington's views see John Esposito, *The Islamic Threat*, Chapter 6; Karen Armstrong, *Muhammad: A Biography of the Prophet*, Chapter 1; Jürgen Todenhöfer, *Why Do You Kill?* 155–160.
4   For further discussion on this topic, see Jack Shaheen, *Reel Bad Arabs*.
5   For further discussion on how consents are created among citizens see Noam Chomsky, *Manufacturing Consent*.
6   Abdullah Elshamy, https://www.aljazeera.com/programmes/aljazeeraworld/2017/05/ islamophobia-usa-170501131435789.html.
7   https://www.mintpressnews.com/iraq-and-beyond-how-many-millions-have-been-killed -in-american-wars/239468/. Also see https://ctc.westpoint.edu/eighteen-years-war-ter ror-comes-age/.
8   Gore Vidal provides the list of conflicts in *Perpetual War for Perpetual Peace*, 22–41. For an individual intervention see William Blum, *Killing Hope*.
9   Edward Said, *Orientalism*, Chapter 1.
10 Said, ibid.
11 Mark LeVine, *Why They Don't Hate Us*, 61.
12 https://www.countercurrents.org/polya050713.htm https://www.politifact.com/truth-o-meter/statements/2014/mar/31/facebook-posts/viral-meme-says-united-states-has-invaded -22-count/https://www.smithsonianmag.com/smart-news/brits-have-invaded-nine-ou

t-of-tcn-countries-109283469/ For a detailed discussion see Vidal, *Perpetual War for Perpetual Peace.*
13 Albright interview with Leslie Stahl, noted by Tariq Ali in *The Clash of Fundamentalisms*, 254.
14 Bernard Lewis, *What Went Wrong?* 1151–1160.
15 Imbesat Daudi, *Civilization and Violence*, 326–334.
16 Matthew White, *The Great Big Book of Horrible Things*, 505–507; also see Robert Fisk, *The Great War for Civilization*, Chapters 3, 9.
17 Ibid.
18 Albright interview with Leslie Stahl (note 13).
19 https://www.youtube.com/watch?v=omnskeu-puE; https://fair.org/extra/we-think-the-price-is-worth-it/.
20 https://www.democracynow.org/2004/7/30/democracy_now_confronts_madeline_albright_on.
21 Project Censored, "Drones are Big Business," 2012, https://www.projectcensored.org/drones-are-big-business/.
22 Ibid.
23 https://www.thenewamerican.com/usnews/foreign-policy/item/26359-award-winning-journalist-says-syria-did-not-use-chemical-weapons; https://www.globalresearch.ca/syria-un-mission-report-confirms-that-opposition-rebels-used-chemical-weapons-against-civilians-and-government-forces/5363139.
24 Chalmers Johnson, *Nemesis*, 54–89.
25 Ibid., 275–277; Johnson, *The Sorrows of Empire*, Chapter 2; Vidal, *Perpetual War for Perpetual Peace.*
26 Deepa Kumar, "Play it Again (Uncle) Sam; A Brief History of US Imperialism, Propaganda, and the News," *Censored 2015*, 299–300.
27 Kumar, 295–314.
28 https://www.salon.com/2007/10/12/wesley_clark/; https://www.globalresearch.ca/we-re-going-to-take-out-7-countries-in-5-years-iraq-syria-lebanon-libya-somalia-sudan-iran/5166.
29 https://www.concernusa.org/story/foreign-aid-explained/. Also see Mike Lewis, "Oxfam Exposes how AID is Used for Political Purpose," *Censored 2012*; also Daniel Wickham, "Top 10 US Aid Recipients All Practice Torture," *Left Foot Forward,* January 30, 2014, http://www.leftfootforward.org/2014/01/top-ten-us-aid-recipients-all-practice-torture.
30 Agence France-Presse AFP, "Timeline of the July War 2006".
31 http://americanfreepress.net/iraq-war-about-oil-or-israel/; http://www.thedebate.org/thedebate/iraq.asp For a detailed discussion see Naomi Klein, *The Shock Doctrine*, Chapter 6; also see Christopher Bollyn, *The War on Terror.*
32 https://www.huffpost.com/entry/pentagon-devours-money_b_5a958750e4b0f2c735654d75 also see Bollyn, *The War on Terror.*
33 Edward Herman, "Still Manufacturing Consent: The Propaganda Model at Thirty," *Censored 2018*, 209–224. For details see Edward Herman and Noam Chomsky, *Manufacturing Consent.*
34 Abraham Eraly, *The Lives and Times of Great Mughals.*
35 https://www.counterpunch.org/2018/03/19/us-empire-on-decline/; also see Joseph Tainter, *The Collapse of Complex Societies*, Chapter 6.
36 Johnson, *Nemesis*, Chapter 7.
37 https://reviewcanada.ca/magazine/2018/07/theres-no-plan-b-chris-hedges-on-the-collapse-of-america/ https://www.truthdig.com/articles/the-end-of-empire/. Also see Chris Hedges, *The Farewell Tour.*
38 Alfred McCoy, *In the Shadow of the American Century*, Chapter 8.
39 Thomas Jefferson, quoted by Johnson, *Nemesis*, 18.
40 https://www.huffpost.com/entry/pat-buchanan-blames-brita_n_103992; for a detailed study see Pat Buchanan, *Churchill, Hitler and The Unnecessary War.*

41 William Engdahl, *A Century of War*. For further discussion on this topic see Jim MacGregor and Gerry Docherty, *Prolonging the Agony*.
42 Carroll Quigley, *Tragedy and Hope*; for its abridged version see Joseph Plummer, *Tragedy & Hope 101*.
43 Ibn Khaldun, *The Muqaddimah*, 245–247.
44 Gwynne Dyer, *Future: Tense*.
45 https://www.pbs.org/newshour/economy/is-your-money-safe-at-the-bank-an-economist-says-no-and-withdraws-his; For a detailed discussion see Joseph Plummer, *Dishonest Money*.
46 https://spacenews.com/report-u-s-aerospace-a-trade-winner-but-tariffs-threaten-future-exports/ https://www.businessinsider.com/top-25-us-defense-companies-2012-2. https://www.usatoday.com/story/money/business/2013/03/10/10-companies-profiting-most-from-war/1970997/. For a detailed discussion see Mike Lofgren, *The Deep State*, Chapter 5.
47 https://www.countercurrents.org/puniyani041107.htm https://www.economist.com/asia/2016/10/29/an-uncertain-community.
48 "Fragile Peace: Sri Lanka is beginning to reckon with the Aftermath of a Brutal Civil War: Tens of Thousands Homeless, Tens of thousands Still Homeless," *National Geographic*, November 2016.
49 https://www.jacobinmag.com/2016/09/bill-clinton-hillary-superpredators-crime-welfare-african-americans/; also see https://www.huffpost.com/entry/hillarys-superpredator-comment_b_9655052.
50 https://www.washingtonpost.com/news/post-politics/wp/2016/02/25/clinton-heckled-by-black-lives-matter-activist/.
51 https://www.theguardian.com/commentisfree/2016/apr/15/bill-clinton-crime-bill-hillary-black-lives-thomas-frank; also see http://www.blackwestchester.com/clinton-mass-incarceration/. For a detail discussion on mass incarceration of black Americans, see Michele Alexander, *The New Jim Crow*.
52 Joel Andreas, *Addicted to War*.
53 https://hangthebankers.com/map-countries-united-states-invaded/.
54 https://www.politifact.com/truth-o-meter/statements/2014/mar/31/facebook-posts/viral-meme-says-united-states-has-invaded-22-count/. Also see Blum, *Killing Hope*.
55 Bollyn, 99–100.
56 Johnson, *Nemesis* 243–247; also see Hedges, *Empire of Illusion*, Chapter V.
57 https://www.ptsd.va.gov/understand/common/common_veterans.asp https://www.vanityfair.com/news/2015/05/ptsd-war-home-sebastian-junger.
58 Amos Leon, "Introduction," in Hannah Arendt, *Eichmann in Jerusalem*, xii–xiv; https://www.newyorker.com/magazine/1963/02/16/eichmann-in-jerusalem-i.
59 Ronald Takaki, *Strangers from a Different Shore*. For European attitude towards Indians see Christopher Hibbert, *The Great Mutiny India 1857*.
60 https://www.webmd.com/parenting/features/tv-violence-cause-child-anxiety-aggressive-behavior https://www.psychologytoday.com/us/blog/reading-between-the-headlines/201309/violence-the-media-and-your-brainhttps://www.dailymail.co.uk/news/article-1159766/Cartoon-violence-makes-children-aggressive.html.
61 https://www.huffpost.com/entry/number-us-mass-shootings-2019_n_5d4849d9e4b0aca34121ad19.
62 McCoy, *In the Shadow of the American Century*.
63 Lindqvist, *Exterminate All the Brutes*.
64 Lindqvist, *Terra Nullius*.
65 Hannah Arendt, *The Origins of Totalitarianism*, Chapter 6.
66 Lindqvist, *Exterminate All the Brutes*, 125–129. Also see Richard Knox, Chapter 6.
67 Lindqvist, *The Skull Measurer's Mistake*, 42-47.
68 https://beyondforeignness.org/4758.
69 Lindqvist, *The Skull Measurer's Mistake*, 143–149.
70 https://thewire.in/communalism/vajpayees-goa-speech-april-2002.

71 https://www.thenews.com.pk/latest/475755-indian-elections-2019-muslims-in-543-strong -lok-sabha.
72 https://thediplomat.com/2014/05/indias-muslim-soldiers/.
73 Daudi, *Civilization and Violence*, Chapter 5, Table 5.9 and 5.10.
74 https://www.theworldreporter.com/2015/02/us-involvement-ukraine-crisis-disturbing-pr oblem-solving.html.
75 Robert Pape, *Dying to Win*, 285–286.
76 https://www.thenation.com/article/sugar-mama-anti-muslim-hate/ http://www.islam ophobiawatch.co.uk/who-funds-the-islamophobes/. For a detailed discussion see Nathan Lean, *The Islamophobia Industry*.
77 Lindqvist, *Exterminate All the Brutes*.
78 John Esposito, https://www.youtube.com/watch?v=E6cKvPo4Dv8.
79 Mike Davis, *Late Victorian Holocausts*, 296–310.
80 https://www.theguardian.com/world/2015/jul/12/british-history-slavery-buried-scale -revealed.
81 Ibid.
82 Ibid.
83 https://www.rt.com/uk/418814-slave-compensation-bristol-taxpayer/.
84 https://www.theguardian.com/news/2018/mar/29/slavery-abolition-compensation-when- will-britain-face-up-to-its-crimes-against-humanity.
85 https://atlantablackstar.com/2013/08/26/17-major-companies-never-knew-benefited-sla very/.
86 Davis, Chapter 9, Figure 9.1.
87 Davis, 6-11, also see Table P1 for estimated famine mortality during the Victorian period.
88 Davis, 32–33.
89 Davis, 392–394.
90 Davis, 172.
91 Huntington, 51.
92 Kumar, Chapter 10.
93 Lindqvist, *Exterminate All the Brutes*. For mass incarceration of Black Americans in contemporary America, see Michelle Alexander, *The New Jim Crow*, Chapter 1. For the policy of forced labor of Black Americans between the Civil War and the Second World War, see Douglas Blackmon, *Slavery by Another Name*.
94 Chomsky, *Manufacturing Consent*; https://atlantablackstar.com/2013/08/26/17-ma jor-companies-never-knew-benefited-slavery/.

Epilogue

I. Major inferences

This book contains several verifiable facts and data. What inferences can be drawn from them? The following observations stand out: the West has invaded every group of nations in the last three centuries (Chapter 2); occupations have resulted in the capture of resources of the defeated nations; their wealth was transferred to their colonial masters and now to transnational mega-corporations (TNMCs) based in the West. The irony is that victims were blamed for being violent, and those who perpetrated the worst crimes are branded as progressive and respectful of human rights. That has not changed in the twenty-first century. Based on these observations, the following inferences can be drawn.

A. "Is Islamic civilization violent?" – an inappropriate question?

There is an ongoing debate on the so-called clash of civilizations between the West and Islam. The prevailing perception is that Muslims are inherently violent, intolerant of other people, and their violent behavior stems from Islamic doctrine. However, as noted in Chapter 2, facts speak otherwise. If so, how did this image become ingrained in the Western perception?

As noted in Chapters 3, 4, and 5, the answer lies with the demonization of Islam and Muslims. However, it may partly be due to how the question was framed by prominent journalists, authors, and opinion-makers during debates. The popular media took over discussions without going through objective evaluation. They did not raise any objection when innuendos replaced arguments. A proper algorithm of this issue should have been as follows:

1   Since nations belonging to every civilization have engaged in acts of violence in the past – some more, some less – the proper question should have been: which civilization is more violent? Since Muslim countries have been inappropriately defined as Islamic civilizations, a better question could have been formulated are Muslim countries *more* violent than their cohorts. We could have found the answer by quantifying violent conflicts of each country or civilization and then compare with acts of violence of other cohorts.

DOI: 10.4324/9781003323105-8

The promoters of the concept that Islamic civilization is violent have failed to present such a comparison. If they did, it was inappropriate.

2 If it was confirmed that Muslim majority countries (or nations belonging to Islamic civilization, as defined by neoconservatives) have indulged in more violent conflicts, only then should Muslims be characterized as violent. That is not the case (Chapter 2). Since it was not true that Muslim countries had indulged in more acts of violence, the question of whether their violent behavior is due to or in spite of the Islamic doctrine is redundant.

3 Acts of violence are due to extrinsic factors, which are common to all civilizations. Greed seduces humanity to capture land that belongs to others, and power lures humankind to become violent. The West formed the most powerful alliances; they were better organized, and by the middle of the nineteenth century, they had acquired more powerful and effective weapons. That explains their success on and off the battlefield. No civilization is inherently violent.

4 Neoconservative and other pro-war ideologues had framed conflicts between the West and Muslim majority countries as a clash of civilizations between the West and Islam or Islamic civilizations. This metaphor is inappropriate since on the one side of the battle-line is the West, which is a political and military alliance; on the other side, it is Islamic civilization, which is not a political entity but only a socio-religious unit. To complicate the matter further, these two terms, Islam and Islamic civilizations, have different meanings to different people.

5 Putting the violent conflicts as a clash between the West and Islam is also unfair from another perspective. The above two terms suggest that religious dogma is important to Muslims but not to the West. This has helped to define Muslims as a monolithic unit. This is a gross generalization of Muslims and Islamic civilization, which has helped the promoters of wars to characterize Muslims as fanatics and the West to be in the post-religious enlightened state. Ideally, these authors should have compared Islamic civilization to Western Christian civilization and Western nations to Muslim nations.

Instead of asking which civilization is more violent, the discussions on this topic usually begin with the question of whether Islamic civilization is violent. These are examples of the power of suggestion. Since these assertions are constantly repeated in every media format, they leave an impression that maybe, Islam is a violent religion or, at the least, it should be viewed as violent. This is the implicit message, which has been effective in stereotyping Muslims as violent. The impression of Muslims being violent is already anchored in the perceptions of readers and viewers even before the discussion begins.

The impression created by these assertions has far-reaching consequences. By framing the question in this way, the actual cause of conflicts, violent or otherwise, was not addressed; violent behavior of Islamic civilization was never proven. Nevertheless, the alleged violent behavior of Muslims became the primary focus of the discussions, and the actions of perpetrators and their reason to use violence became an irrelevant issue. Furthermore, the question raised in this format has left Muslims in a defensive mode, which has created different sets of problems. Some Muslims feel that their religion and way of life are being demonized; therefore, they must defend the sanctity of their faith. Others are reacting to the condescending attitude shown by Western leaders and the media.

The invasions of Iraq and Afghanistan and the War on Terror have been justified by the above concept. President Bush and members of his administration had framed the reason to go to war by asserting that Iraq had weapons of mass destruction (WMDs), even though no valid proof was presented. Apologists of the U.S. policy claimed that acts of violence against Islamic civilization were essential, as Muslims are violent, fanatic, and irrational. They promoted the notion that Muslims would not listen to reasons; therefore, force is the only way to deal with Muslim societies.

Although no WMDs were ever found in Iraq, Iraq was invaded and occupied; close to five million people have been killed; forty million had to flee their homes. Since the invasions were based on false assertions and made-up evidence, the invasions were war crimes. Rhetoric and justifications of acts of violence have no legal standing. Therefore, those who planned the invasion should be declared war criminals. The President of the United States is beyond the law; how about the minions who had planned the invasion of Iraq even before President Bush was elected (Chapter 3)?

By associating civilizational violence with Islam, promoters of violent conflicts have led readers and viewers to assume that the nation (civilization) in question may be violent. That has created chaos, which has built an atmosphere of confusion, anger, hatred, and fear of Muslims in the West. Muslim communities are also apprehensive about the West. Since Muslims have been dehumanized in the most virulent form by the West, there is frustration, resentment, alienation, and disgust with the West. For the last three decades, Muslims have been presented as the problem; that is not a coincidence. They are the perfect targets: they are weak and divided (into sixty nations), and they are sitting on 75% of the world's oil reserve.

One can only wonder what would have happened if the events of 9/11 had been designated as a criminal event, which it was, and not a civilizational clash. In that case, acts of violence of Al Qaida, ISIS, or other similar groups could have been discussed objectively. Confusion would not have taken a foothold in the West. Maybe, American public opinion might not have been in favor of wars for solving complex problems of a diverse and complex world. Furthermore, American citizens might not have accepted that the United States, Britain, and their allies should invade Iraq and bomb half a dozen countries in the name of the War on Terror.

In that case, American taxpayers would have saved $6.2 trillion, which was spent on wars of the last two decades. If so, there would have been losers as well. The military-industrial complex would have lost hundreds of billions of dollars, which they received from the treasury; their board members and executives would also have been poorer by tens of millions of dollars; thousands of people might not have well-paying jobs. Is that the reason why objective discussions on this topic were difficult, if not impossible? Iraqis, Afghans, Libyans, and others became homeless; their countries were destroyed. Was the destruction of their homes their Manifest Destiny, or was it planned? If so, how? Who created the atmosphere?

B. *The actual perpetrators of wars are not blamed for violence*

Wars and invasions of countries committed once or twice by one specific nation over half a century or more, no matter how extensive or brutal, can be viewed as a mistake or a blunder. In that case, certain acts of violence can even be justified in exceptional circumstances, but that is not the case here. The West has been in a perpetual state of war, which has a different etiology from sporadic acts of violence. In the latter case, blame for a specific violent conflict can be placed on an individual leader or exceptional circumstances. However, if a nation or a group of nations is sending its troops to invade other countries year after year, occupying them for centuries, and looting the resources of the defeated nations, then it is neither an oversight nor a blunder; it is a planned strategy of plunder. Capturing the resources of other people by violence is not only a robbery but an armed robbery.

The West has chosen the path of violence for apparent reasons: they are far more powerful than the victims, and the latter is sitting on valuable pieces of real estate. Those whose lands were occupied and their homes destroyed are the real victims; their resistance is feeble, at best. Notwithstanding, the victims are blamed for putting up resistance against the invaders and branded as violent and savages. However, if acts of violence of the perpetrators are justified centuries after centuries by blaming the victims with sophisticated arguments, these are a strategy to justify the transfer of wealth from the victims by force. The excuses are put in place long before invasions begin.

Foreign nationals are not the only victims of a permanent state of violence. Wars require an investment that comes from the nation's coffer. If the military claims a larger share of the budget of the country, while its sizable population is mired in poverty, this is also a robbery; more money for the military ends up in diverting tax dollars to the military-industrial complex, which is run by a small group of people. That money belongs to the entire nation, but it is doled out to the TNMCs engaged in weapon production, post-war disaster management, and acquiring mercenaries. Since half of the discretionary budget of the United States is reserved for the preparation of wars and military, less money is available for the safety net for the poorest segments of American society. Their share of tax dollars is shrinking. Those who can afford the least have a higher proportion of burden.[1] The wealthiest segment of the United States is receiving the most handouts and tax breaks.[2] Welfare dollars for the poor are limited and contracting. But the welfare for TNMCs and the rich, who run these corporations, is ballooning.

If viewed from the perspective of the most disenfranchised groups of the nation, they are being blamed for being poor. It results in resentment. If one in four children in the United States live in a food-insecure household,[3] and their family welfare checks continue to shrink, it creates an existential problem for the destitute. Remaining poor for generations may not be entirely their fault, which causes anger, frustration, and desperation. It is dangerous for the country. A perpetual state of war and an endless demand for funding for foreign wars indicate a problem of its political system; it affects many aspects of society. The underlying issue is the influence of the military-industrial complex, financial sector, and TNMCs. They are owned and controlled by super-elites from the West. Their number may be small, but their influence and power are as vast as one could imagine.

Simply put, the crux of the problem is that wars are the cause of extreme disparity not only among countries but also within the wealthiest country. It has created an underclass. Media elites were demonizing the needy, whose numbers have grown steadily, causing resentment. Ridiculing their inability to manage their finances, which is beyond their control, is not going to solve the problem. If victims are blamed, even though they are not the culprit, it is an open invitation to civil discords. There is enough evidence to claim that a tiny group of elites, which control the financial system, are the cause of the disparity. They are the problem, not the poor; the latter are the victims of the nation's financial system.

Those who control the system have justified the policies of permanent war with noble causes – the nation's security, protecting their way of life, financial system or religious dogma, or any such concepts. Occasionally, important members of the war cabinets of the United States have acquiesced in a state of reflection or guilt, perhaps, that the stated reason to invade other nations had nothing to do with facts.[4] The decision to invade is always taken after careful deliberation.[5] The goal behind their arguments in justifying their acts of violence and demonizing the victims is to divert the attention of citizens from the real issue and from the illegal activities of leaders who take their nations to war. The Western media does not discuss which factors prompt super-elites to start a war and justify acts of aggression.

We know why the West has pursued its policy of perpetual war: it wanted to plunder the resources of the defeated nations. That is not an enigma; the enigma is that the West has gotten away with justifying violence for centuries, and only a few have taken them to task. Even in the twenty-first century, the West continues to justify its act of violence with great success; the world is still a bystander even though children and innocent civilians die in the war zones. Even if there are blatant wrong-doings, nothing happens to the perpetrators.

For example, Mrs. Madeleine Albright, the then Secretary of State under the Clinton administration, which was engaged in bombing Iraq in the 1990s, gave an interview on the ABC, an American broadcasting channel. The United States had also placed sanctions after the First Gulf War; consequently, half a million Iraqi children died from hunger and starvation. Albright was asked in the interview if bombings and sanctions were worth the effort of removing the Iraqi President. Her answer was affirmative.[6] She showed neither empathy nor regret for the deaths of half a million children. Was it because they were deemed "others?"

In a later interview, Albright was asked to clarify her statement. She had plenty of time to think it through. She claimed that the blame should go to the Iraqi President for opposing the United States; the bombings, which killed innocent civilians and children, should not be blamed. Even then, her political career did not suffer; she finished her tenure as the Secretary of State. She is now a respectable icon of the "formers," retired senior officials who retire temporarily, joining industries and using the revolving door between the two. They continue to have a voice in foreign policy. She is also a sought-after political commentator and runs an influential think-tank.

The demonization of victims and justifications of violent conflicts are a multi-billion-dollar industry. Its narratives are controlled by those who run the media. Other players in justifying wars are the military-industrial complex, homeland security industry, intelligence-gathering corporations, and financial sectors. These groups benefit from wars and a surveillance state. They are financed and controlled by the same tiny groups of plutocrats who own and manage a few dozen major financial institutions, public-relations firms, and the mainstream media. There is a high degree of connectivity among board members.[7] Those who control megabanks bankroll the war projects and preparation of wars. They also sit on the board of almost every major corporation.[8]

According to David Rothkopf, the number of super-elites may be a little over 6,000.[9] Of course, they are billionaires, but not all billionaires make it into the small core of global power elites.[10] Having a few billion in the bank here and there is not enough to find a place among the managers of the world order; the entrance to this exclusive club requires control of over a trillion-dollars' worth of assets. Most of them control asset management companies and pension funds. Their influence comes from their control of the financial order. The money belongs to citizens and their pension plans, but the management has the sole discretion to invest in any TNMC they like. That gives them control over the world economy.

Peter Phillips, in his book, *Giants*, claims that the total number of people who control the world economy may only be in three digits.[11] He is right, as only 199 people control seventeen asset management firms, managing over $41 trillion[12] (the total wealth of the world is nearly $240 trillion).[13] Power does not come from having money in the bank; money's influence stems from controlling the right to invest. Chris Hedges argues that many political leaders and their supporters in the media and public relations firms do not work for the country; they are working for big money. Are plutocrats aware of the consequences of their policy? Do they understand that the demonization in the twenty-first century, which is directed against Muslims, has cost five million lives worldwide, and $6.2 trillion to U.S. taxpayers; a large chunk has gone to the TNMCs.

The American policy of perpetual war is based on innuendo, which may be the primary cause of Islamophobia prevalent in the West, Israel, and India. However, Muslims are not the only target. Anyone who challenges the world order will encounter the same rhetoric with full intensity. For example, Jawaharlal Nehru, the first prime minister of India, was one of the pioneers of the non-aligned movement. He was an icon of the twentieth century, but he was defined as a problem. His daughter Indira Gandhi was called a b**** by President Nixon; she often defied the United States. However, the current Prime Minister Narendra Modi is welcomed in the West with open arms. The first two prime ministers were challenging the world order set up by the West; the latter is a part of that world order.

The current world order is being enforced by the United States and its allies. NATO has become their military arm. In the last few decades, the West has also established half a dozen private military corporations, which provide well-trained mercenaries on demand.[14] The plutocrats also own these corporations; they have also become profitable entities; their stock values have soared. War is a profitable business. Financial institutions are heavily invested in this segment of TNMCs. For many plutocrats, violent conflicts of the twenty-first century were the ticket to the accumulation of unprecedented wealth. They will not change their stand on the policy of perpetual war, which has made them rich and powerful. At the same time, their approach has led to the invasions and bombings of a dozen countries; they have been decimated. Millions of people have lost everything which they had accumulated over generations.

Therefore, it is a waste of time and energy to analyze the causes of current conflicts and discuss them with those who benefit from wars and capture wealth. The demonization of victims is an essential step in pursuing the policy of continuous war. That is expected to continue. Muslims happen to be the target in the twenty-first century, but that can change quickly; others will take their place. That explains the sudden explosion of Islamophobic ideas. These super-elites have no incentive to end violent conflicts. Discussions will not resolve the issue of the demonization of Muslims. The chances are that they are determined not to be swayed by peaceniks even if valid arguments are presented. Discussing any aspect of today's wars, except how to end them, will only divert the attention of the citizens from the real problems.

C. Capture of wealth has continued in the twenty-first century; so have wars

As documented in the previous chapter, the West has been in a perpetual state of war for over three hundred years; that trend has not changed in the twenty-first century. Even in the last two decades, the United States has managed to jump from one war to the other.[15] There is no controversy on this topic. Even the diehard apologists of the British Empire, other former colonial powers, and the United States agree with this assessment.[16] The dispute is about the reason behind the acts of violence of the West.

Even though wars have cost enormous resources and millions of lives, the West has continued to pursue war as its central policy. Apologists and their critics have divergent views, at least formally, on this issue. The critics claim that the sole purpose of a handful of European nations was to capture the wealth of the rest of the world. Consequently, colonial wars have made the West prosperous. Neither the incidence nor prevalence of violent conflict has changed in the twenty-first century. Besides, the arguments used by warmongers as an excuse to invade other countries are the same as those they had used in previous centuries during colonial expansion.

In contrast, the apologists claim that the Western presence in colonies was for altruistic reasons; colonial powers merely wanted to teach the virtues of civilization to what they described as *lesser humans* scattered around the world. They have further argued that in the process, the West may have eliminated a few million people here and there, but their intention was pious. They intended to get rid of savages and subhumans who were a menace or had the potential to be a menace to humanity.[17] The other stated reason for the extermination of colonial subjects was to improve the genetic pool of the human race by eliminating unwanted elements.[18]

Who decides which genetic pool is better? Those with better weapons, of course. Incidentally or otherwise, people with deadly weapons also wanted to settle on the land that belonged to "other" people. Is it a coincidence that those who were exterminated had no modern weapons? They were also people of color or with flat noses or both.[19] That could be possible factors, but the main reason may have been that the victims were sitting on the valuable pieces of land which the colonial powers coveted. Europeans were willing to go any distance to control the resources of the newly acquired land. More deadly weapons helped to exterminate the victims.

Arguments to justify massacres of colonial subjects were based on concocted facts and pseudoscience. They argued that weak and inferior species die out in nature and are replaced by stronger and more adaptable ones; therefore, they argued that the extermination of vulnerable subjects is not against the law of nature.[20] The supporters of the colonial-industrial complex called their concept *the survival of the fittest,* a term coined by Charles Darwin to explain evolution. Genocide followed; the media blitz supporting these concepts was vicious. In the process, European colonial powers established their control over colonies in the rest of the world. A.R. Wallace, another well-known author of that era, opined that *natural selection*, a term which Charles Darwin also used, justified occupation of the alien land and extermination of other races.[21]

The apologists had taken those words from Darwin's seminal works, *The Origin of the Species* and *The Descent of Man.*[22] Darwin, by then, had become a respected figure. Associating the extermination of weak and vulnerable people with the most well-known intellectual and accomplished scientist of the nineteenth century gave credence to their bizarre idea.[23] Darwin never endorsed this view, but neither did he refute it. He remained silent as his name was recited to justify each massacre.[24] These ideas were enthusiastically embraced by elites who controlled the slavery-industrial complex. A tiny group of intellectuals raised the alarm, but they had no shrillness in their voices. Still, they protested, but their protest vanished as soon as it began.

Even by the middle of the twentieth century, very few people comprehended the fallacy of such ideas, but Hannah Arendt did; she had understood that the financial and political system created for colonialism was instrumental in justifying massacres of colonial subjects. The silence of ordinary citizens was equally important. Even those who did not benefit from the slavery-industrial complex did not protest. Arendt explained the crux of the problem in simple terms. She pointed out that nineteenth-century scientists and philosophers were assuming that the natives, who were branded as savages, were the forerunners of Europeans.[25] Of course, there was no evidence to suggest that.

Nevertheless, this concept was propagated with great enthusiasm with deadly consequences. Close to 95% of the original inhabitants of the Americas and Australia were subsequently eliminated.[26] Were they a threat to Europeans? Of course not; they had no means to cross the Atlantic or Pacific and attack Europe and the United States. Or was it because the natives owned the most desirable land on which colonialists aspired to settle?

The assumption that aboriginal Australians, Native Americans, and Africans were subhuman was based on a false premise, assumption, misinformation, disinformation, and in most cases, on concocted data.[27] For example, an anatomist from Scotland, Robert Knox, who was the pioneer in making racism an accepted norm in Europe and the Americas, examined only one skull. Still, he claimed that African skulls are smaller than European skulls.[28] There were two false assumptions: a larger skull equals more intelligence, and a bigger brain equals more grey matter. There was also a problem with his method: whose skull did he study? We do not know. Indeed, there are similarities between the ideas of Knox, who branded Africans as savages, and Bernard Lewis's hypotheses, which branded Muslims as violent people. The former justified slavery, and the latter the clash of civilizations. Both hypotheses were based on pseudo-science; both resulted in unprecedented violence.

Samuel Morton, a physician from Philadelphia, had an extensive collection of human skulls. He also claimed that Africans have smaller skulls and, therefore, are less intelligent. His methodology was equally flawed. He did not compare male skulls with male skulls of different races, nor did he consider the size of the body, which is the single most crucial factor of the size of skulls.[29] Still, apologists of the colonial-industrial complex had argued that since *subhumans* were being exterminated by colonial powers, they are merely assisting Mother Nature to get rid of the unwanted elements.[30] Conservative activists such as Richard Knox[31] and progressive reformers such as Herbert Spencer[32] supported ideas that justified slavery, the slave trade, and genocide during the middle of the nineteenth century.

According to Pankaj Mishra, critics of colonialism also emerged at the same time.[33] Jalaluddin Afghani, Rabindra Nath Tagore, Sun Yat-Sen, Liang Qichao, and others challenged the colonial narratives. They argued that Asians and Africans, with a seven-thousand-year history of functioning civilizations, did not need any lesson on civilization from colonial powers who had left a trail of blood wherever they went. Foremost intellectuals of the century argued that being told how to run the country was arrogance or hypocrisy or both.

During the fading phase of the Mughal Empire, the verbal resistance from Indian aristocrats was still caustic. As the historian William Dalrymple points out, a Mughal noble, Narayan Singh, bitterly complained that Indians have to take orders from those who have not yet learned to clean their behind.[34] However, by the end of the nineteenth century, even the verbal resistance of colonial subjects had become muted. As European weapons became more lethal and colonial forces became more numerous due to innovation in mass transportation, the three Asian powers, India, China, and Japan, were decisively defeated. Subsequently, English industries devoured the Indian and Chinese economies. The colonial bureaucracy became the largest employer in the country, which silenced the remaining opposing voices. Protests were confined to few but prominent voices such as Rabindra Nath Tagore, Dada Bhai Naoroji, Syed Qutub, Ho Chi Minh, and others who used their intellect to challenge the proponents of colonialism.[35] Their voice had no strength at the time; still, their role was vital in ending colonialism; they laid the foundation on which anti-colonial movements were formed.[36]

In the last seventy years, the United States has continued the same policy which the British Empire had pursued a century ago. The most powerful country is also in a permanent state of war; it provides excuses, which are similar to the reasons of the former colonial powers. The British Empire used to invade other lands in the eighteenth and nineteenth centuries with the pretext of bringing civilization; the United States argues that it is bringing democracy to the rest of the world. In the process, millions of people were killed.

Today, countries that are being singled out, incidentally or otherwise, own three-quarters of the world's oil reserves under their sand. The critics of U.S. policy argue that the invasions of Iraq and Afghanistan were based on assertions that were found not only to be false but also to be confabulations. The War on Terror, which has meant indiscriminate bombings of half a dozen countries, is being conducted on the pretense of fighting terrorism. They are equally illegal and immoral acts. Do these nations need a lesson in democracy? Maybe so, but not from the West, which has a track record of supporting autocratic rulers and executing *coups d'état* against democratically elected governments. The West has used every excuse to invade and occupy other countries and install pliable regimes.[37]

Therefore, the opponents of the current world order argue that the Western claim of occupying the rest of the world in a state of narcolepsy[38] or for altruistic reasons[39] is sheer nonsense. They claim that Western arguments are only an excuse to control the resources of other people. That may be changing. Now, even apologists concede in a muted form that these arguments were an excuse to stay in colonies as long as they could. The real reason for their presence was to plunder the resources of colonies. Only now have a few intellectuals, political thinkers, and activists started writing about the atrocities, but that has not reached the perception of ordinary folks in the West yet.

There is an irony behind being demonized for three centuries. The West had portrayed Aboriginal Australians and Native Americans as savages and uncivilized. That stereotyping has become deeply ingrained in the Western psyche. Why were they demonized? Was it because they lacked modern weapons? True, the victims had only spears, sticks, bows, and arrows, no rifles or guns. Should that make them more civilized or uncivilized? Since colonial powers had modern weapons that could kill hundreds of people in minutes, should that make them more civilized? There is no logic to this argument, but innovation in deadly weapons established the hegemony. Consequently, the West took over 85% of the planet; the British Empire alone ruled over one-quarter of the world's population.

Modern weapons established the new world order. Colonial powers forced their cultural and social norms on colonial subjects. At the time, there was no one to challenge the West intellectually except a few brave souls. Those who dared to challenge the colonial system were branded unmodern, primitive, and imbecilic. However, a hundred years later, it has become evident that the policy that the British Empire had put in place, and the United States has nurtured after the Second World War, is unsustainable. Both nations are perceived to be enlightened and at the cutting edge of modernity. That may be true, but are they wise?

Their followers around the world copy their lifestyle, which is a drain on precious resources of the planet. In contrast, the ways of Aboriginal Australians and Native Americans, whom the apologists of the colonial industrial complex had characterized as savages, primitives, and subhuman, are far more environment-friendly. Their lifestyle is also sustainable, progressive, and more enlightened than that of the people who occupied their land and exploited the resources. In the process, Western nations have been destroying the planet at an unprecedented scale.

The irony is that the two most ridiculed and dehumanized groups of people have shown us how to live without destroying the planet. The extinction of humanity due to climate change and perpetual war is becoming a distinct possibility in our lifetime. The lifestyle and holistic principles of Native Americans and Australians are the answer to the survival of humanity.

D. Unrestricted growth is destroying the human habitat

The current financial system is based on unrestricted economic growth, which is uniquely a Western concept. This may also be at the root of all violent conflicts. The growth is based not on the needs of society, but on desires and cravings that can never be satisfied. This Western phenomenon of insatiable greed is being copied worldwide, even by those who have thousands of years of history of their own economic system. That is not surprising. Ibn Khaldun, in his seminal work, *Muqaddimah*, pointed out almost 800 years ago that those who had been conquered copy their former masters with great enthusiasm.[40] That is also the reason why there is a lingering perception of Western superiority in many countries even after the departure of colonial powers. This perception has made it difficult to argue against the influence of capitalism without being labeled as an opponent of modernity. Opposing the Western-style economic system carries a negative connotation.

The current financial system, which has taken centuries to evolve into a powerful force, is taking the planet to its sixth extinction, which would be an entirely human creation. The other five extinctions were celestial or geological events. However, this extinction, which is unfolding in front of our eyes, is caused by humans only. It is being engineered by the super-elites who have the money to control and exploit the resources of the entire planet in any way they want, even to the detriment of humanity. These billionaires may be intelligent and capable of creating a wealth of unprecedented magnitude and managing money and people, but are they wise?

That is questionable, as intelligence, knowledge, education, college degrees, management skills, and wisdom are not the same. Although the proof of an impending disaster is unfolding in front of our eyes and the data are available to anyone who seeks them, the decision taken by these multi-billionaires is causing catastrophic events all over the planet. Those who run the world are responsible for degrading the planet. Do they still not care? Probably, but why? We do not know, but climate change will affect them as well. Maybe, they think they have the resources to hide behind barbed wire and gated communities. Can they be safe? Probably not; it is only a question of time before angry hoards come after them with pitchforks and torches.

The world has a serious problem. These plutocrats, who run the world, are either denying reality, which means they are in a state of delusion, or they are incapable of evaluating facts with an open mind, which means they lack the power of analysis or wisdom. Both states of mind are equally dangerous and problematic. Whether it is sheer ignorance on their part or paralysis associated with fatalism or addiction to an insatiable craving for more money may never be known until it is too late. However, there is enough scientific evidence to conclude that it is already too late for the survival of humanity as we know it today.[41] The new evidence in peer-reviewed scientific journals shows that the planet is staring at the abyss, but these men (and a few women) are happily proceeding with *hara-kiri*. Unfortunately, the rest of humanity has no choice but to follow them to our collective apocalypse.

Consider the following facts: scientists agree that up to 350 parts per million (ppm) of carbon dioxide in the atmosphere can sustain life on the planet; we have already passed that stage. The world is currently at 415 ppm of carbon dioxide. This level is already causing deaths and other catastrophes due to the destruction of the atmosphere. The trapped gas at this level ensures that its concentration will continue to rise. It is expected to rise at least to 450 ppm within a decade, even if we do not release any more carbon dioxide starting this moment. President Trump, former leader of a country that is the second-biggest emitter of greenhouse gases, did not believe that the rising temperature across the planet is due to human activities.

Enough carbon dioxide is already trapped under the canopy. It has nowhere to go. Valid data support the assertion that the atmospheric temperature is going to rise. According to scientific studies, any rise of two degrees Celsius above the pre-industrial era is bound to have a catastrophic impact on the climate. An overwhelming majority of the scientific community believes that we are already above that level; they are not sure how high the temperature can go – anywhere between two and four degrees, but it could be even higher.

We may have an inkling of what is stored in the future, as we have already seen the hottest temperature recorded in the last two years.[42] This is only the beginning. We would be looking at disasters of such magnitude that hurricanes, typhoons, forest fires, floods and droughts, and shortage of water and degradation of soil, which are being encountered today, will look like insignificant events. The world of the twenty-first century would look like a paradise. Chris Hedges cites Roger Hallam from his book, *Common Sense for the Twenty-First Century*[43]:

> "Let's be frank about what 'catastrophe' actually means in this context," Hallam writes. "We are looking here at the slow and agonizing suffering and death of billions of people. A moral analysis might go like this: one recent scientific opinion stated that at 5°C above the pre-industrial mean temperature, we are looking at an ecological system capable of sustaining just one billion people. That means 6–7 billion people will have died within the next generation or two. Even if this figure is wrong by 90%, that means 600 million people face starvation and death in the next 40 years. This is 12 times worse than the death toll (civilians and soldiers) of World War Two and many times the death toll of every genocide known to history. It is 12 times worse than the horror of Nazism and Fascism in the 20th century. This is what our genocidal governments around the world are willingly allowing to happen. The word 'genocide' might seem out of context here. The word is often associated with ethnic cleansing or major atrocities like the Holocaust. However, the Merriam-Webster dictionary definition reads 'the deliberate and systematic destruction of a racial, political, or cultural group.'"

E. The current economic system promotes violent conflicts, seizure, and transfer of wealth

The two most critical inferences of this book are a) even in the post-colonial period, unbeknownst to its citizens, the West continues to be in a perpetual state of war, as it had been in the last three centuries; and b) resources from former colonial territories are still pouring into the West and finished products are going in the other direction. The surplus values of the final products are higher than they should be for two reasons: a) the West or TNMCs, and not the market, decides the prices of both raw material and the end product and b) the West arbitrarily decides the labor cost at both ends. Both these factors are against the free-market economic model.

In other words, the West has a monopoly on the financial system; it controls the prices of products and the cost of labor. Consequently, the West, which is still functioning as a cartel, is getting richer, and many former colonies remain as poor as they were during the colonial period. In some cases, they are becoming poorer. Not much has changed on these fronts, except that a few new allies have been accepted into the cartel; others are desperate to get in. Those who become insiders follow the same path to achieve their economic goals. In the process, they too demonize their victims.

This phenomenon merely confirms the hypothesis that the current economic system may or may not be the cause of violence, but it promotes violent conflicts and initiates the demonization of the victims. The irony is that violent clashes are not essential to capture resources, especially if they belong to the weaker nations. The transfer of resources and the capture of wealth can be done more efficiently without violence with currency and market manipulations.[44] Even then, the West in general and the United States, in particular, are still engaged in one violent conflict after another. One would think that since pursuing an avoidable war is irrational behavior, the West, in its infinite wisdom, would refrain from violent conflicts. Wars are a drain on its economy and a factor in the destruction of the planet, which could exacerbate further economic problems.

The United States can bomb any country to submission, except a handful of nations, but it does not have enough manpower to put boots on the ground. It may have successfully invaded a dozen countries or so in the last quarter of a century, but it has been unable to occupy any one of them if the population happens to be relatively large, say twenty million or more. The data may suggest that the United States has reached its capacity to occupy other nations. The most powerful country was in Afghanistan for twenty years, but it could not force the most impoverished nation on the planet into submission. The War on Terror has continued for twenty years; there has not been a clear winner here either.

Despite losing billions of dollars in the wars in the Middle East, the United States was close to invading Syria and has continued to threaten to bomb Iran. Western leaders are either incapable or unwilling to avoid violent conflicts. They are still pursuing unproductive wars. Maybe, it is because a perpetual state of war is beneficial to influential segments of the country, such as TNMCs, which influence its political process. It appears as if wars have become an addiction for the West or invisible forces are compelling it to undertake unproductive wars and other acts of violence. Maybe, something else is going on that citizens cannot comprehend. Ibn Khaldun would describe this phenomenon as the senility of the dying empire.[45] Is it also true for the United States? It is still the most powerful country; it is expected to remain so for the foreseeable future. If so, what is going on?

Therefore, there is another way to look at the ongoing wars around the world. The United States consumes 30% of the planet's resources, even though it only has 4% of the world population.[46] Therefore, the American apprehension could be that other countries are catching up. Until recently, these newly independent nations were not competing with the West for resources, but now they are. They have made it clear that they would also like to enjoy the fruits of capitalism, crony or otherwise. That may explain the need to control the resources of the world.

Can a method other than violence accomplish the goal of controlling resources that belong to other people? We do not know, but violence is the easiest solution to enforce the wishes of powerful nations. There may be other factors as well. There is a difference between reality and its perception, which can be exploited by those who are in favor of wars to solve complex issues. More so, if the most powerful nation believes in its rhetoric of exceptionalism, and other nations do not fear American power anymore, or not as much. There is also a lag phase between the introduction of the technology of war and its comprehension by the leadership. This could cause them to make wrong decisions, which have serious consequences.

For example, in the last century, the technology of killing machines advanced at an accelerated pace, which military theorists could neither imagine nor comprehend. Since senior officers belonged to the upper class, they may not have cared about their soldiers, who generally belonged to the bottom of society. Since generals might not have anticipated the firepower of modern weapons or did not care, they let soldiers be slaughtered. Examples are the battle at Omdurman (40,000 casualties in two hours of action), Gallipoli (almost a quarter of a million on each side), the fire-bombing of Tokyo (more than 100,000 in one day), and of course, Hiroshima and Nagasaki. In these wars, the West inflicted casualties on those whom the West considered "others," but after the Boer War, there were no restrictions on killing white folks. The Battles of the Somme and Leningrad may have seen hundreds of thousands of casualties. The Two World Wars had a combined figure of eighty to a hundred million; the wars in Vietnam and Korea may have cost between three and four million lives each. They are the two next deadliest conflicts of the last century.

In contrast, wars of the twenty-first century have resulted in a significant decrease in casualties. Is this a sign of progress? Possibly, but even though wars should be an outdated concept today, people are still being killed at the rate of hundreds of thousands a year, if not in millions. Violence has taken a different form. In the twenty-first century, the world has been inundated with refugees. Humanity is on the move, not because they want to, but because they have to. The underlying reasons for the refugee crises and wars are the same: violence to control the world's dwindling resources. Refugees are the living manifestation of both violence and a failed world order.

Consider the following numbers: five million people have been killed during the occupations of Iraq and Afghanistan and the War on Terror. At the same time, close to sixty million refugees are on the march to find a new homeland. They have lost their homes either due to violent conflicts or from other human-induced calamities. In both cases, most of the displaced people were innocent and weaker bystanders. The war in Iraq has produced close to four million refugees;[47] the number of people who had to abandon their homes after the U.S. invasion of Afghanistan is close to 5.7 million,[48] and another four million have fled from the Syrian conflict.[49] Between ten to fifteen million or even more are internally displaced in these wars. The rest have been forced to move due to environmental calamities, which human activities have caused. Acts of violence by states end up devouring resources, belching greenhouse gases into the atmosphere. In contrast, the total number of refugees during the First World War was close to two million; twenty million were made homeless during World War II.

Since most of these massacres and destructions have been caused by Western nations and their allies, could one argue that Western civilization is inherently violent? That may not be true, as Japan had an equally lousy record during the Second World War; it exterminated close to thirty million Chinese during the occupation. Nanjing alone witnessed millions of casualties. Similarly, the Soviet Union had annihilated forty million people under Stalin. Ukraine alone witnessed between ten and twenty million massacres in the first few years of the Soviet occupation. Millions of Chinese were exterminated during the Cultural Revolution. In Buddhist Cambodia, Pol Pot murdered one-quarter of its population. These facts indicate that massacres are not confined to one civilization.

The only common factors among nations that have undertaken massacres of this magnitude are a) their military capability to kill, b) the financial capacity to invest in the killing machines, and c) the political ability to get away with their acts of violence, which in the current system requires approval of the West. Those who do not play by the rules set by the world order have to pay the price. For example, Saddam Hussein, the President of Iraq, was hanged for killing 200 people. However, President Suharto of Indonesia may have been responsible for the massacre of over 200,000 people in East Timor alone, but he was alive and well until 2008; he died at his home. The most outstanding achievement for any dictator is to die peacefully among their loved ones, which he managed to do. President Bush is responsible for killing over a million people in Iraq alone. President Obama is responsible for the deaths of tens of thousands of people in Libya and Syria. Both former presidents are revered statesmen. The media seek their opinions on how to avoid violent conflicts; they are also responsible for the targeted killings of thousands of people in half a dozen countries.

Indeed, there is confusion behind violent events of the twenty-first century. It arises partly because hardly anyone knows who is behind the chaos, who is to be blamed for acts of violence, and who is benefiting from the perpetual state of war. The translucency is by design. Is there secrecy about who is pulling strings? Who is initiating violent conflicts? Are they politicians or financial elites? Confusion about the origin of violence is causing chaotic conditions, which yield uncertainty. This, in turn, is responsible for the fear that has gripped the world.[50] Fear promotes irrational behavior, anger, and hatred. The political and economic system that has been in place since the Second World War is not working, or maybe not working properly, for the rest of the world. In contrast, the current world order works very well for the West and small ruling elites of developing countries.

The driving force behind capitalism is the perpetual expansion of capital; this creates vicious cycles – some bad and some not as bad, but still bad enough. The policy of generating profit at any cost promotes violence against resource-rich but militarily weaker countries. Those who control (large) capital control the system; those who do not have to take orders. The rest have to remain subservient to those who have the capital. That can promote a clash of interests. Therefore, the current economic system can initiate violent conflicts since violence and credible threats of violence supported by the military are required to capture wealth. Since violence requires the demonization of the victims, who are sitting on the precious resources, branding of a civilization as violent and savage is the natural sequela of capturing of resources of other people. As long as capitalism is the sole guiding principle of the world order, violent conflicts will continue, and victims will continue to be demonized. Wars and demonization of victims go hand in hand.

The face of the potential victims may change depending upon which resources are in demand. This is what has happened with the Muslim world since the 1990s, as 75% of the crude oil is located in Muslim countries. As long as hydrocarbons are needed, countries with crude oil reserves could be branded as primitive and violent if those countries do not follow the diktat of the world order. Tomorrow, if the demands of petroleum products are replaced by other resources such as lithium or another metal, the focus could shift towards countries that have been endowed with those elements. That may be happening in Bolivia, Argentina, and Congo. There are reports that Afghanistan is sitting on a trillion-dollars' worth of precious metals (tantalum, tin, and tungsten, known as the "three Ts," and lithium). If the reports are accurate, Afghanistan's future is bleak. They are looking for another round of violence which could be in the name of one of many noble causes such as teaching democracy or some other virtues.

II. Making sense of Islamophobia

The issue raised in this book is either about an imagined association of violence with so-called Islamic civilization or a clash of civilizations between the West and Islam. The arguments and counter-arguments may be focused on these two topics, but the underlying issue is neither Islamic civilization nor the theology of Islam; they are irrelevant themes within the realm of irrelevant discussions as far as Islam and violence are concerned. Nevertheless, these two issues have altered the images of Muslims in the Western perception. Even though they may not have anything to do with reality, their impact is deeply entrenched in the Western psyche. As noted in Chapter 5, this perception will be arduous to eradicate.

The real issue is not Islam; it is this: even in the twenty-first century, the West has repeatedly pursued wars to achieve its economic goals, even though occupying lands and capturing the wealth that belongs to other people are considered illegal activities. Since thefts or lootings are perceived as immoral and even amoral acts, the aggressors are forced to justify their presence in the alien lands. Western nations have invaded the rest of the world for three centuries to capture the wealth of other countries, but they have always managed to blame others, which was usually done by demonizing the victims. This is not unexpected. The real problem is that an overwhelming majority of people, even those who were demonized, believe the excuses of their tormentors. The demonization of Muslims as violent people by the United States is unique to the twenty-first century; this should be seen from the following historical perspective.

Ever since Bernard Lewis suggested an association of violence with Islamic civilization (1990), Muslim countries have been invaded and occupied. In the prelude to the invasions, Muslims have been dehumanized and their religion demonized. However, in the bigger scheme of things, Muslims are the latest victims only. They are not the exclusive targets; neither would they be the last. Other nations have also been invaded, occupied, and their resources captured. They were also demonized with similar intensity by blaming either their cultures and religions, political institutions, or their ways of life. How the victims are demonized and what arguments could be used by neoconservative and neoliberal activists to demonize their targets depend upon the *Zeitgeist* and circumstances.

Like other wars of the colonial era, the current conflicts between the West and Muslim countries are not a clash of civilizations. They are battles for controlling the resources that belonged to defenseless victims. Their lands have been invaded, occupied, and their resources stripped and transferred to the West. These countries were invaded not because the inhabitants practice Islam but because they have natural resources, which the West desperately needs to maintain its advantages. These wars have nothing to do with religion. Neither of the two combatants, the West and the non-governmental Islamist (for the lack of a better term) entities, want to convert their opponents.

Therefore, the problem is not political Islam, radical Islam, Islamofascism, Islamism, Islamist ideology, the Islamic State of Iraq, Syria or Maghreb, or the Ba'ath Party, Ba'athification, deba'athification, or the Taliban, and Talibanization of the Muslim world, or similar nomenclatures. These eye-catching terms have been invented and intermittently presented with great fanfare in the last quarter of a century in the popular media. These terms are vacuous; they bring no value to the debate. These fancy terms grab the attention of Western citizens for a limited period; they are discussed on the 24-hour news channels by so-called experts of Islam and terrorism who have no credentials to be an expert.

Then, the terms unceremoniously disappear from plain sight. They are forgotten; a new term emerges, which also has no value; it too would be replaced by some other nonsensical but equally fancy adjectives. Eventually, they would all become irrelevant, but they leave a bitter after-taste that lasts for a long time. The current perception of Muslims being inherently violent is not going to vanish if we consider that racism emerged to justify industrialized slavery three centuries ago. However, implicit racism is still an integral part of Western civilization in the twenty-first century.[51] Similarly, anti-Semitism is only skin deep in many parts of the West. Scratch a little deeper; maybe one could see an unadulterated anti-Semite with Swastika in the basement and *Mein Kampf* in the closet.

Similarly, the core issue of the debate on an association of violence with Islam is neither Islam nor Islamic values, whatever these two terms mean to different people. The issue is obviously not the Islamic doctrine, which have been followed for 1,500 years. Until recently, problems with Islamic doctrine were neither raised nor encountered by the West even though the West and Muslim countries have been at war off and on with each other. However, it was not for spreading religion or converting their opponents. A few individuals may have the ambition to convert whom they may consider the lost souls, but the number of such activists is minuscule. That is true for both sides.

Indeed, the almost 1.8 billion ordinary folks who follow Islam are not to be blamed for wars of the twenty-first century. On the contrary, they are the victims. The data are unambiguous: the driving force behind conflicts is not any religion, religious group, or religious philosophy; it is the control of resources. Therefore, the culprits are those who initiate and manage wars for profit. The dehumanization of the victims of violence is a part of the strategy to garner support from ordinary citizens. In other words, demonization is not the symptom; it is the disease of the new world order by which the world continues to be run in the twenty-first century. The cycle of violence and its justification and demonization of a target will continue until the root cause of violence is addressed.

The allegations of inherent violent behavior of Muslims, which we frequently encounter in the mainstream media, are designed to confuse the pathophysiology of wars and other forms of violence conducted solely by the authority of powerful nation states. Blaming Muslims and Islam are diversionary tactics, as argued by prominent intellectuals such Edward Said, Chris Hedges, Nathan Lee, Deepa Kumar, Christopher Bollyn, and others. The demonization of victims has been a proven strategy to divert the focus from the real issues. It appears that successive U.S. administrations and their supporters have succeeded in their effort. Instead of pointing out the fallacies ingrained in the demonization of victims, both laypeople and intellectuals are busy defending Islam. These activists attempt to prove to the skeptics that their religion abhors violence by citing the religious text, which their opponents do not care about.

Neoconservative ideologues and other supporters of the military-industrial complex are promoting violent conflicts as the only solution to complex problems of the world. They do not care about the validity of arguments even if they are rational, evidence-based, and to the point. Their goal is different. The political agenda of neoconservatives is to maintain Israel's control over Palestinian land. Spreading chaos through violent conflicts in Israel's neighborhood is the strategy to preserve its control. So far, they have succeeded in their endeavor. The Arab world is divided, and the Middle East is in chaos. Iraq was the most prosperous nation and had the second most powerful army in the Arab world. Wars and sanctions have destroyed it; Iraq's bureaucracy is deliberately decimated.[52] They have to rebuild the system from scratch; it is an arduous task and could take one or two generations or even more. So is the situation in Libya; it is engulfed in a civil war with no end in sight. Syria has survived, but barely, but many of its areas are in ruins.

The goal of the military-industrial complex is profit. Like any other corporation, a TNMC wants to sell its products. Peace is not a good business model for their products. Weapons can only be used during violent conflicts and bought during the apprehension of an impending war. Warmongers are not focused on Muslim countries. Their weapons are not designed for Muslims alone. Weapon producers may want violent conflicts to continue; it helps their bottom line. So do the disaster management companies. The extraction sector of the modern economy is equally involved in promoting chaos. Instability in resource-rich countries, many of them Muslim majority, helps to garner contracts for TNMCs from the local elites, which may be detrimental to the local economy and environment but highly profitable to the TNMCs. Most of these mega-corporations are located in the West. They have a firm grip over the public relations corporations and the mainstream media – both are in the business of perception management.

Supporters of these corporations view the arguments of Muslim intellectuals merely as a tool to portray Islam as an outdated religion. To them, it does not matter what arguments are presented by Muslim activists; the apologists of Israel's expansionist policy and the military-industrial complex are going to oppose their arguments by any means, as we had seen during the invasion of Iraq. The Bush administration rejected evidence that Iraq did not have WMDs; instead, they began a demonizing campaign of Iraqis, Arabs, and Muslims. Therefore, even evidence-based arguments are bound to fall on deaf ears.

Those who are convinced that Islam is violent are not going to change their mind, and those who view Islam sympathetically do not need to be convinced that Islam is not a violent religion. They are sure that Islam stands for peace and justice. Besides, the current atmosphere is not conducive to rational thinking on this topic (Chapter 5). Defenders of Islamic doctrine may satisfy their emotional needs by defending Islam from its demonization, but they are wasting their time and energy on issues that are irrelevant to the discussion on an imagined connection of Islam with violence. Islam, or any other religion, does not need to be defended; it has to stand on its own, although its followers may have an emotional need to defend their faith from the criticism, which they believe is an attack on their religious belief and way of life. For them, expressing their views is an emotional issue.

However, if any religion needs to be defended, maybe, that faith has lost relevance to its followers; it also indicates an existential problem for its religious dogma. Nevertheless, there is a need to counter the anti-Muslim rhetoric with a clear understanding that these debates do not serve any purpose except to demonize the victims. The primary strategy should be to present facts and expose the intention of TNMCs and the actions of elites who run these mega-corporations. They are the ones promoting violent conflicts. That is how the narratives of the Islamic activists should be presented. This would be the actual damage control.

Historically, the twenty-first century is not the worst period of Islamic history. Muslim societies have experienced much worse calamities, and Islam has faced equally harsh innuendos in its 1,500 years of history. For example, Genghis Khan massacred forty million people; he wiped out almost 10% of the Old World population.[53] Most of his victims were Muslims from the Middle East and Central Asia; a quarter of the Muslim population was wiped out. He was especially hostile to Muslims whom he considered elites with a condescending attitude towards uneducated Mongols. Hulego Khan, his grandson, killed 80,000 people in just one week in Baghdad as its army entered the city.

However, only a few decades later, their progenies converted to Islam and established four separate empires across Central Asia, China, and the Indian Subcontinent. Genghis Khan's descendants ruled these countries for five centuries. Similarly, Crusaders may have slaughtered thousands of inhabitants of Jerusalem, but 150 years later, they were gone.

Other disasters that affected Muslim societies are the Inquisition in the Iberian Peninsula, colonialism, and industrialized slavery (20% of slaves were Muslims), forced migration of young people that destroyed their country's economy. Colonialism was the worst adversity for Muslim societies. After the First World War, all Islamic nations, except four, remained under Western occupation; three were barely independent (Iran, Saudi Arabia, and Afghanistan); the British Empire controlled foreign affairs and defense. Only Turkey managed to remain a sovereign nation. Islam has survived these calamities. Its followers still find solace in its ethos and logos, which is the best, if not the only parameter, to judge the relevance of any religion.

Different groups of people have raised issues about Islam and Islamic doctrine after 9/11. They will probably continue to do so, as it is in their interest to demonize Muslims. However, as noted earlier,[54] no matter how vehemently the apologists of the current world order might argue, their narratives will remain irrelevant for one reason: they are wrong. Facts do not back their arguments. Islam, or for that matter, any mainstream religion, is not the cause of wars, although it may be used as a rallying point to resist invasion. Since warmongers need to demonize their victims, they can always find excuses to allege the existence of inherent violent behavior of people practicing a specific religion, believing in another political ideology, or finding faults in their race, ethnicity, or nationality. In the past, imagined savagery of other cultures had been used to justify the occupation and colonization by colonial powers.

Therefore, the issue goes far beyond Islam, any particular religion or Islamic civilization or religion-based civilization, or any classification of civilizations if they are based solely on a solitary identity. Such notions are an outdated concept; it is also fundamentally flawed. Therefore, the attention of the defenders of Islam should be focused on the real issue, which is the occupation of their land and a subtle yet effective dehumanization of people justifies invasion. Financial reasons or demonization of a religion or political philosophy are at the root of conflicts. Warmongers sell wars, that is their profession; they want to promote a specific economic agenda that suits their objectives. Hidden behind the veneer of noble causes is the transfer of wealth from one group of people to another.

Indeed, the transfer of wealth from south to north has continued in the twenty-first century and is expected to continue in the near future. The only difference is that, in the past, wealth flowed from colonies to the treasury of the colonial powers. Now, the transfer of resources is taking place not only from former colonial territories to TNMCs located in the West but within the country from one group to another as well. The national budget of the country has become the biggest cash cow.[55] The nation's wealth is being transferred to

TNMCs, which the plutocrats of the country control. According to Peter Phillips, they are a tiny minority; they are less than a fraction of 1% of the world's population and individual countries.

A permanent state of confusion

Simply put, in the twenty-first century, the enemy of the West may seem to be Islam, whatever the term Islam means and whatever people understand by Islam. However, animosity among nations is not permanent. Tomorrow, any other group of people, civilization, or people adhering to another political philosophy or religious beliefs could be declared savages, uncivilized, violent, fanatics, or opponents of modernity and democracy. These adjectives would be added if the interests of people who control and manage the world-order were to clash with the targeted nations.

The Western media may be discussing an association of violence with Islam in the twenty-first century, but only a few decades ago, the mainstream media were discussing in equally demeaning and condescending terms the imagined violent and aberrant behavior of other nations and societies or political philosophies. We may be witnessing that the focus of the media has shifted from Muslims to Russia and China. Therefore, Islam is not the problem. If it is not Islam or any religion, culture, or similar factors, what are those factors which manufacture disasters?

Pankaj Mishra provides an answer in his book, *Age of Anger: A History of the Present*. He has examined the prevalence of fear in today's world. He believes that there are fear and anger towards "others" but also remarkable similarities in the underlying political philosophy and social ethos.[56] Fear may fuel passionate hatred in such diverse groups as radical Islamists, Hindutva hyper-nationalists, secular as well as right-wing religious Zionists, right-wing Christian fundamentalists, and Chinese super-nationalists if their interests clash. These groups may be sworn enemies of another group and may go at each other's throats, but they tend to behave similarly if they are in power or in the majority. These groups also act in an identical pattern if they are in the minority and defend their culture or way of life.

What are they afraid of? Mishra believes that that may not be apparent to them. To him, the source of their anxiety appears to be an apprehension that the cultural influence of the West threatens their way of life. Each may be equally concerned with the political dominance of the West, which they can manage. They may feel that they have already survived colonialism. In most cases, one group may have been supported by the West at the expense of the other. Those who are allied with the West also feel threatened by Western influence. Cultural dominance of the West is a different story; it creates intense anxiety.

Indeed, it appears that there is a common enemy: it is *westernization*, which has been presented as *modernization*. They are not the same; on the contrary, the difference between the two is drastic. Whereas the former could cause upheaval within traditional societies, the latter can build cohesive units.

Modernization depends on intrinsic forces, which are the building blocks of communities. On the other hand, Westernization has meant copying the western system without changing the fundamentals on which Western societies function.

Mishra believes that all these groups are resisting Westernization, which is the primary cause of their anxiety. Since the source of the threat to their culture or religion is not apparent to everyone, these groups tend to blame modernization, or they find a scapegoat. They tend to blame other groups, such as their neighbors or minorities living in the country. They can be easily targeted, especially if they are a visible minority and disenfranchised. Ironically, all groups are equally affected by the same forces. In most cases, visible minorities, who are the prime candidates for becoming a scapegoat, may have already been marginalized.

Psychologists may define the phenomenon of blaming someone else for the cause of fear of an unknown as a transference, or projection;[57] both are harmful defense mechanisms. Lay people would even claim it to be insanity. No matter how it is described, it is a pathological state of mind. These groups may feel *Schadenfreude* when their object of contempt is targeted for demonization or violence by another group, but they could also be the next target. Ironically perhaps, there is also a common bond among those who have been affected by westernization. The connection is mostly negative, but instead of joining forces, these groups are fighting each other. Arendt described such emotion as *negative solidarity* among victims, which also represents a pathological mindset.

Every group is putting up resistance against the onslaught of some form of westernization, which they all argue, is toxic. One way to look at the problem is that the toxicity is due to the apprehension of losing their identity. It could be more traumatic if identity is perceived to be formed by a single character or source.[58] Humankind has multiple identities; the notion of a solitary identity is false,[59] but it makes it easier to dehumanize the target and create a sense of an existential threat. Those who have been left behind in Western societies are equally angry and resentful. Their resentment has been present for decades, as their livelihood was shifted to other countries.

By the turn of the twentieth century, the West had established itself as the leader of the social, cultural, and political hierarchy. Their success led many non-European countries to embark upon westernizing their societies to catch up with the West. Even Turkey, which had decidedly defeated the Western army in at least two major battles during the First World War (Gallipoli and Kut al Amra), outlawed wearing eastern attire, including a hijab or a Fez in government offices. The Turkish language adopted the Roman script and left the Arabic alphabet at the height of colonialism. That reflects the soft power of the West. Indian aristocrats who were comfortable in Indian attire switched to suits and ties and started using knives and forks; western attire became the sign of modernity; it was a symptom of westernization. Indians headed north to study in Britain. Those who stayed behind emulated Western-trained intellectuals.

Arab and Iranian intellectuals did the same, but a clash of values was brewing. As the changes went beyond cosmetic alterations, the fundamentals of a deeply traditional society did not change. Iran was the poster child of rapid westernization, which was based on urbanization. The development plan was put forth by corporations based in the West and financed by Iran's oil wealth, which British companies controlled. Urban development, which was promoted as modernization, became the mantra, which may be a normal process during globalization across cultures. Consequently, there was a mass migration of rural poor to cities, which is also similar to the changes we see in the twenty-first century in rapidly developing economies. However, not all went well. There were repercussions for Iranian society.

The Iranian author, Jalal Ale Ahmad, who grew up in Tehran, was a witness to those changes. He had first-hand experience of the westernization of his society, which he described in his work *Gharabzadgi* and other essays.[60] He called the psychological changes in its victims *Weststruckness*.[61] It was prevalent among new immigrants to the West. Its milder form (for lack of a better term, let us call it *Westitis*) emerges when the new arrivals make it in the top echelon of the corporate world or other Western institutions. Its toxic form results in rootlessness among immigrants; that may be called *Westoxification*.[62]

Ahmad also noted that the disconnect from their roots was pervasive among the migrants who moved from rural areas into the cities. According to Ahmed, the toxic atmosphere he witnessed among migrants was caused by rapid westernization; it was associated with rootlessness, which ordinary people could not digest in one generation.[63] Ahmad may be right, as similar rootlessness is seen among rural migrants to the cities in India and China after rapid urbanization. These changes have been created by globalization in the last decades of the twentieth century.

A century ago, westernization had become a goal for the world, as it is today. Many Western ideals may be an alien concept for traditional societies, but they were being copied worldwide. Ahmad also witnessed similar rootlessness among many Western citizens. They, too, were at a loss at the rapid pace of change, which their societies experienced during the explosive expansion due to industrialization. Traditional jobs were lost. He describes his observation, as he settled in the West:[64]

> And now I, not as an Easterner, but as one like the first Muslims, who expected to see the Resurrection on the Plain of Judgement in their lifetimes, see that Albert Camus, Eugene Ionesco, Ingmar Bergman, and many other artists, all of them from the West, are proclaiming this same Resurrection. All regard the end of human affairs with despair. Sartre's Erostratus fires a revolver at the street blindfolded; Nabokov's protagonist drives his car into the crowd, and the stranger, Meursault, kills someone in reaction to a bad case of sunburn.

Ale Ahmad was a very perceptive individual. It is reflected in his writings. He described the fictional characters of Camus and other great writers of the early twentieth century with incisive precision. Their vision of the society they lived in was formed at a time when the West reigned supreme. One could argue that

Western citizens had no reason to go berserk; the West was wealthy, prosperous, influential, and powerful; they were either respected or hated or both by so-called *others*. It is similar to what we perceive the West in general and the United States, particularly at the turn of the twenty-first century.

However, all was not well with Western societies even though financially they were doing very well. Neither is it today. Camus and many of his contemporary writers were describing events that transcend time and space. Indeed, it might even appear that these authors were describing events of our time, as the West is still rich, powerful, and prosperous, but things are wrong as well. Those random acts of violence of fictional characters are no different from the events of the twenty-first century.

For example, on August 4, 2019, Conner Butts, like Sartre's fictional character, *Erostratus*, opened fire at random on the street in Dayton, Ohio. He killed nine people.[65] In 2017, James Alex Fields rammed his truck into a crowd assembled at Charlottesville, Virginia, to protest against the Ku Klux Klan.[66] Fields killed one person and injured many. Was he emulating Nabokov's fictional character? On November 11, 2014, Zachary Gonzales shot and killed Donavan Arzola[67] because he wanted to pick a fight with someone. He found Arzola, who refused to fight, but he was still killed. The victim had the misfortune of traveling on the same bus. Did Gonzales have a bad case of sunburn like Nabokov's fictional character? On November 19, 2018, Drew Armstrong was walking alone; he saw a car flashing its lights. Assuming that there might be an emergency, he walked towards the car to help. Suddenly, he was hit by a bullet in his face. Two young men, Danial Amato and Hunter Boucher shot him with a B.B. gun; they were seeking a thrill. Armstrong survived, but the shooting left him blind.[68] Butts, Fields, Gonzales, Amato, or Boucher may not have heard of those fictional characters, but the dynamics behind the actions of both groups of people may not be any different.

True, these are anecdotal events; a better picture will emerge with time and after the conclusion of formal studies. These events should be evaluated with long-term observations. However, there are indications that a far more serious problem is lurking underneath the surface. Almost 69,000 people died from opioid overdose in the United States in 2020 alone.[69] This has been going on for some years. There have been frequent incidences of random acts of violence every day in which three or more people had been killed, injured, or shot. Close to 40,000 people die of gun violence each year, out of which 24,000 deaths are due to suicide.[70] The background in which these events had unfolded a hundred years ago and are unfolding today are similar. The similarities suggest that random acts of violence are not the cause; they are merely a symptom. They will continue unless the cause is addressed. The problem may be that violence is an integral part of the system, which has to erupt at a regular interval. Otherwise, it could explode like a volcano, which could be far more violent than humanity could imagine, as weapons have become more potent.

The world order that the European nations had put in place during the peak of the colonial era was based on the extraction of the wealth of colonial subjects by force. The violence committed by the West remained unanswered in the twentieth century; colonial subjects could not match the firepower of occupiers. However, it fueled resentment among the victims. Colonial wars supported the prosperity of a handful of European nations. The crack in the system came as other empires also wanted to have a bigger piece of the pie. The result was the First World War. Since this war did not resolve the fundamental issue of inequitable distribution of wealth among European powers, the treaty of Versailles became an armistice and not a permanent solution. Consequently, the world witnessed the worst slaughter of human history. Both the victims and perpetrators were Europeans.

What was behind the conundrum that the authors described a hundred years ago? Is there a similarity with the events of the twenty-first century? In theory, both sets of acts of violence are different: one is real, the other fictional. However, both appear to be senseless, but are they nonsensical? Mishra argues that there are reasons behind random acts of violence; these acts may appear to be irrational and meaningless to us, but they are real to the people affected by changes to which they cannot adjust. Such feelings transcend time and space. Indeed, Westerners alone should not be blamed for senseless acts of violence. In China, there have been numerous reports of car drivers intentionally killing injured pedestrians if they survived the initial accident.[71] Many of the victims could have been saved. There is a perception that it is better for drivers to kill during road accidents than to injure; it has been reported that drivers have, therefore, reversed their vehicles and driven over the victims to make sure they are dead.

One could argue that the perpetrators of violence have lost their humanity in the twenty-first century, but respecting the rights of individuals who cannot defend their rights may only be a temporary and exceptional phenomenon in human history. These events, which relate to random acts of violence, may not make any sense to those who witness the events from a distance. To them, there may be a sense of surrealism; it may also be related to the intense demonization of victims.

Is there a struggle to catch up with modernity? Maybe so, but being demonized as people affects their perception of reality, which damages people if they cannot adjust to the changes that modernity brings. Ahmad's comments are poignant, as he argued that these events represent psychological damage that modernity brings:[72] "These fictional endings all represent where humanity is ending up in reality, humanity that, if it does not care to be crushed under the machine, must go about in a rhinoceros's skin." Those who have succeeded in the West by breaking glass ceilings and climbing to the top of the ladder within the current world order have developed a thick skin to cope with the pressure in boardrooms and workplaces.

Despite a widespread sense of rootlessness, there is hope. As Mishra points out, the right-wing Christian fundamentalists, Islamists, Zionists, Hindu, and Chinese hyper-nationalists may feel and believe that their existence as a society and their way of life is at stake, but these varied groups have based their opposition to the Westernization on the same guiding principles, which laid the foundation of humanist movements. All these groups may be at each other's throats today, but they derive their philosophical strength from the same liberal traditions once spearheaded by Western philosophers.[73] Mishra also points out that the same movement also transformed Russia from a feudal society to a modern state, made Germany the most productive and industrialized nation in Europe, and brought modernity to Japan. At the same time, it also brought the worst form of totalitarianism, such as in the Soviet System and Maoist China, and pathological forms of nationalism and fascism in Germany, Italy, and Japan.[74] Even the most progressive movement may go either way. Therefore, the challenge is how to manage modernity and discard Westernization.

Take-home message

The West has remained the most dominant group of nations or civilizations (if we follow Huntington's classification of humanity) in the last few centuries. It is expected to remain so in the future. Despite the enormous strides made by China and Russia, another undeniable fact is that the United States still remains at the cutting edge of innovations. This also indicates that the United States is firmly in control of its future. Chinese miracles are partly fueled by American tech giants. China may be mass producing i-phones, but the Apple Corporation is an American TNMC, which ultimately controls the production and distribution; so are other tech giants. American hegemony is intact, although it is being challenged by several countries. Whether its adversaries will succeed cannot be answered now. In other words, the prevalent theory of American diclinism may only be wishful thinking.

Therefore, peace and prosperity in the world will depend upon the United States and its policy; it will not depend on people like Osama bin Laden, Abu Mosab al Zarqawi, or Anwar al Awlaki. They are the creation of chaos and bitterness. Take the clutter out of the equation, and these people will also wither away to nothingness. They come and go; they would be merely a footnote in history books. Besides, they can only remain at the periphery of the power structure. They do not have the money or resources to get into the multi-billion-dollar club that manages the world. In contrast, drug lords have found their way into the shortlists of power elites of the world.[75] They control billions of dollars. Neither does peace in the world depend on organizations like ISIS, Al Qaeda, the Taliban, Boko Haram, or other entities, which pop up intermittently, nor would it depend on Iran or Venezuela, or any other middle-income countries. Peace will depend upon the policy pursued by the most powerful government and its allies. The rest of the world can only react. Until now, the United States has acted as the policeman of the world; it has also followed the policy of exceptionalism, which is at the root of resentment across the deprived world.

The West may have rejected the idea of being one among the equals, but there are many laudable accomplishments of Western civilization; it has moved humanity forward on many fronts. The Western impact on science and technology is outstanding, which catapulted the West to the front row. Historical data support this assertion. However, in many cases, the West was only a conduit for furthering the benefit to humanity. Certain values have been with us for eternity, such as equality and human rights. Still, its credit should go to the West.

For the last three centuries, Western philosophers have taken the lead in providing intellectual stimuli for the expansion of human rights, although until recently, those rights were confined to Europeans only; "others" were deprived of those rights. They had to struggle to get what was due to them. Other nations are still engaged in that struggle. Nevertheless, the ideas of the European philosophers formed the nucleus on which other societies had based their demand for equality during the colonial period. It is still the guiding principle of the entire humankind.

There are equally serious problems with the West. It has put in place its economic and political systems by which the world has been run and managed after the Second World War. The United Nations, IMF, the World Bank, and many other international entities, which are essential for free trade and commerce, are neither neutral nor independent. The crux of the problem is that these organizations cater to the interests of the West in general and the United States in particular. That creates resentment across the world. The economic and political systems, which the West has put in place, leave much to be desired.

The West has introduced capitalism and communism in the economic area and democracy and fascism in the political field. Communism and fascism have been abandoned as failed systems. The realization that two out of the four systems have been utter failures became apparent only after each of the two had devoured more than 100 million people. How about the other two? As noted earlier, capitalism is the guiding principle of the current world order. It has caused severe strain to the disenfranchised segments of the world and those who could not or do not abide by the world order.

Democracy, which is being followed by many countries, has been promoted as the solution to every problem, including the excesses of capitalism. Is it true? Is democracy the solution? A better question should be: can democracy act like an antidote against the powerful people of society? Probably not, at least not according to data. In the twenty-first century, democracy has been transformed into a majority rule – of the majority, by the majority, and for the majority – even in countries where democracy was established for centuries. The other component of democracy is minority rights, which are equally vital for democracy to survive, but have been abandoned even by the established democracies. Today, for lack of a better term, democracy can only be called *majoritarianism*.

Democracy has been unable to challenge the forces which control big money. Neither can it tame populism and populist leaders who have a penchant for demagoguery. One could argue about the pathophysiology of its transformation, but the virtues of democracy need to be acknowledged. Also, it is also a mistake to consider that democracy is entirely a western concept. However, its current form, based on the Magna Carta, may be a Western phenomenon. It ensures the rights of property owners and not the equality of all citizens.

Equality in a democratic setup has appeared only periodically. That makes democracy a fragile and temporary institution.

Its other form is known as the Athenian democracy; its origin is more diverse than its name suggests. This form of democracy came into existence thousands of years before the Magna Carta was established as a political ideology. Some form of Athenian democracy is still practiced in places where westernization has yet to arrive. Many Native American and Aboriginal Australian societies still follow this system in different forms. Nelson Mandela mentioned in his biography how it was practiced in his native village. The Islamic system of Shura was also based on the same principles. The advantage of this form of governance is that it gives equal rights to the disenfranchised segments of society. Of course, it too can be manipulated. Therefore, it could never become a permanent feature of a society.

Greek proponents of democracy had more in common with Indian and Iranian philosophers than any society in Western Europe. Democratic setups of this type, which may be the genuine democracy, have never lasted more than forty years in any place. Powerful segments of society eventually learn how to exert their influence. In the past, democratic nations have often been overtaken by demagogues. They turn out to be fascists in the garb of democratic warriors. Many democracies were transformed into fascist states within a short period. The transformation from democracy to fascism appears to be a natural sequela, as fascism crops up at the same time in different places. Even the most enlightened nations have fallen prey to populist politicians and demagogues.

That may be the reason why Aristotle and Plato spoke out against establishing democracy. These Greek philosophers were afraid that if an uninformed populace were allowed to make laws, it could only bring disaster, probably in the form of autocratic rulers. Two centuries ago, Alexander Taylor argued that democracy could only be a temporary phenomenon. The current state of democracy around the world merely confirms Taylor's assertion. That may be the reason why James Madison, one of the framers of the American Constitution, advised citizens to be vigilant. We may be seeing the same transition – from democracy to fascism – in the twenty-first century.

Capitalism may have given prosperity but it has also given colonialism, slavery, and the slave trade. Combined, these events may have killed as many millions as communism and fascism together. Both World Wars were the sequelae of colonialism. The Second World War had caused between sixty and eighty million deaths. Neo-liberal policies, which were dominant during the Cold War era, may have caused another twenty million casualties. The wars of the twenty-first century can be placed in the account of neoconservative ideologues, who have promoted crony capitalism. They have caused over five million deaths in the last fifteen years. The current climate change can also be directly attributed to capitalism. It could be the greatest disaster the planet has ever encountered. All other atrocities would be nothing in comparison. That alone could be the reason for the annihilation of humanity as we know it.

These events were due to the excesses of the capitalist system. Historical data are unambiguous on this issue. Democracy as a system has never controlled global capital. As Yannis Varoufakis argues, democracy and capitalism could not exist together; if left alone, he believes, capitalism could devour democracy.[76] Those who control big money also control all three pillars of democracy. Financial elites have always figured out how to influence and manipulate the system. The most critical factor for their dominance is the accumulation of capital in fewer hands, which creates debt and captures wealth from the poor and transfers it to plutocrats. The dynamics are similar in the international arena: the wealth is also transferred from developing countries to a handful of Western plutocrats. During the colonial period, citizens of Western nations were kept safe from the predatory practices of the capitalist class, but not anymore. Today, Western citizens are also inundated with debt, which controls their existence.

The Western dominance of the world has lasted over centuries; consequently, its apologists have found it easy to spread the notion that Western civilization is superior to other cohorts. That narrative appears to have been ingrained in the American psyche ever since the United States took over the world order from the British Empire. Both neoliberal and neoconservative wings of U.S. foreign policy establishments have justified the use of violence on American exceptionalism. They argue that the United States is an *exceptional nation*; therefore, it has the right to force its way of life on others and punish other countries if they do not follow American advice. Until recently, the British Empire and the United States could push through their agenda.

Can the West continue the policy of exceptionalism? This is a six trillion-dollar question: the cost of wars of the twenty-first century for the United States. Even the fate of the planet depends on the answer to this question. There are two distinct options for the United States and its allies. The West can either continue to follow the same policy of dominating the rest of the world or accept that it is one among equals. The latter option will require a change in the mindset of financial elites. Political elites are not the issue; they follow the money. In most cases, they serve as the mouthpiece of plutocrats. The problem lies with financial elites.

The other option is to accept that other countries have the same rights and obligations as the West. It is not a new concept. Many intellectuals have been arguing in favor of this policy. Wilfred Cantwell Smith, a Canadian theologian, was one of them. After the failed invasion of Egypt of 1956 by the combined forces of Britain, France, and Israel, he suggested:[77]

> The fundamental weakness of our civilization in the modern world is our inability to recognize that we share the planet not with inferiors but with equals. Unless Western civilization intellectually and socially, politically and economically, and the Christian church theologically can learn to treat other men with fundamental respect, these two, in their turn, will have failed to come to terms with the actualities of the 20th century.

This is easier said than done. The status quo has its own dynamics. Its roots, once established, are difficult to dislodge. Those who control western establishments were born and grew up with the idea that the country has the right to take a decision at the expense of the world. This concept is no different from the principle of *might is right*, which formed the basis of colonialism and lasted until the birth of the United Nations. The policy has cost over a hundred million lives. The West has repeatedly found an excuse to impose its will on others who cannot afford to challenge the economic system.

The Secretary of State, Madeleine Albright, argued that the United States had the right to bomb Iraq because it is an exceptional nation. Similarly, after 9/11, President Bush gave a clear choice to all other countries in a Biblical phrase: they are either with "us" or against "us." He also claimed that he does not understand why other nations do not see how good the United States is. He had the power to ignore what others were saying, which was this: how could you not see that your decisions are not only immoral but amoral? But then, the world is not run on moral grounds.

Neoconservative intellectuals had a field day after 9/11. They let their imaginations wander. Tom Friedman explained that the fast-food chain, McDonalds, could only survive if the United States can afford to have McDonald Douglas, the manufacturer of fighter planes. Michael Ledeen, a neoconservative ideologue, was more forthright, as he suggested that the United States should pick up a country and throw it against the wall once in ten years so that the world knows that it means business. It was called the Ledeen doctrine.

The apologists of the colonial-industrial complex expressed similar sentiments. At the turn of the twentieth century, Rudyard Kipling, who grew up in India after the war of 1857, expressed his reasons why the United States should become a colonial power and stay in the Philippines:[78]

> Take up the white man's burden
> Send forth the best ye breed
> Go bind your sons in exile
> To serve your captive's need;
> To wait in heavy harness,
> On fluttered folk and wild
> Your new-caught, sullen peoples,
> Half devil and half child.
> [...]
> Take up the white man's burden
> And reap his old reward;
> The blame of those ye better,
> The hate of those ye guard ...

It is not any different today. The world of the twenty-first century is also filled with chaos: a clash of civilizations between Islam and the West, the emergence of China as the next economic superpower, Russia's emergence as a competing military power, challenges by Iran to the dominance of the United States and its allies in its backyard, Zionism versus Palestinian rights in the Holy Land, hyper-nationalism, Hindutva, and rights of Kashmiris of self-determination, or potential confrontation between India and Pakistan, the two nuclear-armed nations, North Korea with its nuclear arsenals, military junta and death squad in South America against the rights of indigenous people, and other much smaller chaos around the world. These events fuel intense anxiety globally, which can turn into fear, anger, and violent conflicts.

We can discuss the validity of these issues till kingdom come, but that will not change the reality, which is this: hidden underneath the chaos, arguments, and counterarguments of bad intentions of "others," xenophobia and Islamophobia or Hindu phobia, there is an undeniable fact that the entire humanity – all seven billion of them – share a single planet. Hopefully, those who manage the current world order understand and accept their limitation, which is this: nobody can deport all unwanted elements to other planets, at least not yet, or even in the foreseeable future. There are no penal colonies on Mars or any other planet. The other option may be genocide – the extermination of "all the brutes" (using Joseph Conrad's term);[79] but for all practical purposes, that is not an option anymore.

Powerful countries may create unlivable conditions for those who own valuable properties but have no weapons to fight back. Still, the problem of slum dwellers of the rest of the world will eventually engulf the whole of humankind. No one, no matter how rich and powerful, can live in complete isolation. The world is already witnessing mass exodus from war zones of Africa and the Middle East into Europe. Most of the castaways of humanity find a tent city in the neighboring countries, but a tiny percentage make their way to the West, which could be large enough to change the demography of Europe. It is causing a state of intense anxiety. For some reason, the West is terrified of a molecule called melanin; although it is an immobile molecule and not a virus, it remains hidden underneath the skin and gives it a black or brown hue.

Capitalism in its current form is also a failed system. It serves the interests of a tiny group of plutocrats or the upper 1% of the world population at the cost of the world at large or 99% of the people; it creates resentment. Consequently, it has resulted in numerous violent conflicts in the past; it will continue to do so if left unchecked. Indeed, the current system is in the process of creating another round of wars and conflicts, which could even result in nuclear annihilation and ecological catastrophe. If so, that would be the final gift of capitalism to humanity before the planet earth would experience its sixth extinction. Would the West, which has created this monster, survive its impact? If viewed from a different perspective, the question should be: can the political system control the excesses of the financial plutocrats who manage the world? That is a trillion-dollar question; the fate of humanity depends on it.

Notes

1 https://www.pbs.org/newshour/economy/column-much-poor-actually-pay-taxes-probably-think.
2 https://www.bankrate.com/finance/taxes/tax-deductions-favor-rich-1.aspx; also see https://www.washingtonpost.com/news/wonk/wp/2018/03/30/the-richest-americans-get-a-33000-tax-break-under-the-gop-tax-law-the-poorest-get-40/.
3 https://www.childtrends.org/indicators/food-insecurity.
4 https://www.motherjones.com/politics/2011/12/leadup-iraq-war-timeline/.
5 https://www.independent.co.uk/news/world/middle-east/wmd-just-a-convenient-excuse-for-war-admits-wolfowitz-106754.html.
6 https://www.dailymotion.com/video/x2s4k4p.
7 Peter Phillips, "Global One Percent Exposed," *Censored 2013*, 235–237.
8 Peter Phillips and Brady Osborne, "Exposing the Financial Core of the Transnational Capitalist Class," *Censored 2014*, 315–329. Also see Phillips, *Giants*, 235.
9 Phillips, ibid. For a detailed discussion see David Rothkopf, *Superclass*.
10 Phillips, *Censored 2013*, 233–239.
11 Phillips, *Giants*, 9–13.
12 Phillips, *Giants*, 11–12.
13 Phillips, ibid.
14 Peter Phillips, "Twenty-First Century Fascism: Private Military Companies in Service to Transnational Capitalist Class," *Censored 2016*, 255–276.
15 Discussed in Chapter 2; also see Imbesat Daudi, *Civilization and Violence*.
16 Daudi, ibid., Chapters 4, 5, and 6. His data are confirmed by Niall Ferguson in *Empire* and by Samuel Huntington in *The Clash of Civilizations*, Chapter 4.
17 Sven Lindqvist, *Exterminate all the Brutes*, 100.
18 Ibid. For a detail discussion see Richard Knox, *The Races of Men: A Fragment*.
19 Lindqvist, ibid., 111–112.
20 Lindqvist, ibid., 118, 120, 126, 135.
21 Lindqvist, ibid. 132.
22 Lindqvist. ibid.,116.
23 Lindqvist, ibid. 139–141.
24 Lindqvist, ibid., 136.
25 Hannah Arendt, *The Origins of Totalitarianism*, 183.
26 https://www.history.com/news/native-americans-genocide-united-states.
27 Lindqvist, *The Skull Measurer's Mistake*, 42–47; also see Lindqvist, *Exterminate All the Brutes*, 114.
28 Lindqvist, *Exterminate All the Brutes*, 125; also see Knox, *The Races of Men*.
29 Lindqvist, *The Skull Measurer's Mistake*, 42–47.
30 Lindqvist, *Exterminate All the Brutes*, 129–133.
31 Ibid.
32 Lindqvist, *The Skull Measurer's Mistake*, 138.
33 Pankaj Mishra, *Age of Anger*.
34 William Dalrymple, "The East India Company: The original corporate raiders," *The Guardian*, August. 13, 2015.
35 Mike Davis, *Late Victorian Holocausts*, 54–59. For detailed discussion on the anti-colonial movement see Mishra, *Age of Anger*.
36 Mishra, Prologue, 1–28,
37 Daudi, 378, 381.
38 Ferguson, *Empire*, 205.
39 Edward Said gives a detailed account of justification of the presence of the West in his book *Orientalism*.
40 Ibn Khaldun quoted by Adam Hochschild in *King Leopold's Ghost*, 304.

41 https://www.climate.gov/news-features/understanding-climate/climate-change-atmosp heric-carbon-dioxide.
42 https://www.climatecentral.org/gallery/graphics/the-10-hottest-global-years-on-record.
43 Roger Hallam, *Common Sense for the Twenty-First Century*.
44 James Rickard, *The Currency Wars*.
45 Ibn Khaldun, *The Muqaddimah*, 244–246.
46 https://www.tapatalk.com/groups/peoplespoliticsiii/u-s-consumes-30-of-world-s-resourc es-while-it-make-t22641.html.
47 https://www.unhcr.org/figures-at-a-glance.html.
48 https://www.unhcr.org/figures-at-a-glance.html.
49 https://stepfeed.com/a-look-at-24-refugee-crises-from-the-last-century-6525.
50 Mishra, *Age of Anger,* Chapters 1 and 2.
51 Ian Haney Lopez, *Dog Whistle Politics*, 1–5, 212.
52 Naomi Klein, *The Shock Doctrine*, Chapter 6.
53 Steven Pinker, in *NOVA: The Violence Paradox* (video), https://shop.pbs.org/nova -the-violence-paradox-dvd/product/NV61903.
54 Chapter 3.
55 https://www.huffpost.com/entry/pentagon-devours-money_b_5a 958750e4b0f2c735654d75.
56 Mishra, *Age of Anger*, Prologue and Epilogue.
57 Clifford Morgan et al., *Introduction to Psychology*, 524-526.
58 Amartya Sen, *Identity and Violence*, Chapter 3.
59 Sen, Chapter 3.
60 Mishra, 119–124.
61 Ibid.
62 Mishra, 120.
63 Ibid.
64 Mishra, 123.
65 https://nypost.com/2019/08/04/suspect-killed-after-mass-shooting-in-dayton-ohio/.
66 https://www.washingtonpost.com/news/post-nation/wp/2017/08/14/was-the-charlottes ville-car-attack-domestic-terrorism-a-hate-crime-or-both/.
67 https://www.expressnews.com/news/local/article/Man-who-shot-killed-stranger-on-VIA -bus-gets-40-6328786.php.
68 https://torontosun.com/news/crime/man-shot-with-bb-gun-just-wanted-to-help.
69 https://www.cdc.gov/nchs/pressroom/nchs_press_releases/2021/20210714.htm.
70 https://www.bradyunited.org/key-statistics.
71 https://slate.com/news-and-politics/2015/09/why-drivers-in-china-intentionally-kill-the-p edestrians-they-hit-chinas-laws-have-encouraged-the-hit-to-kill-phenomenon.html.
72 Mishra, 122.
73 Mishra, 44–46.
74 Mishra, 26–32.
75 Phillips and Osborne, *Censored 2014*, 317. For a detailed discussion see Peter Dale Scott, *American War Machine*.
76 https://www.youtube.com/watch?v=GB4s5b9NL3I.
77 Karen Armstrong, *Muhammad: A Biography of the Prophet*, 266.
78 https://www.shmoop.com/white-mans-burden/poem-text.html.
79 The title of Lindqvist's book is from a sentence written by the main character in Joseph Conrad's book *Heart of Darkness*.

Bibliography

Akbar, M.J. *The Shade of Swords*. New Delhi: Roli Books, 9th edition, 2008.

Akbar, M.J. *India: The Siege Within*. New Delhi: Roli Books, 2008. Alexander, Michelle. *The New Jim Crow: Mass Incarceration in the Age of Colorblindness*. New York: TheNewPress, 2010.

Ali, Tariq. *The Clash of Fundamentalisms: Crusades, Jihads and Modernity*. London: Verso, 1st edition, 2002. Andreas, Joel. *Addicted to War: Why the U.S. Can't Kick Militarism*. Oakland, CA: AKPress, 2004.

Arendt, Hannah. *Eichmann in Jerusalem: A Report on the Banality of Evil*. New York: Penguin Books, 1963.

Arendt, Hannah. *The Origins of Totalitarianism*. San Diego: A Harvest Book, 1968.

Armstrong, Karen. *Muhammad: A Biography of the Prophet*. San Francisco: Harper Collins, 1992.

Armstrong, Karen. *Islam*. New York: Harper Collins, 1992.

Armstrong, Karen. *The Battle for God*. New York: Harper Collins, 1992.

Axelrod, Alan. *The Complete Idiot's Guide to World War I*. New York: Alpha Books, 2000.

Bacevich, Andrew. *The New American Militarism: How Americans are Seduced by Wars*. New York: Oxford University Press, 2005.

Berger, John. *How Ideas Spread* (Audio). New York: Recorded Books, 2015.

Bernays, Edward. *Propaganda*. London: Routledge, 1928.

Black, G. *The Good Neighbor*. New York: Pantheon Books, 1988.

Blackmon, Douglas. *Slavery by Another Name: The Re-enslavement of Black Americans from the Civil War to the Second World War*. New York: Doubleday, 2008.

Blum, William. *Killing Hope: US Military and C.I.A. Intervention Since World War II*. Monroe, ME: Common Courage Press, 2004.

Bollyn, Christopher. *The War on Terror: The Plot to Rule the Middle East*. 2017.

Buchanan, Patrick. *Where the Right Went Wrong*. New York: St. Martin's Press, 2004.

Buchanan, Patrick. *Churchill, Hitler and the Unnecessary War*. New York: Crown Books, 2008.

Bulliet, Richard. *The Case for Islamo-Christian Civilization*. New York: Columbia University Press, 2004.

Chomsky, Noam. *Manufacturing Consent: The Political Economy of Mass Media*. New York: Pantheon Books, 1988.

Churchill, Ward. *A Little Matter of Genocide*. San Francisco: City Lights Books, 1997.

Clodfelter, Micheal. *Warfare and Armed Conflicts*, Jefferson, NC: McFarland, 4th edition, 2017.

Cole, Juan. *Muhammad: Prophet of Peace amid the Clash of Empires*. New York: Bold Type Books, 2018.

Crossen, Cynthia. *Tainted Truth: The Manipulation of Facts in America*. New York: Touchstone Books, 1994.

Curtis, Mark. *Web Of Deceit*. London: Vintage, Random House, 2003.

Curtis, Mark. *Unpeople*. New York: Random House, 2004.

Danner, Mark. *Torture and Truth*. New York: The New York Review of Books, 2004.

Daudi, Imbesat. *Civilization and Violence: Islam, the West, and the Rest*. Presque Isle, ME: QED Books, 2014.

Davis, Mike. *Late Victorian Holocausts: El Niño Famines and the Making of the Third World*. London: Verso, 2002.

Diamond, Jared. *Guns, Steel and Germs, The Fates of Human Societies*. New York: Norton & Company Inc., 1999.

Dyer, Gwynne. *Ignorant Armies*. Toronto: McClelland & Stewart, 2003.

Dyer, Gwynne. *Future: Tense. The Coming World Order*Toronto: McClelland & Stewart, 2004.

El Fadl, Khaled Abou. *The Place of Tolerance in Islam*. Boston, MA: Beacon Press, 2006.

Elkin, Carolyn. *Imperial Reckoning: The Untold Story of Britain's Gulag in Kenya*. New York: Henry Holt & Company, 2005.

Engdahl, F. William. *A Century of War: Anglo-American Oil Politics and the New World Order*Palm Desert, CA: Progressive Press, 2012.

Eraly, Abraham. *The Lives and Times of Great Mughals*. Delhi: Penguin Books, 1997.

Esposito, John. *The Islamic Threat – Myth or Reality?*New York: Oxford University Press, 3rd edition, 1999.

Esposito, John and Mogahed, Dalia. *Who Speaks for Islam? What A Billion Muslims Really Think*. New York: Gallup Press, 2007.

Esposito, John and Kalin, Ibrahim (eds.). *Islamophobia: The Challenge of Pluralism in the 21st Century*. New York: Oxford University Press, 2011.

Farah, Caesar E. *Islam*. Hauppauge, NY: Barron's Educational Series, 6th edition, 2000.

Ferguson, Niall. *Empire*. London: Allen Lane, 2002.

Fisk, Robert. *Pity the Nation*. London: Touchstone, 2002.

Fisk, Robert. *The Great War for Civilization*. New York: Barzoi Books, Knopf, 2005.

Fromkin, David. *A Peace to End All Peace: The Fall of The Ottoman Empire and the Creation of the Modern Middle East*. New York: Henry Holt and Company, 1989.

Fukuyama, Francis. *The End of History and the Last Man*. London: Penguin Books, 1992.

Gates, David. *The Napoleonic Wars, 1803–1815*. London: Edward Arnold, 1997.

Gerson, J. and Birchard, B. *The Sun Never Sets*. Boston, MA: South End Press, 1991.

Goldberg, J.J. *Jewish Power: Inside the American Jewish Establishment*. New York: Perseus Books, 1997.

Goodwin, J. *Lords of the Horizons: A History of the Ottoman Empire*. New York: Henry Holt, 1999.

Hallam, Roger. *Common Sense for the Twenty-First Century*. London: Chelsea Green Publishing, 2018.

Haney Lopez, Ian. *Dog Whistle Politics: How coded Racial Appeals Have Reinvented Racism & Wrecked the Middle Class*. Oxford: Oxford University Press, 2014.

Headrick, Daniel. *The Tools of Imperialism*. London: Oxford University Press, 1981.

Healy, David. *U.S. Expansionism, The Imperialist Urge in the 1890s*. Madison, WI: University of Wisconsin Press, 1970.

Hedges, Chris. *War is a Force That Gives US Meaning*. Philadelphia, PA: Public Affairs, Perseus Books, 2002.

Hedges, Chris. *American Fascists*. New York: Free Press, 2006.

Hedges, Chris. *Empire of Illusion*. New York: Nations Books, 2009.

Hedges, Chris. *The Farewell Tour*. New York: Simon & Schuster, 2018.

Herman, Edward and Chomsky, Noam. *Manufacturing Consent*. New York: Pantheon Books, 1988.

Hibbert, Christopher. *The Great Mutiny India 1857*. London: Penguin Books, 1978.

Hochschild, Adam. *King Leopold's Ghost: A Story of Greed, Terror, and Heroism in Colonial Africa*. Boston, MA: Mariner Books, 1999.

Huff, Mickey and Project Censored (eds.). *Censored*. New York: Seven Stories Press, 2013–20.

Huntington, Samuel P. *The Clash of Civilizations and The Remaking of World Order*. New York: Touchstone, 1997.

Johnson, Chalmers. *Blowback*. New York: Metropolitan Books, 2004.

Johnson, Chalmers. *The Sorrows of Empire*. New York: Metropolitan Books, 2004.

Johnson, Chalmers. *Nemesis: The Last Days of American Republic*. New York: Metropolitan Books, 2006.

Kagan, Robert and Kristol, William (eds.). *Present Dangers: Crisis and Opportunity in American Foreign and Defense Policy*. San Francisco: Encounter Books, 2000.

Keegan, John. *The Second World War*. London: Hutchinson, 1989.

Khaldun, Ibn. *The Muqaddimah: An Introduction to History*, trans. Franz Rosenthal. Princeton, NJ: Princeton University Press, 1969.

Kinzer, Stephen. *All the Shah's Men: An American Coup and the Roots of Middle East Terror*. Hoboken, NJ: John Wiley and Sons, 2003.

Kinzer, Stephen. *Overthrow: America's Century of Regime Change from Hawaii to Iraq*. New York: Henry Holt and Company, 2006. Klein, Naomi. *The Shock Doctrine: The Rise of Disaster Capitalism*. New York: Metropolitan Books, 2007.

Knox, Richard. *The Races of Men: a Fragment*. London: Renshaw, 1850.

Kumar, Deepa. *Islamophobia and the Politics of Empire*. Chicago: Haymarket Books, 2012.

Lake, Marilyn and Reynolds, Henry. *Drawing the Global Color Line*. Cambridge: Cambridge University Press, 2008.

Lando, Barry M. *Web of Deceit: The History of Western Complicity in Iraq, From Churchill to Kennedy to George W Bush*. New York: The Other Press, 2004.

Larzig, Marnia. *Torture and the Twilight of Empire*. Princeton, NJ: Princeton University Press, 2008.

Le Cour Grandmaison, Olivier. *Coloniser, Exterminer: Sur la Guerre et l'etat Colonial*. Paris: Fayard, 2005.

Lean, Nathan. *The Islamophobia Industry: How the Right Manufactures Fear of Muslims*. London: Pluto Press, 2012.

Leonard, Richard. *South Africa at War*. Westport, CT: Lawrence Hill & Co., 1983.

LeVine, Mark. *Why They Don't Hate Us*. Oxford: Oneworld Publications, 2005.

Lewis, Bernard. *The Jews of Islam*. Princeton, NJ: Princeton University Press, 1984.

Lewis, Bernard. *What Went Wrong?* New York: Oxford University Press, 2002.

Lewis, Bernard. *The Assassins: A Radical Sect in Islam*. New York: Weidenfeld & Nicholson, 2003.

Lewis, Bernard. *The Crisis of Islam: Holy War and Unholy Terror*. New York: Clarity Press, 2003. Lindqvist, Sven. *Exterminate All the Brutes*. New York: The New Press, 1992.

Lindqvist, Sven. *The Skull Measurer's Mistake*. New York: The New Press, 1997.

Lindqvist, Sven. *A History of Bombing*. New York: The New Press, 2001.

Lindqvist, Sven. *Terra Nullius: A Journey Through No One's Land*, trans. Sarah Death. New York: The New Press, 2005.

Lofgren, Mike. *The Deep State: The Fall of the Constitution and the Rise of a Shadow Government*. New York: Penguin Books, 2016. Lyndall, Ryan. *The Aboriginal Tasmanians*. Sydney: Allen & Unwin, 1997.

Maalouf, Amin. *The Crusade through Arab Eyes*. London: Saqi, 2006.

MacGregor, Jim and Docherty, Gerry. *Prolonging the Agony: How the Anglo-American Establishment Deliberately Extended WWI by Three-and-a Half Years*. Waterville, OR: Trine Day LLC, 2018.

Mamdani, Mahmood. *Good Muslim, Bad Muslim*. New York: Pantheon, Random House, 2004.

Mann, Michael. *Incoherent Empire*. New York: Verso Books, 2003.

Mann, Michael. *The Dark Side of Democracy: Explaining Ethnic Cleansing*. Cambridge: Cambridge University Press, 2005.

McCargo, Duncan. *Tearing Apart the Land: Islam and Legitimacy in Southern Thailand*. Ithaca, NY: Cornell University Press, 2008.

McCarthy, Justin. *Death, and Exile: The Ethnic Cleansing of Ottoman Muslims 1821– 1922*. Princeton, NJ: The Darwin Press Inc., 1995. McCoy, Alfred. *In the Shadows of the American Century: The Rise and Decline of US Global Power*. Chicago: Haymarket Books, 2017.

Mearsheimer, John and Walt, Stephen. *The Israel Lobby and U.S. Foreign Policy*. New York: Farrar, Straus and Giroux, 2007.

Meyer, Karl. *The Dust of Empire*. New York: Public Affairs, 2004.

Miller, Judith. *God Has Ninety-Nine Names: Reporting from a Militant Middle East*. New York: Simon and Schuster, 1996.

Mishra, Amresh. *War of Civilizations*. New Delhi: Rupa Books, 2008.

Mishra , Pankaj. *From The Ruins of Empire*. New York: Picador, 2013.

Mishra , Pankaj. *Age of Anger: A History of the Present*. London: Allen Lane, 2017.

Moore, Michael. *Dude, Where's My Country?*New York: Warner Books, 2004.

Moore, Michael. *Fahrenheit 9/11, The Official Reader*. Lawrence, KS: University of Kansas, 2008.

Morgan, Clifford *et al*. *Introduction to Psychology*, Tokyo: McGraw-Hill Kogakusha, 1979.

Netanyahu, Benjamin (ed.). *International Terrorism: Challenge and Response*. New Brunswick, NJ:Transaction Books, 1981.

Olender, Piotr. *Russo-Japanese Naval War 1904–1905*. Hampshire: Mushroom Model Publications, 2010. Pakenham, Thomas. *The Scramble for Africa: White Man's Conquest of the Dark Continent from 1876 to 1915*. New York: Perennial, Harper Collins, 2003.

Pape, Robert. *Dying to Win*. New York: Random House, 2005.

Patai, Raphael. *The Arab Mind*. New York: Hatherleigh Press, 2002.

Patnaik, Utsa and Patnaik, Prabhat. *A Theory of Imperialism*. New York: Columbia University Press, 2017.

Perkins, John. *The New Confessions of an Economic Hitman*. New York: B.K. Current Books, 2016.

Perloff, James. *The Shadows of Power: The Council on Foreign Relations and the American Decline*. Appleton, WI: Western Islands Publishers, 1988.

Phillips, Melanie. *Londonistan*. New York: Encounter Books, 2006.

Phillips, Peter. *Giants: The Global Power Elites*. New York: Seven Stories Press, 2018.

Pipes, Richard. *Russia under the Bolshevik Regime.* New York: Penguin Books, 1997.

Plummer, Joseph. *Dishonest Money.* dishonestmoney.com, 2009.

Plummer, Joseph. *Tragedy & Hope 101: The Illusion of Justice, Freedom, and Democracy.* Brushfire Publishing, 2014.

Polk, William R. *Understanding Iraq.* New York: Harper Collins, 2004.

Pravel, K.C. *Indian Army after Independence.* Lancer, 1987.

Quigley, Carroll. *Tragedy and Hope.* GSG & Associates, 1966; for its abridged version see Plummer, *Tragedy & Hope 101.*

Rabin-Havt, Ari. *Lies, Incorporated: The World of Post-Truth Politics.* New York: Anchor Books, 2016.

Rampton, SheldonandStauber, John. *Weapons of Mass Deception.* New York: Jeremy P. Tarcher/Penguin, 2003.

Reeves, Minou. *Mohammad In Europe: A Thousand Years of Western Myth-Making.* New York: New York University Press, 2003.

Rickard, James. *The Currency Wars: The Making of the Next Global Crisis.* New York: Penguin Books, 2012.

Rothkopf, David. *Superclass: The Global Power Elite and the World They are Making.* New York: Farrar, Straus and Giroux, 2008.

Rummel, Rudy J. *The Blue Book of Freedom: Ending Famine, Poverty, Democide, and War* Nashville, TN: Cumberland House Publishing, 2007.

Said, Edward W. *Orientalism.* New York: Pantheon Books, 1978.

Said, Edward W. *Covering Islam: How the Media and the Experts Determine How We See the Rest of the World.* London: Random House, 1997.

Saunders, Doug. *The Myth of the Muslim Tide: Do Immigrants Threaten the West.* New York: Vintage Books, 2012.

Scobie, James. *Argentina, a City, and a Nation.* New York: Oxford University Press, 1964.

Scott, Peter Dale. *American War Machine: Deep Politics, the CIA Global Drug Connection, and the Road to Afghanistan.* Lanham, MD: Rowman & Littlefield, 2014.

Sen, Amartya. *Identity and Violence: The Illusion of Destiny.* New York: W.W. Norton & Company, 2006.

Shaheen, Jack. *Reel Bad Arabs; How Hollywood Vilifies a People.* Northampton, MA: Olive Branch Press, 2009.

Sheehi, Stephen. *Islamophobia: The Ideological Campaign Against Muslims.* Atlanta, GA: Clarity Press Inc., 2011.

Singh, Anurag. *Giani Kirpal Singh's Eye-Witness Account of Operation Bluestar.* New Delhi: B. Chattar Singh, Jiwan Singh, 1999.

Tainter, Joseph. *The Collapse of Complex Societies.* Cambridge: Cambridge University Press, 1988.

Takaki, Ronald. *Strangers from a Different Shore: A History of Asian Americans.* Boston, MA: Back Bay Books, Little Brown, and Company, 1989.

Todd, Emmanuel. *Welt-Macht USA Ein Nachruf.* Munich: Piper, 2002 (German edition).

Todenhöfer, Juergen. *Why Do You Kill? The Untold Story of the Iraqi Resistance.* New York: The Disinformation Company Ltd., 2009.

Valentino, Benjamin A. 2004. *Final Solutions: Mass Killing and Genocide in the Twentieth Century.* Ithaca, NY: Cornell University Press. Vidal, Gore. *Dreaming War: Blood for Oil and the Cheney-Bush Junta.* New York: Nation Books, 2002.

Vidal, Gore. *Perpetual War for Perpetual Peace: How We Got to Be so Hated.* New York: Nation Books, 2002.

Vidal, Gore. *Imperial America.* New York: Nation Books, 2005.

Viorst, Milton. *Sandcastles: The Arabs in Search of the Modern World*. New York: Knopf, 1994.

White, Matthew. *The Great Big Book of Horrible Things*. New York: W.W. Norton, 2011.

Woodham-Smith, Cecil. *The Great Hunger*. Readers Union/Hamish Hamilton, 1964.

Wurmser, David. *Tyranny's Ally: America's Failure to Defeat Saddam Hussein*. Washington, DC: AEI Press, 1999.

Yergin, Daniel. *The Prize: The Quest for Oil, Money & Power*. New York: Simon and Schuster, 1991.

Zakaria, Fareed. *The Post-American World*. New York: W.W. Norton & Company Inc., 2010.

Zinn, Howard. *A People's History of the United States*. New York: Harper Perennial Modern Classic, 2005.

Index